Also by ARTHUR MITZMAN

THE IRON CAGE:

An Historical Interpretation of Max Weber

1970

THIS IS A BORZOI BOOK,

Published in *New York* by *Alfred A. Knopf*

Sociology and Estrangement

SOCIOLOGY AND ESTRANGEMENT

Three Sociologists of Imperial Germany

ARTHUR MITZMAN

Alfred A. Knopf   New York
1973

THIS IS A BORZOI BOOK
PUBLISHED BY ALFRED A. KNOPF, INC.

Copyright © 1973 by Arthur Mitzman

All rights reserved under International and Pan-American Copyright Conventions. Published in the United States by Alfred A. Knopf, Inc., New York, and simultaneously in Canada by Random House of Canada Limited, Toronto. Distributed by Random House, Inc., New York.

Library of Congress Cataloging in Publication Data
Mitzman, Arthur. Sociology and estrangement.
Revision of the author's thesis, Brandeis.
Includes bibliographical references.

1. Michels, Robert, 1875–1936. 2. Sombart, Werner, 1863–1941. 3. Tönnies, Ferdinand, 1855–1936. I. Title.
HM22.G3M55   1973   301'.092'2   71-111240
ISBN 0-394-44604-6

Manufactured in the United States of America

FIRST EDITION

To Phyllis

I was in a Printing house in Hell & saw the method in which knowledge is transmitted from generation to generation.

In the first chamber was a Dragon-Man, clearing away the rubbish from a cave's mouth: within, a number of Dragons were hollowing the cave.

In the second chamber was a Viper folding round the rock & the cave, and others adorning it with gold silver and precious stones.

In the third chamber was an Eagle with wings and feathers of air: he caused the inside of the cave to be infinite: around were numbers of Eagles like men, who built palaces in the immense cliffs.

In the fourth chamber were Lions of flaming fire, raging around & melting the metals into living fluids.

In the fifth chamber were Unnam'd forms, which cast the metals into the expanse.

There they were receiv'd by Men who occupied the sixth chamber, and took the form of books & were arranged in libraries.

—WILLIAM BLAKE,
from *The Marriage of Heaven and Hell*

Contents

Preface and Acknowledgments	xi

PART I: *Sociology and Estrangement*

Introduction	3
1. Varieties of Estrangement: *Reification and Self-Alienation*	6
2. Antimodernity: *Bourgeois, Mandarin, and* Mittelstand	27

PART II: *Ferdinand Tönnies (1855–1936)*

3. Approaching a Theory Through Its Author	39
4. Tönnies' Life and Education to 1878	41
5. Tönnies and Paulsen: *1878*	50
6. The Sources of *Gemeinschaft und Gesellschaft*: *Tönnies' Rediscovery of the* Heimat	63
7. Tönnies and Romanticism	101
8. Tönnies and Durkheim: *Estranged and Engaged Sociology*	108
9. The Evolution of Tönnies' Social and Political Views to the First World War	112

PART III: *Werner Sombart (1863–1941)*

10. The Problem: *The Many Ideologies and the One Gyroscope*	135
11. The *Verein für Sozialpolitik* and Sombart in Italy	137
12. Industrialism versus Patriarchalism: *1890–1900*	151
13. Socialism and the Beginnings of a Voluntarist Ethic: *1890–1900*	161
14. Sombart's Voluntarism: *An Overview*	168

Contents

15. *Dennoch!: The Trade Unions and Community* — 175
16. Modern Capitalism: *The Origins of the Capitalist Spirit* — 186
17. The German Economy: *Nostalgia for the Whole Man* — 194
18. The Estrangement of a Modernist: "A Man of Culture, He Who Hates All Culture" — 207
19. Voluntarism and the Theory of Antiprogress — 234
20. The Celebration of the Entrepreneur: *1909* — 238
21. The Two Faces of the Bourgeois: *1913* — 243
22. Sombart's Values and *Der Bourgeois: The Hero and the Merchant* — 254

PART IV: Robert Michels (1875–1936)

23. Introduction: *The Iron Law and Its Legislator* — 267
24. Michels' Youth: *The Destruction of the Cologne Patriciate* — 271
25. The Path to Syndicalism and Back: *1901–1907* — 282
26. Scholarly Retreat, Social Pedagogy, or Elitism? — 310
27. From International Socialism to Italian Nationalism — 315

Conclusion — 339
Abbreviations Used — 345
Notes — 347
Index — *follows page* 376

Preface and Acknowledgments

Most of this work was written some ten years ago as a doctoral thesis in the history of ideas. Numerous passages have since been grafted on or excised, and the introductory section has grown from a humble thousand words to its present immodest proportions. I have, however, steadfastly resisted repeated urgings to cover more closely the lives and works of my subjects in the period after World War I. My concern is less with the beginning, middle, and end of their lives than it is with the counterpoint between those lives and the social, political, and cultural framework of Imperial Germany (or, in Michels' case, its echoes in prewar Italy). The end of the counterpoint is the end of the book.

Although the general theoretical significance of this study became apparent to me only in the decade since its completion, the method of approaching individual biography and history of ideas as interrelated phenomena was suggested to me by a number of my teachers in the History of Ideas program at Brandeis University. Frank Manuel, whose seminars were an invariably exhilarating and sometimes overwhelming experience, suggested the basic approach. Herbert Marcuse was a towering giant of Socratic energy and an inspired transmitter of the best European traditions of cultural criticism. Lewis A. Coser supervised the writing of the thesis with a remarkable store of patience, humanity, and wisdom, without which it could probably not have been done at all.

Other colleagues have commented helpfully on all or part of the manuscript over the years. Ned Polsky and Juan Linz analyzed it in detail and offered some invaluable suggestions. H. Stuart Hughes read the Michels section; Stephen Berger and Herman Lebovics read the Tönnies and Sombart chapters. Hayden White and Charles Tilly commented most helpfully on other parts of the manuscript. I have nonetheless, for perverse and sometimes trivial reasons, ignored much of the advice given me, so it should be clear that none of the infinite number of possible defects in the work are to be attributed to these friends, colleagues, and teachers (except to the extent that none of them advised me to burn the manuscript).

The staffs of the Bayerische Staatsbibliothek in Munich, of the Westdeutsche Bibliothek in Marburg, and of the Harvard and Dartmouth libraries were generous in permitting me the use of their facilities. Particularly valuable, for their collections of unpublished letters, were the International Institute for Social History in Amsterdam, and the Schleswig-Holsteinische Landesbibliothek in Kiel. Götz Langkau, of the Amsterdam Institute, offered invaluable assistance in enabling me to read Werner Sombart's letters to Otto Lang.

Part of the Introduction and a version of the chapter on Tönnies' evolution before World War I have been published, respectively, in *Social Research* (1966) and *The Journal of The History of Ideas* (1971).

ARTHUR MITZMAN

The University of Amsterdam
January 1973

PART I

Sociology and Estrangement

Introduction

THE CENTRAL HISTORICAL EXPERIENCE of our time has been the transformation of the dream of social and technological perfection into the nightmare of bureaucratic petrification and ecological apocalypse. In politics, the buoyant popular nationalism of the French revolutionary era has led, as Tocqueville and Burckhardt predicted, to highly centralized and regimented power states; at their best, they have conferred upon us the mixed blessings of affluence and corporate liberalism; in their more maleficent forms, the totalitarian tyranny of the party-state. But in both cases, the assumed compatibility between the development of individual personality and the development of national social organization seems to have turned into polar opposition. In economics, laissez-faire and technological progress in the democratic West have permitted the concentration of industrial power in the hands of a few giant corporations under some degree of state supervision, a situation only marginally different from the planned state economies of the totalitarian East. Militarily, the splitting of the atom and other gifts of scientific progress threaten to make any major war the funeral pyre of mankind. Ecologically, we have learned that the industrial progress hailed by earlier generations as the gateway to utopia may, if unchecked, suffocate us, poison all living things, and end by turning our once lovely planet into a lifeless refuse heap.

This book discusses three men who lived during the historical transition from dream to nightmare, who experienced it in their changing perceptions of their age and its potentialities.

As sociologists nurtured in the culture of Imperial Germany, they were enabled by their calling and their location to anticipate and to analyze with passionate wisdom some of the problems that sociologists now perceive as the bitter fruit of modernity: the accelerating fracturing and disintegration of communal bonds, the transformation of economic life from means to end, the continual absorption of movements to transform decaying societies into constituent elements of the decay. Their sensitivity to these issues stemmed from their temporal location in the generation that grew to intellectual maturity before World War I and their geographical location in the German Empire, the European state that excelled all others in the rapidity of its transition from agriculture to the machine age and its consequent social dislocation and psychic pain.

These men were, of course, neither unique nor wholly original in their presentiments of disaster. Throughout the nineteenth century a breed of sorrowing prophets decried the then fashionable equation of material improvement with moral progress; Carlyle, de Maistre, Schopenhauer, Kierkegaard, Nietzsche, and Burckhardt are only the better-known ones. Not only these men, but whole classes of impoverished artisans and small tradesmen stood in bitter opposition to the inexorable advance of the new age. In none of the countries of Europe was opposition so strong as in Germany.

Little affected in the first half of the century by the changes that swept through England and France, Germany was the political bulwark of reaction, the economic bastion of a firmly entrenched tradionalism,° and intellectually the purveyor of a completely dif-

° For an excellent discussion of the German artisanry and its relationship to political currents before and during 1848, see Theodor S. Hamerow, *Restoration, Revolution, Reaction* (Princeton, 1958), pp. 21ff. Regarding the dissolution of a traditional, guild-centered economy, Hamerow says: "In Western Europe, the transition from a handicraft to a mechanized method of manufacture was more gradual and the process of social adjustment to the factory system less difficult than in central Europe. For whereas by 1789 the guilds of England and France had lost much of their economic importance, in the Holy Roman Empire they still enjoyed full possession of their ancient rights. It was the French Revolution which opened a new era in the development of Germany by violently thrusting upon it the tenets of liberalism, nationalism, and industrial freedom."

ferent kind of rationalism from that prevalent in Western Europe. German romantic and preromantic poets and scholars rejected the idea that the contemporary age was one of "Enlightenment," and sought their ideals in the past rather than in the future. And the highest flower of German idealism, the philosophy of Hegel, saw the progress of the rational Idea as emerging only through a chaotic history of convulsive catastrophes, and only for the benefit of the small fraction of mankind selected by the providential World-Spirit. Indeed, attainment of universal happiness, that chimerical *telos* of so many eighteenth-century *philosophes,* was neither prospect nor possibility to the *Philosophen* across the Rhine.

Brilliantly illuminating the Lutheranism behind the German philosophic ethic of consciousness and spiritual liberty, Frank Manuel has described the characteristic pessimism of German thought:

> If Hegel's spirit triumphs, it triumphs amid the death of cultures. . . . The Germans were always conscious of the bloody travail of history, while among the French the philosopher's eye was focused on the growing ease and the new rationality. The Germans, even the secularists among them, were weighted down by a sense of inborn evil. The baubles of French civilization they rejected with the moral righteousness of a Rousseau negating the arts and sciences.[1]

The latter part of the century, it is true, saw the attempted reconciliation of the traditionalist ethos, as represented by the Prussian state system, with the contemporary trends of rapid capitalist expansion and political liberalism. But the frequent barbarism resulting from this amalgam drove not a few of Germany's finer minds to despair and estrangement from the world around them. Such estrangement was by no means limited to philosophers and historians like Nietzsche and Burckhardt, nor to the *Völkisch* ideologists discussed by Fritz Stern and George Mosse, all more or less remote from the new social sciences. It was rampant among the very founders of the sociological discipline. The significance of this endemic estrangement in the work of Ferdinand Tönnies, Werner Sombart, and Robert Michels, three of the founding spirits of modern sociology, is the theme of this book.

1

Varieties of Estrangement

Reification and Self-Alienation

INSPIRED BY A FEAR for the survival of the individual personality in the midst of an overrationalized world, the estrangement of Tönnies, Sombart, and Michels from their age fits into a dual pattern discernible in a large portion of German thought from Schiller to Max Weber. This dualism may be understood both theoretically, insofar as "ideal types" of estrangement can be constructed, and historically, in the context of the actual evolution of those types in European and especially German history.

The most important criteria for defining the theoretical models of estrangement are: the type of personality the theorist values and whose loss he fears; the specific threat rationalization poses for this type; and the solution proposed, if any. One such personality type, prominent throughout the last five hundred years of Western history, strives unceasingly to expand the power of the individual will over the world of nature and of man, so as to experience it with maximum intensity, to combat it with maximum heroism, to know it with maximum intelligence, and to master it with maximum ruthlessness. This type embraces both Nietzsche's Dionysos and Goethe's Faust.*

---

* These are two sides of the same coin. In both, the goal is mastery, but in the Dionysian model, one hopes to achieve mastery through passionate exercise of will, whereas in the Faustian model, one hopes to master through

It appears as well in the *Sturm und Drang*, in the "infinite striving" that is one aspect of early romanticism, in Marx's apotheosis of the struggling proletarian, in Weber's "goal-rational" politician and Sombart's aggressive entrepreneur.

The effect of rationalization that most concerns those who value such personalities is the "reification" of an objective world of culture and the consequent transformation of the reified cultural forms from means to ends in themselves. Hans Freyer frames the problem of reification:

> The functions of knowledge, grown from the direct needs of life and originally woven into its practice, break loose from life and become reified in an autonomous, purely theoretical world of science; religiosity, in itself a purely subjective relationship, strives to objectify itself in dogmas, rituals, cults; every moral attitude solidifies into Morality and ethical norms; every aesthetic attitude toward the world becomes a style, every living humanity, a type. Now since these forms not only have objective stability but claim to prevail normatively, while contrariwise, creative life, comparable to a torrent, can never stop, can never let itself be bound by such temporally-based norms, the question is raised of the relationship between the creative powers and the created forms, between subjective and objective spirit.[2]

The suggestion that the means, the techniques, which were originally only supposed to provide for the security and prosperity

---

rational exercise of will. Though Weber's voluntarism is primarily of the more rational, Faustian variety, the best studies of Weber's thought have noted the similarities to Nietzsche. See Karl Löwith, "Max Weber und Karl Marx," *Gesammelte Abhandlungen* (Stuttgart, 1960), pp. 10, 13, 29; Wolfgang Mommsen, *Max Weber und die deutsche Politik, 1890–1920* (Tübingen, 1959), pp. 54, 62, 115, 142, 144; idem, "Universalgeschichtliches und historisches Denken bei Max Weber," *Historische Zeitschrift*, vol. 201 (1965), 557–612. Nietzsche's own discussion of the Dionysian spirit, of course, begins with *The Birth of Tragedy*, but continues throughout his work. An excellent discussion of Apollonian and Dionysian elements in early German romanticism appears in Ricarda Huch's *Blütezeit der Romantik* (Leipzig, 1908), pp. 81–116. A major polemical work identifying German irrationalism from the romantics on with the Dionysian spirit is J. H. W. Rosteutscher's *Die Wiederkunft des Dionysos, der naturmystische Irrationalismus in Deutschland* (Berne, 1947). The relationship of Goethe's Faust to the daemonic spirit of Dionysos is discussed on pp. 15–18.

of the subjects who created them, have become hypostatized to ends in themselves—the premonition of permanent domination over man by the world of things—has been worked out in its most general significance in Simmel's "Der Begriff und die Tragödie der Kultur"; it was used by Werner Sombart in his critique of the high capitalist spirit, which no longer has any other goal than accumulation itself; by Marx in his similar concept of the fetishism of commodities; by Michels in his critique of socialist parties, which were created as means of liberation, only to become ends in themselves; and by Weber in his concept of the bureaucratic threat to individuality.

The various solutions proposed for this problem have as their common denominator the demand for an unremitting struggle against the objectification of what men have produced. The most profound and consistent representative of this position, Nietzsche, proposes to do away altogether with the archetypal embodiment of the objective spirit, the moral code embodied in what psychoanalytic theory calls the superego. Weber and Sombart see some small hope for rescue from bureaucratic stultification through charismatic entrepreneurial and political figures. Marx, grasping the problem in its most material aspect, defines reification, in the *Economic-Philosophical Manuscripts*, as the estrangement of the proletarian producer from his product, but in opposition to his later view of the bourgeois in his analysis (in *Capital*) of the fetishism of commodities, Marx assumes that the worker will struggle to regain control over it.

Marx's view of the problem, however, differs in a number of important respects from the model just outlined. For one thing, the agent of struggle for Marx is class rather than individual action. Furthermore, the goal of this struggle—and accordingly the underlying notion of estrangement—is by no means clear. For we cannot be sure whether, in his very important early work, he values struggle for its own sake, or for the sake of the good, and presumably more peaceful, society it can achieve. In the *Economic-Philosophical Manuscripts* of 1844, for example, he discusses the estrangement of the proletarian both in terms of his lack of control over what he produces (reification of the object) and the meanness of his work (alienation from his activity). But it is impossible to ascertain whether Marx's principal concern over the worker's alienation from the act of producing is because producing does not bring to the proletarian that reward of enhanced control over the objective world which his alienated, specialized labor brings to the bourgeois order that purchases it (or should bring, barring the fetishism of commodities), and which Marx's voluntarist emphasis on social struggle would suggest is his ultimate goal, or because such alienated labor is intrinsically dehumanizing.

A similar problem of basic values underlies the confusion over the phrase "*Aufhebung der Arbeit,*" in the *German Ideology*.[3] If Marx means here "transcendence of labor," in the sense that labor would have a completely different meaning where the workers directly controlled the means of production, then his basic ideal of personality would be striving, Faustian man, simply projected from the individual to the collective level. On the other hand, if Marx literally means "abolition" of labor, which he occasionally implies, then alienation from the act of producing is objectionable regardless of the social framework, the personality ideal is the spontaneous enjoyment of one's powers, and Marx's idea of human nature shows more similarity to Schiller's and Tönnies' than to Nietzsche's and Weber's. The likelihood is that Marx never clearly decided one way or the other in his early work and dismissed the whole question as unrealistic shortly after writing the *German Ideology* in 1846.

Nonetheless, in one side of Marx's ambivalent reaction to rationalization, we do find values similar to those of Nietzsche, Simmel, Weber, and Sombart: a celebration of the Faustian, Dionysian qualities of man, a great concern over the reification of culture as the source of the estrangement of man from the world, of subject from object, and a solution centered on struggle.

The other principal mode of estrangement has as its basic premise the value of the harmonious, Apollonian personality, which seeks not mastery over, but reconciliation with, nature, and especially with its own nature. Such personalities are spontaneous, unreflecting, completely attuned to their psyches' demands for spiritual or physical gratification. Schiller's conception of the naïve, the Pietist quest for a religious community of love, the romantic notion of a brotherhood founded on the community of state or nation, all anticipate Tönnies' conception of "organic will" (*Wesenwille*), which, nurtured by customary community, does not enter relationships with other wills for the sake of some carefully calculated gain, but only for the direct satisfaction they give to basic needs of the psyche.

The greatest threat that rationalization poses to such personalities is not so much reification as alienation from their own activity. For rationalization, presupposing a struggle for existence, imposes a sharp separation of means from ends as the techniques for winning that struggle. Spontaneity, impulsiveness, direct gratification of instinctual desires, action for its own sake, fantasy unrelated to practical needs, have no place in the combat. For victory, whether the prize be social status, economic gain, or political power, sober calculation is needed. If any or all of these goals can be obtained by marriage to a dull and ugly woman, or by working at a totally uninteresting job, the *goal*-conscious man, the striving individualist, accepts the means to attain the end. It is symptomatic of the increasingly sharp division between goal-oriented and activity-oriented types that the spiritual ancestors of this striving individualist, Faust and Dionysos, demanded a great deal more pleasure along the road to mastery.

Tönnies uses the term *Willkür* to designate this type of personality and in so doing presupposes the kind of estrangement from oneself that I am outlining here. *Willkür* means arbitrariness or capriciousness; but Tönnies' societal man, the bearer of *Willkür*, is certainly not capricious or arbitrary in relation to the goal he has set for himself—indeed, the effect of every move is carefully considered in advance. He is, in fact, very similar to the *"zweckrational"* (goal-rational) type in whom Max Weber sees the only hope against reification, the only kind of man capable of keeping ultimate control over his social destiny both from his baser emotional impulses and from bureaucratic regimentation.[4] But for Tönnies, such a man's actions are completely arbitrary in relation to the *Wesenwille*, the organic will, of communal man, which is Tönnies' real, though unstated, measuring device and which develops only through the *intrinsic* satisfactions of its activity.

Weber's puritanical identification of freedom with goal-rational behavior, and his scorn for "that romantic-naturalist version of the 'personality-idea' which contrariwise finds the real sanctuary of the personal in the dark, undifferentiated, vegetative 'underground' of the personal life, i.e., in that . . . irrationality which the 'person' shares completely with the animal," is specifically directed against Treitschke in the essay on Roscher and Knies,[5] but is equally applicable to Tönnies' conception of *Wesenwille, insofar as the latter might be upheld as an ideal*. It is a reflection of Weber's retreat (after 1910) from his apotheosis of goal-rational behavior, as well as of Tönnies' relatively objective presentation of *Wesenwille* and *Willkür* in *Gemeinschaft und Gesellschaft*, that Weber refers to Tönnies' book as "lastingly important" and lauds "the beautiful work of F. Tönnies."[6]

The solutions offered by those who oppose rationalization because it produces alienation, estrangement from the self, usually center around the belief, or tacit presupposition, that the source of the goal-oriented will that deprives the personality of spontaneity and human activity of intrinsic value is the struggle for survival. Liberation of the personality from the effects of this struggle is contingent on the establishment of some social context that will delimit the scope of the individual will and provide a much greater degree of secure satisfaction for both spiritual and material needs than is offered by a society of competing, goal-oriented egoists. One finds two such social contexts in nineteenth-century thought. In one of these, most strongly represented by reactionary romanticism, the struggle for existence is softened by customary procedures, upheld by some ethnic or state community and requiring little or no intentional willfulness. The other, exemplified by the socialist solution, obviates this struggle by the widespread use of machines, and posits the social community rather than the community of state or nation.*

---

* On Marx and community, see the sharply critical treatment of Alfred von Martin in *Ordnung und Freiheit* (Frankfurt, 1956), p. 203: "But the belief in the 'jump' from the 'society' tied to the state of necessity, into the 'free com-

In brief, we have two basic personality types. One seeks internal peace, the other, the mastery of subject over object. The danger of rationalization to the first is estrangement from one's own activities—alienation; the danger to the second, estrangement from the world—reification. The solution sought by the first is social; by the second, individual.

With this rough schematization in mind, the historical reference point of the two basic personality types should be evident. It is the change from medieval to Renaissance man, "the evolution of the individual subject from the enclosed community, protected from chaos, to the isolated experience of an infinite perspective, softened by nothing, held together and closed by no transcendental idea."[7]

Certainly the predominant inspiration for the concept of the harmonious personality stems from the Middle Ages. Schiller, who saw his "naïve poet" in Homer, was exceptional. Romantic admirers of the spontaneous, noncalculating type, such as Novalis, Adam Müller, and Joseph von Görres, found their examples in the Germanic Middle Ages.[8] The early Marx, though far from any romantic veneration of feudal institutions, did admit, by clear implication, that the relatively feeble division of labor in the medieval guild system permitted unalienated labor,[9] and the Guild Socialists around William Morris went considerably further in their glorification of medieval craftsmanship. Finally, Tönnies saw the highest forms of community, apart from the *polis,* in the free cities of the Holy Roman Empire.

On the other hand, it is in the precise antithesis of medieval harmony, the Renaissance princes depicted by Burckhardt, that one finds the historic prototype for the nineteenth century's opposition to cultural reification, from the early romantic glorification of unrestrained aesthetic expression, to Nietzsche's contempt for conven-

---

munity' is belief in miracle: belief in the miracle of the paradise which is to return at the end of history." A similar view of Marx may be found in Karl Löwith's *Meaning in History* (Chicago, 1957), pp. 41–42: "Eventually the whole realm of life's necessities will be replaced by a 'realm of freedom' in a supreme community of communist character: a Kingdom of God, without God on earth, which is the ultimate goal and ideal of Marx's historical messianism."

tional morality, to the charismatic entrepreneurial and political figures in whom Sombart and Weber saw the only hope for the rescue of culture from bureaucratic stultification:

> Audacity, the fundamental evil of all communal culture, becomes an absolute value, the superman becomes the model, the numerous small and great heroes of the modern age, the followers. On this basis is to be understood, in the final analysis, the origin and the evaluation of the economic superman in the modern age. The mass worships the great men who hover before the age as its ideal.[10]

The evolution of social forces and ideas which led to the two modes of estrangement evident in nineteenth-century German thought begins with this turning point from medieval to Renaissance. The destruction of the medieval order was, in a sense, accomplished by an alliance of reason and will. It was the dissolution of this alliance, the perception that modern culture, the creation and objective embodiment of reason, was antagonistic to the free personality, which produced the twin modes of estrangement sketched above. If the value lay on the all-sided, harmonious personality, the threat was seen in the divisiveness of modern culture: first, the separation of church from state; then, because of the ever-growing division of labor, the increasing estrangement of men from their potentialities and the attendant loss of pleasure and involvement in work; finally, the destruction of all bonds between people but contractual ones, the spiritual isolation of the individual from church, state, nation, and local community. Against this divisiveness, one upheld some kind of organic communal unity, usually based on the medieval model. If, however, the value lay on the creativity of the personality, the threat was seen not in the divisiveness but in the unified power of culture, indeed in its *reification*—the hostility of cultural forms to change, to further creativity, the dangers posed by accepted dogmas and entrenched bureaucracies. Against the menace of cultural reification, one upheld the Renaissance genius; against the creations of reason, their creator. In short, the solution was unceasing individual struggle.

But initially, as mentioned, the man of the Renaissance saw no antagonism between reason and will. Reason offered to the will of the absolute monarch Roman law and the rudiments of rational administration; to the merchant, double-entry bookkeeping and inventions in navigation; to the soldier, gunpowder; to the scientist, techniques of experimentation; to the humanist, rediscovery of ancient tongues and methods of analyzing old manuscripts.

Initially, what reason and will had to contend with was the archaic, the unplanned, the customary modes of thought and life. Only in the course of creating out of the chaos of medieval remnants a world of pattern and order did the cultural forms of government, aesthetics, and social convention unforeseeably become independent of their creators; only then did they seem to develop a life of their own and even begin to appear antagonistic to further creativity. Thus did the problems of alienation and reification appear on the spiritual horizons of Western man. The first signs of disquiet over this phenomenon may have appeared in the aesthetic quarrel between the ancients and the moderns in seventeenth-century France: Were the rational aesthetics of Aristotle, only in the last century imposed on the French stage as a perfect complement to the rational absolutism of the French monarchy, to be accepted as the permanent criterion of artistic perfection, or was a broader scope to be given to the creative impulse of the dramatist? About the middle of the eighteenth century a more resounding blow was struck against the rational edifice of human culture in the early discourses of Rousseau. But it was in Germany that, only a brief generation later in the 1770s, an intellectual movement first arose in conscious opposition to the works of the human intellect: the *Sturm und Drang*, which sought to cast off the shackles of civilization through furious and passionate exposure of the emotional side of man. And it was also in Germany, two decades after the *Sturm und Drang*, that the herald of nineteenth-century European romanticism appeared, the *Frühromantik* of the Schlegels, Novalis, and Hölderlin. In both of these movements the two modes of estrangement appear side by side as evidenced by, on the one hand, an idealization of the striving ego —that Dionysian response to the reification of culture—and on the other, the cultivation of love and friendship, of personal relationships as ends in themselves—the Apollonian answer to the alienation of man from his own activity.* Nonetheless, it is probably true that in the *Sturm und Drang*, Dionysian protest predominated, while in the *Romantik*, the Apollonian vision of love was more important.

It is not hard to see why Germany should have been the center of resistance to the rationalization of life, of outspoken antimodernism. For the spiritual impact of Lutheranism, so sharply delineated by Manuel, was magnified many times by social and political developments. The commercial classes, one of the most important instruments of the rationalism that dissolved the medieval unity, were, soon after the beginning of the sixteenth century, all but destroyed by the discovery of the Cape route to the Indies. About the same period religious wars resulted in a politically dismembered Germany for the next three centuries. Thus, the centralized state, which brought internal peace, and the middle class, which brought increasing prosperity, the two forces that in France and England used rational procedures for the public welfare, and so tended to lessen the antagonism between the impulses of the individual and the constraining forms of objectified Reason, were either absent or miserably enfeebled in Germany. Instead, in the swarm of principalities that inherited the Holy Roman Empire, rationalism was pressed into the exclusive service of petty absolutism. The citizens of these states were utterly powerless to do anything but obey the oppressively close bureaucratic machinery of the state, which paralleled in miniature, but without any of the ameliorative features, the larger state absolutisms. Ernst Troeltsch, for example, has argued that "for practical purposes, the natural-law ideas of Western Europe only affected Germany in the sadly attenuated form of enlightened despotism."[11] According to Roy Pascal, "All the states were governed by despots, and the more efficiently they were managed, the more despotic was the government."[12] And Franz Schnabel awards to the Prussian army of this period the honor of completing an absorption of the personality "by the organized mass, by the rationalized operation," which was only "anticipated in the development of the modern state."[13]

---

* Roy Pascal, *The German Sturm und Drang* (Manchester, 1959, p. 306) suggests the appearance of both medieval-communal and Renaissance-individualist elements.

Thus, the rationalist social criticism of the French Enlightenment saw hardly the feeblest of counterparts across the Rhine, not just because of the lack of a middle-class base, but because Germany knew only the harshest side of objectified social rationality. Whereas in France, the rational spirit that had created the French state (against the willful opposition of the aristocracy) was still alive in the wrathful criticism of the king's more articulate subjects, in Germany the subjects of the territorial princes were not the bearers but exclusively the victims of the rational spirit.

Complementing this concentration of rationality in the repressive instrumentalities of the territorial prince was a congenital weakness of the urban spirit which aggravated Germany's difficulties in coping with the problems accompanying rationalization. Of this weakness Helmut Plessner has written:

> It is, of course, obvious that the complaints about growing institutionalization and bureaucratization, and the increasing difficulties of adapting Natural Man (or human nature) to the industrial milieu are by no means limited to Germany. But in a society that cultivates urbanity, narrower limits will be drawn to the hatred for civilization, and responsibility for the decreasing spontaneity and the growing estrangement of man will not be heaped on the process of civilization alone. No wonder that in our land, which saw and sees itself relegated as a whole to the military and authoritarian state mold of its recent history, while the urban traditions remain limited to the narrow horizons of its early history (unpopularity of the metropolis, dominance of the local press), the lower middle class and peasant strata, in which the comparatively older economic methods are conserved, react correspondingly when the whole approaches them with its impositions. No wonder that just these strata were and will remain most sensitive to the myth of blood, earth, and national community, so long as there is no success in opening them up to the spirit of urbanity.[14]

The result of this victimization in the nineteenth and twentieth centuries was a particularly acute and prevalent form of cultural pessimism, which Talcott Parsons has analyzed in functionalist terms in "Democracy and Social Structure in pre-Nazi Germany."[15] Parsons emphasizes the fact that the development of industrial capitalism in Germany was more rapid and brutal than elsewhere in Europe, and that the antecedent social framework in which it grew, unlike the egalitarian "economic individualism" of England and the United States (or, he might have added, the aristocratic individualism of the Latin countries), was dominated by Prussia's highly rationalized, semifeudal, bureaucratic civil service and army. Thus, elements of romantic irrationality in personal life, which elsewhere in Europe could find support in various traditions of individualism—bourgeois, Puritan, or aristocratic—were untenable within the overstructured society of Imperial Germany and, more often than elsewhere, they tended either to be projected outside the given social world into realms of fantasy, or to find satisfaction only in completely separate asocial and apolitical spheres of activity.

Pietism expressed this tendency a century before the Prussian-controlled unification and industrialization of Germany. As a refuge from the unredeemed harshness of political and social life under the territorial princes, and as an alternative to both the dry orthodoxy of German Lutheranism and the "natural theology" of the German Enlightenment, Pietism offered to German Protestants a religious life that "was not a matter of knowledge, but of self-communion and moral purification and the exercise of the love offered by the redeemer" and which "raised individualism to the level of a subjective religion of feeling."[16] It is thus comprehensible that many of the *Stürmer und Dränger* should have come from Pietist backgrounds, and that two of the leading representatives of early romantic reverence for love and personal community, Novalis and Schleiermacher, should have been brought up in a Pietist sect, the *Herrenhüter*.[17]

Philosophical currents as well as religious fed into the mainstream of romantic subjectivism in Germany. The Kantian insistence on the permanent unknowability of the thing-in-itself shifted the prime concern of philosophy from the known object to the knowing subject and, by positing as the goal of his ethics the unending quest for absolute moral perfection, Kant provided German romanticism with the basis of one of its crucial concepts: the infinite striving of the individual. Only the mediation of Fichte and Schiller was required to make this material usable in the archsubjective constructions of early romanticism. Of Fichte's role, Arthur Lovejoy tells us that he

> had, by 1794, converted this Kantian conception of the moral ideal as an endless pursuit of a forever unattainable goal into a metaphysical principle, and had represented the very nature of all existence as an insatiable striving of the Absolute Ego, whereby it first sets up the external world as an obstacle to its own activity, and then gradually but endlessly triumphs over this obstacle. The notion of infinity thus took precedence in philosophy over that of the finite and determinate, the category of Becoming over that of Being, the ideal of activity over that of achieved completion, the mood of endless longing over that of quietude and collectedness of mind.[18]

Schiller, too, contributed to the early romantic aspiration to infinite striving. Friedrich Schlegel was greatly stimulated by Schiller's argument that the sentimental poet was in endless pursuit of an ideal of naïveté, which, precisely because it was his ideal rather than his nature, he could never attain.[19] Nonetheless, Schiller's greatest significance for romanticism and for later German social thought is not that of a direct influence, but rather of a strongly articulated anticipation of both the modes of estrangement I have suggested above.

In Schiller's "Über die ästhetische Erziehung des Menschen" and "Über naive und sentimentalische Dichtung" one may discern antagonism to contemporary rationality occasioned both by concern over the phenomenon of reification and, as mentioned, by a stubborn adherence to the ideal of spontaneity. The way in which Schiller deals with the opposition between the creative individual (subjective spirit) and the existing edifice of culture (objective spirit) is particularly noteworthy, since, in locating the problem in specialization, the division of labor in both material and spiritual endeavors, he forges a link to that other unfortunate result of rationalization: loss of enjoyment in work, estrangement from one's own activity:

> Those many-sided natures of the Greek states, where every individual enjoys an independent life and, if necessary, can re-

produce the totality, give way to an artificial clockwork, where, out of the piecing together of an unending number of lifeless parts a mechanical life of the whole is formed. State and Church are now rent asunder, as are laws and customs. *Enjoyment is cut off from work, means from ends, and effort from compensation.* Eternally bound to only a single small fraction of the whole, man perfects himself only as a fraction, eternally hearing only the monotonous din of the wheel he is turning, he never develops the harmony of his substance, and instead of showing humanity in his nature, he becomes a mere image of his business, of his science. But even the mean, fragmentary participation that still ties the single members to the whole does not depend on forms which they create for themselves (for how could one entrust such an artificial light-shy clockwork to their freedom?) but is prescribed to them with scrupulous strictness, by a formula through which their free insight is held in bondage. *The dead letter replaces living understanding* and a practiced memory is a surer guide than Genius and sensitivity.[20]

Though the solutions offered by different schools of thought and individuals are most varied, this view of the underlying problem of modern culture is a common theme of German thought in the nineteenth century. Hans Freyer says of the passage just quoted:

> Schiller's solution, that the path from the barbarism of civilization to the moral ideal leads through aesthetic education (for it is a question of refinding the lost wholeness of man and man is said to be complete only when he plays) is the general solution of the problem to the extent that all who share in the construction of the classical world of thought, from Pestalozzi to Humboldt, from Fichte to Goethe, orient their educational concept to the goal of totality. Totality of humanity is the goal of all, and for all the path is: free activity. This is the core of the reproach against the system of civilization: it has torn apart the inner organization of human nature, it has ruined the unity of that nature's harmonious powers, because it has imposed on their free self-activity the mechanical rules of its soulless concerns. It is clear that this critique of the present must be mainly a critique of the economic sphere, for here, civilization has conquered completely.

[Freyer then recapitulates the passage from Schiller I have quoted in the text, and adds:] How well this criticism strikes the core of the enemy's intellectual position. The division of labor, which we perceived as the a-priori of the liberal system, the objectification of culture and of existence which we saw as its necessary characteristics, are here revealed as the a-priori of corruption.[21]

Schiller himself, and idealist social philosophy in general, saw the solution to the problems caused by excessive rationality in the sphere of a new transcendent art and reason: *"weil alle ohne Unterschied durch Vernünfteley von der Natur abfallen müssen, ehe sie durch Vernunft zu ihr zurückkehren können."**[22] In the essay on naïve and sentimental poetry, the aesthetic aspects of this return are fully explored, Greek man being used here no longer just as the example of cultural many-sidedness, but also as that of spontaneous man, analogous to the child, in which means and ends, enjoyment and activity, and effort and compensation are fused. That the modern, "sentimental" poet is also fully legitimized should not obscure the fact that what makes him sentimental is his yearning for the irretrievable spontaneity of the "naïve" poet.

In German romanticism, the same problem of lost totality and spontaneity is handled in two ways, corresponding to the literary movements conventionally dubbed "Early Romantic" and "Young Romantic." Early romanticism represents a retreat from the rationalized objective world to the personal, emotional life of the subject. But, as suggested above, there are two sides to this early romantic emotionalism which, though often found in the same individuals, are clearly distinguishable according to the two theoretical models established above. One side, individualist and Dionysian, strives, through heightened aesthetic experience, for infinite expansion of the ego. The other, social and Apollonian, seeks, through love, to develop a personal community of devoted friends. While neither aspect is at all concerned with the problems of society at large, the latter, catalyzed by the Napoleonic destruction of traditional politi-

---

* "Because all men, without exception, must be cut off from Nature through clever rationalizing (*Vernünfteley*), before they can return to it through reason (*Vernunft*)."

cal forms in Germany, can and does expand into the social philosophy of the "Young Romantics," with its quest for a state community, and ultimately, through diverse paths, leads to Hegel, Marx, Lorenz von Stein, and Tönnies. The former, the purely subjective viewpoint of early romanticism, rather anticipates the egoistic anarchism of Max Stirner and the lonely individualism of Friedrich Nietzsche, and is distantly echoed in the voluntarist ethics of Werner Sombart and Max Weber.*

With these two modes of estrangement sharply defined both theoretically and historically, the groundwork is prepared for some summary remarks on the relation to them of Tönnies, Michels, and Sombart. I have suggested above that, on the one hand, the approach that sought a social rather than an individualist solution to the prob-

* On the basic distinction between an "individualist" early romanticism and a "collectivist" young and late romanticism, see Fritz Lübbe, *Die Wendung vom Individualismus zur sozialen Gemeinschaft im romantischen Roman* (Berlin, 1931). The thesis of this work is stated on pp. 8–9. Franz Schnabel discusses the basis for the changed attitude, using in particular the examples of Fichte and Schleiermacher, on pp. 261–62, 237–38, 267, and 251 of Band I of his *Deutsche Geschichte im neunzehnten Jahrhundert*. Paul Kluckhohn discusses the romantic subjectivism in *Die Liebe in der Romantik* (Halle, 1922), of which chapters 6–9 (pp. 343–640) offer detailed studies of romantic authors, but he does deal with the transition in his last chapter: "Even from the extreme individualism which some of the romantics cultivated in their youth, almost all of them found the way to community, the community of marriage, state, church, etc. And they had no need to surrender the essential convictions of their youthful idea of love" (p. 633). Kluckhohn's *Persönlichkeit und Gemeinschaft* (Halle, 1925) opposes the sharp distinction between the early and young romantic movements by arguing for a consistent identification of personality with community throughout romanticism. Oscar Walzel's *German Romanticism*, trans. by A. W. Lussky (1931), specifies a new interest in political and social matters around 1805: "The romanticists began to take a stand against Napoleon; not only in the aesthetic, but also in the political sense, they became conscious of their national peculiarities" (pp. 134–35). Friedrich Meinecke discusses Novalis and F. Schlegel exclusively from the standpoint of national consciousness in *Weltbürgertum und Nationalstaat* (Munich and Berlin, 1917), pp. 62–92.

The best treatments of Max Weber's individualist values are the essays by Wolfgang Mommsen and Karl Löwith cited above. Alfred von Martin's essay "Zum verhältnis von Mensch und Gesellschaft (Karl Marx–Carl Schmitt–Max Weber)," in his *Ordnung und Freiheit* (Frankfurt, 1956), pp. 186–249, is also excellent. A valuable, though rather general, treatment of Sombart and Weber in the context of the historical trend from *Gemeinschaft* to *Gesellschaft* is the already-cited work of Erich Fechner, "Der Begriff des kapitalistischen Geistes bei Werner Sombart und Max Weber und die soziologischen Grundkategorien Gemeinschaft und Gesellschaft," *Weltwirtschaftliches Archiv*, vol. 30, 1929.

lems of estrangement branched off in two directions: romantic reaction, which celebrated custom and ethnic community as the means of protecting the personality from an egoistic social order, and socialism, which advocated the widespread use of machines and a classless social community of self-transcendent proletarians. It was the sad accomplishment of Tönnies and Michels to illustrate in their theoretical work the ultimate bankruptcy of each of these conceptions. Sombart's work, on the other hand, while acknowledging the general historical obsolescence of the "heroic" solution, argued on racial grounds that Germany was an exception to this obsolescence.

Tönnies' position can only be understood in the context of the latter evolution of romantic and neoromantic state theory. In the wake of the Napoleonic destruction of the old order in Germany, the "Young Romantic" movement, departing from the apolitical personalism of the "Early Romantics," had desired the construction of a new German state that would respect, encourage, and revive the earlier corporate forms of German life. The general thesis was that the new forms of economic life, based on the rational pursuit of profit, would, if no expression of the common national will were able to bridle them, lead to a continuation of the destruction, carried on by the enlightened despot of the eighteenth century, of the old customary communal ways. The new German state must create a new spiritual-political *Gemeinschaft*, in other words, it must cherish and protect the old folkways and put a sharp brake on socially disruptive economic practices.

The German state of the restoration period gave meager satisfaction to the demands of romantic political theory.[23] The states of Austria and Prussia resumed their previous policies of enlightened despotism, and spurred by economic development elsewhere, the internal economy of the German lands slowly shook off the centuries-old accumulation of guild regulations and internal tariffs and prepared for the explosive capitalist activity of the second half of the century. In fact, most of the popular support for the German revolution of 1848 came from unemployed guildsmen, whose fundamental lack of sympathy with the liberal goals of the revolutionary leadership, once it became clear, was perhaps the principal reason for the defeat of the revolution.[24] At the same time, however, that the policies of the restoration monarchs were destroying the old social and political order, their ideological pronouncements gave continuing encouragement to adherents of late-romantic political theories. An overwrought public statement by the King of Prussia in 1847, assuring his subjects that no piece of paper (a constitution) would ever come between him and them, showed that the Prussian monarch himself was thinking in romantic terms.

Although the decade of reaction after 1849 revealed the impossibility of combining the economic and social conceptions of reactionary romanticism with the development of a new and powerful state, Bismarck's abandonment of this brief experiment by no means signified the rejection of romantic state theory. The new regime, after all, while it accepted the capitalist order as the source of economic growth and power, insisted on retaining the social and political pre-eminence of the Prussian Junkerdom. Thus, the Bismarckian *Reich*, with all that it signified in reverence for the past, became the center of hope for most representatives of neoromantic and historicist political economy. All the social problems of the new age—that of the atomization of a bourgeois competitive society, of individualistic utilitarianism, of the split between the wretched, alienated lower class and the rest of the nation—all these social sicknesses could be healed by the benign influence of the state, the traditional bearer of the spirit of *Gemeinschaft*.*

Tönnies agreed with the diagnosis, but denied the possibility of the remedy, particularly the one advocated by the historicists, since for him, the new German state was itself part of the disease ravaging the old social order. For Tönnies, at least in his original understanding of *Gemeinschaft* and *Gesellschaft,* the state was indissolubly connected with *Gesellschaft* and the forms of will that underlay *Gesellschaft*. Between state and *Gemeinschaft* there was simply no link.

This strict separation of state and *Gemeinschaft* is the key to an understanding of Tönnies' view of his age. It was to establishment of the philosophical or scientific or sociological basis of this view

---

* Tönnies' relationship to the romantics is discussed more extensively in chapter 7.

that Tönnies' original work, *Gemeinschaft und Gesellschaft*, was dedicated—to the assertion, in educated terms, of an antiprogressist view of society, one that saw the better forms of human interaction locked permanently in the past.

The import of Michels' major theoretical work, *Political Parties*, was just as destructive to the socialist notion of a free community developing through the proletariat as Tönnies' was to the romantic notion of community emerging from the state or the nation. Before the socialist parties could save humanity, they had to save themselves. Marx had assumed that the working class would develop into a self-conscious instrument of its own liberation. But it was precisely self-consciousness, consciousness of its full humanity, which the inescapable growth of bureaucracy and oligarchy made impossible. Tönnies and Michels both detested the Prussian spirit in Germany. But each man came to see the instrument of redemption chosen by his own milieu—the German state for Tönnies' milieu of social philosophers and German socialism for Michels'—as inevitably the medium for just that mechanization and regimentation of life that they saw as the epitome of Prussianism: that rationalizing, bureaucratizing phenomenon that Tönnies then claimed to be inseparable from modern society and Michels, from any would-be democratic mass organizations.

But if Michels showed great similarity to Tönnies in declaring the futility of any social solution to the alienation of men from their own acts, he also apprehended, if indirectly, that other mode of estrangement—estrangement from an objectified world of culture, from reification—that has been discussed in these pages. Marx had shown his sensitivity to the problem in his discussions of the fetishism of commodities and the estrangement of the producer from his product. Whereas Marx, however, expected the worker not to fall prey to the bourgeois worship of instrumentalities, but to overcome his estrangement from control over his culture through struggle, and then enter the promised realm of happiness and harmony,[25] Michels saw the proletarian as subject to a fetishism very similar to that of the bourgeois, though now it was the political party rather than the almighty commodity to which men bowed in worship.

Werner Sombart did pass through stages of sympathy both for

the socialist movement and for Tönnies' veneration of community. But the unifying impulse of his life's work was a voluntarist emphasis on the striving, Faustian side of man which ultimately led him to look to heroic entrepreneurial figures as the guardians of society against reification. Franz Schnabel excellently presents the historical setting for Sombart's values:

> The individual began to grasp himself as a problem; in the centuries of modern history, the idea of the sovereign personality worked itself out in all spheres of life. Thus originated the types of the modern way of life, unknown to the High Middle Ages, who comprise in their numerous realizations the varicolored wealth, but also the confusion, of modern culture and history. There is the restless and ruthless entrepreneur in state, society, and economy, who, through knowledge of the forces of nature and through mastery over them, seizes a field of unlimited expansion for his will to live, to rule, and to construct. In the course of Western history, these figures crop up, from Leonardo and Lord Bacon to the absolute princes—those first entrepreneurs and leaders of large-scale state enterprises, with their following of adventurers and charlatans—and finally down to the captains of industry of the Americanized world.[26]

If theory and experience had shown to Tönnies and Michels the historical obsolescence or impracticality of their social ideals, Sombart's analysis of the entrepreneur in *Der Bourgeois* (1913) revealed him to be similarly out of tune with the contemporary spirit. In modern capitalism, the swashbuckling adventurer who organized great enterprises was overshadowed by his more passive counterpart, the trader and financier. Max Weber had a similar pessimistic conception of the prospects for individual heroism and free creativity. But whereas Weber asserted the impulse towards rationalization and regimentation of life to be inherent in all of Western culture, Sombart, trapped in a racist mythology, deeply believed it to be alien to the German soul. Weber could hope to create as much breathing space as possible for the autonomous, responsible German through a program of national imperialism, and he might look down on the Slavs, as he did before 1905, as on a lower level of culture, but he never dreamed of justifying his nationalism as Sombart did, by allegations of a superior racial capacity for preserving the entrepreneurial and withstanding the commercial spirit. Sombart, in thus appealing to racial superiority, opened the way for the strange and frightening fusion of the neoromantic concept of the state community with the aggressive, charismatic hero which appeared in his wartime polemic, *Händler und Helden*. Strange, because in so joining together the medieval concept of the harmonious community with the Renaissance hero, the audacious master of man and nature, Sombart was placing the lamb next to the all-devouring wolf; frightening, because, without close examination, the combination appeared to offer total redemption to a people who suffered more than most from both varieties of contemporary estrangement, and because within a generation National Socialism was to offer to the German nation an image of itself and its enemies which, though cruder, was by no means dissimilar to the one created by Werner Sombart.

Nonetheless, in its most sophisticated form, the estrangement of the sociologists was quite distinct from that of the ideologists of the *Volk*. Though estrangement from their age produced in most of the cultural critics of prewar Germany a hostility to modernism, the antimodernism of the sociologists expressed in theoretical terms the estrangement of *fin-de-siècle* bourgeois radicals from the rigid social code of the Prussianized bureaucratic state. As such, it was akin to that of the pre-World War I German vitalists and expressionists influenced by Nietzsche and Slavic nihilism, but dissimilar in crucial respects both to the "Germanic critics" analyzed by Fritz Stern and George Mosse and to the "orthodox Mandarins" of the German academy dissected by Fritz Ringer.* Further, the profound extent of this estrangement was in large measure the result of the evaporation of

---

* For an outstanding essay on Nietzsche as a manifestation of the estrangement of "spirit" from the German power state, see Otto Westphal, *Feinde Bismarcks, Geistige Grundlagen der deutschen Opposition, 1848–1918* (Munich and Berlin, 1930). On the cultural significance of German expressionism, see Walter H. Sokel, *The Writer in Extremis* (Stanford, Calif., 1959). On the Germanic critics, see Fritz Stern, *The Politics of Cultural Despair, A Study in the Rise of the Germanic Ideology* (Berkeley, Calif., 1961); and George Mosse, *The Crisis of German Ideology* (New York, 1964). On the German Mandarins, see Fritz Ringer, *The Decline of the German Mandarins, The German Academic Community, 1890–1933* (Cambridge, Mass., 1969).

their generation's youthful hopes for the regeneration of modern society by reform from below, either through socialism or some other mixture of politics and scientific philosophy.

Indeed, the fact that antimodernism appears in the work of the sociologists only after an ardent embrace of social radicalism suggests that the source of their malaise may have been less modernity itself than the singularly intractable and repressive form taken by modernity in German culture. We have already discussed the unique sources of Germany's harshly repressive modernity. What remains is to indicate how the cultural criticism of the German sociologists may serve as a point of departure for distinguishing sharply among the varying social bases of antimodernity in Imperial Germany.

2

Antimodernity

Bourgeois, Mandarin, and Mittelstand

APART FROM THE SPLIT between Faustian and Apollonian varieties of estrangement, which appears among sociological as well as non-sociological representatives of the antimodernist position, a second split distinguishes the German sociologists as representatives of a particular antimodernist social perspective. It may be useful to distinguish among: a) the antimodernist stance of the sociologists, who, though hostile to the established powers, generally did not—apart from the period of World War I—accept the assumption of the folkish ideologists that some kind of merger between "tribal nationalism"[1] and the state authority was a realistic solution; b) the antimodernism of most other social scientists (e.g., Gierke, Schmoller,

Gneist, and Wagner) who, because they accepted the conservative posture of the German Empire at face value and saw it as either accomplishing or potentially accomplishing the goals of traditional nationalism, were thoroughly establishmentarian; and c) the folkish ideologists themselves, exemplified before 1914 by Paul de Lagarde and Julius Langbehn, who shared the sociologists' mistrust and sporadic hatred for Imperial Germany's establishment and echoed their more subtle cultural pessimism, but tended to think in a framework of utopian and nationalist fantasy that was remote from the systematic theorizing of the sociologists.*

The ideological bent common to most of the social strata who were bruised, psychologically and materially, by the onslaught of industrial capitalism was to perceive the problems created by industrial society in Germany exclusively in terms of their international character, as the result of pernicious universalist intellectual principles and/or economic practices emanating from England and

---

* Diagrammatically, the variables which enable us to distinguish between these three varieties of antimodernism appear as follows:

	Antimodernism or Cultural Pessimism (belief that rationalization of life leads to cultural decline)	Belief that German state and social order reflect antimodernist conservatism	Belief that merger of state and national "community" is a realistic goal
A. Orthodox social scientists (academic insiders: Gierke, Schmoller, Wagner, etc.)	+	+	+
B. Unorthodox social scientists (academic outsiders: Tönnies, Weber, Sombart, Simmel, etc.)	+	−	−
C. Extrauniversity folkish ideologists	+	−	+

The *George-Kreis*, a neoromantic group of poets and critics centered around the poet Stefan George, cut across B and C, both in its membership and in its conviction that elite communities of artists could establish a counterculture to the prevailing decadence in the absence of significant political or social change (whose prospects they recognized as hopeless).

France, and to ignore the extent to which the earlier bureaucratic structure of Prussian feudalism had compounded and magnified these problems in a characteristically German way. Nonetheless, the distinction drawn above between the cultural pessimism of academic insiders, academic outsiders, and extrauniversity critics represents three fundamental modes of adaptation to or reaction against this bureaucratic structure by the fractured segments of Germany's Third Estate, modes that indeed define the historical role and ambitions of these segments.

In general, we are dealing here with the ideological exponents of three groups, two of which initially appeared on the horizon of German politics in 1848 to challenge the third—on the one side, the divided revolutionary classes of '48, whose conflicting interests undermined the insurgent forces: the retrograde *Mittelstand* (the old middle class of artisans, shopkeepers, and free peasants, which wanted a return to a protected economic status), and the liberal bourgeoisie (the new upper-middle class of property owners, bankers, professionals, etc., which strove for freedom of enterprise and a constitutional order); on the other side, those who took the part of the feudal, military, and bureaucratic caste of the established state power, particularly Prussia.

In the next seventy years, the German academy, though in some ways it enjoyed an independent status, continued to be funded by the bureaucratic state, and to a large extent served as its ideological voice. Given the failure of the revolution of 1848, it tended to attract and absorb, in a manner that strongly suggests what Pareto called the circulation of elites, much of the intellectual energy both of the *Mittelstand* and of the bourgeoisie.

Nonetheless, residual groups of intellectuals who identified with one or the other of these strata remained aloof from the "orthodox" *Weltanschauung* of the Mandarins: the view that Germany's destiny was inseparable both from a core of timeless spiritual values and from Bismarck's bureaucratic monarchy.[2] In the 1870s and early eighties, *Mittelstand* ideologists and politicians such as Lagarde, Meyer, and Stöcker attacked Bismarck's opportunistic alliance with liberal bankers and Jews as a betrayal of the *Volk*.[3] Folkish agitation waned as Bismarck made clear his genuine conservatism and illiberalism toward the end of his chancellorship, but in the next decade other dissident intellectuals, identifying themselves with the liberal bourgeoisie of 1848 and the 1860s, began to protest the voluntary subordination of the social and political goals of German liberalism to the interests of an alliance with the agrarians, and within the conservative academy they staked out what Ringer has called the "modernist" position: the demand that the Mandarins accommodate to, rather than resist, the new social forces of industrialism, technology, and scientific rationalization.[4]

There are two points to be noted about these fringe groups: generational conflict as an historical force of unknown dimensions; and—related to Parsons's point about the hyperrationalization of German life—the tendency of both groups, in the absence of a social base strong enough to force concessions and compromises from the Imperial regime, to slip over into extreme and, from the standpoint of the original class goal, suicidal positions.

The folkish and anti-Semitic agitation of the late seventies and early eighties seems to have brought to conservative nationalism "those disgruntled members of the *Mittelstand*, the 'small men' whose fathers had manned the barricades in 1848 and who, since the crash of 1873, had really been politically homeless."[5] And the most energetic among the modernist Mandarins of the nineties, Sombart and Weber, were reacting against the failure of *their* fathers, men of the generation of the sixties, to break through the social order of Prussian patriarchalism and create a genuinely modern, liberal state. How much of the rebelliousness of both groups was a projection of Oedipal hostilities—severe and harshly repressed in the extremely authoritarian social order of Imperial Germany—is a question we can do no more than raise.

The problem of the lack of a social base from which to engage in "realistic" politics is intimately related to the absence of a German political tradition of resistance to royal centralization comparable to the French or English. The *Mittelstand* of Berlin, having never joined with the radical bourgeoisie in shedding noble blood like the sansculottes of Paris, seems to have been incapable of joining with the bourgeois liberals to play the role of an insurgent "national" class

Antimodernity   31

in German history.* Efforts around 1880 to organize the Berlin *Mittelstand* against Bismarckian "liberalism" were only partially and momentarily successful. Most of the *Mittelstand*, doomed though it was by the economic forces unleashed under the Empire, accepted the conservative appearance of the Empire as genuine coin. The *Mittelstand*'s tendency to recoup its diminishing corporate status through identification with the *Volk* found satisfaction only through the *Volksgemeinschaft* ideology of 1914–18 and 1930–45, when it fused its sense of self to the image of the Prussian warrior.

The modernist Mandarins also tended to slip off to extremes in the absence of any real perspective of bourgeois hegemony. Both Sombart and Weber, after vigorously championing, in the nineties, the new industrial age against obsolete Junker patriarchalism, withdrew from politics in the decade before World War I, emitting overtones of cultural criticism and despair which occasionally made them sound like expressionists with Ph.D.'s. Indeed, it is arguable that, given the lack of a meaningful framework for the bourgeois opposition to Wilhelmian sham-constitutionalism, the only feasible alternative to the rigid social and political structure of the Empire was not a political variant of Anglo-Saxon pluralism, as Ringer has implied,† but rather that escape into Nietzschean pessimism and Slavic nihilism which did in fact tend to dominate the intellectual life of the bourgeois "outsiders" in the years before World War I.‡

Thus, the years 1900–14 reveal a general decline of faith in the modernist option among the younger intellectuals and a channeling of formerly political energies into movements of apolitical aesthetics

---

* On the concept of "national class" in Marx, see George Lichtheim, *Marxism, An Historical and Critical Study* (New York, 1962), pp. 86ff.
† Ringer, *Decline of the German Mandarins*, pp. 46–47, 159. Ringer's suggestion that the political correlate of the modernist position was liberal pluralism would seem to be undermined by his own *caveat* against viewing "English developments as a norm" (p. 15).
‡ Sokel, *The Writer in Extremis*, pp. 62–65, 95, 100–102, 151–56. Paul Honigsheim, an intimate of Max Weber in the prewar years, saw Slavic culture in general and Dostoevsky in particular as having a major impact on Weber's circle in Heidelberg: "I don't remember a single Sunday conversation in which the name of Dostoevsky did not occur" (Paul Honigsheim, *On Max Weber* [New York, 1968], p. 81). Also see Leo Löwenthal, "Die Auffassung Dostojewskis im Vorkriegsdeutschland," *Zeitschrift für Sozialforschung*, III (1934), pp. 344–81.

and philosophical speculation. These were the years of the youth movement, expressionism, *Lebensphilosophie*, and the *George-Kreis*. Two of Sombart's closest friends of this period, Carl Hauptmann and Max Scheler, were vitalists.* And two of his most eminent colleagues, Georg Simmel and Max Weber, who were also modernists in the nineties, developed along lines strikingly similar to his own.

Very much like Sombart, they saw and exemplified in their lives the abrupt cleavage between the formal structures of their society and the pressing emotional needs of the bourgeois scholar who could neither fit into the academy of the orthodox Mandarins nor secure a viable base outside it for engaging in political activity. Simmel, who in 1905 was the only social scientist Weber could think of who had contributed (anonymously) to the official Socialist press,[6] was excluded from a permanent academic position because of his overly "critical" viewpoints and his Jewishness.[7] But even his perspective can hardly, on balance, be considered modernist. Never on good terms with the orthodox Mandarins, his extra-academic orientation was, like Sombart's, modernist in the nineties: sympathetic to "materialism, mechanism and similar conceptions of primarily English origin," i.e., to the anti-Bismarckian ideology shared by left-liberals and socialists in what Paul Honigsheim has called "the unofficial Berlin culture."[8] Moreover, his closest friend of the nineties (and later) was the modernist Ignaz Jastrow, a close associate of Heinrich Braun.[9]

But after the turn of the century, through a shift which paralleled Sombart's at that time and Tönnies' after 1878, he became close to the circle of modernity-hating poet-seers around Stefan George, and thereby to what Honigsheim defines as "the antirationalistic protest against urbanization, rationalism and materialism."[10] As part

---

* Sombart mentions his friendship with the brother of Gerhart Hauptmann in a letter to Otto Lang dated 29/7/06. Carl Hauptmann appears to have replaced Lang as Sombart's intimate between 1900 and 1910 (see pp. 224–25). The Scheler-Sombart relationship was discussed in Katharina Kanthack, *Max Scheler* (Berlin-Hannover, 1948), pp. 22, 59, 62. Sombart applies Scheler's interpretation of the Nietzschean concept of *Ressentiment* in *Der Bourgeois*, pp. 439ff. And Scheler discussed Sombart's *Bourgeois* in a number of essays on capitalism and the capitalist spirit. See Max Scheler, *Vom Umsturz der Werte* (Berne, 1955), pp. 343–95, and John Raphael Staude, *Max Scheler, 1874–1928* (New York, 1967), pp. 57, 65–66, 72, 143.

of his involvement with the *George-Kreis*, Simmel developed a prolonged extramarital intimacy with Gertrude Kantorowicz, the only woman whose poetry George published in his journal, and had an illegitimate child by her.[11]

Weber, who has generally been extolled as the heroic puritan of the German academy, underwent a similar development in the *fin de siècle*. In the nineties, like Sombart, he attempted to use his brilliant ascendancy in the academy to further a generational revolt that was both political, in that he opposed his own brand of modernism to what he viewed as the social bankruptcy of the Junker-industralist alliance then in power, and intimately personal, in the context of his family quarrel with his National Liberal father.[12] In 1897, after their first and only open argument, Weber's father stalked out of his son's house and some weeks later died of what may have been an ulcerated colon.[13] Shortly after, Weber suffered a nervous collapse. From 1898 until 1918, he was incapable of fulfilling academic duties, although he recommenced scholarly work in 1903 and undertook administrative responsibilities in the first year of World War I.[14]

Weber differed from Sombart in the rigor of his thought and his sense of personal responsibility for those near him. But like the other sociologists I have discussed, he found the organized, officially sanctioned roles of Imperial Germany stifling. As a husband, though he always seems to have retained a profoundly chivalrous respect and affection for his wife, he was sexually impotent. Yet he had an extramarital affair in his last decade which may well have been even more significant in his intellectual growth than Sombart's affair with the woman under whose influence he wrote the neoromantic *Deutsche Volkswirtschaft*. Indeed, it is difficult to conceive of a more brilliant exposition of what the later Simmel called "the tragedy of culture" than Weber's exploration of the effects of rationalization on erotic and intellectual activity in "Religious Rejections of the World and Their Directions," published in 1915.[15] And it is noteworthy that the polarity of charisma and rationalization, which some of Weber's most astute interpreters have viewed as the core of his approach to the evolution of society,[16] appeared at just the time that this affair was most intense—in the years before World War I when he was working on *Wirtschaft und Gesellschaft*.

One of the important tests for establishing the degree, kind, and seriousness of antimodernity among the various groups of thinkers of Imperial Germany is their approach to Nietzsche. Fritz Ringer has noted Nietzsche's "rather poor showing in the standard handbooks of German academic philosophy," and writing about the popular revival of Nietzsche, he says that it "had no marked repercussions in the German academic world,"[17] which is all the more reason for locating the sociologists—culturally—outside of that world. Tönnies' early enthusiasm for Nietzsche is clear both from his "Autobiography" and from his *Nietzsche-Kultus,* an effort to rescue the philosopher from his overzealous admirers.[18] Sombart's application of the Nietzschean concept of *"Ressentiment"* in *Der Bourgeois* (1913) followed on Scheler's *Das Ressentiment im Aufbau der Moralen* (1912), and both works probably inspired Weber's remarks on Nietzsche and *"Ressentiment"* in *Wirtschaft und Gesellschaft* and the "Einleitung in die Wirtschaftsethik der Weltreligionen" (written in 1914). Weber in turn had earlier read and annotated Simmel's *Schopenhauer und Nietzsche* (1907).[19]

The acute interest in the philosopher-prophet by the most important sociologists of Imperial Germany underscores their unique antimodernism. The powerful impression Nietzsche made on the sociologists and the lack of such impact on the orthodox Mandarins probably stems from the accessibility of the sociologists to Nietzsche's unqualified, irremediable pessimism. Sombart's analysis of the world created by the capitalist spirit, Tönnies' view of *Gesellschaft,* Weber's perception of inescapable bureaucratization, and Simmel's notion of *objective Geist,* in their suggestion of reified structures hostile to the emotional and aesthetic qualities of the human spirit, are all fundamentally of a piece with the young Nietzsche's brilliant *aperçu* into the desiccation of human emotion by abstract conceptual language:

> Language . . . is now simply no longer capable of doing that for which it is there: to bring understanding of the simplest needs of life to the suffering. In his misery, man is no longer able to perceive himself by means of language, and thus cannot truly unburden himself. In this darkly felt condition language has everywhere become a power unto itself, which now

grasps men as with ghostly arms and pushes them where they really do not want to go. . . . Under this compulsion, no one is any longer capable of revealing himself, of speaking naively.[20]

Thus, in the extraacademic circles of bourgeois intellectuals and Bohemians, who before the war found their deities in Nietzsche and Dostoevsky, we discover the polar opposite of the modernist position; and yet, it was among such people that many of the sociologists felt most at home in the decade before 1914. For both in the pessimistic insights of the sociologists and in the aesthetic-intellectual opposition to Wilhelmian society epitomized in the *George-Kreis* and in German expressionism, we find a sense of estrangement from their age which is compatible neither with the xenophobic qualities of the conventional folkish indictment of modernity, nor with the orthodox Mandarin's identification of Germany's bureaucratic Empire with the preservation of eternal cultural values. Whether in the academy or out, the bourgeois antimodernists experienced estrangement largely as the result of their own intimate—and similar—experience of disillusion with their society. In Schiller's words, "Civilization itself inflicted these wounds."[21]

I do not wish to exaggerate. Neither Tönnies nor Michels nor Sombart was as single-minded in his opposition to the new age as certain extraacademic philosophers and *literati* of the period, such as Nietzsche, Lagarde, and Langbehn. All more or less committed themselves to the use of scientific techniques; all made lasting contributions to sociology as a discipline. And all three were at one time or another, and in varying degrees of importance for their life's work, attracted to the regenerative promise of socialism. But in the light of this positive aspect of their work, the value-laden negative basis of much of their thought has been largely ignored by contemporary sociology.

In the preceding pages I have attempted to lessen this ignorance—to present in broad outline the relationship of Tönnies, Sombart, and Michels to currents of estrangement that may be traced back at least as far as Rousseau and the *Sturm und Drang*. The following chapters will continue this work of *dévoilement* by scrutinizing in detail, through the lives of Tönnies, Sombart, and Michels, the obscured, estranged roots of German sociology, and by tracing both the historical strata that nourished these roots, and the intellectual organisms that grew from them. Further, this study will show the relationship between their estrangement and the sometime commitment that all of these men made to the socialist cause. For the tendency of all three men to look at the evils of modern society as beyond cure, as generic to the society itself, was, as I have suggested, partially balanced by their varying hopes that social democracy might prove a possible cure for the ills of society. In short, in addition to elucidating the sources of their discontent, I shall depict in all three men a dialectic of internal discourse between criticism of the evils of modern society and criticism of modern society *as evil*.

Tönnies, Sombart, and Michels, despite the different disciplines in which they were trained and the differences in the nature of their scholarly production, share with one another, and with many others of the generation born between 1855 and 1875, a common heritage, a common experience, and a common aversion. All three were nurtured in the patriarchal life of preindustrial Germany; all three saw the irreversible and rapid march of industrial civilization and the consequent destruction of older cultures and values; all three developed theories to account for what they came to see as an abhorrent mechanization of life; and all three were, for the greater part of the period I shall discuss, estranged from a world that had become alien and uncontrollable.

PART II

Ferdinand Tönnies (1855–1936)

For a new helmsman steers Olympus.
By new laws Zeus is ruling without law.
He has put down the mighty ones of old.
　　—AESCHYLUS, *Prometheus Bound*

3

Approaching a Theory Through Its Author

FERDINAND TÖNNIES' MAJOR WORK, reprinted six times from its original appearance in 1887 to 1936, the year of his death, was *Gemeinschaft und Gesellschaft (Community and Society)*. The title of the work suggests the contrast between two ways of life which is its theme. *Gemeinschaft,* originating in primitive human groupings based on kinship ties, reveals a pattern of action motivated by natural impulse (*Wesenwille*), rather than calculation of advantage, and regulated by customary law. The *Gemeinschaft* style of life can develop from its origins in the primitive household, through the village level, into quite advanced urban civilizations, such as those of the Greek *polis* and of the free German cities of the Middle Ages. Traces of *Gemeinschaft* may survive well into the modern era, wherever a noncalculating, natural volitional pattern survives, such as within the immediate family, and especially among women and children. *Gesellschaft,* on the other hand, is the way of life characterizing modern commercial society. In such a society, no ties exist between individuals except those consciously created for the attainment of agreed goals, including such fundamental ones as the maximizing of pleasure and profit, and the minimizing of pain and loss. The volitional pattern, then, is one of ceaseless calculation of advantage. The legal system is positive law usually based on some interpretation of natural law, rather than the customary law that regulates *Gemeinschaft* relationships.

Tönnies' distinction between these two life styles is by no means original. It was assumed, in one form or another, by a major part of German social thought from the romantics to Tönnies' own day. There was, however, a fundamental difference between Tönnies' conception of *Gemeinschaft* and that of romantic and neoromantic political theory. The latter groups contended that the state could be the means for the restoration of community. Tönnies, through a critical confrontation with most of the political and social theory of his day, concluded that state and community were no more compatible than fire and water, that, on the contrary, the forms of will on which the activities of the modern state were based were the same as those underlying the capitalist *Gesellschaft*.

The evolution in Tönnies' thought that brought him to this formulation of his basic concepts and then gradually led to their modification resulted from four interacting elements, as they appeared in or influenced Tönnies' mind: Tönnies' intellectual experiences, especially his reaction to Hobbes; his reaction to the political events and social trends of his time, in particular to the outlawing of the German Socialist party in 1878; his personal milieu and local origins, particularly his friendship with Friedrich Paulsen and Theodor Storm and his North Frisian ancestry; and his position in the German academic world, at first marginal, later secure.

Materials for a study of Ferdinand Tönnies' early life and ideas have, until recently, not been abundant. Unlike Robert Michels and Werner Sombart, whose intellectual development in the ten years preceding their major works was clearly outlined by their many articles on political and sociological problems, Tönnies did not begin to write political articles until five years after the publication of *Gemeinschaft und Gesellschaft*, and his scholarly writings before this work were restricted to a long, serialized essay on Hobbes,[1] and a briefer one on Spinoza.[2] Nevertheless, certain invaluable documents relating to the early period did appear later. These include a thirty-five-page "Autobiography," written in 1922;[3] most of Tönnies' correspondence with Theodor Storm, dating from 1872 to the poet's death in 1888;[4] several pages of perceptive remarks by Tönnies' close friend and early mentor, Friedrich Paulsen, in Paulsen's *Autobiography*; various papers and speeches written by Tönnies to the memory of Storm;[5] and, most important and essential, the recently published edition of the Tönnies-Paulsen correspondence.[6] The two hundred forty pages of letters written between these men in the years 1876–87 provide an indispensable basis for a close study of the intellectual evolution that led Tönnies to the writing of *Gemeinschaft und Gesellschaft*.

4

Tönnies' Life and Education to 1878

IN 1855, FERDINAND TÖNNIES was born of Frisian parents in the parish of Oldenswort, district of Eiderstedt, duchy of Schleswig. We are not told whether Tönnies' father was one of the *Interessenten* who ran the affairs of the parish,[1] but it seems likely from Paulsen's description of the man that he was at least quite wealthy: "As a matter of fact, his father had long ceased to be a farmer, if he ever was one. He was much more at home at Hamburg, where he engaged in financial operations on the Stock Exchange."[2]

Tönnies tells us nothing of his childhood, except that when he was ten years old, his parents moved from Eiderstedt to the nearby town of Husum[3] (population in 1860: 4,816).[4] He entered the Husumer *Gelehrtenschule* at a very young age. From the few things he says about his education, it is apparent that he was taught early to think in terms of conceptual opposites (e.g., such notes as "Understanding distinguishes, draws limits. Reason sees the unity in things"),[5] and that he was early familiar with and impressed by Plato's doctrine of ideas.[6] He was also impressed with a history teacher, Otto Kallsen, who filled his students with the glories of the free German cities of the Middle Ages.

In the *Gelehrtenschule*, Tönnies had as a friend and schoolmate Ernst Storm, the son of the poet Theodor Storm.[7] The elder Storm was sufficiently impressed with his son's friend to ask his help in reading the proofs for an anthology of German poetry he was preparing for publication.[8] With reverent awe, the young Tönnies did so, thus beginning an all-important relationship with the older man, who was a living representative of the old traditions of the Schleswig marshland.[9]

Nevertheless, from all that Tönnies says of himself, and from all we can deduce about his attitudes at this period, he was far from captive to any nostalgia for the past of his native land, and felt no enmity toward the new Bismarckian state. In his last year at the *Gelehrtenschule* he subscribed, with another boy, to a new weekly called *Im Neuen Reich*, which, in its first editorial, gave full support to Bismarck's creation and roundly condemned the looseness of South Germany's ties to the Reich.[10] His choice of a university also indicates conformity with the prevailing enthusiasm for the new Reich. He tells us that he was moved by considerations of "high German consciousness" to attend the newly opened University of Strasbourg.*

Tönnies did not remain in Strasbourg after the dedication ceremonies of May 1872, being frightened away by the poor "living conditions in the old imperial city, which had not become cleaner as a French fortress."[11] He registered for the summer semester at the University of Jena and was not long in adapting himself to the fraternity life there.[12] He had early, at twelve, shown his independence from the religious orientation of his mother, who was the daughter of a leading Holstein clergyman.[13] In his first years of college he continued to show his "negative interest in theology" by reading D. F. Strauss, who was then fashionable as a result of his patriotism in 1870.[14]

---

* Tönnies, "Autobiography," p. 4. Tönnies may have been influenced, apart from the general enthusiasm, by his teacher Kallsen, whose *Deutsche Städte im Mittelalter* (Halle, 1891) reveals a most patriotic attachment to Strasbourg, and also by two articles in *Im Neuen Reich*, dealing with the re-creation of the German university in the regained city.

Tönnies attended several courses in "modern philosophy" (the term, of course, included everything from Descartes on), but his main interest in his first years of university study was classical philology. It was through this interest that he seems to have been attracted to the thinker who first suggested to him the basis for a critical attitude toward the new state: Friedrich Nietzsche. In the summer of 1873, he read "with enjoyment, indeed, almost with the feeling of a revelation," Nietzsche's *Birth of Tragedy*.[15] The following winter, while studying in Liepzig, he read the first part of Nietzsche's *Unzeitgemässe Betrachtungen,* which began with a blistering attack on the prevailing identification in Germany of military victory with cultural superiority:

> Of all the bad consequences, however, which the late war with France brings in its trail, perhaps the worst is a widespread, indeed general error: the error of public opinion and of all the publicly opining, that German civilization was also victorious in that struggle, and therefore must now be decorated with garlands appropriate to such extraordinary events and results. . . . It is not a matter of victory of German civilization, for the most simple reason that French civilization continues as before. . . . Strict war discipline, natural bravery and endurance, superior leadership, unity and obedience among the led, in short, elements that have nothing to do with civilization, helped us to victory over opponents who lacked the most important of these elements.[16]

Though Tönnies' recollection that this was "the first [critique] which made a strong impression on me" may have related principally to Nietzsche's criticism of Strauss,[17] the latter criticism is certainly carried out in the framework of Nietzsche's overall attack on contemporary German culture. Nietzsche's early writing, then, probably did have some importance for the critical stance vis-à-vis modern society that Tönnies was gradually to develop. The emphasis on the aesthetic harmony of Greek culture, as opposed to the barbaric individualistic hodgepodge of modern culture, may very well have prefigured the polarity of *Gemeinschaft* and *Gesellschaft.*

I do not wish to overemphasize the Nietzschean influence. Tönnies certainly had less sympathy for the master's later writings, and in 1896 he devoted a small book to an attack on "the Nietzsche cult."[18] Furthermore, he could have found the same reverence for Hellas in the German romantics, with whom he later became familiar, or developed it independently. But he did write with considerable enthusiasm about his early reading of the young Nietzsche.

As was the custom among German students, Tönnies moved frequently from one university to another. After spending the winter semester of 1873-74 in Leipzig, where he "zealously heard the lectures of Ritschl and Curtius," he moved to Bonn. When his favorite teacher in Bonn announced that he intended to spend the following semester in Italy, Tönnies, probably weary of tramping from one university to another, decided to use the next year to dispose of his period of compulsory military service. He was apparently not sufficiently attracted by the military life to devote all his time to it, and paid heavily for his lack of interest:

> It was to my detriment that I wanted to unite the barracks with the saloon, the fusilier with the fraternity student. Moreover, . . . I began at the same time with the *Critique of Pure Reason* and the fourfold root of the proposition of sufficient cause. In January, on the occasion of a drink-fest, I collapsed. Since then, I have suffered attacks of violent headaches.[19]

Tönnies quickly recovered and advanced in rank, but, being physically too weak for field duty, was dismissed in the summer of 1875. He was never recalled for service, though he often dreamt (presumably without pleasure) of this prospect.[20]

The summer of 1875 saw, in addition to a close reading of Schopenhauer, the publication of Tönnies' first writing, a fifty-page pamphlet defending the existing fraternity structure.[21] This work, described half a century later by its author as "pretty worthless,"[22] is another indication of the probable conservatism and orthodoxy of Tönnies' student outlook. Tönnies spent this period at home in Husum, and only returned to university life in the winter of 1875-76 at Berlin. When he resumed his studies he was no longer primarily interested in classical philology and history. Although a continuing interest in Greek antiquity made him a temporary disciple of Georg Curtius, and although he received a doctorate at Tübingen a year later for a work on the Greek god Zeus, his main interest in Berlin turned to modern philosophy.*

Thus, it was here, in Berlin, that he made the acquaintance of Friedrich Paulsen, a young lecturer in philosophy whose first seminar on Kant Tönnies attended with about a dozen other students. Paulsen, born on the west coast of Schleswig, was also of Frisian ancestry, and because of this and other affinities the twenty-year-old Tönnies and the twenty-nine-year-old Paulsen began a personal and intellectual relationship that was crucial to the development of Tönnies' thought. Paulsen was an adherent of Ferdinand Lassalle, and he regularly engaged in lively after-class discussions on social questions with Tönnies and Kuno Francke, another countryman, who later became Professor of German Literature at Harvard.[23] These discussions may have been Tönnies' first occasion for serious thought on the social problems of Wilhelmian Germany. Paulsen's views were not uncharacteristic of the prevailing notions among *Kathedersozialisten* of that period, and the confrontation with these ideas, both through Paulsen and through Adolf Wagner and Rudolph Gneist, was most important in the development of Tönnies' thought.[24] Paulsen later wrote about his early beliefs:

> I had read Lassalle's speeches, probably as early as 1873 or 1874. . . . His vigor and self-confidence impressed me as much as his socialistic interpretation of State and Society, which found support at all points in my own old-established views, as based on those of Gneist, Wagner, Hobbes and Carlyle. He described the state as being not merely a legal institution but an all-inclusive union for the purpose of the self-preservation of society as a whole, and for the advancement of the culture and welfare of all its citizens. Sentiments harking back to my old homeland, age-old feelings of equality traditional among the North Frisian farmers, induced a favorable response on my part to his political views, which culminated

---

* Tönnies, "Autobiography," pp. 7–8. Paulsen, in *Friedrich Paulsen, An Autobiography* (New York, 1938) tells us that Tönnies tried to obtain his doctorate in Berlin in 1875–76, but failed his examination because "in his high-mindedness—or was it high-handedness?—he had never troubled to find out exactly what would be required of him in the examination" (p. 289). This failure, according to Paulsen, precipitated his decision to move into the field of philosophy.

in his idea of a "social monarchy," this being the obverse of his positive antipathy against "vulgar" liberalism, the Manchester school, and the doctrine of laissez-faire. The era of the bubble companies, with its excesses, the plebeian literature, the maudlin farces on the stage—*in short, all those things which made young Nietzsche turn his back on his times* [my italics], had not failed to make a strong impression on me too. I have reason to believe that these personal sentiments and convictions made their influence felt on the younger friends around me.[25]

Tönnies, in his autobiography, maintains that Paulsen's enthusiasm for Lassalle rubbed off only partially on himself, "but his view of the history of philosophy, his natural scientific and historical perceptions, and even more his personality, filled with a pure sense of truth and a social conscience, left behind in me deep and fruitful consequences."[26] Actually, the relationship in both areas was more complicated than this and, as the letters between the two men show, underwent an important evolution. To anticipate this evolution, we can say that throughout, Tönnies shared Paulsen's concern over the atomized and debased character of modern society, but that precisely on the basis of the Hobbesian concept of state and society, which sees the state only as a rationally contracted truce in the war of all against all, and which he also shared with Paulsen, he gradually rejected the idea (which he originally accepted from Paulsen) that the state could or would unify society, or be anything else than an expression of the fundamental disharmony of society. But this development only became clear some years later.

To avoid the sweltering heat in Berlin, Tönnies went to the University at Kiel for the summer of 1876.[27] Here he apparently planned to take his doctoral exams, which he had just failed in Berlin, but changed his mind at the last minute,[28] probably because of the headaches that caused him to break off his studies before the end of the term.[29] In any case, his manifest dislike for the North German university anticipated the discomfort and embarrassment he was to endure when he was for decades stranded there as a *Privatdozent*. Paulsen urged him to return to Berlin for the winter of 1876–77, and he did so, only to find that Paulsen himself was in the hospital with typhus for most of the semester. In the summer semester of 1877, Tönnies finally received his doctorate at Tübingen.

As a result of his poor physical condition, Tönnies had been reconciling himself to philological work on a *Gymnasium* level, a goal from which he felt "internally alienated."* But after obtaining his doctorate, he retired to his parents' home in Husum and reconsidered. Considering his youth (he was only twenty-two), he felt little hesitation in changing his field to "philosophic or cultural-scientific research"[30] and his career to university teaching. His father agreed to support him for an unlimited time; he was furthermore able to rely on a considerable inheritance from a wealthy uncle, and he felt that if he proved inferior to his task, he could always prepare later for the *Gymnasium* teacher's examination.[31] Meanwhile, he planned to spend that winter of 1877–78 in Husum, studying Hobbes. In response to Paulsen's suggestion that he investigate the relation between Descartes and Hobbes, Tönnies asked Paulsen for other, similar topics to work on and mentioned his reading of Adam Smith and Wilhelm Roscher.

The letters between the end of December 1877 and the middle of March 1878 are all concerned primarily with a discussion of Tönnies' work on Hobbes. They reveal his complete absorption, after making the decision to enter a university career, in obtaining a thorough grounding in the history of philosophy.

It is clear that the guiding mind behind the Hobbes work was Paulsen's. Paulsen suggested as a basic area of concentration the relation of Descartes's, Hobbes's and Spinoza's theories of perception and will.[32] And this, indeed, was the main focus of the essay on Hobbes that Tönnies wrote in 1879.[33]

Paulsen's influence is clear in the content of the work as well. Tönnies adopted Paulsen's unitary conception of the history of philosophy (from Descartes up to the nineteenth century) as rationalistic

---

* T-P, 26/11/77. Paul de Lagarde, the antimodernist ideologue and philologist who was Tönnies' senior by a generation, similarly reconciled himself to this fate but, unlike Tönnies, was forced to endure it for over a decade. Although he enjoyed the work, he felt exiled. Fritz Stern, Lagarde's biographer, reminds us that Ranke, Droysen, and other important German scholars of the nineteenth century taught precollege students, "to the inestimable benefit of the *Gymnasia* and without real harm to themselves" (F. Stern, *Politics of Cultural Despair*, pp. 13–14).

and shaped particularly by Hobbes and Spinoza.[34] Tönnies' view that Spinoza systematized Hobbes' thoughts on the relationship between inertia (the basic principle of physics) and self-preservation (the basis of a rational ethics) was suggested in a letter of Paulsen's where he said of "the absolute ruling will to life in the animal realm": "The beginnings are in Hobbes; the system in Spinoza."[35] Another indication of influence appeared in Tönnies' view of the similarities between Hobbes and Spinoza: "But they agree in the decisive proposition that the concepts of good and evil, which determine the will, are themselves determined not through thought, but through desire and aversion."[36] Paulsen had said, in the same letter cited above, that "*bonum et malum* are determined not through the conception [*Vorstellung*], but through the will," the notion of "will" here being the seventeenth-century one, which included the affects of desire and aversion mentioned by Tönnies.

Apart from the concentration of Tönnies' attention on Hobbes, as the political and ethical philosopher of the modern epoch, perhaps the most significant point to emerge from this early correspondence is Tönnies' enthusiasm over an essay of Paulsen's, "Kultur und Religion." Though the work itself was apparently never published, the editors of the *Correspondence* believe that its main features are reproduced in Paulsen's introduction to the German translation of Hume's *Dialogues on Natural Religion*. Tönnies' laudatory remarks tell us nothing of the actual content, but he does say that he shares "the historical conception presented there in all essential points," and that he finds "new and excellent the juxtaposition of both tendencies according to their effects on life-view and life-conduct."

What these two tendencies are we do not discover from Tönnies' letter, but Paulsen's introduction to the *Dialogues* reveals a juxtaposition that is highly suggestive of Tönnies' psychological opposition of *Wesenwille* and *Kürwille*. It is the opposition of "two conceptions, clear in themselves, of the essence of God and his relation to the world." On the one hand is the rationalistic-theistic conception of the artisan God, who exists before the world, who considers how he wants to make it and, after deciding, sets it apart from himself. From then on, he occasionally acts on it, and it occasionally reacts on him. This is a goal-oriented relationship that suggests and prefigures Tönnies' *Gesellschaft-Willkür* complex. On the other hand is the pantheistic conception, Spinoza's God, who

> is not before the world, considering how he wants to erect it, for he is not before himself, considering how he wants to develop; he is not next to the world, regarding it and occasionally acting on it, but he is internally present in each thing, in every process. *The whole separation of intent and realization has no place in this view:* God himself experiences the content of world history. He has not, though, put it together beforehand in unreal imagining, so as to then set up afterwards the puppet play of reality.[37]

Thus, while Paulsen's dichotomy of "intent and realization" suggests precisely that separation of ends from means which later characterizes Tönnies' *Willkür,* the lack of this dichotomy, acting without reflection or intent, but rather according to some inherent principle of development, is the characteristic mark of *Wesenwille.* Whether or not these two conceptions of God represent the particular juxtaposition that Tönnies was excited by in the unpublished essay, there can be very little doubt, considering the closeness of the intellectual relationship between the two men, that Tönnies was at least aware of his friend's notion.

In April and May, it appears, Tönnies visited Berlin, apparently to see Paulsen and to hear some lectures of Rudolf Gneist on political economy.[38] But of much greater importance for the evolution of Tönnies' thought than his personal or intellectual experiences in these months were the political events that shook all of Germany. As a result of an assassination attempt on the Emperor, the Reichstag, on May 23, 1878, began debate on a bill to outlaw the Socialist party. Later that year, after another such attempt, the bill was passed. All those disciples of Lassalle whose goals of social peace and progress in Germany had depended on a gradual reconciliation between the Socialist party and the monarchy were suddenly deprived of hope in the future. Both Tönnies and Paulsen were, of course, among these. Although Paulsen soon swung to a more conservative, pro-Bismarckian position, Tönnies' disillusionment at this event pushed him to an ever more despairing democratic radicalism which turned, in the course of the period 1878–80, into a total spiritual and intellectual alienation from the modern age. And this, of course, was the spirit behind *Gemeinschaft und Gesellschaft*, a draft of which Tönnies wrote in 1881.

5

Tönnies and Paulsen
1878

Before 1878, Tönnies' Schleswig *Heimat* had little or no influence on him, as his initial enthusiasm for the Prussian victory over France indicates. But after his rejection of the new German state, he rediscovered his roots in the land and customs of his forebears. From then on, his homeland, its traditions, and particularly the living embodiment of those traditions, the poet and novelist Theodor Storm, were to assume increasing importance in Tönnies' work and personality.

There was as yet no suggestion of this rediscovery in May 1878, when Tönnies and Paulsen, in the midst of continued discussion of their plans for future scholarly work, began to exchange thoughts on the political and philosophical significance of the burgeoning antisocialist hysteria. But their correspondence suggests that the different directions their scholarly interests took in the eighties were in large measure a function of the different conclusions they drew from the sudden change in the political climate.

From May to October 1878, Tönnies was on a visit to England, where he discovered two unpublished manuscripts of Hobbes. The correspondence in these months is concerned, apart from Hobbes, with three topics of major significance: judgments on the contemporary political and social situation; reflections on the meaning of history (in large part stemming from the impact of events); and plans for scholarly work, partially connected with the first two. Because of the crucial impact of these months on Tönnies' intellectual development, a close scrutiny of the lengthy exchanges with Paulsen—a kind of joint diary—is in order.

Tönnies' first letter after returning to Husum from Berlin reveals a "plague-on-both-your-houses" attitude towards the conflict between the government and the Social Democrats. Since their recent encounter, "many thousand Germans have again gone mad, agitators and rulers; both types do so easily. One would have to thoroughly despair of human reason, if there were not still others, who, however, let less be heard of themselves."[1]

Paulsen's opinion of recent events is quite the same as Tönnies':

> These incidents are a national misfortune, which, together with the unreason of the masses and the mendacity of their leaders, unavoidably blocks the natural development. Worst of all, it could be that the monarchy will thereby be further pushed away from its social tasks and be driven back into the arms of the remnants of feudalism and clericalism.[2]

The question for Paulsen is whether the monarchical ship of state will be "enlightened" enough, in the true eighteenth-century sense, to perceive that it can only escape a revolutionary shipwreck if it turns to "the other group . . . supporting state and society," presumably state socialists like himself. Paulsen's hopes for a social monarchy, meager though they are, center on the Imperial Crown Prince.[3] The philosopher heaps sarcastic rage on the National Liberal press for demanding, in the name of the German people, the suppression of all "disturbers of the peace." Right, he says: "And the New Testament should be forbidden, that shameful peace-disturbing book! How can the police have allowed this revolutionary of Nazareth, this prophet of the proletariat, to do as he liked for so long! Inconceivable!"*

Yet Paulsen is far from despair about the ultimate course of things. Though God has left the daily history of man, full of lies,

---

* Paulsen-Tönnies, 20/6/78, p. 28. Seventeen years later, Friedrich Engels made the same comparison between the persecutions of early Christianity and the attacks on German socialism in the last paragraph of his introduction to the 1895 edition of Marx's *Klassenkämpfe in Frankreich*.

stupidity, and violence, to the devil, Reason, in the long run, is visible: God himself takes care of the millennia. Paulsen turns to revealed religion for a solution to the problem of evil: perhaps this life is only a testing period for another, to let God see whether the individual chooses to serve Himself or the devil. The true life begins only after this temporal history in the community of the elect. "Oh, dear Tönnies," he cries, "what a splendid life that will be if no one lies any more!"

Tönnies' long reply of July 9, 1878,[4] with the exception of a concluding paragraph about his work on Hobbes, is devoted entirely to political problems. He begins by quoting Theodor Storm on the contemporary scene, "this age of great adversity, this golden age of scoundrels," and he joins in Paulsen's condemnation of the German press by asserting the impossibility of finding in it "a grain of truth ... a breath of justice ... a drop of conscience." Unlike Paulsen, however, Tönnies does not fall back on theological explanations for social evil. The fault lies in the educational system, and the responsibility for transforming it lies with themselves and their youthful colleagues. He speaks of "young souls who are becoming free and would like to become *kaloi kagathoi* [true and beautiful]," and urges an untiring struggle "to implant that glowing Lassallean hatred against the pitiful, shameful journalistic culture." Tönnies is convinced

> that scattered everywhere men still live who feel the sharp affliction of the times just as painfully and angrily as we, that they are as yet silent like us, but are as firmly decided as we to devote their lives to the education of strong and bold heroes, who, armored with an iron philosophy, will take up again the Herculean struggle of Reason and struggle on.

What this Reason is to achieve, and what Tönnies hopefully glimpses on the horizon, is "a new age of Enlightenment ... a time of religious enthusiasm for a real moral-aesthetic civilization, whose firm foundations would be laid in social production of commodities, whose walls, therefore, would be a general, equable prosperity." Tönnies believes a great number of the despised socialist workers want just such a future. The task of philosophy is to teach them the Hobbesian "*suprema lex naturae et rationis* ... that war is to be hated and peace to be striven for." The practical consequence of this doctrine in the existing situation is that the socialists, despite their ideal of a socialist republic, should leave the abolition of the monarchy to the distant future, since it is now too firmly rooted in the past and thus cannot be abolished peacefully. Indeed, "the more the party abstains from useless attacks on the monarchical principle, against whose power it can accomplish exactly nothing, the sooner will it be able to win by legal means a just and rational constitution." Presumably to improve the "legal means," Tönnies advocates the extension of universal suffrage to all individual states and communities. For despite its "unorganic" character, universal suffrage "may nevertheless be the only just way for this epoch."

Tönnies had been heartened by the growing strength, in recent years, of the more moderate elements in the Socialist party.[5] But he fears that "after the shameless behavior of the ruling classes in this period, the real rebellion-seekers will again gain the upper hand."

From the side of the monarchy, Tönnies does not expect

> a social monarchy with its own initiative [here, too, he differs with Paulsen]—but merely an understanding one, which wants to have peace with its people. Or rather, such an empire [*Kaisertum*]. For the whole peaceful revolution, which bears the future in its womb, as well as the whole work of decentralization, can only proceed from the Reich; for Germany at least, it must be universal and simultaneous.

Apparently riding the crest of an inspirational wave, Tönnies then proceeds to a theoretical destruction of the existing German constitution and the building of a new one, which, as he notes at the end of this passage, is both Hobbesian and Platonic. The present imperial constitution is an absurdity, primarily because of the duality of power; both the Reichstag and Bundesrat have apparently equal legislative authority. Since the Reichstag is democratically elected and the Bundesrat a collection of princely favorites, "in a serious split no legislation would be possible and the institution would actually be pregnant with rebellion." The fact that, as Tönnies understood the situation, one house (presumably the Bundesrat) has gained the right, at its discretion, to send the other one home, does not improve the situation.

His solution to the problem of divided sovereignty is, apparently, to do away with the Bundesrat, and to give the Reichstag the right to elect a lifetime Kaiser from among the German princes. But this is only the beginning of Tönnies' reform. Once the general spread of Reason has brought science and philosophy into the Reichstag as well as the representative assemblies of the individual states, an "organic, social and political transformation of the whole" can begin. The Reichstag will dissolve itself and transfer its power to a council of elders, each of whom has been elected by one of the state assemblies, which in turn consists of representatives of regional assemblies, etc., down to the local community meetings of all qualified electors.

In short, Tönnies remarkably if inadvertently anticipates democratic centralism. The Platonic elements appear in the qualifications he sets for public office: Only the wisest and best of those over fifty may be chosen for the highest council. A minimum age must also be set for the lesser councils, with a lower limit of thirty for the local assembly of citizen electors. Until that age, citizens must go through a comprehensive physical and mental training, with the last years before thirty devoted to political science. To complete the rationality of his utopia, Tönnies proposes that at a certain point, the council of elders should elect a president from their own ranks, rather than from the German princes. The whole, he calls "an aristocratic Democracy or democratic Aristocracy."

As soon as he had put all this down on paper, Tönnies obviously began to worry about how his scheme would look to Paulsen. Immediately after summing up his political concept by modestly calling it a "Hobbesian-Platonic state," he says "I fear I have bored you with it." Twelve days later, without waiting for Paulsen's reply, he apologizes for the "somewhat confused scribbling of my last letter."[6]

In the same letter, Tönnies comments bitterly on an article in *Der Staatssozialist*, which gave the theory of one Moritz Carrière on "the moral world order."

> In this moral world order, the starving Chinese eat their children, and the factory owners in Germany, thanks to the thrice-cursed law of capital property, throw out their workers. . . . Moritz Carrière apparently identifies the new German

Reich with the Reich of the spirit and of freedom. What a pure philosopher Most is, compared with Moritz Carrière.*

Paulsen's following letters of July 24 and 28 restate his philosophy of history, with Darwin taking over from God most of the responsibility for the progress of Reason. Human history reveals

> a process of development from bestiality to humanity . . . Darwin brought it to my consciousness. The unreasonable is also the impossible; it comes into the world, but only to go under. And, conversely, if a thing has Reason in it, it will survive. If the work of social reformation is from God, then it will stand, even if there are as many dailies and national newspapers as tiles in the roofs of Berlin.[7]

A hopeful sign of progress for Paulsen is the son of the Crown Prince, second in the line of succession, whose mother has insisted on sending him to England in the company of a well-known historian, so as to broaden his horizons: "She does not want her son to meet only with officers; he must learn to have other viewpoints for things than military ones, etc." Heartened by his burst of Panglossian optimism, Paulsen has come to be much less troubled than Tönnies over the moves to outlaw the Socialist party. Even in this legislative error, the hand of Reason is hidden:

> Persecution is a salutary stage of purification and strengthening of a reform movement. It must all be fulfilled, what stands written of the son of man: he must be surrendered into the hands of the heathen, and they will condemn, crucify, and kill him—and on the third day he will rise again.

In the weeks following this letter, Paulsen paid a visit to Theodor Storm in Husum, and to his own parents, who lived in the same general area,[8] at just the time that Tönnies himself went to England for two months of research on Hobbes. Tönnies' first letter from London, apart from telling about his discovery of two lost manuscripts of Hobbes,[9] is more pessimistic in its condemnation of modern civilization, German society, and the course of Reason than anything he has previously written.

---

* Johann Most was a socialist who, after expulsion from the German Socialist party in 1880, emigrated to England and the U.S. and became an anarchist.

London gives Tönnies the impression of a bloated, hedonistic civilization, resting on rotten foundations of human misery. "Every morning," he writes,

> I look down from the raised omnibus bench, half with anger, half with melancholy sympathy, on the small dirty lads, who, in constant danger of being crushed by the rattling wagons, are dully occupied in shoveling up the horse dung—in truth, a very useful thing, but worth being purchased with the misery of young men, *of our brothers?*

For Tönnies, the well-being of human individuals is the highest value. So far only a small number had discovered that, in history, the heightened well-being of the few has been achieved only by the sacrifice of the many. Nevertheless, Tönnies, for a fleeting moment optimistic, thinks it probable that "a time will come when one views this sacrifice as just as barbaric as the human sacrifice of savages or the tortures and auto-da-fés of Christians." Of course, the relatively enlightened state of public opinion in England provides more hope for this millennium than does that in Germany. Exposés of mass misery occasionally appear in the English liberal press, and apart from the press, there is generally, for Tönnies, a refreshing honesty in the Englishman's picture of himself. "It is most common for them to describe their fatherland as a 'country of drunkards.' Such things appear among us only from bitter enemies of the Reich. Otherwise it is, 'Our nation, finally strong in pomp and glory, united against external and internal enemies, etc. etc.' Only Beaconsfield speaks like that here and, indeed, when he is drunk." The press is "with all due respect completely incapable of comprehending the profundity of Bismarckian state wisdom. . . . The leading paper said of the 'thought control' Law [the bill to outlaw the Socialist party]: one must of course not view it as the monster it *would* be in England."[10]

At the end of this letter, Tönnies returns more soberly to the question Paulsen has raised of the unfolding of Reason in history: Who guarantees Paulsen that all the objectionable sides of human reason, for example, the willingness to lie and deceive, will not be strengthened from one generation to the next by the struggle for survival? Does anything but wishful thinking tell them that civilization is possible on some other basis than legal, or economic and moral, slavery? The course of Reason may lead to growing inequality, if increasing population makes it necessary. In disillusion and despair, the young Tönnies asks whether the final goals of Reason "have not ceased to be morality and art, on which the matured Reason looks back as on the dream-like ideals of a foolish youth," but have rather become the goals of "making life ever more comfortable, more lazy, and more soft, in other words, more insensible, for its cavaliers."[11]

Paulsen's reply is devoted to convincing Tönnies of the ultimate victory of Reason. At the outset, he establishes rapport with Tönnies' sensitivity to social misery by citing his own horrified reaction to the abrupt class differences in the landed estates on the eastern coast of Holstein, where he is vacationing. In this "divine order," everyone, from the four hundred beaten near-slaves to the proprietor, is miserable, but holy laws require that anyone who questions the perfection of the situation will be punished as a criminal. Paulsen goes so far as to attack the slaughters of the Franco-Prussian War as serving the interest of the ruling classes, and expostulates, "Oh, God, that is divine order? That is a disorder, crying to heaven. And it should and can and will not persist, as long as your holy name, Reason, is still named on earth . . . with reverence."

Tönnies should not despair of Reason. Her reign will yet come. As for Tönnies' fear that the struggle for existence will encourage the unsocial characteristics of man, Paulsen denies this. It is society as a whole, not its individual members, that experiences and reacts to events, and therefore society as a whole that learns from its experience and progresses. And the task of the philosopher is to spare society any unnecessary evils by helping it to know its proper course on the basis of the fewest possible experiences.

Paulsen tries to convince Tönnies of the immanence of Reason by a rapid sketch of recent German history. Germany must now decide between the interests of a ruling group, including the remains of feudalism and the bourgeoisie, and the interests of the vast majority. But it is able to confront this decision clearly only because the question of the external shape of the German nation was solved by Bismarck in 1866 and 1870, because most of the old feudal and clerical institutions have been reduced to insignificance, and because the masses, whatever the motive, have been given the vote. "Reason is cunning, says Hegel; it even knows how to use Prussian Junkers and lieutenants to obtain its goal."¹² The accession of the Crown Prince will tidy up all the loose ends.*

Thus fortified by Hegel's *Vernunft* and its purported incarnation in the future Emperor, Paulsen's optimism rebounds from the doubts of the earlier part of the letter to new paeans of praise for the status quo: "The National Liberals justly have a feeling of satiety. . . . How can anyone still be dissatisfied?"

Tönnies, meanwhile, has spoken at length with Johannes Heller, who had accompanied the future Wilhelm II to England, and has heard enough to be able to say in his answering letter,

> The prince seems to be pretty much of a blockhead. . . . My opinion is thereby confirmed: the monarchy is played out. Whatever its intrinsic value, it now sticks together with all grotesque, half-dead institutions and together with them we shall have to bury it. Whatever the intrinsic value of democracy, it is the only possible regime for a future civilized state. If we join in the struggle for democracy, we are no more rebels than the *logos* demands us to be. . . . Practically speaking, the political task of the coming period—and the Social Democrats are (as almost always) right; without this, no social task can be solved—is to bring the monarchy to renounce voluntarily, but completely, its "rights of sovereignty."

Tönnies comes back to the question of meaning in history and roundly denies that there is any. Nonetheless, he does allow for a modified form of Reason, which though not closely defined, would seem to be much more a matter of individual possession and cultivation, especially in art and philosophy, than Paulsen's Hegelian Reason. He also allows that the individual reason he does accept suggests the desirability of an ideal state, apparently the fusion of Hobbes and Plato he had mentioned earlier, but he considers the possibility of achieving this state to be remote.

* Johannes Heller, the professor chosen by the court to accompany the Crown Prince's son to England, was a close friend of Paulsen, and after Paulsen heard a personal report from Heller on the mind and demeanor of the future Wilhelm II, his hopes seem to have vanished (Paulsen, *Autobiography*, p. 286).

The next letter from Paulsen and the following one from Tönnies, the last before the two friends meet again in Berlin, simply restate and sharpen their respective political positions. Paulsen acknowledges the justice of Tönnies' critique both from the Hobbesian standpoint of a single sovereignty and from the less theoretical one of misrule. Yet he can see no alternative to the monarchy. He finds it the only possible internal means of holding the nation together. Only a slow education of the people can prepare them for a new political framework. Tönnies repeats his Hobbesian argument that there can be only one sovereign power in the state and says that the monarchical democracy in Germany, really an oligarchy, is actually the bitter enemy of both monarchy and democracy. In a brief "personal credo," he adds,

> Now, that oligarchy (as it exists in England and only a little less openly in Germany) is a product of the economic power of capital and a guarantee of its permanence. If one wants to struggle against this oligarchy, that is possible only from the extremes; one must pull on the end of kingship or of democracy. *My* heart becomes warmer every day for democracy; the ugly period of public life in which we now move has significantly nourished my hatred against the "existing state and social order."

Considering the letters of this five-month period as a whole, most obvious is the overpowering significance of Hobbes and the lingering influence of Plato on Tönnies' thought on the ideal state. And certainly Paulsen, who had directed Tönnies to work on Hobbes, was also impressed by Hobbes. Of modern German thinkers, they both seem, at the beginning at least, to share a high regard for Lassalle; Paulsen obviously has an affinity for Hegel, and Tönnies reveals a trace of Nietzschean influence. But apart from these three figures, neither man shows any interest in, or knowledge of, German nineteenth-century thought. Paulsen twice shows antipathy;[*] Tönnies

---

[*] P-T, 20/6/78: Writing of his research in the history of education, Paulsen says, "With much edification, I have again tarried in the eighteenth century. How superior its healthy rationalism is to the mindless reaction of the nineteenth century." 3/8/78: "I believe the historical concern with the seventeenth and eighteenth centuries can do pretty much to free us from the Restoration flood of the nineteenth century."

simply does not mention it. Both men, on the other hand, are much attracted by contemporary or recent English thought. Paulsen tries to work Darwin into his history of philosophy. And Tönnies, at one point, impressed by "the theory of development," says he is contemplating a study on the evolution of human thought, which would investigate such things as the separation of prose from poetic thought, the beginning of scientific thought, "in other words, the history of civilization from the viewpoint of logic,"[13] a task partially fulfilled in *Gemeinschaft und Gesellschaft*. Other English thinkers with whom Tönnies is concerned in this period are James Mill and Ricardo,[14] and from earlier centuries, Adam Smith[15] and William Petty.[16]

Two questions arise from these exchanges. To what can one attribute the political difference between Tönnies and Paulsen that develops in this period? And what relation, if any, is there between Tönnies' views in this period and the conceptions found in *Gemeinschaft und Gesellschaft*?

The first question is the more difficult. Tönnies' evolution to a position of democratic radicalism appears at first sight to be a consequence of his Hobbesian demand for a single sovereign power. But Paulsen also saw himself as a Hobbesian, yet did not feel compelled to reach such a radical conclusion. Was Tönnies, then, simply more consistent? In general, this is true; he did take a more undeviating approach than Paulsen, whose thinking became thoroughly entangled with Hegel, Darwin, and revealed religion. But at one point, Tönnies logically deduced from Hobbes' requirement of social peace a recognition by the Socialists that the monarchy was there to stay. At a later stage, Tönnies deduced from Hobbes' requirement for a single sovereign power the need for the party of democracy to eliminate the monarchy altogether.

If, however, the key to Tönnies' growing radicalism is unlikely to be found in the realm of pure theory, it may be discovered in personality and in social setting. Paulsen himself later referred to Tönnies' "way of looking at things in a melancholy light and more especially his pessimistic interpretation of the course of history," and explained both by a generally sickly physical constitution.[17] While there may be much to this insight, the differing social situations of the two men may also have been important in their diverging political views. Paulsen, after all, was an established young academician in Berlin, who, for all the sincerity of his social convictions, had been well treated by "the system" and could look forward to a successful career in it. Tönnies, on the other hand, was a marginal man. He had failed his doctoral examination in Berlin, been too sick to take it in Kiel, and finally had to take it in Tübingen. His choice of a field of study, originally classical philology, was now unsettled. His native Schleswig, where he had recently been living and studying, had a long history of hostility to alien state powers, which had turned it against Prussia in the 1860s and produced a socialist protest vote three times the national average in the 1870s.[18] His close friend Storm, who had written in 1864 of the "system of brutal power rule that appears inseparable from the Prussian state,"[19] had very likely discussed the antisocialist law with Tönnies.[20] Finally, Tönnies' marginality became externality when he visited England and saw the German press and political system through the eyes of English liberals.

Thus, the two men related their intellectual arsenals to their personal experiences in very different ways. Though their theoretical equipment and their perceptions of social misery and political inadequacy were similar, Tönnies, lacking any stake in things as they were, used his intellectual arsenal to equip his personal experiences with a shattering firepower of radical criticism. Paulsen, however, who had no desire to destroy the comfortable prospects of the *status quo*, was continually constraining his experience and dampening the powder in his intellectual magazine.

As for the relation between Tönnies' views in this period on the one hand, and in *Gemeinschaft und Gesellschaft* on the other, there are several elements of relationship and one of total nonrelationship. The notion of writing a history of the development of logical thought, though not connected to anything else in the letters of this period, ultimately, as mentioned above, found its way into the later work. The sudden disillusion with the course of history that appeared in the letter of August 21, 1878 was, if only in temperament, closely related to Tönnies' *Hauptwerk*. More importantly, Tönnies' "hate for the 'existing state and social order'" provided a harshly critical distance from contemporary society which was to facilitate greatly his coming emotional leap into the past. And Hobbes, though his doctrines later ceased to be an absolute ideal for Tönnies, and were made relative to the mental framework of modern society, always remained for him *the* political philosopher of *Gesellschaft*.

Nevertheless, Tönnies' upholding of state sovereignty—even a democratic state sovereignty—indicates that he was as yet remote from the duality for which he became famous. Indeed, this remoteness was still evident a year later, in Leipzig, when Tönnies wrote a conclusion for his essay on Hobbes that barely distinguished between *Gemeinschaft* and *Gesellschaft*, and to the extent that it did so at all, retained the Hobbesian framework intact. Showing a complete ignorance of the meaning customarily given to *Gemeinschaft* by most nineteenth-century thought, not to mention by his own later theory, he used the word to refer to Hobbes' commonwealth.* The only distinction he did make was between what he called a *Gemeinschaft* state, in which the communal will was expressed by the absolute sovereignty of an unlimited monarchy, and a *Gesellschaft* state, in which *Gemeinschaft* (presumably meaning the permanent embodiment of the social will in absolute monarchy) was considered unnecessary and was replaced by "two-sided relations, equally binding and revocable, of men to each other." Both concepts, according to Tönnies, were derivations from Hobbes' theory, and if we recall Tönnies' last letter from London, in which he wrote to Paulsen that the sovereign power had either to be embodied in an absolute monarch *or* in a democratic electorate, with all compromises logically excluded,[21] it is not difficult to see that Tönnies himself was the deriver. In any case, in October 1878, and perhaps later, he explicitly preferred the *Gesellschaft* state and bitterly opposed the "*gemeinschaftliche*" monarchy. A greater contrast to his later denial that theories of absolute monarchy, or for that matter, any theory of state power, could in any way be connected with *Gemeinschaft*, to his later insistence that all such theories and

---

* F. Tönnies, "Anmerkungen über die Philosophie des Hobbes," *Vierteljahresschrift für wissenschaftliche Philosophie*, V (1881) (hereafter referred to as Tönnies, "Anmerkungen"), pp. 194–204 passim, e.g., "All *Gemeinschaft* is thought to have originated from contracts of individuals, as with Hobbes."

such state systems were products of *Gesellschaft,* and to his later unqualified admiration for the values and life style of *Gemeinschaft,* can scarcely be imagined.

6

The Sources of *Gemeinschaft und Gesellschaft*

Tönnies' Rediscovery of the Heimat

TÖNNIES SPENT THE WINTER SEMESTER of 1878–79 in Berlin. He was particularly interested in the seminar of Alexander von Oettingen on social statistics and also did a paper on socioeconomic relations in Greek antiquity for Adolf Wagner. The latter led him into a study of Rodbertus, author of a history of Roman agrarian development in the Imperial period and an early state socialist who counted Wagner himself among his disciples. Since the antisocialist bill had just been passed, discussions on the social question were lively and tense in Wagner's seminar. And of course, Tönnies spent much time with Paulsen, who had recently married:

> I visited his new home very often, and many walks, in and outside of Berlin, brought endless discussions on philosophical and on political-social problems, in the course of which we exchanged our quite radical thoughts, in no way friendly to the regime.[1]

Paulsen says that Tönnies spent Christmas and New Year's Day with him,[2] so that it is no great surprise to discover that when they resumed their correspondence in June 1879 (Tönnies having returned to Husum), they used the familiar *du*. This closer personal relationship to Paulsen was not the only thing Tönnies brought back from Berlin. Apparently the discussions and the exposure to the ideas of *Kathedersozialisten* such as Wagner, with notions similar to those of Paulsen, had stimulated Tönnies to begin thinking of a work of social criticism of his own.

From this seed *Gemeinschaft und Gesellschaft* was to grow. Indeed, the six-year period between Tönnies' departure from Berlin, in the spring of 1879, and his lectures at the University of Kiel, in the summer of 1885, encompasses all the preliminary stages in the formulation of his own social theory. On July 31, 1879, Tönnies revealed the first intimation of this theory when he wrote to Paulsen: "The continual evil of this age has been plaguing me to write down in one place my opinions on economic and political things. But I am too slow at creating." By January 9, 1881, he had finally decided that the work he was preparing to hand in to the philosophy faculty at Kiel as his *Habilitationsschrift*, and which was an outgrowth of that earlier hesitant intention, would bear the title *Gemeinschaft und Gesellschaft*. And his lectures in 1885 presented the theory in a form practically identical with the book of 1887.

Nevertheless, the working out of his own theory, though a recurring theme, was far from being the only object of his attention in this period. The completion and revision of his long essay on Hobbes occupied him at least until November 1879 and possibly as late as March 1880.[*] Sometime in late 1880 and early 1881 he interrupted his work on the first draft of *Gemeinschaft und Gesellschaft* to write a paper on Plato, which, however, he was unable to publish.[3] (As with the Hobbes manuscript, it was Paulsen who suggested the latter topic to Tönnies.[4]) In 1883, he devoted time to a brief monograph on the development of Spinoza's thought.[5]

There were other interruptions. Several times during this period,

---

[*] On June 25, 1879, writing of the revision of the first section, Tönnies complained, "It is a tortured draft. But it was [sic] now too late to completely rework it. Since we have similar taste, you will also find it bad. What fortune, that the periodical columns are not marble tablets!" The last article in the *Vierteljahrsschrift für wissen. Philos.* (1881) is signed "Leipzig," where Tönnies stayed, according to his letters, from November 1879 to March 1880.

Tönnies, apparently driven by his headaches to despair over his creative theoretical efforts, switched his main interest to a study on social statistics.[6] After the first such change, Paulsen chided him,[7] and Tönnies dropped the study. But instead of going back to his major work, he became temporarily involved in a project for a periodical to which Nietzsche and his circle and Tönnies, Paulsen, and their circle were jointly to contribute. The goal of this journal was to form a "community of thinkers" (*Denkergemeinde*) to influence university students and *Gymnasium* teachers: "There are here [Leipzig], as I have heard today (*entre nous*), not a few students who, from embarrassment and bitterness, secretly read the Zürich *Social-Democrat*; these we want to guide and edify."[8] But despite Paulsen's encouraging offers of support,[9] the project foundered, and Tönnies returned to his theoretical work. Five months later, immediately after a long defensive lament about his headaches, which Paulsen seemed to think were exaggerated in Tönnies' mind by his lack of self-discipline, he was again talking about his *"Lieblingsplan"* for a comparative study of national crime statistics.[10] And again, though he sandwiched in a brief period of work on the theoretical opus,[11] this was succeeded by a phase of intense interest in the establishment of some kind of community of scholars for the propagation of the social gospel.[12]

Despite the frequent interruption of Tönnies' work on *Gemeinschaft und Gesellschaft*, the elements of sentiment and intellect that went into it unfolded steadily between 1879 and 1885. Since Tönnies was a man whose social passions clearly shaped his intellectual directions, it may be useful to distinguish between these passions—the term *Weltanschauung*, implying an emotionally charged view of the world, is appropriate—and the intellectual structures based on them.

The components of Tönnies' *Weltanschauung* were a total alienation from modern society (going back to his reaction to the antisocialist law); the development of a new and positive view of the Middle Ages; and, as a psychic corollary to his alienation from modern society, the quest for a new community, which he sought at first in a utopia of intellectuals, then increasingly in his attachment to his native land and its bard, Theodor Storm. The principal theoretical inclinations nourished by this *Weltanschauung* were: first, Tönnies' discovery of, and gradual immersion in, the late nineteenth-century anthropology of primitive life, which, in stressing the communal aspects of primitive society, gave an altogether different picture of the state of nature than did Hobbes; second, his investigations into modern theories of the relation between human will, natural law, and political economy; and finally, his increasingly polemical stance toward modern theories of the state, which viewed it as transcending the divisions of *Gesellschaft*.

In the actual development of Tönnies' thought, of course, many of these elements appear side by side and are actually dependent on one another. It is often impossible to be just to the origin of the ideas that went into *Gemeinschaft und Gesellschaft* without showing this interdependence. Again the correspondence with Paulsen provides a diary of Tönnies' intellectual evolution. In the first letters written by Tönnies after his return from Berlin (June 25, July 31, and October 30, 1879), we see the intertwining of two of the elements that are to destroy Tönnies' previous political and historical attitudes and prepare his new *Weltanschauung*.* In Tocqueville and Carlyle, he finds condemnation of the political, social, and economic trends of modern society, and in Emile Laveleye's book on primitive property,[13] he finds an extensive discussion of village and house communities as the universal basis from which more advanced civilization developed.

The new turn appears vividly in the same paragraph that informs Paulsen of Carlyle's "gripping and provocative sermon" (*Past and Present*). Here, Tönnies for the first time expresses his intention to set down his own "thoughts on economic and political things"; in this same letter, Tönnies describes "misunderstanding and scorning of the Middle Ages, economic and moral individualism," as "some of the most striking weaknesses of the Enlightenment."

A similar close relationship appears between the reading of the Laveleye book and the resumption of the historical pessimism of

---

* Tönnies himself sanctions the use of the term "*Weltanschauung*" in reference to his conceptions in his first draft of *Gemeinschaft und Gesellschaft* (1881). See Ferdinand Tönnies, *Soziologische Studien und Kritiken* (Jena, 1924–27), 3 vols., I p. 4. Henceforth referred to as SSK.

his earlier letter to Paulsen, in which he feared that the main trend of modern life was going away from moral and aesthetic ideals to luxury for its own sake.[14] The development of Tönnies' alienation from that earlier letter to this one is strongly suggested in that, whereas before, luxury and its vices had been seen as opposed to social equality and moral-aesthetic goals, now Tönnies fears that even if socialism and the idea of equality should triumph, the evil of modern life will persist: "If that is so, if men *remain selfish* in socialism, *inclined* more to luxury and idleness than to moral companionship and labor—then what use is it?"[15]

Of further interest in this letter is the concept of *Gemeinschaft,* which Tönnies has only recently used in the essay on Hobbes to characterize absolute monarchy (bad); here it is used to characterize socialism (good). But perhaps the most significant element in this transitional phase of Tönnies' *Weltanschauung* is that changed attitude toward the Middle Ages to which I have alluded above.

The favorable view of the Middle Ages that Tönnies clearly had implied in his letter of July 31, 1879, was adopted by Paulsen, who rather abruptly altered his earlier dislike for that period,* and taken up with redoubled vigor by Tönnies in his letter of October 30, 1879, where, most significantly, his new valuation of the Middle Ages brought him to think in terms of a synthesis of the contemporary intellectual shadow of the Middle Ages—romanticism—and the rationalism of which he had hitherto been such a stern advocate.

* Paulsen-Tönnies, 12/7/79: "What a feeling of well-being in the seventeenth and eighteenth centuries! Is it not like that of the convalescent, who, after fifteen hundred years of deathly illness, gradually feels health stream through his members again?" Just one month later (13/8/79), Paulsen wrote: "If we are ordained to stay where we are, if the present structure is not transitional, then one would have to view the whole development since the 16th century, that is, the tendency of accumulation, which destroyed first the political, then the economic life of the Middle Ages, as degeneration. . . ." For Paulsen, the keynote of the modern epoch was "increasing collectivization of production, increasing individualization of consumption." Under the old rural economy, perhaps twenty separate producers made all the necessities of life for the patriarchal household. But in the modern period, "Through the development of commerce (of capitalist production) it has become possible to consume the productivity of all these men without ever seeing one of them, without any kind of *Gemeinschaft,* not even that of direct purchase, much less of house *Gemeinschaft,* occurring." The positive value Paulsen placed on *Gemeinschaft* undoubtedly reinforced the idyllic picture of the *Hausgemeinschaft* that Tönnies was soon to receive from Laveleye's *Ureigentum* (T-P, 30/10/79).

Again discussing the Middle Ages, Tönnies wrote,

> It is a world which to us—to us as a people—is irretrievably lost. The men in whom these feelings were still living were more decent and generous than we. And don't we meet a certain elevation of mind ... together with simplicity, loyalty, and most blessed cheerfulness in the Middle Ages. It was precisely the period of growth and blossoming of our people. I am more and more convinced of this, especially on the basis of economic considerations. That is romanticism. Yes, it is romanticism, and I think too that we must bind romanticism and rationalism into a higher synthesis, i.e., not as our whole generation has done since the thirties, to a muddle in practice —there rationalism must prevail quite pure and unfalsified— but rather we may permit the romantic manner of thought in our theoretical observations (in ethics, sociology and the philosophy of history) to the extent that we justly appreciate the moral power of religion against that which, until now, reason has shown in the history of men.

The religion he is talking about, he continues, is not religion formulated in terms of more or less rational dogmas, but rather the "actually superstitious religion" that

> accompanied the life of peoples as long as it rested on healthy and rational ... economic and social circumstances, and also perished or decayed with the same, and became an object of mockery or falseness. In the history of community, belief was in fact higher than reason, or was itself the highest reason; so that one could perhaps say that reason only rose to the human mind after it had escaped from below, from the heart or the will.

Tönnies tells Paulsen of his current preoccupation with these ideas ("more than ever before") and indicates in a parenthetic remark that he seems to be coming back to the *Weltanschauung* of his early years as a university student: "scorn for Darwinism and denial of the progress of mankind." Then follows the passage mentioned above, in which he fears that socialism may only deepen moral decadence.

The significance of these letters from June to October 1879 can scarcely be overestimated. In the first place, they reveal a new historical perception in contradiction to his Hobbesian assumptions. The transfigured vision of the Middle Ages, and especially of popular religion, is most important here. There seems, in addition, to be a new and non-Hobbesian view of the state of nature, with the term *Gemeinschaft* now being used, for the first time, more or less consistently with his own later usage, to describe the primitive human condition. There is also the resumption of his previous pessimism regarding the possibility of any embodiment of moral-aesthetic ideals in future society, and a linking of this current in his thought with an earlier rejection of the idea of Progress and of Darwinism (otherwise unelaborated, but probably related to his youthful period of intense admiration for Nietzsche). All in all, we might say that Tönnies is increasingly finding value not in that democratic transformation of the present which he had previously hoped for, but in the communal and religious institutions of an irretrievable past.

But in addition to showing just how and when Tönnies first displayed the *Weltanschauung* that underlies *Gemeinschaft und Gesellschaft*, these letters also indicate important sources of his early thought on that work to which he later gave scant treatment in his many prefaces to *Gemeinschaft und Gesellschaft* and in other writings on the origins of his thought. These sources include, in addition to Tocqueville—whose work on the continuity between royal absolutist and modern democratic centralization of social and political life is today well known—Carlyle and Laveleye. Thomas Carlyle, in his *Past and Present*, offered an evaluation of the Middle Ages and the contemporary scene that fitted perfectly into Tönnies' own mood of the moment. All the anger and despair at the poverty, unsound institutions, and moral decadence of modern society that had been growing in Tönnies since the antisocialist law seemed to cut off all hope in the future was mirrored in this book, and to place modern conditions in their true perspective, Carlyle had artfully and lovingly re-created the mood of the Middle Ages through the pages of an ancient English monastery chronicle:

> How much is still alive in England; how much has not yet come into life! A Feudal Aristocracy is still alive, in the prime of life; superintending the cultivation of the land, and less consciously the distribution of the produce of the land, the

adjustment of the quarrels of the land. . . . How silent, on the other hand, lie all Cotton-trades and such-like; not a steeple-chimney yet got on end from sea to sea! . . .

Our religion is not yet a horrible restless Doubt, still less a far horribler composed Cant; but a great heaven-high Unquestionability, encompassing, interpenetrating, the whole of Life. Imperfect as we may be, we are here, with our litanies, shaven crowns, vows of poverty, to testify incessantly and indisputably to every heart, That this Earthly Life and *its* riches and possessions, and good and evil hap, are not intrinsically a reality at all, but *are* a shadow of realities eternal, infinite; that this Time-world, as an air-image, fearfully *emblematic,* plays and flickers in the grand still mirror of Eternity. . . . Which testified or not, remembered by all men or forgotten by all men, does verily remain the fact, even in Arkwright Joe-Manton ages. But it is incalculable, when litanies have grown obsolete; when *fodercorns, avragiums* and all human dues and reciprocities have been fully changed into one great due of *cash payment*: and man's duty to man reduces itself to handing him certain metal coins, or covenanted money-wages, and then shoving him out of doors; and man's duty to God becomes a cant, a doubt, a dim inanity, a "pleasure of virtue" or suchlike: and the thing a man does infinitely fear (the real *Hell* of a man) is, "that he does not make money and advance himself,"—I say it is incalculable what a change has introduced itself everywhere in human affairs.[16]

This continual juxtaposition of medieval and modern, always to the disadvantage of the modern, cannot but have appealed to Tönnies, who had been prepared from his *Gelehrtenschule* days to think in terms of such oppositions,[17] and who certainly must have been looking for such a basis as Carlyle offered for his attack on German life. Indeed, shortly after the appearance of *Gemeinschaft und Gesellschaft* (1887), Paulsen encouraged Tönnies to do a comparative study of Carlyle and J. S. Mill, saying, "Perhaps there is no man to whose way of looking at things you stand closer than Carlyle."*

---

* P-T, 1/1/88. Tönnies did not seem especially taken with the comparison (see T-P, 12/1/88).

Nevertheless, there was an essential difference between Carlyle and Tönnies. The Englishman was at heart a literary man, a publicist, who in his disdain for modern science felt no need for any other technique of reaching the truth than soul-searching and the ancient and honorable methods of literary humanism. Tönnies, while sharing many of his values, was committed to the rationalist methods of modern scholarship. Thus, he could not leave his values at the level of mood and assertion, as Carlyle had done, but felt compelled to deal with contemporary social theories and to establish such a theory of his own, based so far as possible on scientifically established fact. In particular, any conception of human nature or the original human society that ran counter to the atomist premises of Hobbesian and post-Hobbesian social theory would have to be based on a comprehensive historical refutation of the Hobbesian conception of the state of nature. Emile de Laveleye's work on primitive property, in the German edition of the political economist Karl Bücher, supplied such a refutation, gave Tönnies two of the basic categories of *Gemeinschaft*, and furthermore referred Tönnies to other recent works of the same genre.[18]

Laveleye's thesis was that in the origins of every people, land was the property not of the individual, but of the community. The book was an early example of historical anthropology, using existing studies of a comprehensive range of cultures.* It dealt, for the most part, with village community (*Dorfgemeinschaft*) and home community (*Hausgemeinschaft*), thus suggesting to Tönnies two of the three forms of *Gemeinschaft* he was to describe in the first section of his book.† And in doing so, it certainly must have offered a convincing alternative to the Hobbesian picture of primitive man as a savage fighting a war of all against all.

Other insights dealing with legal and economic development, though less important to Laveleye's work, may have been of considerable value to Tönnies. The following account of the origin of

---

* Nations mentioned in the table of contents are Russia, Java, India, Germany, Switzerland, Finland and Scandinavia, the Netherlands, Belgium, France, America, Greece, Rome, Ireland, England, China, and Turkey.
† Ferdinand Tönnies, *Gemeinschaft und Gesellschaft* (Leipzig, 1887), Book I, Section I, par. 10–18. The third form is the city community (*Stadtgemeinschaft*).

law in *Gemeinschaft* is certainly very close to Tönnies' own later theory, and in any case directed him to the man whom Tönnies did mention as his principal inspirer:[19]

> Sir Henry Maine believes that the application of the same methods [comparative historical research] to the beginnings of law could cast a whole new light on the original phases of the development of civilization; one would clearly perceive that the laws are not the arbitrary product of human will, but are on the one side the consequence of certain economic needs, on the other the expression of particular ideas of justice originating in moral and religious feelings.[20]

In Bücher's chapter on existing remnants of the old German agrarian constitution, there is another passage dealing with the historical forces opposed to the old community, which may also have stuck in Tönnies' mind:[21] "As a result of the encroachments of the landlords, the interference of the absolute state, the influence of the Roman law and of individualistic political economy, the community of *Markgenossen* was first limited and then finally destroyed." Tönnies, whether or not he was inspired directly by Bücher on the matter, certainly developed a similar notion of the antagonism between the old peasant community on the one hand and the absolute state, Roman law, and atomistic political economy on the other.

Indeed, Tönnies wrote that along with other studies of primitive agrarian communism, the Laveleye work gave "new confirmation [to] the historical school of law, which found its favorite in customary law and invoked the feeling for law and the quietly working powers of the popular spirit."[22] This certainly points toward another of the problems that preoccupied Tönnies during this period: finding a new conception of natural law to replace his heavily battered Hobbesian one.

In that same very important letter of October 30, 1879, Tönnies replied to Paulsen's suggestion that he write down his thoughts on politics and social doctrine by announcing his desire, if he had the strength, to write a small book under the title "The Law as a Philosophical Problem." It was to contain a brief history of natural law, a refutation of some of the crudest errors on the subject, and his own theory, presented in connection with an evaluation of recent literature. The work he seemed most concerned with was Rudolf Ihering's *Zweck im Recht,* the first volume of which had appeared in 1877. Although appalled by Ihering's inflated presentation, he found intelligent insights scattered throughout and agreed with the basic thought of the second half, which saw the state as an ordering force over a society based on the wage principle.

Three months later he wrote that he had held two lectures on "The Renewal of Natural Law Through Ihering and Wagner," and further noted that he had been reading the second volume of August Schäffle's *Bau und Leben des Sozialen Körpers* and found it "far superior both in philosophical understanding and in energy of thought to both Ihering and Wagner."[23]

On April 1, 1880, Tönnies supplied a new outline for his work on natural law. It was to contain a logical evaluation, partially finished, of Ihering's *Zweck im Recht*; "an essay on the scientific view of law in general," which differed from his previous outline in that he now included in addition to the natural law school, "romanticism and its aftereffects," and a section "on the comparative legal research of our time in connection with economic history, influence of Darwinism and of socialism"; and "critique of all these directions and characterization of future tasks." He now seemed determined to confront directly his old preconceptions with the new historical insights he had gained from Laveleye and perhaps others.

Of great importance in mediating this confrontation, of preventing a complete rupture between the old and the new, was the application to his two sets of theoretical conceptions of recent Darwinian evolutionary theory, which he found especially well stated in Schäffle, and which was to allow him to view the Hobbesian, atomized *Gesellschaft* as part of a process of social development leading out of, and distinct from, earlier communal forms of existence. In the light of his own developing theory, however, he had also to condemn the basic conceptions of Ihering and Schäffle, who both thought in terms of a single pattern of social existence, leading up to the state as a new bulwark of *Gemeinschaft.*

Ihering and Schäffle were to Tönnies not nearly as important for the contemporary German theory of the state as Lorenz von Stein

(1815–90) and Rudolf Gneist (1816–95). On May 2, 1880, a month after writing the previous letter, Tönnies had a new plan to present.

He now wanted to attack his problem from the standpoint of the concepts of "state" and "society," dealing principally with Stein and Gneist,* only secondarily with Schäffle, but emphasizing his own views rather than his critique of others. Furthermore, as opposed to a concern with abstract state and legal philosophy, the object of his work was to be predominantly historical material, though the treatment would be philosophical. In brief: "It will be situated rather under the discipline of the philosophy of history than under that of the history of philosophy."[24] Tönnies planned to submit the work as his *Habilitationsschrift* to the University of Kiel.

Eight months later, Tönnies finally decided on the title his work was to bear.

> Hopefully, by the end of February, enough of my work—which was again interrupted by the Plato article and moreover has cost me many hours of externally unsuccessful cogitation—will be completed to hand in to the faculty. I have no time tonight to discuss it and only want to tell you that, under the title *Gemeinschaft und Gesellschaft,* I deal with the antithesis which the newer people (Stein, Gneist, et al.) have handled as that of *State* and Society, and in my opinion in a liberalistically false way; which one can also generally characterize as that of order and freedom or as connection through duties and connection through interchange. But I work it out differently. And I see myself compelled first to develop a number of elementary concepts, through which the theme will touch on Ihering's *Zweck im Recht,* vol. 1, to which I also refer.[25]

In April 1881, Tönnies wrote the first draft he had been talking about. But it showed little of the fireworks he had been promising. As he himself confessed to Paulsen, it contained nothing to indicate

---

* When Tönnies finally did write such a critique, he dealt with Gneist as a disciple of Stein ("Der Begriff der Gemeinschaft," 1919, SSK, II, 266–76). For Stein's theory, he used the "Einleitung" to Stein's *Geschichte der sozialen Bewegung Frankreichs seit 1789* (Leipzig, 1850).

his relation to other theorists, nor any hint of concrete applications. What, then, was it?

The first draft of *Gemeinschaft und Gesellschaft* is some thirty pages of conceptual hairsplitting.[26] The first third establishes Tönnies' conception of the nature of *Kulturwissenschaft* and of philosophy. His notion of philosophy is particularly revealing, since it throws into relief two of the contradictory characteristics of his lifework: his concern with developing strong, abstract concepts, and his belief that philosophy must be concerned with evaluating and must be practical:

> Amidst all difference of opinion on the goal and value of philosophy, one thought appears to remain central: philosophy is to bring forth and represent a *Weltanschauung*, and by that is to be understood a connected and uncontradictory *unity* of clear concepts and firmly based judgments. . . . I think that I posit a correct notion of philosophy when I say that its actual goal, towards which it must direct all its efforts, is not theoretical, but of a completely *practical* nature, that it is the foundation of a *life-ideal*, which the philosopher declares valid and binding for himself and for all who share his evaluation of life.[27]

I say these two notions are contradictory because we are used to relating abstract form—the kind of strict and sometimes arbitrary concept-formulation Tönnies is urging—with abstract content, airy discussions of metaphysical problems. But Tönnies explicitly demands that his highly abstract conceptual categories serve as the basis for a *practical* philosophy; his goal is a life-ideal that compels action.

This contradiction and its attendant confusion dominate the next two sections of this draft, where Tönnies attempts to establish the basic psychological categories of his voluntaristic philosophy. In the first of these two parts, a series of concepts is developed to describe various layers of the human volitional apparatus. At the bottom are the feelings of pleasure and pain. Then, when one becomes conscious of the future, the category of wish becomes part of the will. A further refinement on wish is reflection—the choosing from several different alternatives of pleasure and pain. The last paragraph of this section deals with a question that had also preoccupied Ihering, though Ihering's name is not mentioned: that of altruistic, nonegoistic behavior. Tönnies simply denies that such behavior is possible, if it is alleged to contradict the general principle of pleasure and pain.

Having brought up the question of the relation between people, Tönnies devotes to it his third and concluding section. There are two kinds of relations between wills: hostile and friendly. Although the hostile relation—basically antisocial—aims at causing pain and destruction, while the friendly relation strives to give pleasure, both relations can be the basis of peaceful social patterns. Even if the underlying relationship is one of hostility, "every man is ready to abstain from hostilities against others, just as long as they too are ready to abstain, and to do things for others on the condition that they do something equivalent for him."[28] This is the foundation of *Gesellschaft*. The friendly relation as the basis of social interaction means that "inside of a group of men, abstention from (certain) hostilities and carrying out of (certain) services occurs for the sake of particular lasting relationships which prevail between the wills of men in such a way that, as a result of this carrying out and that abstention, they have a permanent even course." This is *Gemeinschaft*.[29]

In the following pages, Tönnies discusses, without concrete reference, various possible relations of wills as they fall into *Gemeinschaft* or *Gesellschaft* patterns. Such phenomena as trust, obedience, coercion, obligation, fear, reverence, request, command, and contract are presented, but without any systematic treatment. Only in the last paragraph does Tönnies finally pull together some of the preceding material to show the main direction of his thought:

> Just as *Gemeinschaft* rests on custom and consciousness of duty, *Gesellschaft* rests completely on desire and fear, or on wishes: however not on wishes alone, but on those bound to the reflection that forbearance or performance are the most useful for their fulfillment. The will itself, as feeling or as wish, has in the present case nothing to do with any other human being than oneself. Whether it is bent on a possession

of foreign objects, or on making something happen (foreign activities), it is completely objective and not personal; the accessory reflection here affirms the alien will only as long and as far as the aim conceived in the consciousness makes it necessary or appears to require it. As far as that consciousness is concerned, it is a matter of total indifference whether this [alien will] exists, and whether it feels joy and sorrow. It is observed not at all as an end in itself but purely as a means and a tool for whom the accident of being alive and being human makes necessary a characteristic way of acting. The *hostile* tendency perceives the other as hindrance to its goal and seeks, therefore, to destroy it, or seeks its pain as a goal in itself, and wishes to deal it such pain; the societal [*gesellschaftliche*] renounces both; it establishes itself on a footing of equality, discovers that the other is not an unconditional hindrance, but may, under certain circumstances, even be of service, provided he himself ceases to show a completely hostile will. He is so much the more useful, if he grants benefit [*Leistung*] for benefit. It [the societal tendency] therefore wants to preserve or even encourage him, to whatever extent necessary, in order to dispose his choice [*Willkür*] to such behavior. This relationship, considered as a complete type, is a purely rational one, i.e., it is established on the basis of rational calculation of use and convenience. The more it deviates from this type, the less is it a societal one. It approaches the hostile, the more the feeling of superiority or (on the other side) fear, takes part in reflection and codetermines the specific relationship. It approaches the friendly, the more the purely benevolent, loving, and sympathetic impulses of man toward man are determinate. And it approaches community to the extent that custom of similarly disposed wills [*in gleicher Willensrichtung*] and the feeling of mutual obligation enter into the motivation. Nevertheless, it is understandable, and it follows most clearly, that just as *Gemeinschaft* is more closely related to friendship, so *Gesellschaft* is more closely related to hostility, and that in this index, origin of the one from the other is easier.³⁰

For all his careful analysis of psychological categories, however, Tönnies does not yet present his fundamental concepts of *Wesen-*

wille and *Willkür*. *Wesenwille* is not mentioned at all, and *Willkür* is only loosely associated with *Gesellschaft*.*

In the letters there is no further outline of his planned work until June 1885, when he tells Paulsen of his lectures at the University of Kiel, which, as it turns out, approximate the scheme of the finished volume:

> Like a true desperado, I have now begun to lecture on my own theory, *mentibus praejudiciis minime occupatis,* and am always astonished that they bear it patiently and do not protest loudly against curious concepts and words. First the psychological: the distinction of *Wesenwille* and *Willkür*; to which I shall attach that of *Gemeinschaft* and *Gesellschaft*, of nationality [*Volkstum*] and statehood [*Staatstum*], of organic and mechanical structures, of family spirit, morality and religion on the one hand and the economic-political-scientific powers that dissolve them on the other. . . . I want to show that the well-known dichotomy, so vigorously maintained in Germany, between the historical and the rationalist view of social, political, etc., earthly affairs is false, to the extent that now one, now the other, can be adequate to these things and their constitution: in other words, to those which really are analogous to organic-living structures, one such observation (the biological); contrariwise to the whole class of institutions of a mechanical character which are to be understood by the analogy to pure tools, *mechanai,* the other, technical-rationalist investigation.[31]

What has happened in the four years since the first draft? Tönnies had expressed his antipathy to the conventional distinction between the historical and rationalist approaches as early as 1879.[32] The basic polarity of *Gemeinschaft* and *Gesellschaft,* and the view

---

* Paulsen's remarks on this first draft of *Gemeinschaft und Gesellschaft* mirror its extremely difficult style and manner of presentation:

> With difficulty I have read to the end; I can hardly say thought to the end. It became very difficult for me. You delineate in this section the fields on which your thoughts should move. That, it seems to me, is a matter which everyone must carry through for himself. . . . The division and limitation of sciences is the most inappropriate business for common discussion. But the thought-beast that one drives into the fields is an object of negotiation. . . . Either the abstract discussion has not grasped me properly, or I have not grasped it. It is, I believe, not easy to follow (P-T, 15/10/81).

of the state as a product of *Gesellschaft,* appeared in his plan of January 1881, where he first stated the title of the work. He had suggested the idea of organic and mechanical structures in his proposed reconciliation of historicism and rationalism. It appears that the major accomplishment of those four years was the working out of the psychological antithesis, *Wesenwille-Willkür.* This seems odd when we recall that the psychological foundation of his theory was the almost exclusive object of his concern in the draft of 1881. And this concern in turn becomes strange when we recall that what Tönnies set out to write in 1881 was a refutation of existing state theory and the establishment of his own opposing conceptions. But Tönnies himself later depicted his conception of *Wesenwille* as central to his thought.* Why was this psychological underpinning so essential? What relation did it have to Tönnies' original political and social concerns?

There can be little doubt that Tönnies' basic concern in this period was with the state, with refuting the mass of contemporary social theory that posited the state as the savior of mankind from itself, and with establishing an alternate value structure and ideology. In truth, all the paths of contemporary social and political theory led up to the state.† Schäffle, the Social-Darwinist and follower of Spencer, treated the survival of states as the highest phase of natural selection. Ihering, concerned with human behavior in relation to end-goals and at a loss to explain altruistic behavior, posited the

---

* "The core of my thought was to reveal the root of *Gemeinschaft* in pre-rationalistic (perhaps also transrationalistic) thought and will, which I have designated as *Wesenwille*" (Tönnies, "Autobiography," p. 13).

† For the origins of glorification of the state in German thought in Schelling, see Carl Schmitt, *Politische Romantik* (Munich, 1925), pp. 156ff. Hegel's early conception of the state (1800–1801) is discussed in Herbert Marcuse, *Reason and Revolution* (New York, 1954), pp. 49–56. The development in Germany from "the old pantheistic deification of the state" to "a blind worship of success and power" is discussed in Ernst Troeltsch, "The Ideas of Natural Law and Humanity," in Otto Gierke, *Natural Law and the Theory of Society, 1500–1800* (Boston, 1957), pp. 214ff. On the importance of the state in nineteenth-century German thought, see also Friedrich Meinecke, *Weltbürgertum und Nationalstaat* (Munich and Berlin, 1917), pp. 10ff; Heinrich O. Meissner, *Die Lehre vom monarchischen Prinzip im Zeitalter der Restauration und des deutschen Bundes* (Leipzig, 1913), p. 290, and, for the state-centered character of early German sociology (post–1850), Heinz Maus, "Simmel in German Sociology," in Kurt Wolff, ed., *Georg Simmel, 1858–1918* (Columbus, O., 1959), pp. 183ff.

state, with compulsion (*Zwang*) as its means, as the regulator of a society based on *Lohn* (wage), and wandered for five hundred pages in search of a moral state system. Wagner, the follower of Rodbertus, looked to the state to heal the social divisions of society, as did Lorenz von Stein, who saw community only in the action of the state against the social ills and divisions of society.*

But for Tönnies the "state" was the Prussian state, the Bismarckian state, in which he could see neither morality, nor a social panacea, nor, in terms of the reading he had been doing in the anthropology of primitive life, anything vaguely like the spirit of *Gemeinschaft*. To develop his own theory, which clearly had its origins in explicit hatred for the very "state" all other theory was so bent on glorifying, he had to destroy these other theories, in his own mind at least. And as a basis both for the all-important destruction of the old and for the construction of the new, he had to supply himself with a sound theoretical foundation.

He created this foundation by reducing all human actions to psychological patterns. All social phenomena, actions, institutions, he viewed as dependent entirely on human will. Opposing the "objective" social philosophy stemming from Hegel, and going back to the "subjective" tradition of Hobbes, Hume, and Kant,[33] he measured all social aggregates by the one criterion of how they related to the wills of the individuals composing them. He discerned two fundamental volitional patterns: *Wesenwille* and *Willkür* (after 1912, *Kürwille*). *Wesenwille* was a will that dictated action for its own sake; action was not a means to an end, but an end in itself. *Willkür* was action for the sake of a goal beyond the action. Thus, in the *Wesenwille* pattern one might love another person without having any goal beyond that love; one might take a walk for the sheer pleasure of it. Economic activities, although always involving the external end of self-preservation, would be closer to the *Wesenwille* pattern if accompanied by some joy in the act of producing and if the producer consumed his own product. In the *Willkür* pattern, however, love was excluded—one dealt with others as objects toward

---

* Tönnies, in one of many references to the sources of his theory, later said, "The chief concepts were also conceived in continual critical relation to the theories of Lorenz Stein, Ihering, and Schaffle" (SSK, II, p. 98).

an end. Marriage, in the *Willkür* pattern, would be undertaken not for love, but for social advancement, business contacts, etc. Economic activities would be dictated by the principles of exchange and rational calculation of profit and loss. The big landowner who never saw his crop growing but spent his time arranging for the most profitable sale of it would be another example of *Willkür*.

In using these volitional patterns as the exclusive criteria for defining social structures, Tönnies attacked at its foundation the view of the state as an organism, a super-*Gemeinschaft*, or, at least, as in some way antithetical to the atomistic nature of society. He did not completely rule out the notion of a social "organism," but he dealt with the idea very critically. If the way in which the social group originated and developed was similar to that of a biological entity, then perhaps the analogy could hold.[34] And he certainly was fascinated by the application of Darwinian notions of natural development to the social scene. He viewed the whole Social-Darwinist conception as a necessary step beyond the somewhat static Hobbesian paradigm, and his idea of a development from *Gemeinschaft* to *Gesellschaft*, his notion of civilization growing old, certainly reflects this. But he insisted that the group was defined by the way the conscious wills of its members participated in it.*

His volitional patterns, of course, led him to another point of cardinal importance. While he could not in any way associate *Gemeinschaft* with the pattern of *Willkür* that underlay state and society, he could associate it with the antithetical pattern of *Wesenwille*.

Gesellschaft, on the other hand, was based on the *Willkür* pattern. *Willkür* means arbitrariness in German: it was often used to describe the sovereign will of the territorial despot. For Tönnies this kind of will was arbitrary because no matter how carefully its practitioners adjusted means to ends in rational calculations of ad-

---

* "What gives a quasi-organic character to a human group can be only the perception, the feeling, the *will* of the grouped men themselves. Through this foundation, my theory sharply distinguishes itself from the otherwise current 'organic' doctrines, which do not notice that, insofar as their biological analogies have any basis, they remain within even an expanded biology, and lack the specific character of sociological facts" (Tönnies, "Zur Einleitung in die Soziologie," SSK, I, p. 12).

vantage, their actions had no relationship whatever to the affectual *Wesenwille,* that "organic will" that underlay actions undertaken for no ulterior motive, actions for their own sake, in *Gemeinschaft.* The state was a product of this societal *Willkür,* a contract among the participants to observe certain rules in their mutual dealings for the sake of social peace—in short, it was the completely unromantic Hobbesian state. *For Tönnies, there was no other state.*

It was, then, impossible for him to view the state as some mysterious power above the struggle, as the source of a new *Gemeinschaft.* At one time or another in his later writings on the history of recent social thought, he explicitly came out with refutations of Schäffle,[35] of Stein and Gneist, and of the German historical school,[36] all for making this same impossible definition of the state as in some way antithetical to atomistic *Gesellschaft.*

What is of great significance, however, is that Tönnies, as the result of his intellectual labors, gave birth not only to a polemical counterattack on existing scholarly justifications and glorifications of the contemporary state and society, but to a theory of the will which served as the basis both of a deeply personal philosophy of life—a *Weltanschauung*—and of a sociological discipline, which, together with its underlying volitional theory, was capable of standing quite independently of that *Weltanschauung.*

Thus, to all three—to the *Weltanschauung,* which changed little through Tönnies' lifetime, to the earlier sociology that was based on it, and to the later sociology that was more or less independent of it—the theory of the will was basic. Tönnies' antimodernist *Weltanschauung* required the notion of *Wesenwille* as a psychological model against which to measure and judge prevailing modes of behavior. His sociology was, in its origins, a philosophy of history based on his *Weltanschauung*: the universal course of world history led from *Gemeinschaft* to *Gesellschaft.* Here too, as has been shown, the psychological dichotomy was of vast importance in defining the difference between one epoch, one way of life, and the other. However, because of Tönnies' strong tendency to abstract conceptualization, the two ways of life were presented very much as ideal types, against which the individual phenomena of any society might be measured for the purpose of determining to what extent *Gemeinschaft* and

Gesellschaft relations prevailed. Tönnies did not originally establish his concepts for this purpose, but they increasingly came to have this purely sociological meaning for him rather than that of a philosophy of history. Rene König has expertly traced the change in Tönnies' own view of *Gemeinschaft* and *Gesellschaft* between the first and second editions (1887 and 1912).[37] What is important, though, is that even in the recent purely sociological interpretations of Tönnies, such as that of Talcott Parsons, the relationship between wills remains the essential one.[38]

Now, if our knowledge of, and interest in, Tönnies began and ended with his theory in its properly sociological sense, then the origins of his *Wesenwille-Willkür* distinction might be traced to particular intellectual influences. Tönnies himself, by his indefatigable name-dropping, encourages us to do just that, and J. Leif has done a very fine job of tracing the similarities between the psychological theories of Tönnies and a number of the men he mentions.[39] Since, however, our principal concern is with Tönnies' *Weltanschauung*, and with *Gemeinschaft und Gesellschaft* only as it was originally conceived—as a philosophy of history based on that *Weltanschauung* —we are much more interested in the experiences, milieu, attitudes, and goals of Tönnies' personal life that accompanied his period of most intensive labor on his psychological antithesis. For in this process, which may be reduced to a dialectic of growing alienation from the contemporary and love for the past, especially of his native land, we may find the true wellsprings of his thought.

Indeed, if we keep in mind that virtually everything else of basic significance in Tönnies' intellectual and emotional experience appears in the letters, then it would be wise not to seek the roots of *Wesenwille* in theoretical sources. For while the letters contain much material pointing to a *combination* of social and theoretical influences on Tönnies' evolution toward the other elements in his conceptual apparatus—*Willkür, Gemeinschaft, Gesellschaft*, customary law, natural law—they contain virtually nothing in the critical years 1881–85 to suggest the *theoretical* sources of *Wesenwille*.

In May 1882 Tönnies was reading Bachofen's *Mutterrecht*, which probably was the principal source for his connection of *Gemeinschaft* and matriarchy; in July 1882, Comte, whose importance was probably to present a model philosophy of history against which to work out his own theory; in December 1882, Gierke's *Genossenschaftsrecht,* which was surely of value for the section of Tönnies' work dealing with customary and natural law (T-P, 4/12/ 82). At about the same time, he was reading Morgan's *Ancient Society,* which, like Laveleye, stressed the communistic aspects of primitive society. It is possible that his work on Spinoza in 1883 was helpful for his psychological theory, but he himself did not view it as in any way connected with *Gemeinschaft und Gesellschaft.*

Thus, the lack of any particular reference to theoretical sources of *Wesenwille,* plus the central position that this concept holds in Tönnies' value-charged *Weltanschauung,* virtually directs us to seek out the roots of *Wesenwille* in Tönnies' own experience of and reaction to his age.

Judging by the letters, and by his autobiography, Tönnies' period of most intense absorption in the contemporary political scene was during 1878–79, centering roughly on the antisocialist bill and what it would mean for Germany's political and social future. If after Tönnies' important letter of October 30, 1879, discussed above, his remarks on political affairs became sporadic, it was probably more from loss of hope than loss of interest. A month later, on November 30, he added, as a postscript to a letter suggesting a joint trip to Paris: "What do you think, meanwhile, about things contemporary? It seems to me as though the clouds draw closer and closer over our national life. Will the Lord soon take a look and exterminate the scoundrels?" In a letter of August 29, 1880, Tönnies repeated his question. He was just as detached, but no longer saw the possibility of a positive development. After grumbling about the lack of unity among the liberals in tariff matters and their mixed religious composition (half Lutheran, half Jewish), he confessed to the viewpoint that the future belonged to the radicals (here meaning the small Progressive party) and that the workers' party would be forced to join with them. Under the Crown Prince the regime would become National Liberal, and there would be an increasing tendency toward democracy.

Tönnies showed his disenchantment with the idea of democracy, however, by surrounding it with quotation marks. He summarized his ambivalence in his final remarks: "The whole thing becomes quite repulsive. I am not going along. But: *it will bring the development on its feet.*" Thus, we find simultaneously the idea that there is some sort of inevitable historical process, and definite alienation from this process.

In later letters suggestions of alienation predominate. A letter of November 10, 1880, shows an intemperate antagonism toward the hypocrisy of the German bourgeoisie in aping the religious posture of the petty nobility.[40] On May 15, 1881, Tönnies does reveal a flickering recurrence of political interest when he urges his friend to attend a founding meeting of a new social reform party, probably to be headed by Adolf Wagner.[41] But this is followed by further signs of estrangement:

> Even with the most harmless spirit, one does not escape from nausea against this mutual splitting of fractions that they call practical politics.[42]
>
> ❋ ❋ ❋
>
> If I were independent of family considerations, I would go with an open flag into the camp of the pure Communists. Here would be the only field on which I would hope to see the fruits of honest striving. But since I will hardly ever achieve the decisiveness for that, I think of nothing but how I can honorably achieve a retreat from an arena in which I have found nothing but bitterness and disillusionment; what I exclude from that, you know.[43]

The arena is the academic one. Tönnies was as discontented with the world of scholarship as he was with the world of politics and society. Though the radical political inclination was uncharacteristic of his thought in this period, this feeling of alienation was nothing new. Roughly a year before, on the occasion of another gloomy prediction of the approaching end of civilization, he had exploded with despair and anger over the popular culture of the period and the vulgar anti-Semitism of a student political meeting he attended.

> To expect rescue through reaction or through socialism is also an error. It is not the race of 'forty-eight which approaches its end, but the German, English, French, Austrian, Italian,

etc. The whole glory of Christian history approaches its end. It may to be sure yet last five hundred years, although everything goes faster than earlier. This is my conviction. All new experiences strengthen it. This evening—here is really the immediate occasion for my writing—I happened to drop by the city theater here. In it was given an operetta, *Die Fledermaus*, which has been played a couple of hundred times in Berlin and in every cultured city with limitless applause. I had often heard . . . what a "charming," "amusing" (and all the other modish words) piece it was. I endured hearing and seeing an act of it. I say to you in solemn earnestness: a people which allows such a thing to be produced, and admires and recommends it, which brings its wives and daughters into a theater made into such a whorehouse, a people from which no voice of protest is heard against such ignominy, which simultaneously "takes stock of itself" because of the gesture of a madman against its King (about whom this same people tells spicy anecdotes behind closed doors and whom they would hang if he energetically prepared to take their gold and silver from their fists), and then comes out with lies and calumny— this people is so deeply sunk in meanness that it is irretrievably lost, it deserves nothing but scorn and pity.* —I am deeply convinced that you are also deceived about your "coming generation"; there are perhaps two or three among them who are serious. I had another experience. I attended a student anti-Semitic meeting. There were probably a few people there who feel a dark yearning; but the ones who spoke (I heard a jurist and three theologians, all found enormous applause, each intoxicated the others in the most repulsive way), what a low sort of man has been produced by our *Gymnasium* and newspaper culture, that noble pair. Talk went abundantly on about materialism, mammonism, Jewry,

---

* "Speaking generally, the Frisian is not a man of many words; anyone with a glib tongue runs the risk of being regarded as a trifler and not being taken seriously. While it cannot be said that jesting and merriment are never heard, anyone jealous of his reputation takes good care to keep himself well in hand. Frisians never sing or play games; if any singing is heard, the assumption is justified that it is a case of drunkenness. . . . To find pleasure in play and games is foreign to their tribal character: rather they are given to ruminating, especially about religious questions, and this is apt to lead to brooding and melancholy" (Paulsen, *Autobiography*, p. 11).

the "awakening German youth" was extolled, jokes were cracked about the old beat-up [*rummelige*] synagogue in New Stettin (a nonspeaker but, as I noted, coleader, asked me how do we think in our circle about such things, he and his comrades, they were so enthusiastic that each one would have been capable of setting fire to the old temple), etc., etc. Truly, the people with whom I attended the university, it is not many years ago, but they were more honorable men.*44

Tönnies urges Paulsen to spend his coming vacation in putting his optimism to the practical test of wandering at random through theaters, dance halls, prisons—whatever is accessible to him. Everywhere, he will see "that all bonds of shame fall increasingly to pieces, that the descendants of such a generation, even if one could rescue them from the swamp, will never be free from the poison in their bodies. There goes the people and gapes and exults—*moritur et ridet!*" The few who stand for something better will be of no help against the coming apocalypse: "Sodom and Gomorrah were not spared because of the three just ones."

This acute pessimism concerning the fate of existing society, with its accompanying sense of alienation, sets the underlying psychological tone of Tönnies' life and thought during this period (1881–85). There was, however, a reverse side to this pessimism: the repeated attempt to salvage something from the wreckage, somehow to establish new roots, to relate to something. At first, Tönnies made this effort in the field of pedagogy. The idea of building a group of scholars around a magazine was the first such attempt. The second was his plan for a community of scholars, in the manner of the ancient Platonic Academy of the Stoa. What he ended with, however, was his growing attachment to his native land on the west coast of Schleswig, and his relationship to its poet laureate, Theodor Storm. There are indications that both of these latter attempts were intimately related to the evolution of Tönnies' conception of *Wesenwille*.

---

* Tönnies was by no means unique in his reaction to the anti-Semitic movement. Hellmut von Gerlach, later a prominent liberal publicist, wrote of his experiences a decade later: "The anti-Semites did a better job of curing me of anti-Semitism than the Jews" (Paul Massing, *Rehearsal for Destruction* [New York, 1949], p. 115).

The first suggestion of a community of scholars appears in the context of Tönnies' criticism of Paulsen's essay "Was Kant uns sein kann." Paulsen, in Tönnies' eyes, had moderated his critical political and social comments so as not to offend his readers. Tönnies writes, "I cannot deny that I would have attacked yet more strongly and certainly present conditions, that I would have characterized them with pathos and bitterness."[45] The difference between them, according to Tönnies, is a result of their different goals and hopes. Paulsen seems to hope to win over the whole nation. Tönnies denies the possibility of this and hopes only to bring together a "small community" [Gemeinde] of the already committed, and to "give a word to these which, as a *logos spermatikos*, may here and there germinate and develop and grow." This is their proper task:

> And while it would be now good, for the other goal, to appear mild and conciliatory and hopeful, for this one, it cannot be said violently and penetratingly enough, how badly the noble and decent in our morals and beliefs is decaying and how the common and ugly ever more gains the upper hand; how much more important than fighting and improving false metaphysical and scientific notions it is, now and always, to protect our people from the godless servants of Mammon who want to rule it, and to rescue it from the dirt and dishonor of the proletarian life on the one side and the oriental luxurious life on the other, in which it sinks deeper and deeper, and, as we fear, without hope of rescue.

Their responsibility then, is to open the eyes of the few who are capable of seeing. For all the contamination, even in the extremist movements, by the spirit of the times, Tönnies nevertheless sees the greatest potential receptiveness among the Social Democrats and, with reservations about "most unsavory elements," in the anti-Semitic movement. The conclusion:

> Whoever wants to be a *philosophe* must turn from the spirit of the times with aversion. That is our watchword. With it we must form a firmly closed, organized, and disciplined sect, united in writing and action, not from the people, from the mass—for that we have not enough faith and must await the messiah who may bring it—but from the educated; if we only

become as strong and powerful as the order of the Stoics in late antiquity, we shall have done great things. This thought would so fill me and permeate me, if I write anything, that at least the attentive and sensitive would see it shimmer through everywhere; just as one feels and sees it, and finds it outspokenly in Lagarde, whom I read again this summer with deepest sympathy.*

It is, perhaps, significant that in the same letter, and following directly on this appeal for a sharp break with the spirit of the times, Tönnies writes that he is attempting "to define a real theoretical difference concerning the relation of 'Will' and 'Intellect.'" The editor of the *Correspondence* is almost certainly correct when he calls this "the preliminary distinction of *Wesenwille* and *Kürwille*."

Some five months later, the subject of a community of scholars again arises, this time in the context of a discussion of religion.[46] Belief, Tönnies says, rests on *Gemeinschaft*. Once Tönnies has acquired a family, he wants to join with the Paulsens and other in-

---

* On Paul de Lagarde, see F. Stern, *The Politics of Cultural Despair*, pp. 3–97. Tönnies was attracted to Lagarde, one of the principal pre-Nazi ideologues of the *Völkisch Mittelstand*, by the latter's aversion to the new commercial Germany, by his longing for the community of old, by his hostility to state control over the university system, and perhaps also by his visions of a new religion. Indeed, Lagarde developed, in mid-century, practical proposals, superficially similar to those of Tönnies at a later date, for intentional family communities (see pp. 117–19 and Stern, p. 60) and for communities of scholars (see Stern, pp. 79–80). But fundamental differences between the men preclude consideration of Lagarde as an important influence on Tönnies (argued by Robert W. Lougee in *Paul de Lagarde, 1827–1891* [Cambridge, 1962], pp. 232–34). Lagarde's conception of community involved a "passionate concern for the unity of the German people" (Stern, p. 55) which was absent in Tönnies, except for a brief period around the First World War. Tönnies, too, was a much more uncompromising critic of Prussia and the state system represented by Prussia. There was certainly no suggestion of a "Prussian ethos" (Stern, p. 29) in Tönnies. And Lagarde's notion that the state, though like a machine, could receive, in Stern's words, "the guidance of a spiritual entity that could give it purpose and direction" (p. 56) suggests an interrelationship, a dialectic between the state and the national community, whose very possibility Tönnies denied in *Gemeinschaft und Gesellschaft*. Tönnies would further have rejected Lagarde's intention to use his family community scheme for the creation of a new nobility (Stern, pp. 59–60). One is left with Tönnies' undoubted appreciation for a man who, like the early Nietzsche, anticipated his general direction, and who probably influenced him most strongly on the subject of educational reform.

terested friends in a "philosophical community" [*Gemeinde*]—"a cloistered academy in the rural stillness, where we give the philosophically curious shelter and education." There they can develop "a strong and bold belief. . . . We want to dress it in festive garments, now and then, we want to erect images to it in our homes, but its spirit will be within us, and if one should approach it scientifically and ask for its formula, it will answer something like what the Greek words say: *koina te philon*. That is a high truth, no one can refute it."*

The most detailed exposition of the community of scholars appears in Tönnies' letter of March 28, 1881. Tönnies has lost interest in his project for a journal and is now concentrating exclusively on his academic utopia. Within five years, there will be a mass exodus of philosophy students from the universities. In the countryside will be constructed a group of houses, for families, and a "*Lykeion, Stoa oder Academie.*" Twenty students will be taken annually, for a minimum period of one year. They must be prepared to pay fifteen hundred to two thousand marks per year for upkeep and instruction. Poorer students could earn a part of their tuition by teaching the faculty's children. "The whole thing would rest chiefly on trust, community [*Gemeinschaft*], friendship." Presumably the initial outlay of money would come from Tönnies' substantial inheritance. Kuno Francke, an old fellow student in Paulsen's philosophy seminar, who later became professor of German literature at Harvard, is enthusiastic about the idea. Tönnies is counting on other mutual friends. Above all, though he does not say so, he is hoping to entice Paulsen.

A barren hope! Despite an initially encouraging response,[47] Paulsen evidently was too firmly rooted in Berlin to embark on

---

* In a passage comparing Tönnies with Schopenhauer, J. Leif excellently points out the relationship of *Wesenwille* to just such a community as Tönnies is trying to establish: "The intuition of the profound will [*Wesenwille*] allows us, on the contrary, to grasp the intimate consubstantiality of all beings, and suppresses, to a certain extent, the principle of individuation developed by egoism and knowledge. Thus, the feeling of our pains and pleasures allows us to feel the pains and pleasures of others, and leads, for Tönnies as for Schopenhauer, to sympathy, pity, goodness, and love for our fellow man. In Schopenhauer's philosophy, this modern wisdom leads us to the Hindu Nirvana. In the community, such virtues are expressed by family bonds, morals, customs and religion" (J. Leif, *La Sociologie de Tönnies* [Paris, 1946]).

such a shaky new venture. A year later, Tönnies writes, "If we were only sitting in our free academy. Or do you still hold the universities to be suitable places for philosophizing? Say it boldly; I won't give up hope of your improvement." And he didn't. He was still tugging at his old mentor in 1882, arguing the incompatibility between a state-controlled system of higher education, which was bound to be used as an instrument of the state power, and the "anarchistic ideal" of freedom of conscience. His conclusion: "Philosophy belongs in the shadowed grove of the Academy, not in the Forum Romanum."[48]

But the scheme was, after all, utopian and not practical. Paulsen was not to be budged from his chair in the University of Berlin, and Tönnies himself was not the type of hard-headed administrator to translate his dreams to reality.

As Tönnies' projects for a new academy fade, his ties to his ancestral homeland grow stronger. One of the first signs of this attachment appears in a letter to Paulsen of January 19, 1882, when there seems to be an opening for Paulsen at the University of Kiel:

> The dreariness of this place for me, the fact that the whole sadness of modern life grips me here ever anew and most painfully, that I suffer so much the more from a hollow homesickness the closer I am to the eventful and comfortable life of the parental home and the yet peaceful-solemn roofs of the old city [Husum]—all this will certainly be different if I should have you here. Having your own home and garden will not be very difficult here. And even this Kiel is still venerable as the spiritual capital of the fatherland (though little may be left of either). Your children must also become Schleswig-Holsteiners.

It is noteworthy that "fatherland" here, as elsewhere in the letters to Paulsen, connotes Schleswig-Holstein, not Germany.[49]

Despite Tönnies' praise for old Kiel, however, his preference clearly is for country living. On the occasion of a visit to Theodor Storm's new home in Hademarschen (Holstein), in March 1882, Tönnies writes: "The neighborhood is most charming, a great wood nearby, also close by the castle park of Hanerau. I have really enjoyed the rural life. It is the only truth."[50] A few months later, writing of a night ferry trip from Copenhagen to the *Vaterland,* Tönnies says,

> I left the cabin just after 2 A.M. and saw the mild morning come while wandering alone on the foredeck: the brightening in the east, the full moon dipping and becoming pale, the rosy-fingered Eos, then the red Phoebos himself, slowly climbing, proud and victorious, then the green coasts of our land, shimmering in the young light—everything around me full of Gods. Oh, what we miss, we who no longer begin our daily work with the day! Afterward came abominable men, always cheerily cracking jokes in Old-Markish [Prussian regional] dialect and with Berliner feelings, truly a profane people. But those are our everyday companions, their clamor surrounds us and prevents us from coming to devotion.

Tönnies' love for nature continued to grow throughout this period, and to attach itself ever more securely to the Frisian coastland of his birth. So, however, did his loneliness grow, and his need for the companionship of his friend. His letter of September 23, 1884, gives these sentiments vivid and tender expression:

> 18/9. At the dike. If you were here and lived with me, how happy I would be. I lack nothing but a complete friend, one having time and thoughts, with whom the secret beauty of this place, the stillness of the sea and the twilight, the lonesome birdcry at ebb tide and the power of the waves under the stress of the gale might be completely enjoyed, and long winter evenings chatted through, things written and read and comfortably discussed; in serene and fine contemplation which one can never know in the sea of population; where the presence and press of man overstrains the imagination. Here we would be *autarkeis,* and fruitful in words and deeds. What becomes barren is not the environment, but humanity, which becomes increasingly barren of culture. Alone I am not strong enough against it. But two is $1 \times$ infinity.
>
> 19/9. How your children would thrive here, in the garden air and by the dike, laughing and wandering; nourished with the homeland sentiments: which for me, at least, next to the love of loves, are the most precious to the heart that the earth

offers. And those who live without it seem poor to me, poorer yet, those who grow up without it.

20/9. Between Hockensbüll and Hattstedt. Every day I become more aware of the incomparable wonder of this nature, once unrecognized in the disgusting haze of my schooldays, later often enjoyed with glances that were filled with care and melancholy. I write this in the autumnal evening, on the path between the dike embankments, flies buzzing around me, from a distance sounds the bleating of sheep, before me glows a mild yellow gleam from the departed sun, higher up [it is] compressed to a red shimmer, to my left the soft, bluish-red puffed up clouds in a long layer, with many thin streamers on top; behind me, like a piece of legend, the serious gray houses, there a mill, and enveloped from afar, the city [Husum] to which I am returning. Great and rich is this loneliness.

A few months later, Tönnies returns one last time to his idea of an academic community.[51] But now it has become, rather than a practical project, a transfigured vision, unattainable and so all the more yearned for. Instead of writing books, they should cultivate and propagate their thoughts in a small community—and not in rooms and behind lecterns, but "under the breath of the wind, in sight of the starry heavens, or walking in the forest, or anywhere in nature wonderful and divinely infused." The results should be a "book of books," thought out by the group as a whole in a communal endeavor similar to the Platonic notion of "colonizing a city (*oikízontes tèn pólin*)."

Did this obviously lonely and sensitive man never, in these years, think of marriage? The Tönnies-Paulsen correspondence points to one ill-fated liaison in 1881.* Two years later, he was competing with Hermann Ebbinghaus and Paul Rée for the favor of Lou Andreas-Salomé, but that was also a short-lived relationship.[52]

* P-T, April 18, 1881. An unpublished part of Tönnies' letter to Paulsen of April 16, 1881, in the Tönnies archive in Kiel (Schleswig-Holsteinische Landesbibliothek), refers, extremely delicately and vaguely, to an affair Tönnies seemed to be hoping to turn into a marriage. Tönnies never referred to the woman by name.

At the time of Theodor Storm's death, in 1888, the poet's daughter Gertrud was in love with Tönnies,[53] but it is unclear whether this love was reciprocated. If there was a romance, it must have been conducted from a distance; the Storms had lived since the spring of 1881 in Hademarschen, which Tönnies visited only occasionally.

Thus, with three possible exceptions, there were no women in Tönnies' life until his marriage in 1894 at the age of thirty-eight. This highlights the significance of anyone to whom Tönnies did feel particularly close. Certainly one such person was Paulsen. Theodor Storm was another.

Paulsen was aware of Tönnies' ability and inclination to remove himself from his age and transfer his understanding and sympathy to another way of life.* This faculty was awakened repeatedly in Tönnies by his relationship with Storm. As early as 1878, Tönnies had written to Paulsen, after a meeting between Paulsen and Storm arranged by Tönnies in Husum, "You are right. Theodor Storm is a completely delightful phenomenon. He is not merely a poet with a pen, but his whole soul is graced with a mild twilight gleaming. I continually doubt whether such men will be able to arise in the crude and noisy public life of the contemporary and probably future scene."[54]

Just after Storm's annual visit to Husum, in 1884, Tönnies wrote, "I asked myself, when he left me, how much longer will this summery nature continue to bloom? The young generation is so monotonous and so hard."[55] The sense of estrangement here is of course not merely a question of younger and older generations. Tönnies himself was only twenty-eight in 1884. Storm's visit to Husum the following year evoked a similar lament over the younger generation.[56] And when, in 1888, Storm died, Tönnies wrote, "I have suffered a deeper loss through Storm's departure

---

* P-T, 18/4/84. "In Naumburg the Cathedral was an inspiring sight. . . . How wonderfully did that age know how to give shape to the religious feeling of release from time and space, the same feeling you experienced on the omnibus in Oxford Street." Paulsen also commented on Tönnies' similarity to Carlyle, who clearly had that talent: "Perhaps there is no man to whose manner of looking at things you stand closer than Carlyle" (P-T, 1/1/88). In a letter to Paulsen of November 10, 1880, Tönnies himself refers to "the preference for older conditions and men which has grown powerfully in all of us, I think, during recent years."

than I earlier suspected. He was the last man who still bound me in reverence to the older generation."⁵⁷

The friendship between the talented boy and the mature poet continued to be close from the day in 1869 when Storm asked Tönnies to read the proof-sheets for his anthology of German poetry, at least until 1872, the year of Tönnies' departure for the University of Strasbourg. But the relationship apparently lost importance for Tönnies during his years of university study. Judging by their correspondence, Tönnies became closer to Storm once again after 1878. Although the relationship never approached the intensity of Tönnies' friendship with Paulsen, Tönnies and Storm probably saw one another frequently between the younger man's return to Husum from his university studies in 1877 and Storm's moving to Hademarschen in 1881, and there were regular visits between them after 1881.*

A devoted student of Tönnies' has recently written that the "very profound relationship to the poet . . . symbolized the spiritual root which fastened the young scholar to his homeland and made him always return to the grey city [Husum] as to a harbor."⁵⁸ It is likely that Tönnies came to view Storm as a living embodiment of *Wesenwille*, and that his formulation of this concept may very well have been conditioned by his understanding of the poet's personality. The comments in Tönnies' letters to Paulsen hint at this possibility; the remarks Tönnies made some thirty years after the poet's death strongly imply it.⁵⁹ Tönnies characterized the uniqueness of Storm's work in these words:

> His . . . art is free of intentions. That means: it wants neither to teach nor to shape: it wants to call forth neither sensual, nor moral, nor political agitation and excitement; it wants

---

* Franz Stuckert in his *Theodor Storm* (Bremen, 1955) speaks of "the faithful Ferdinand Tönnies" as one of Storm's first guests in Hademarschen (p. 108). In the second volume of Gertrud Storm's *Theodor Storm* (Berlin, 1912–13), Tönnies is mentioned as being among Storm's guests at Hademarschen in 1884. And we know from the addresses on Tönnies' letters to Paulsen that he made it a point during the 1880s to be on hand every January in Husum for Storm's annual visit to his relatives and friends there. Tönnies mentions accompanying Storm in 1886 on a trip to Weimar (T-P, Easter, 1886, p. 223), and in August 1887, the two men took a three-week trip to Westerland on the Isle of Sylt (Stuckert, p. 113; G. Storm, p. 229). According to Stuckert (p. 108), Storm called Tönnies "the most noteworthy young man whom he [had] found in his life—next to Theodor Mommsen."

neither to flatter nor to make tense, nor to horrify; the author is not concerned—as most of the moderns are—with imposing. For all that he is too naive. He works inwardly, for himself, with the quiet joy in his work, and thus with the conscientiousness of an old master of bronze or ivory sculpture.[60]

To those who insist that the artist address himself to contemporary controversies, that his work have some purpose or goal beyond itself, Tönnies responds, "One must love the beautiful for its own sake, or resign oneself to having no taste for it."[61]

Tönnies explicitly associates Storm with the most fundamental form of *Gemeinschaft*:

> The life of the closest human community has its abode and its poetry in the home. . . .[62] Theodor Storm is a poet of the family spirit in a further sense. For him, the family still has its invisible existence, continuing beyond the grave. Remarkably, it is the matriarchal clan whose community is present to him as a condition of his own life. The figures of his grandmother and great-grandmother often occupy his memory; in them he sees the embodiment of an age sympathetic to his poetic vision. The elegance of the rococo, that mixture of dignity and grace, delights his artist's eye, and casts a transfiguring gleam on the old-Frankish figures of his ancestors.[63]

Tönnies' description of Storm's way of thinking looks, again, like a model of *Wesenwille*: "Storm thought predominantly in intuitions—conceptual thought was more distant from him."[64]

Storm not only signifies *Wesenwille*; he also represents in his own consciousness the hostility between *Gemeinschaft* and state that is explicit in Tönnies' theory. Franz Schriewer writes of Storm:

> "The laws of the land" were no slogan for him, but content. Thus he emphasizes all his life the standpoint of law, and law grounded both historically and in the sense that everything should be legal—related to an absolute law . . . thus his violent aversion to the state as legislator. Apart from all else, that had to sharpen his animosity against Prussia, since this state, after the incorporation of Schleswig-Holstein in 1867, could not help intervening with decrees and laws and did not show a very sparing hand with them.[65]

Schriewer notes further that Storm "came from the patriarchal era, from the era when the state was a sleeping beauty, when sleep was especially deep in Schleswig-Holstein."[66] After the Prussians and Austrians took over Schleswig in 1864, Storm wrote to a friend, "This political situation ruins one internally; to be dependent in one's own homeland on the arbitrariness [*Willkür*] of foreigners, a completely defenseless object, that is yet worse than to be simply cast out, which can also happen at any moment."

The historical background of this fierce local particularism, which Storm knew thoroughly[67] and which he may also have transmitted to Tönnies, illuminates much in Tönnies' comprehension of *Gemeinschaft*.* The western coast of Schleswig, on which Tönnies, Storm, and Paulsen all were born, had a social history that was virtually unique in Germany. Much of this area retained the traditional character of a peasant *Gemeinschaft* until the middle of the nineteenth century.

The west coast of Schleswig is composed almost entirely of marshland that was formed from the North Sea during the medieval and early modern periods. Settlers from the *Geest*, the sandy interior of Schleswig, along with Dutch and Frisian colonists, early established an elaborate system of dikes to increase the amount of land. The many small peninsulas and the dikes made the task of a would-be conqueror a difficult one. The Frisian district of Eiderstedt, in which Tönnies was born, was for a long time particularly successful in maintaining its independence and ancient customs.[68]

The Danish kings attempted several times between 1200 and 1500 to establish their sovereignty over the Eiderstedters, without success. Only after their southern neighbors of Dithmarschen entered an alliance with the Danish kings did the people of Eiderstedt turn to the duke of Schleswig and Holstein for support against the Danes and Dithmarschers. But they took every possible precaution to insure that their customary laws and self-government would not

---

* Tönnies was certainly familiar with the communal constitution of the Eiderstedt Frisians, since he mentions at one point in the letters that he is taking notes on the subject, and alludes to a work on the subject by one Cornils which he probably read (T-P, 16/4/81).

be prejudiced by the new relationship. They made a general agreement with the duke's representative that they would serve in the duke's army in return for the retention of their customary laws. They then prepared a detailed listing of inheritance laws and of the constitution of the people's court (*Volksgericht*). When Duke Heinrich confirmed both documents, they joined his army.

Until the latter part of the nineteenth century, the people of Eiderstedt maintained their traditional freedoms to a considerable degree. True, the dukes succeeded in making considerable inroads in the judicial system, transferring most cases involving fines from the local parish court to one presided over by their agents, and gradually forcing local bodies to give up their lawmaking power. Indeed, Volquart Pauls, an historian of Schleswig-Holstein who probably reflects the local evaluation of this process, describes it as "the struggle between the old German popular freedom (*Volksfreiheit*) and the state authority," and argues that as a result of the *Landrecht* decreed by the dukes in the sixteenth century, "the old traditional customary law, inherited from the fathers, living in the consciousness of the people," succumbed to "a state law, which had absorbed some foreign legal ingredients . . . the spirit of the beginning absolute state." Nevertheless, most of the structure of local self-government was retained. The local agent of the territorial overlord was the *Staller*. In 1590, the Eiderstedters obtained the *Stallerprivileg*, by which the overlord promised that only a non-noble nominated by the district, with his residence and property in the district, would be chosen *Staller*, and that the overlord would never place an intermediary between the *Staller* and himself. In the seventeenth century, the dukes tried to impose a new agent on the Eiderstedters to oversee the dikes—a *Deichgraf*. Within a brief period of time, the people of the district had absorbed this agent completely into the local administration.

The Eiderstedters were able to keep their old ways for two reasons. The dukes of Schleswig were usually poor and the Eiderstedters, raising cattle for export in the fertile marsh lands, usually were able to purchase guarantees for their old liberties. In addition, the Eiderstedters never provided any excuse for outright appropriation of the land. Though firm in their opposition to state domination, they seem to have been civil, and since the dukes realized that their own interests were better served by having the Eiderstedters approach them with moneybags rather than pikestaffs, they did not much interfere.

Thus, for centuries there was little change in Eiderstedt in the economic, political, or social spheres. A large class of relatively well-off gentlemen cattle farmers (*Interessenten*), each with a small number of "hands" drawn from small farmers and landless workers to do the work on the farms, formed an oligarchy that administered the parishes of the district. In 1840, there were 452 *Interessenten* among some two thousand landowners in a total population of seventeen thousand. Kuschert calls this group a "peasant patriciate which has the same significance for Eiderstedt as the bourgeois patriciate in the German cities of the Middle Ages."

Paulsen testifies to the primitive, communal, and democratic character of the village in which he grew up, not many miles from Eiderstedt. Transportation and communication seem to have been on a medieval level. Many people never saw a town.[69] There was, of course, no railroad—neither was there any coach connection, or post office, and the only road was an ancient ox path.[70] In the isolation imposed by these conditions, the self-contained autarchic household which Tönnies posits as the core of *Gemeinschaft* still prevailed.[71]

The social structure of the village was clear and simple: "The village formed a community of life which one could take in as a whole." There were independent farmers, the marsh farmers being the wealthiest; there were artisans, who each had a regular clientele among the farmers; there were a few professionals—pastors, teachers, doctors and officials; there were day laborers; and there were the indigent.[72] However, the unity of the community was not disturbed by the existence of different social classes: "In our own community the transitions between the different levels of property holding were gradual, and the different classes held intercourse with one another and intermarried . . . a hired man who had proved his competence and worth could ask the farmer for the hand of his daughter or propose to the farmer's widow without having to regard refusal as a foregone conclusion."[73] The political affairs of the community were administered by officials who were personally known by everyone.[74] It is not surprising that in the Frisian tongue spoken by Tönnies and Paulsen in their youth, the words "state" and "society" did not exist.[75]

This is the world from which Tönnies emerged at age seventeen, with no apparent attachments, to attend the University of Strasbourg and to which he returned years later, filled with loneliness and despair at the culture of his time, to write his "book of books." How direct an influence on Tönnies' notion of *Wesenwille* was the past and present of his Frisian homeland, and his relationship with Theodor Storm? It is, of course, impossible to say. But when a man who lives on a mountainside paints pictures of mountains, it is possible that there is more than coincidence involved. In any case, for Tönnies, even the mountains were losing their grandeur. For what he sought could no longer be found in the present, not even in Schleswig.

Perhaps the most profound revelation of the community of spirit shared by Theodor Storm and Tönnies lies in a comment of Thomas Mann which, though written about the poet, perfectly describes the sociologist: "I mentioned his love of home, his prepossession for it, his—so to speak—homesickness. . . . In essence, it is a longing, nostalgia, unsatisfiable by any reality, for it is addressed altogether to the past, the lost and sunken backward of time."[76]

7

Tönnies and Romanticism

ALTHOUGH THERE IS LITTLE EVIDENCE of any direct influence on Tönnies during his critical period by any German thinkers before Lorenz von Stein, Tönnies himself later became aware of certain striking similarities.*

The social and historical thought of preromantics and romantics, roughly from Schiller to Savigny, as far as it relates to Tönnies' thought, may be conceived as a two-story building with a foundation. The spiritual soil in which this structure rests is an alienation from and reaction against the prevailing spirit of rationalism, which found its highest expression in the French Revolution. The foundation of the structure is a philosophy of history that views the present as decline and sees hope of progress only in a future overcoming of the existing tendency toward the atomization and rationalization of individual and social existence. This foundation is formed by such preromantics as Schiller and Fichte, and also by romantics who follow their lead. The first floor of this structure takes the pattern of the foundation one step further, to a glorification of the Middle Ages, as the epoch when an organic community completely

---

* Tönnies' views of romantic and preromantic German thought may be found in the preface to the second edition of *Gemeinschaft und Gesellschaft* (1912), in his 1906 essay, "Entwicklung der Soziologie in Deutschland im 19. Jahrhundert" (SSK, II, pp. 63–104), and in his *Schiller als Zeitbürger und Politiker* (Berlin, 1905), 45 pp. Tönnies made known his opposition to the German Historical School of Savigny and Eichhorn, with which he has sometimes been associated (e.g., Gottfried Salomon, *Das Mittelalter als Ideal in der Romantik* [Munich, 1922], p. 85) in his 1894 essay "Historismus und Rationalismus" (SSK, I, pp. 105–27).

antithetical to the modern world still prevailed. This glorification of the Middle Ages may be found in Novalis, Tieck, and Wackenroder. The upper story of the structure presents the logical conclusion of the first two stages—the demand for the reconstruction of society on the medieval pattern. This was the demand of men like Adam Müller, K. L. von Haller, and, to the extent that he sought to reestablish the legal basis of society on its medieval foundations, Savigny.

Tönnies had no hope at all for a restoration of the medieval body politic. In his "Historismus und Rationalismus," he denied any possibility of the historical school's actually overcoming the much-despised *Rationalismus*. For one thing, he saw in the juristic and the economic schools of historicism completely different definitions of the source and support of the traditional and customary. The jurists interpreted customary law as the creation of the *Volk* and viewed any attempt by the state to legislate as *"willkürlich"*— arbitrary, disruptive of the organic character of the customary law.* The state merely had the responsibility of preserving this customary law. The historical economists, however, asserted that *only* through the legislative interference of the state could the disruptive economic individualism of bourgeois society be made to conform to an organic pattern for the good of all. In any case, the social institution to which both wings appealed, the state, was for Tönnies, by definition, an integral part of the modern rationalistic tendency, and could not be otherwise.[1] He maintained a similarly critical attitude toward the historicists of his own day. When in 1888 Paulsen told him that Gierke found his work one-sided, in that it perceived only the disintegrating aspect of modern life, but failed to notice "the new formation of communities and corresponding sentiments,"[2] Tönnies replied, "I knew that Gierke would not go along with me. The excellent man has childish Prussian illusions about the current century. He sees the renewal of the old German popular spirit and law in the blossoming stock corporations."

Even though he denied the possibility of translating their value

---

* Even here, Tönnies noted an internal contradiction in the thought of Savigny, who tried to assert the Roman law—itself of a rationalist origin—as the fundamental law of the people (SSK, I, pp. 105–7).

emphases into normative prescriptions for contemporary society, Tönnies did, of course, share the historicists' positive valuation of customary law and the Middle Ages, and so was often close to the spirit of those who glorified the Holy Roman Empire. If, however, the German romantics were themselves split in their view of the Middle Ages, with some, like the aristocrats Novalis and Schlegel, looking back to the Hohenstaufens and the golden age of knighthood (twelfth and thirteenth centuries) while others, such as the bourgeois Wackenroder and Tieck, looked back to the great Catholic urban culture of the fourteenth and fifteenth centuries,[3] there is no doubt that Tönnies was spiritually aligned with the latter rather than the former.

Indeed, Tönnies' view of feudalism is of a transitional stage between community and society in which the community of the lord and his followers, though originally arising out of the village community, stands opposed to it, and tries to break it down and reduce its members to dependency on the lord. Once this is accomplished, a relationship of lord to serf or tenant ensues which appears to prefigure the societal relationship of state absolutism to an atomized helpless citizenry.* Certainly, Tönnies shares with his fellow Frisians Storm and Paulsen an aversion to the nobility of their own time,† stemming no doubt from the ancient traditions of rural republicanism in their homeland.

---

* "So that as a last extreme, a property of the lord can appear in the *Mark* which is no longer relative, communal and divided, but absolute, individual and exclusive [*alleiniges*]. After all bonds of the community with its dependents are dissolved, either complete serfdom or a contractual tenantry relationship results. The latter can either develop, through the capital and education of the tenant, into complete opposition to serfdom, or be merely a different name and a new legal form of the same. On the other hand, it can also happen that the lord or some external legislation will abolish all dependency of the lower or peasant property, and declare the same to be both individual and absolute, just as the upper property is. In each of these cases, a simple and rational, abstract structure replaces the complicated, living, concrete relationships" (*Gemeinschaft und Gesellschaft*, I, par. 16; p. 32, 1920 ed.).

† See T-P, 25/4/85; Franz Schriewer, "Theodor Storm in seiner politischen Welt," in *Schriften der Theodor Storm Gesellschaft*, Schrift I (Heide in Holstein, 1952), p. 28 ("The noble is [like the Church] the poison in the veins of the nation"; letter from Storm to Brinkmann 18/1/64); and Paulsen, *Autobiography*, pp. 370–71, where the distaste for the Prussian officers' tradition is explicitly related to the democratic social customs of his Frisian forebears.

Be that as it may, Tönnies sees as the true glory of the medieval German cities the same combination of aesthetic, religious, and social harmony that enthralled the romantics.*

The closest similarity between Tönnies and earlier German thought is not, however, in the view of the Middle Ages, but in the underlying philosophy of history, which is actually a common possession of preromantic and romantic thought. In many of the late-eighteenth- and early-nineteenth-century German literary figures—Herder, Schiller, Fichte, Humboldt, Novalis, and Kleist—one discerns implicitly or explicitly a philosophy of history which clearly anticipates that of *Gemeinschaft und Gesellschaft*. Heinrich Popitz depicts the common denominator of these earlier "world-views" in terms that leave no doubt of their similarity to Tönnies' outlook:

> Previous history is the fall from an originally harmonious unity to a disruption of human abilities and powers which, both in the single individual and in human society, has reached its absolute high point in the present, the complete fall from man's original ideal disposition. The censure of the contemporary spirit is unambiguous: "worthlessness," "disorganization," "absolute sinfulness," "anarchy," "destruction of everything positive"—the expression "suffering humanity" returns again and again and is found both in Herder and Schiller, Fichte and the young Hegel.[4]

Thus, Schiller asks:

> Should not approximately the same thing be true of the progress of human culture as we have occasion to notice in every experience? Here, however, one distinguishes three stages:
> 1. The object stands before us in its entirety, but confused and mixed.
> 2. We separate single characteristics and distinguish. Our perception is clear, but limited and isolated.
> 3. We unite what was separated, and the whole stands once more complete before us, however now no longer confused, but illuminated from all sides.

---

* Cf. for example the quote from Wackenroder in Gottfried Salomon, *Das Mittelalter als Ideal in der Romantik* (Munich, 1922), p. 43, with Tönnies' reverent description of *Stadtgemeinschaft* in *Gemeinschaft und Gesellschaft*, I, par. 16; p. 37, 1920 ed.

In the first period were the Greeks. In the second stand we. So the third is still to be hoped for, and then we will no longer wish that the Greeks were back.[5]

In Wilhelm von Humboldt, we find a similar pattern:

1. Unity through the rule of *physical sensuality.*—Unity through crudeness—among all barbaric peoples.
2. Unity of aesthetic powers—among the Greeks. With this, a unity through reason—as with Plato—is united in speculative heads.
3. Lack of unity through great development of the understanding.
4. The highest unity, proceeding from that lack.[6]

Fichte has five stages of world history. In the first, reason rules through instinct. It is an age of primordial innocence. In the second, this instinctive reason has taken the form of compulsion which enforces blind belief and obedience. This is the stage of beginning sinfulness. In the third stage, mankind is liberated both from authority and from the last remnants of reason in any form. This is "the age of absolute indifference against all truth, and of complete unrestraint without any guides: the stage of complete sinfulness." In the fourth stage reason makes a gradual return, truth is recognized and loved above all else. It is the stage of beginning vindication. In the fifth stage, mankind surely and infallibly reconstructs itself in the image of reason. This is "the stage of complete vindication and consecration."[7] Needless to say, Fichte places his own generation squarely in the third stage of "absolute sinfulness."[8]

Kleist provides another version, in his brief story "Über das Marionettentheater," where perfect grace in the dual sense of both physical and spiritual perfection is revealed, via the story of the fencing bear, to be embodied in only two kinds of beings—those whose instinctual apparatus is not weakened by reflection and half-consciousness, or those whose consciousness and knowledge are infinite:

> Therefore, I said, a little nonplussed, we should have to eat once more from the tree of knowledge in order to fall back into the state of innocence?

To be sure, he answered, that is the last chapter in the history of the world.

And in Schiller's essay "Über naive und sentimentalische Dichtung," we have a very similar treatment that directly suggests to us, in the concept of the naïve, Tönnies' notion of *Wesenwille*. Speaking of the attraction that children have for us, Schiller says,

> We love in them the silently creating life, the quiet working from oneself, the existence according to one's own laws, the eternal unity with oneself. They are, what we were; they are what we are again to be. We were Nature, like them, and our civilization should lead us back, in the path of reason and freedom, to Nature. They thus represent to us our lost childhood, which remains always the most precious to us; therefore they fill us with a certain melancholy. At the same time they represent to us our highest completion in the ideal; therefore they transpose us into an elevated emotion.

Tönnies, with the exception of one brief passage, only deals with the initial and middle stages discussed by these earlier philosophies of history. *Gemeinschaft* was innocence, *Gesellschaft*, the fall. But in the one passage where he does mention the possibility of a further stage, he suggests a notion of overcoming reason by reason that could just as well have sprung from the pen of Kleist or Schiller:

> It occurs to us all to value the lack of consciousness in the woman, the pious simplicity of her soul, the secret depths of her temperament and substance: we sometimes suspect what we have lost when we become cold and calculating, flat and enlightened. And yet, here too the fact is confirmed and Nature only completes her destructions to let the powerfully developing elements prosper in a new life. For when science develops into philosophy, man again achieves, through the purest and highest knowledge, that joy of intuition and love which was ruined for him through all sorts of reflections and strivings. But this perspective goes beyond the limits of the observation marked out here.[9]

This similarity is not, after all, very surprising. The earlier philosophies of history cited above were all developed as reactions to the Enlightenment and the French Revolution, those two great bearers of modern rationalism, those two destroyers of all that was holy, natural, and organic. In the century that had elapsed between German classicism and Tönnies, the force of rationalism, in the shape of the industrial revolution and the bureaucratic state, had captured Germany, too. But Tönnies found in his provincial backwater in Schleswig the same kind of refuge from the modern spirit that his predecessors had earlier found in Germany as a whole. The sudden transformation of German society from its idyllic patriarchal ways in the earlier part of the century to its feverish industrial and commercial activism in the latter part, together with the sudden predominance of Prussia and Prussian values over many onceindependent areas, brought the chill of alienation to many of the intellectuals who were born after the middle of the century. Scheler, Sombart, Michels, Simmel, Vierkandt, to name only the most prominent—all revealed this estrangement in varying degrees. The significance of Tönnies lies in the fact that, being of them all the most hostile and marginal to the new Germany and the most rooted to the old, he was the first to express, in the language of sociology, the dichotomy that was to dominate German sociology for half a century. And if he only once and fleetingly mentioned that third stage of history, in which philosophy restores to mankind "the joy of intuition and love," it is because the victory of rationalism and the all-devouring state was too crushing to permit anything more than sad contemplation of the past and cold analysis of the present.

8

Tönnies and Durkheim

Estranged and Engaged Sociology

Examining tönnies in the context of his native milieu and of his relationship to German romantic political thought clarifies much of the irreconcilable pessimism that informs his early work. Comparison with his contemporary, Émile Durkheim, as representative a founding father of the French school of sociology as Tönnies was of the German, is equally illuminating.

Born in 1858, Durkheim, like Tönnies, grew up in a traditional community, linguistically separate on the margin of his national culture—the Alsatian community of Ashkenazic Jews, who spoke Yiddish and Hebrew until after the French Revolution. Attracted like Tönnies to the cosmopolitan culture of the capital city, he educated himself in Paris and sustained great hopes of applying the resources of the new constitutional order to the problems of social dislocation caused by the upheavals of the modern era. He too elaborated in his first major work (*The Division of Labor in Society*, 1893) a distinction between traditional culture on the one hand, based on affective ties and a unifying value system, and modern culture on the other, based on a sharply articulated division of labor; a distinction which neatly paralleled that between *Gemeinschaft* and *Gesellschaft*. Durkheim was as aware as Tönnies of the spiritual problems accompanying the disintegration of traditional community and its supersession by highly individualistic codes of behavior based on the division of labor. And again like Tönnies, Durkheim separated himself from the positivist psychology of his day and insisted upon viewing men not as isolated individuals but in the framework of a social nexus.

Beyond these points of similarity, however, Durkheim and Tönnies held sharply contrasting views. In the vocabulary of late-nineteenth-century European scholarship, beholden to Darwin and eager to be rid of the dry formulas of eighteenth-century rationalism, any use of the dichotomy "organic-mechanical" implied "superior-inferior." For Durkheim, traditional culture had a "mechanical" division of labor, whereas modern society was "organic." For Tönnies the telltale adjectives were reversed (though he only accepted them in a metaphorical sense): *Gemeinschaft* was "organic," *Gesellschaft* "mechanical." These opposed valuations of the modern era reflect major differences between the political cultures as well as the social positions and experiences of the French and German sociologists.

Efforts in France to roll back the tide of nineteenth-century liberalism—the recurrent crises between 1870 and 1900 centering around the figures of MacMahon, Boulanger, and Dreyfus—were uniformly unsuccessful. Unlike their German counterparts, French liberals and radicals emerged from such intrigues with their honor largely intact and their political power supreme. In fact, Durkheim, himself a Dreyfusard, rose steadily within the French educational system; in the favorable intellectual climate of the Third Republic, he became the principal architect of the social science curriculum in the secular educational system created under the radicals Waldeck-Rousseau and Emile Combe. Well before these reforms, he had sparked the interest in sociology of the French Director of Higher Education, the philosopher Louis Liard, whose German equivalent, Friedrich Althoff, seems to have nurtured the ambition of supporting sociology only as, to borrow Lenin's exquisite simile, a rope supports a hanged man. In contrast to the pariah status of the liberal German sociologists, Lewis A. Coser writes:

> During the years 1890 to 1914 the Sorbonne was the center of the intellectual defense of democratic and rationalist values and many of its key professors, with Durkheim in the fore-

front, were the intellectual spokesmen for these liberal trends. Durkheim made the most of the opportunity. He sat in a number of administrative commissions and councils; he became the intermediary between top officials in the Ministry of Education and in the university bureaucracy; he placed a good number of his friends in strategic positions both in administration and in the educational system. He had a key hand in filling vacant chairs in the social sciences both at the Sorbonne and in the provinces.*

Tönnies, as we have seen, recoiled, under the shock of the antisocialist hysteria of 1878 and the liberals' capitulation before it, from the Berlin cultural milieu. Between 1878 and the publication of *Gemeinschaft und Gesellschaft* in 1887, he underwent an emotional return to the values of his ancestral *Heimat* and came stubbornly to reject the views of Gierke, Stein, Schmoller, and Wagner, who saw in the Prussian state the protector of traditional communal organization from the ravages of capitalism. But the surrender of the German liberals to a policy of authoritarian repression in 1878 reflected a larger disparity between the social and political traditions of France and Germany.

France had experienced a revolutionary epoch between 1789 and 1870 in which the political thrust of the liberal bourgeoisie was alternately allied with and antagonistic to that of the preindustrial lower-middle classes. The French Third Republic represented the uneasy alliance of these two groups over their defeated but still powerful enemies—Bonapartists, monarchists, and the decimated Communards of Paris. Threats from ambitious generals and conservative Catholics tended to overshadow, until after the turn of the century, the socialist and anarchist opposition of the fourth estate, and the result was a receptivity, in a society where technological progress and the threat of social upheaval were minimal, to the new discipline of sociology, critical of all the pieties of French traditionalism. Durkheim's meteoric ascent to the pinnacle of the French

---

* Lewis A. Coser, *Masters of Sociological Thought* (New York/Chicago/San Francisco/Atlanta, 1971), p. 170. Comparison with the fruitless efforts of Max Weber to find appropriate university positions for his friends Simmel, Michels, and Sombart, is instructive. See Marianne Weber, *Max Weber, Ein Lebensbild* (Heidelberg, 1950) pp. 277, 395–96.

educational establishment, in a period when his German colleagues —Tönnies, Sombart, Weber, Michels, and Simmel—were denied disciplinary status and largely confined to ill-paid positions on the margins of the academy, becomes comprehensible and highly significant if we consider by comparison the trials of the German third estate.

In the German revolution of 1848, the conflict between the socially reactionary demands of the preindustrial strata and the liberal constitutional and economic goals of the upper middle class froze into permanent animosity after liberal fledgling parliaments invoked the Prussian army to quell the revolt of those "little men" whose French equivalents had rescued the third estate when they stormed the Bastille.[1]

Although insoluble problems of national unification may have made the cause of the German bourgeois revolution hopeless in 1848, the resulting debacle fatally undermined the future aspirations to social and political dominance of Germany's liberal bourgeoisie as well as the demands of the oppressed *Mittelstand* for social justice. The examples of France and England suggest the paradox that the moneyed power of the bourgeoisie can attain hegemony only with the militant support of its fated victims in the preindustrial middle class. Both the German liberals and their victims, unable to rely upon each other for social gain, subsequently turned themselves over as clients to the only power that could further their most elementary economic needs: the Prussian monarchy. Abandoning all hopes of power and supremacy under Bismarck, the principal representatives of both groups approached the state not as conquerors but as supplicants. For those who rejected such roles and retained the critical consciousness of the radical bourgeois, there was no place in the Second Empire. The fate of the Progressives under Bismarck found its microcosmic echo in the fate of the sociologists under Althoff, the Prussian Minister of Education.

Thus, while the German sociologists in general—and Tönnies in particular—may have held methodological assumptions similar to Durkheim's, the Germans whose view of their political and social milieu most closely approximated Durkheim's view of his—whose implicit philosophy of history was similarly shaped by the assumption that the political *status quo* (or progressive extensions from it) could effectively protect their highest values—were not the sociologists, but the conservative "socialists of the chair," Gustav Schmoller and Adolf Wagner, against whose celebration of the German bureaucratic state the sociologists aimed much of their intellectual arsenal. Durkheim strongly suggests this kinship in a lengthy essay he wrote on the German "socialists of the chair" in 1887, and subsequent reviews by Durkheim of Tönnies' work and by Tönnies of Durkheim's *Division of Labor in Society* reveal a consciousness by both men of the differences, as well as the similarities, between them.[2]

9

The Evolution of Tönnies' Social and Political Views to the First World War

I HAVE ARGUED that the basis for Tönnies' sharp historical dichotomy of *Gemeinschaft* and *Gesellschaft* was his attachment to the values of his ancestral homeland and his hostility to the new state and society of Bismarckian Germany. After the publication of his groundbreaking book in 1887, however, Tönnies' opposition to his society gradually softened, and by the time of the First World War he had come to accept a view of the modern German state which he had bitterly opposed in Lorenz von Stein—the state as bearer of *Gemeinschaft*.

Considering this evolution of Tönnies' views toward the reconciliation of what had previously represented irreconcilable historical stages—community and the modern state—it is only natural that when *Gemeinschaft und Gesellschaft* appeared in its second edition Tönnies should have ceased to think of the strict opposition he had established as one of historical stages, and should rather have conceived of it as a purely conceptual opposition.*

But the historical pessimism and social alienation implied by Tönnies' earlier understanding of *Gemeinschaft* and *Gesellschaft* were not completely unambiguous. Tönnies left two loopholes in his theory. With the transformation of *Gemeinschaft* and *Gesellschaft* from an historical to a conceptual opposition, these loopholes were to allow his later reconciliation with the modern world to occur within the confines of his own theory. In the first place, he recognized that the state, apart from being purely contractual, the mere representative of the sellers of goods—the "night watchman state" of English liberalism[1]—might also perform the social role of administering the nation's economy,[2] which approximated the state socialist conception of Stein or Gneist stripped of all *"gemeinschaftliche"* qualities. Between these two forms of sovereignty, Tönnies implied the possibility of conflict.[3] In the second place, when the state was conceived as the representative of the sellers of goods (English model), the creators of the goods, the workers, who had only their labor power to sell, were unrepresented.

> The state is a capitalist institution, and remains so when it declares its identity with society. It consequently ceases to be so when the working class makes itself the subject of the state's will, in order to destroy capitalist production. It follows that the political strivings of the working class, according to their goal, fall outside of the framework of *Gesellschaft*, which includes the state and politics as necessary forms of its will.[4]

For Tönnies, these two escape routes from his completely pessimistic *Weltanschauung* were no more than theoretical possibilities in 1887. The opposition of *Gemeinschaft* to *Gesellschaft* was of

* E.g., the change in the subtitle of the work from "Treatise on Communism and Socialism as Empirical Forms of Civilization" to "Basic Concepts of Pure Sociology."

much greater importance to him than the potential one between *Gesellschaft* and the state. And the very subtitle of the work, which identified communism with the past and socialism with *Gesellschaft*, showed how little hope he had that the working-class movement might destroy capitalist *Gesellschaft*. But by the First World War these theoretical possibilities of 1887 were to become the basis for a significant change in Tönnies' social perspective.

The evolution toward this changed perspective proceeded, as mentioned, slowly. But the first signs of it were visible not long after the publication of *Gemeinschaft und Gesellschaft*. In 1888, Theodor Storm, the probable model of *Wesenwille*, died, and in the same letter in which Tönnies told Paulsen of the deep loss he had suffered from Storm's passing, we also see the first sad acknowledgment that his feeling for Paulsen was weakening: "Never doubt my reverence and love for you, even if you must also know that I do not feel so well understood by you, and do not understand you as well as earlier. That this had to come, given our different conditions of life and natural dispositions, I have foreseen."[5] At the same time, with his "book of books" completed, Tönnies was finally able to break through the loneliness that bound him to his ancestral *Gemeinschaft* and to invest his considerable energies, both scholarly and nonscholarly, in the world around him.

It is no wonder that Tönnies came to realize the power of opposing forces within society, for as soon as he ventured into it, he felt the pull of these forces within his own life and ambitions. He had a profound ambivalence about the German university system. He despised it as an instrument of state and society, felt alienated from it, and yet, spurred on by Paulsen, frequently sought a secure position within it. It was a continuing mortification to him that the system would only accept him on terms that he could not accept. And his attempts, first through the Ethical Society and then through the labor cooperative movement, to strengthen the *Gemeinschaft* elements within *Gesellschaft*, not only made his course within the German academic world more difficult, but ended by involving him deeply in the internal social problems of *Gesellschaft* itself.

Tönnies' most serious attempts to find a permanent position in a university occurred in the period 1888–90. Early in 1888, he tried unsuccessfully to obtain a position at Jena. For a brief period toward the end of that year, he hoped to obtain a position in Basel;[6] like Paulsen, he treasured the old, democratic communal life of Switzerland.[7] In 1889, he was apprehensive about being pushed out of his position as *Privatdozent* in Kiel.[8] In 1890, buoyed up by the departure of Bismarck and the elder Wilhelm from the imperial scene, he wanted to return to Berlin. On being told that even a post as *Privatdozent* was not assured him, he applied to Göttingen. But here too there was nothing open.[9] When Paulsen suggested that he write articles for a nonacademic weekly, he refused: "I have never thought of such a public, and admit to everyone that, in form and content, my book must be repugnant to the general reader. The respect which I await and demand is a purely scholarly one."[10]

In this same three-year period, Tönnies made clear on several occasions his estrangement from and disappointment with the academic world. After abandoning hope of a job in Jena, he wrote:

> I am too certain that I am not suitable for the gentlemen. Other life courses occur to me. What I need is quiet, a life without excitement. . . . In quiet, with time, I would be able to do some not inconsiderable things. If last October, I had applied for the post of Bürgermeister in Garding, it would have been the right post for me. A little administering, which would have claimed 2-3 hours daily, and would have granted insight into the intimate life of a small region. Moreover, free time, no distraction, healthy climate, modest salary, and the possibility of serving men. Compared with that, I would really not like to become a professor.[11]

Eight months later, affairs had not improved. He remained "alien." "The witty conversations with professors and their wives only make me uncomfortable; I yearn for isolated observation and creation."*

---

* T-P, 26/11/88. In *Gemeinschaft und Gesellschaft,* this Rousseauan aversion to social life received theoretical formulation:
  All conventional socializing can be understood analogously to this commerce which rests on the exchange of material values. The highest rule of such socializing is politeness: an exchange of words and courtesies in which each appears to be there for all and all appear to value each other equally. In

In 1889, while waiting for a decision about a possible regular appointment as professor in philosophy at Kiel, Tönnies informed Paulsen of another obstacle to his career—he seriously doubted that he would be willing to take the oath, required by law of all Prussian university professors, of personal service to the Prussian king. The oath would be against his conscience and would deprive him of a "feeling of philosophical freedom."[12] Adding to his discomfort in this period was the unhappy fate of his magnum opus. Two years after publication, *Gemeinschaft und Gesellschaft* had sold fewer than five hundred copies of an initial printing of seven hundred and fifty, and the printer was threatening to pulp the remainder.[13]

The letters of the nineties show a lessening interest in academic possibilities and a more active devotion to social concerns. These concerns slowly altered from the attempt to preserve or resuscitate *Gemeinschaft* units within *Gesellschaft* to involvement, through the labor movement, in the social problems of society itself.

I have mentioned Tönnies' earlier attempts to develop some sort of intellectual community among like-minded philosophical critics of the new Germany. Shortly after the publication of *Gemeinschaft und Gesellschaft*, he entered an association of local workmen, in which he hoped to find a congenial milieu, open to his insights, and remote from the enlightened deviousness of scholarly society. His description of his relationship to this group illuminates well the state of mind of the young sociologist:

> I do not mean to say that I would limit myself entirely to studying and thinking. Rather I want to undertake for myself the social affairs of a narrower sphere of life so as to take part in it, and have taken the first step by attending the general meeting of the Worker-Colony Union and becoming a member of it. That this thing increasingly falls into the hands of the Pietists and internal missionaries does not bother me. It re-

---

truth, though, each thinks of himself and tries to assert his significance and advantages in opposition to all others. So that for everything that anyone does for anyone else, he expects indeed demands at least an equivalent: consequently, he calculates his services, flattery, presents, etc. exactly as to whether they will have the desired effect (*Gemeinschaft und Gesellschaft*, I, par. 25; pp. 62–63, 1887 ed.).

mains sympathetic to me and in many respects interesting. If, then, they will not be able to use my views, still, perhaps, here and there my insights, since naturally only a few take an active part. From this viewpoint too—I mean participation in life—I would not willingly leave our beautiful homeland. I would rather break with the whole professional crowd and achieve a firm, regular mode of life, for which I would perhaps choose another area than Husum if I did not feel myself drawn there by my mother. That is of course not the only thing; I have many ties there among the inhabitants, also among the workers, among whom I find much understanding and trust, if I could ever find the occasion to be helpful to them. So I feel in my natural sphere there, while here I am a nothing, whom everyone assumes to bear in his heart the most violent desires for a professorship.[14]

But it was not until the formation of the Society for Ethical Culture in 1892 that he saw a public arena large enough for the significant implementation of his social views.

Tönnies' relationship to the Society for Ethical Culture is one of the least-known aspects of his life's work. This is regrettable, since it was through the Ethical Society that Tönnies was involved in his most specific activity—or attempt at activity—as a social reformer, and ignorance of his activities here has furthered the widespread illusion that Tönnies never seriously desired or entertained hopes for a return of *Gemeinschaft*.[15] Tönnies' value bias in favor of *Gemeinschaft* has been clearly shown. But it would seem to follow from his conception of *Gemeinschaft* and *Gesellschaft* that there is an historical inevitability in the succession from one to the other, and that consequently any conception of a return to *Gemeinschaft*—such as the Nazi version—was something Tönnies could never have accepted. The Nazis' *Volksgemeinschaft* represented a total perversion of Tönnies' ideas, which he steadfastly rejected, and his prevailing attitude toward the disappearance of *Gemeinschaft* was the submissive, "Can one help becoming old?"[16] Published articles from the year 1893, however, testify that at this time Tönnies had definite plans for counteracting the ills of *Gesellschaft* through the development, on the basis of new family associations, of a new community.

The most explicit suggestions for such an "intentional" community appeared in an article of September 16, 1893,[17] in which Tönnies proposed that the Ethical Culture Society establish "associations [*Verbände*] or partnerships [*Genossenschaften*] of families, which would have as their direct task the cultivation of the family spirit." He distinguished between two conceivable types of such groups: groups by nature (blood-relationship) and groups by choice. Though he knew of an already existing natural family union, founded five years earlier in Frankfurt, he advocated family groups based on choice, because of the great dispersion of blood relations in contemporary society.

What Tönnies envisaged, then, was

> the partnership of choice-selected families, who commonly declare their faith in Ethical Culture and set themselves as a direct goal a renewal of family life. Three thoughts must bring forth this goal: 1. making the way of life simpler and healthier; 2. shaping a more serious meaningful companionship; 3. raising the understanding between the male and the female manner of thought. That is enough. For common ethical activity in other directions follows necessarily from these. ("Fünfzehn Thesen zur Erneuerung des Familienlebens," *Ethische Kultur*, September 16, 1893.)

Tönnies thinks groups of families should be formed very loosely at first, to keep out any artificial formality. The number of families in each group shall be no less than three and no more than five. Three is best, because it allows the formation of a majority and also makes the departure of one family so dangerous to the existence of the group that, in all important matters, a majority of two will be inclined to compromise.

Through the gradual development of mutual trust and companionship, Tönnies saw the possibility, as a further step, of providing an economic basis for the group. First, he envisaged the common purchases of supplies; then, their common use. This, he wrote, would be facilitated by neighborly, if not communal, living arrangements. In addition, he would propose a set of by-laws which would be sworn to by all.

Evolution of Tönnies' Social and Political Views   119

As a final stage of organization, three to five of such family groups would join to form a larger unit,

> which would serve a broader companionship, and particular goals of a moral and economic variety, and which would do well to establish an advising and administrative authority that would watch with wisdom, fidelity and tenderness over the weal of this family community [*Gemeinde*]. It must activate its common spirit in regular and extra meetings, meditations, and artistic exercises, in the manner of a religious belief. All religion [*Kultus*] is originally a religion of home and hearth.° Around home and hearth may religion also revive. Only in such inner communities can the beautiful be cultivated, the good, thrive, and the true be kept holy.

Other writings of the period 1893–95, though less explicit, suggest the same view of the Ethical Society as a medium for the reestablishment of community.[18] But by mid-1895, Tönnies had to admit that the hoped-for rejuvenation of *Gemeinschaft* had not occurred: "The ethical societies are still remote from a community of life."[19]

Another, better-known aspect of Tönnies' social concern—his sympathy for the sufferings of the working class at the hands of *Gesellschaft*—also appeared in his articles in *Ethische Kultur*. Here too he hoped to see the Ethical Culture Society become an instrument of social reform. Side by side with his most specific proposals for developing new communities of families appeared demands for the abolition of private property in urban real estate, for the prohibition of child labor, for the limitation of the working hours of women and youth, for the inspection of factory conditions, for total state insurance against all forms of personal emergency, for the shortening of labor hours to allow parents more time for the education of their children, and—a demand which shows the continuing incompatibility between Tönnies' *Gemeinschaft* ideal and

---

° This idea is found in Tönnies' description of *Gemeinschaft* (*Gemeinschaft und Gesellschaft*, Leipzig, 1935, 8th ed., I, par. 18, p. 37). Through many of the articles of this period there runs the assumption that ethical culture itself, conceived by Tönnies in some pantheistic sense of a philosophical understanding of man's proper, harmonious relation to nature, would form the basis of a new, *Gemeinschaft*-like religion.

the ideals of even the most "progressive" or socialist forces of *Gesellschaft*—for the "greatest possible increase in agricultural activity, which is physically and morally healthier, and serves the needs of all, at the cost of industrial and commercial activities, and of personal services, which to a great extent only serve the luxury of the few."[20]

Since Tönnies' demands for social reform required much less active participation from the Ethical Culture Society than his proposals for the reactivation of family communities, its inactivity in pressing for social reform was not quite as obvious as its lack of enthusiasm for the artificial creation of family communities. It consequently took somewhat longer for Tönnies to realize that there was immovable opposition within the Society to its serving as a liberal advocate for what he conceived to be the cause of the worker, than to perceive that it would not submit to the role of social guinea pig. By 1899, however, his disillusion with the Ethical Society on both scores was evident. In that year, he described the two main goals of the Ethical Society as the maintenance of European peace and the spread of popular education. As for his own desire to see the Society attack a social system based on private property, he noted that the Society had no unity of opinion on the subject.[21]

In his autobiography, written twenty-five years later, he discussed briefly his part in the Ethical Society. He accepted election to its first committee in 1892 because he liked "the general direction of a humane idealism" and tried to chart a clear course for the Society. "However, the Society persisted in its ambiguities. In 1898, I proposed a change of name to 'Verein für Sozialethik'; I thought thereby to give the program a more socialistic-popular direction, as I had earlier attempted to do, but I found little sympathy and approval."

By the time Tönnies was urging a new name on the Ethical Society, he had become considerably more committed to the workers' cause than he had been in 1893. He had earlier of course, as his open letter to Mehring showed,[22] had strong sympathy for the Socialist movement, and hoped to see the Ethical Society mediate between the just demands of the workers and a largely ignorant middle-class public opinion.²³ But in 1896 occurred a harbor strike in Hamburg, among longshoremen and seamen, about which Tönnies agreed to do a series of studies for Heinrich Braun's *Archiv für Soziale Gesetzgebung und Statistik*.²⁴ His research seems to have drawn him into a personal involvement with the labor movement that he had never felt before. Being an eyewitness of many of the events of the strike, and undoubtedly acquainting himself with many of its leaders, he was morally outraged at attempts by the employers to link the strike to an international socialist plot. This tone of outrage crept into his articles on the subject, both in Braun's *Archiv* and in *Ethische Kultur*, and, together with other public advocacy of the strikers' cause,* won him the unmerited reputation of being a Social Democrat.†

Needless to say, this reputation was of no use whatever to Tönnies in his sporadic efforts to secure for himself a position in the German university system. But by 1897 it could do him little harm, for as early as 1893, Tönnies was a marked man. The one person who had more control over Prussian university appointments than anyone else was Friedrich Althoff, who from 1882 to 1897 was the chief adviser on university affairs to the Prussian Ministry of Education, and from 1897 to 1907 was director of the Ministry. In 1893, Tönnies turned down an offer from the Ministry of Education to become an *Extraordinarius* (assistant professor) with prospects of a full professorship.²⁵ Paulsen considered this refusal an act of foolish pride on Tönnies' part—an unwillingness to accept less than a full professorship.²⁶ But Paulsen was unaware of the strings attached to the offer: in a letter that Tönnies was instructed never to discuss with anyone, and which was only found in his *Nachlass*, Althoff told Tönnies that the offer of a post at Kiel was contingent

---

* P-T, 4/2/97. Even Paulsen was moved by the press slanders against the strikers to contribute to their support. Lili Braun recounted sympathetically the passion behind Tönnies' article in her husband's journal, in L. Braun, *Memoiren einer Sozialisten, Kampfjahre* (Munich, 1911), pp. 202ff.

† "I was now [1897] considered by the superficially educated [*Viel-aber-leichtgebildeten*] as a Social Democrat; I never was one, openly or secretly, because my way of thinking deviated considerably in some points from the Erfurt Program, and because I had a great aversion to losing myself in practical politics" (Tönnies, "Autobiography," p. 21).

on his giving up all activity in the Society for Ethical Culture. Naturally he refused.[27] It was not until the year of Althoff's death (1908) that Tönnies received his first permanent appointment at Kiel.

Tönnies was aware of the incompatibility not only between his professional ambitions and his social militancy, but also between the latter and his generally pessimistic *Weltanschauung*. In 1898, when Tönnies again tried to obtain a position at the University of Berlin, Paulsen warned him that he would be expected to show more reserve than previously in his public behavior.[28] Tönnies' reply shows his attempt to grapple with both incompatibilities:

> If there is anything for which I reproach myself in politics, it is that, as a citizen who understands something of it, I have concerned myself too little with it. Not in the slightest have I ever concerned myself publicly with politics! I have only acted in purely human and moral concerns, thus, in the matter of the Hamburg strike, for negotiation and mediation against the principle, proclaimed by the employers' league, of Civil War. If people don't want to understand that, it is very sad, but alters nothing. If the scholarly, and the unscholarly, think I am a Socialist, I must insist that my view of history and the contemporary conditions stands further from Social Democracy than that of the social politicians [*Sozialpolitiker*]. They all hold the recognized sickness of the social condition to be curable—these through petty speeches and laws, those (in part) perhaps only through "blood and iron"; I have always held the same sickness to be incurable. That is why Höffding wrote about my book under the title "Social Pessimism." To a degree, I have personally rescued myself from the hopelessness of this thought through the conviction that the progressing dissolution of modern culture can proceed in two different forms: a) through forcible preservation of its obsolete forms, thus as petrification or ossification, b) through adaptation of the forms to the actual content, thus as relative rejuvenation and regeneration. The former the victory of the bourgeoisie, the latter, the victory of the labor movement. I believe it is a moral and, if you will, patriotic duty, to stand on the side of the labor movement and, as much as we are able, to educate

it. I stand just as far from the theoretical foundations of Social Democracy, at least as it is conceived in political practice, as from their illusions.

The notion of "adapting" the forms to the content signifies the two influences that were to draw Tönnies' thought and activity into the main framework of German society and make of him a staunch defender of his nation's position in the First World War. On the one hand, Tönnies, like most other thinkers in this period, was struck by the implications for society of Darwin's theory of natural selection and survival through adaptation to a changing environment.[29] As a citizen, he increasingly came to feel that, though the society to which he belonged was doomed, some of its better features, such as its cultural heritage, could be saved by accepting without violent struggle the inevitability of the new social content, the supremacy of the working class in industrial society. In short, spurred in part by Darwinian ideas, he thought it possible to insure cultural continuity in the revolutionary social changes ahead through popular education and the cooperation of the more enlightened elements of liberalism with the working class.[30]

On the other hand, the general nature and inevitability of these revolutionary changes was determined for him by Marxian notions: the primacy of economic base over social superstructure, the view of the state as an instrument of the dominant economic class, and the labor theory of value which he used to explain the economics of *Gesellschaft* in *Gemeinschaft und Gesellschaft*.

But this concern with the affairs of *Gesellschaft* remained for a number of years sporadic and did not result in any major restatement of his social outlook. Indeed, after his active involvement in the Hamburg harbor strike, he seems to have resumed his earlier predisposition to evaluate the world in terms of his *Gemeinschaft–Gesellschaft* dichotomy. The application of this dichotomy to the history of ideas may be seen in his brief but remarkable study of Rousseau[31] and, more importantly, in the form of a critique of contemporary political trends. In a pamphlet of 1901 entitled *Politik und Moral*, Tönnies attacked the spread of a dog-eat-dog morality in economic and political life, and placed a great deal of the blame on the amoral imperialism of the contemporary state. The critique was conducted entirely within the framework of Tönnies' "*gemeinschaftliche*" value system. An article of 1901 on political developments in England showed his apprehension that the result of the modern social struggle would be the destruction of parliamentary democracy by a one-party military state, imperialist externally, Caesarist internally. With the incipient decline of the Liberal party, Tönnies saw this fate in store for "the classic land of the Magna Charta Libertatum," to which only three years earlier he had considered emigrating.* In 1904 he was still so concerned with the dangerous affinity between Caesarism and the modern state that he saw the abolition of the three-class voting system in Prussia—an urgent demand of the Socialists—as a potential aid to the growth of a popularly supported Caesarist regime in Germany.[32]

Tönnies' articles in the years from 1904 to 1908, however, suggest a gradual shift from *Gemeinschaft*-centered to *Gesellschaft*-centered concerns. An article of August 1904 sees new hope for liberal idealism in Germany.[33] A study written in English on German political parties reveals strong sympathy for the revisionist wing of the Socialist party, and also for the cooperative groups within the labor movement.[34] In the following year, the Ruhr miners' strike enlisted his renewed support for the trade union movement. Interestingly enough, despite his tendency to think of the motives of the strikers in terms of *Wesenwille* and of those of the state in terms of *Willkür*,† he nonetheless hopes, "as a friend of man and Father-

---

* T-P, 29/7/98. Earlier, in 1895 and 1897, Tönnies had told Paulsen he must spend some time in England to see just how bad German rule was (T-P, 9/2/95; T-P, 6/7/97). The English role in the Boer War, too, which he strongly disapproved of as imperialist, dampened his earlier enthusiasm for English parliamentarism (T-P, 27/2/01).
† About the strikers, he wrote: "Great strikes have more the character of natural phenomena than of considered human action. . . . They have less the character of a willed means to a predetermined end than that of an immediately willed demonstration" ("Ein Rückblick auf den Streik im Ruhrkohlenrevier," FW, 5 [1905] pp. 893–900). About the state's attempt to improve the workers' lot only for the sake of preventing the spread of socialism: "It is always unpleasant when men devote themselves exclusively to the pursuit of isolated ends and views. . . . The focusing of all senses on the *one* goal, the intellectual fixation with one point, blinds and deafens one to all intervening conceptions, it subordinates all ideas to the one idea, it degrades everything which really has value in and for itself to a purely banal and unworthy means" ("Glück Auf!" signed "Normannus," FW, 5 [1905], pp. 49–52).

land" that "the spread of a *social ethical spirit*" may allow the coming struggles to be led "in a spirit of reconciliation, of the general welfare."[35] In the following year an article on England shows once more the old euphoric Anglophilia, catalyzed by the acceptance of a trade unionist into the English cabinet: the goal of a democratic, peaceful reconciliation of labor and capital "is set not for this land alone, but for all of Europe, which must finally realize that only a planned application of scientific thought to legislation and government can check the immeasurable evils which have accumulated everywhere in consequence of our technical progress."[36]

Other indications of new involvement in the concerns of society now appear. Coupled with a strong note of European cosmopolitanism in these years[37] comes an increasing concern for the maintenance of peace, both between classes and between nations.[38] This concern leads him, on the one hand, to oppose in 1905 any spread of the Russian revolutionary fever to German soil,[39] and on the other, to oppose the dangerous paranoia of "encirclement" developing in German conservative circles.[40] Tönnies shows the attempt to reconcile his growing attachment to the German fatherland with both his concern for world peace and his old enmity to the modern state, by channeling all his old hostility to the modern state against militaristic Prussia: "Militarism in the German Reich is not national. It is essentially Prussian, and even old Prussian. It has its social support in the estate of the great landlords."[41] In 1907–1908, this anti-Prussianism is further manifested by the abandonment of his earlier reservations against doing away with the three-class voting system in Prussia. In three articles of these years, he strongly advocates its abolition.[42]

In the autumn of 1908, a thoughtless interview given to the London *Daily Telegraph* by Wilhelm II so badly jeopardized Germany's international position that a public outcry arose for a reform of the imperial constitution. Probably influenced by these events, Tönnies in the same year wrote two articles that threw into sharp focus the modifications of his social perspective which had ensued since 1887. The old unity of state and *Gesellschaft* has been sundered, and the polarity of *Gemeinschaft* and *Gesellschaft* has been blurred to the point where, whatever its sociological significance, it no longer has social relevance: Tönnies has come to see the important historical and social conflicts in other terms. In place of these former conceptions, Tönnies now posits two historical oppositions against the absolute state: the opposition of the Reich idea, which he sees as implicitly democratic, and the opposition of the self-governing municipality, whose character now appears as something of a cross between the older notions of city *Gemeinschaft* and the egalitarian side of *Gesellschaft*.

Tönnies now sees "a principle of life and health" in the development of *Gesellschaft*. In "the critique of the state through the *Gesellschaft*,"[43] he sees

> the idea of a democracy which is organically built up, which lets the state rule only so far as the common interest of all make it necessary, which develops a counterbalance against the state through the new formation of political municipalities. ... The latter have the purpose not of limiting the state, but of living in harmony with it, of variously developing legislation and administration in smaller districts, of preparing and exercising the capacity of popular self-rule in narrower, easier spheres, closer to common sense.[44]

In an article on the crisis of the imperial idea in Germany, Tönnies goes even further than the separation of a democratically inclined *Gesellschaft* from the state. He actually identifies the nature of the state with its subservience to the democratic will of the populace:

> That the state has its existence through the will of the collectivity [*Gesamtheit*] of its citizens ... is its essential, necessary and rational existence. ... As a state it [the Reich] has no existence outside of the will of the united German nation. ... As a state [it exists] by virtue of the sovereignty of the people, of all free members of the German nation. ... All contemporary theoreticians attempt to construct this concept without admitting Natural Law, in whose sense alone one may represent the essence of such associations as the state; for its essence does consist in Natural Law, i.e., in practical social reason.[45]

Tönnies believes this normative, democratic conception of the state to be realizable within the framework of the Reich as a whole.

But against this conception of the Reich stands that of the Prussian state and the Junkers, whose arrogant hatred for the Reichstag and for the Reich idea itself had created the crisis that is the subject of Tönnies' article. For the principles of the Prussian state in no way correspond to the ideal he has established: "The thought behind the system is unconditional subordination, separation between regime and subjects in all branches of administration. It is primarily put into practice as absolute obedience in the army, separation of the army from the people, rule of officials over municipalities."[46]

If Prussia has its way and makes of the Reich little more than an instrument for the extension of its own power, then there is little hope for the idea of the democratic nation-state in Germany. For Prussia opposes to the conception of the imperial *state* that of the imperial *alliance* of separate states, in which of course Prussia remains the prime mover.

Tönnies has both hope and misgivings about the role of the Social Democrats in bringing about the kind of Reich he wants. Insofar as they represent the urban and industrial masses, the Socialists have a great chance to become the leading national party in Germany. If they were to correctly understand their position, they would have to support the Reich, because it alone can undertake major social welfare programs. Indeed, "Perhaps only the Reich—much though it is conditioned by capitalism, indeed, like every state is dependent on it—can after long struggling become stronger than capitalism, and separate from it." But he is doubtful that the "revolutionary" party would ever consent to give the necessary support to even a democratic Reich (voting the military budget) that would allow it to represent itself as a genuinely national party.

The most striking indication of the change in Tönnies' outlook from the publication of *Gemeinschaft und Gesellschaft* to the articles of 1908 is in his attitude toward Otto Gierke. We have already noted (Chapter 7) how Paulsen, in 1888, relayed to Tönnies Gierke's objection to the "one-sidedness" of his presentation—and Tönnies' retort: "The excellent man has childish Prussian illusions about the current century. He sees the renewal of the old German popular spirit and law in the blossoming stock corporations."[47] Twenty years later, however, Tönnies was quoting approvingly and hopefully Gierke's stated goal of "the reconciliation of the cooperative basis and the authoritarian top in the contemporary state."[48]

The two articles of 1908 remain the clearest indication of the changes in Tönnies' attitude toward state and society until the brief but incisive study of 1914, "Rechtsstaat und Wohlfahrtsstaat." Here Tönnies posits a new dialectic: the historical alternation of state systems based on contract with state systems based on law. In the first, it is assumed that social and economic relations will be regulated by contracts between individuals, who have jointly contracted to establish the state as a kind of watchman, to insure observance of contracts. In the second, the state itself regulates social and economic relations by law. Fundamentally, these two forms are the ones discussed toward the end of *Gemeinschaft und Gesellschaft* as the two possible relations of state and society. But whereas earlier, conflict between them was only implied, and was insignificant compared with the overriding conflict of both forms with *Gemeinschaft*, here *Gemeinschaft* is ignored and the conflict between the two is the very substance of history. In addition, the strivings of the working class are now no longer seen as lying outside of *Gesellschaft*: even if successful, they can do no more than give a somewhat different twist to the pattern of society.

Tönnies sees mercantilism and enlightened absolutism as an early incarnation of the welfare state (*Wohlfahrtsstaat*). The contractual state (*Vertragsstaat*) which replaced it arose out of the demands of large-scale agriculture (e.g., the physiocrats) and of large-scale industry for free trade and the abolition of state regulation of economic practice. The free contractual society which then arose under the protection of the "watchman" state did not, however, fulfill its promise, since in one major area of contractual relations, that between the worker and his employer, the "great inequality of means"[49] took all but the ghost of freedom from the contract. Thus, the demand has arisen for state interference in the labor contract, for the protection of the worker, and this limitation of contractual freedom for the sake of social welfare has led to many others. The trend is definitely towards a new welfare state. The question is not whether such a welfare state is necessary, but whether its goal should be the preservation of the existing order of society and property, or the transformation of this order so that ownership of the means of production should be transferred from private to public authorities. The first is the "*bürgerliche*," the second the "proletarian" view of social reform. It is noteworthy that Tönnies chooses Adolf Wagner as a theoretical exponent of the more radical view of state social reform, the man whose views on a social monarchy he had disparaged in 1885 as "this tolerated variety of military-aristocratic conservatism" and a "'Christian' royal Prussian social reformer."[50] What was formerly anathematized had now become eminently desirable.

But Tönnies is also willing to grant that the new welfare state will itself be superfluous if the working class should prove capable of forcing private capital to accept an equitable social order. The three possibilities he envisages are codetermination of industry by the trade-unions—the idea of a harmonious cooperation of labor and capital in "the constitutional factory," which we shall also encounter in Sombart;[51] the seizure and exclusive control of the factories by the working class—syndicalism; and the spread of the cooperative movement into production so as to create a "cooperative commonwealth"[52] from the base up. All three of these solutions obviate any need for the state to do more than oversee economic agreements made between private groups in the society. What is most interesting, however, is that none of these solutions are really seen as breaking out of the mold of *Gesellschaft*. Even the last, the cooperative commonwealth, which Tönnies would earlier have thought of as a renovated *Gemeinschaft*, is now explicitly called *eine neue Gesellschaft*.

Nevertheless, it should be clear that both the *Rechtsstaat*—the one most closely in harmony with the *Gesellschaft* concept of 1887— and the *Wohlfahrtsstaat* may nurture elements of *Gemeinschaft*: the *Rechtsstaat* if the contracts within it are between communally organized groups of workers, or between the latter and the erstwhile capitalists; the *Wohlfahrtsstaat* if it simply fulfills its definition, i.e., legislates for the welfare of the mass of the population. Thus, in both cases, the *Gemeinschaft-Gesellschaft* polarity has ceased to be relevant.

Tönnies, like most other German intellectuals, was caught up in the great national enthusiasm occasioned by the outbreak of World

War I. Much of his writing in the years 1914–18 was devoted to polemics on the culpability of Germany's enemies for the outbreak of the conflict. But in 1917 appeared a more theoretical work, comparing the English and German state systems.[53]

Tönnies had by then come full circle. He quoted Gierke approvingly as saying, "The essence of the modern German idea of the state rests in the identity of state and people."[54] And Lorenz von Stein, whose conception of the state as the bearer of *Gemeinschaft* Tönnies had once thought to refute by his own theory of *Gemeinschaft*, was now acknowledged as a reputable authority in political theory.[55] In effect, what Tönnies had earlier defined as the *Wohlfahrtsstaat* he now accepted as the historical reality of the German state system; the contractual state, however, he had come to view as a characteristically English phenomenon. The *Gemeinschaft–Gesellschaft* polarity thus returned, not as the opposition of historical stages, but as that of national cultures. The English contract state was clearly the offspring of *Gesellschaft,* and the German state was just as clearly the offspring of *Gemeinschaft*:

> The *Volksgemeinschaft* is a fact. It is bound together by speech, custom, and law, by art and science, by tradition and history, but also by the life of the state. Endangered and sometimes disorganized by the whole societal development, by the growth of trade and the capitalist mode of production, it still struggles for its existence and preserves itself as living strength in the *national* state and in national-popular institutions; and therefore it cultivates and increases them. In the sociological sense, one can call the state the organized nation [*Volk*], above all if it stems, as the German Reich does, from the wish and will of a living *Volksgemeinschaft*.[56]

Wartime polemics have often brought out the worst in their authors, and if we compare Tönnies' piece with others of the same genre—Sombart's *Händler und Helden,* for example[57]—it does stand out as one of the better ones. His ingrained distaste for Prussia gives to his chapter on the Prussian constitution a tone of cool objectivity which certainly must have been rare in contemporary German discussions of the subject. Indeed, what we see in Tönnies' wartime conceptualization of German state (neo-*Gemeinschaft*) versus English state (neo-*Gesellschaft*) is only the development of a line of thought whose origins are visible at least as early as 1904—a line of increasing optimism about the moral worth and potentiality of the world he lived in that was probably furthered by his finding a secure post in the German academic world in 1908, and which had as its inescapable corollary the change, already noted, in the nature of his *Gemeinschaft–Gesellschaft* dichotomy: from historical stages to "concepts of pure sociology."

PART III

Werner Sombart (1863–1941)

> *May the scholar above all keep in view the fact that he is basically a pitiful wretch who can do nothing better than cover the thousandfold life with a barren formula; a fearful creature in whose hand what formerly had a living breath must wither. . . . The offense which every science commits against life can only be expiated if it itself kindles a new life in its creations, in that it strives to shape them as works of art.*
>
> —Werner Sombart,
> Der Moderne
> Kapitalismus

10

The Problem
The Many Ideologies and the One Gyroscope

WERNER SOMBART'S CAREER as economist and sociologist encompasses a period of more than fifty years.* He became famous—and notorious—in the nineties as one of the few academic celebrators of modernity and reformist socialism; after the turn of the century his work on modern capitalism, especially its peculiar "spirit," preceded Max Weber's investigations of the subject by two years; in 1913, his application of the Nietzschean concept of *Ressentiment* to economic and social life also found an echo in Weber's sociology. Though his flirtation with fascist ideology after World War I has irreparably tarnished his reputation and his attempts to fuse historicist economic theory with the emerging discipline of sociology have been superseded, his historical importance in the *fin-de-siècle*

---

* His first published work appeared in 1888. Judging by his posthumously published *Noosoziologie* (1956), he seems to have been active until his death in 1941.

There are few works on Sombart in English. Morton Plotnik's *Werner Sombart and His Type of Economics* (New York, 1937) and Vincent P. Carosso's "Werner Sombart's Contribution to Business History," *Bulletin of the Business Historical Society*, 26, (1952), pp. 27–49, are not to be recommended. Much better than either of these is the brief treatment by Talcott Parsons in *The Structure of Social Action* (Glencoe, Ill., 1949). But Parsons restricts himself to a synoptic presentation of Sombart's analysis of capitalism as expressed in *Der Bourgeois* and the second edition of *Der Moderne Kapitalismus* (1916). Herman Lebovics devotes a fine chapter to Sombart in his *Social Conservatism and the German Middle Classes* (Princeton, 1968), but he is essentially concerned only with Sombart's ideas after World War I.

culture that nurtured the less timeworn efforts of Tönnies, Weber, Simmel, and Michels cannot be disputed. Above all, he was a weathercock for the creative winds of his age.

This study is primarily concerned with the development of Sombart's social theory up to the First World War, pointing out the convergence of personal and social background and using the man as a mirror to his age, and the age as a key to understanding the man. In the case of Ferdinand Tönnies this attempt could be centered around the background to his single outstanding work, *Gemeinschaft und Gesellschaft*, from whose major outlines his thought deviated but slightly. For Sombart, the task is more complex, for he decisively altered his social and political perspective at least once every decade during the period 1888 to 1915. Therefore, this section will trace a thread through Sombart's frequent changes of allegiance on the ideological battlefields of the modern age: the hidden gyroscope that guided his peregrinations from evolutionary Marxism and a profound belief in modern industrial civilization as the agent of progress, to rejection of modern civilization and nostalgic love of community, to the exaltation of the entrepreneur and the hero, and ultimately to a position not far removed from Nazism.

This study will not examine closely every aspect of Sombart's work. It will not be concerned with evaluating Sombart's work on modern capitalism from the standpoint of economic theory, nor will it make more than passing reference to Sombart's contributions to the methodological problems of "ideal-types" and a value-free sociology which, though of importance to the history of sociological theory, have only tangential relevance to our concerns. The period covered excludes any study of Sombart's later ardent nationalism and support for the Third Reich. I shall, however, develop two hypotheses that may elucidate Sombart's sharp changes in attitude; one concerning his relationship to the older generation of social theorists and reformers (a milieu in which his father was prominent) as a possible explanation for his changing orientations in the first twelve years or so of his career, and another, connected to the first, concerning his involvement in the Europe-wide trend from a rationalist to a voluntarist theory of social change.

11

The *Verein für Sozialpolitik* and Sombart in Italy

AT ITS VERY INCEPTION, the new German Empire created by Bismarck faced two major social problems, both of which arose from the rapid industrialization then in progress. One was the danger that the new working class, plagued by the appalling working conditions that had elsewhere accompanied the industrial revolution, would succumb to the socialist virus, and so divide into warring classes a nation that had just been united out of quarreling principalities. The other was the threat of obsolescence and impoverishment that the older middle class of merchants and artisans (*Mittelstand*) faced from the competition of new and efficient capitalist combines.

To prevent the impoverishment of the traditional middle class, to give the workers some legitimate role in the political and social life of the nation, and to keep them from the agonies of applied Manchesterism, in October 1872 an important group of political economists formed the *Verein für Sozialpolitik*. The group hoped to accomplish its aims by preparing detailed studies of the social problems raised by the new economic era, and by lobbying among economic conservatives and in the government for reform proposals based on its studies. They thus attempted to substitute themselves for social forces that were the outcome of successful revolutions in England and France, and in so doing they continued a long tradition of academic involvement in the affairs of the Prussian state.[1]

The new group, which numbered among its leading figures Gustav Schmoller, Adolf Wagner, and Lujo Brentano, was attacked by German protagonists of free enterprise even before the official founding of the *Verein für Sozialpolitik*.[2] The term *Kathedersozialismus*—"lectern socialism"—first appeared in an article published in December 1871. It was quickly accepted by the objects of the epithet as a title of honor, and was borne by academic social reformers until the First World War.

If any one figure may be said to have incorporated in his person the ideas of the early *Kathedersozialisten*, it was Gustav Schmoller. In his polemic against Treitschke, Schmoller revealed his fundamental concern over the moral function of economic activity, and his belief that technical advances could not be called progress if they occurred at the expense of the moral character of the producers:

> Every particular economic organization has not only the goal of producing goods, but also that of being the container, the moving cause, the support for the creation of moral qualities, without which society cannot live. It is a question in every concrete kind of division of labor and of profit, does it properly educate the youthful powers of labor, does it bring about in the growing person diligence, thrift, self-reliance, honesty, good family life, so that here too progress is secured and the sources of future well-being are not squandered?[3]

Thus, Schmoller, in opposition to the classical economists as well as to Marx, denied that the level of economic technique "naturally" determined the economic order; this order, he insisted, had to be imposed on the levels of technology by the moral, social, and political will and values of society. He demanded a distinction "between natural-mechanical and spiritual-moral, psychological causes."[4] In Aristotelian terminology, we could say that for Schmoller, the material cause was the technology; the formal cause was the moral-economic order; the efficient cause was human will; and the final cause was human progress, the increasing perfection of the moral order. Adolf Wagner had a roughly similar standpoint.

In many areas of economic life, Schmoller and his friends in the

Verein für Sozialpolitik urged government intervention to preserve pockets of the old patriarchal artisan and small-trade economy from suffocation at the hands of large factory owners. They also advocated measures for the protection of the new working class. A further problem preoccupying some of the *Kathedersozialisten* was the condition of agriculture in the eastern provinces of Prussia, always a major object of concern to social reformers of the Wilhelmian era.* The dominant form of cultivation in this area was the large estate of the Prussian nobleman. Before the French Revolution, the area had been a powerful stronghold of high feudalism. In the wake of Prussia's humiliating defeat by Napoleon in 1806, apostles of reform, particularly Stein and Hardenberg, were able to legislate a sweeping abolition of the feudal system. Serfdom was ended and land was made alienable. But making the law was not the same as carrying it out. After Stein and Hardenberg were pushed out of office at the instigation of the French, their legislation was only feebly enforced by the reactionary regimes that followed Napoleon's fall. In 1850, the legislation was revived, but it quickly became apparent that unless the state actively intervened to foster the settlement of peasants, free competition would only serve to fatten the still dominant large estates.

In the 1880s, the semifeudal rural regime in the East Elbian areas remained a stain on the conscience of all forward-thinking Germans. Instead of outright serfs providing the manpower to cultivate the large estates, it was now done partly by migratory day laborers, partly by sharecroppers. Neither group was considered the proper breeding ground for the nobler social virtues. Furthermore, the meager independent peasantry was increasingly bought out, to make way for sugar-beet plantations, or forced off the land, unable to compete with the low prices resulting from technical innovations and cheap labor on the estates. And Polish seasonal laborers were taking jobs away from Germans in the area, because of their willingness to work at lower wages and their employers' knowledge that they would be too frightened of deportation to complain of either

---

* The following material is based on the essay of Lujo Brentano, "Agrarian Reform in Prussia," *The Economic Journal*, 7 (1897), pp. 1–20, 65–84.

bad pay or working conditions. Thus, many Germans were fearful that Prussia's work of centuries in Germanizing this once-Slavic area was about to be undone.*

The solution proposed for this situation by worried reformers was *innere Kolonisation*, the establishment in the East Elbian territories of settlements of Germans subsidized by either the state or private individuals.

At its Frankfurt meeting in 1886, the *Verein für Sozialpolitik* devoted half of its time to the theme of *innere Kolonisation*. There were two speakers on the subject, both of them founding members of the *Verein*, and, judging by the jointly drafted resolution they presented, which asked for an extension of existing government assistance to the internal settlement schemes, both of them of similar ideas. One was Schmoller. The other was A. L. Sombart, estate owner, Reichstag deputy, and father of Werner Sombart.

Anton Ludwig Sombart† was born on a Westphalian rural estate in 1816. His paternal ancestors had probably been French Protestants who emigrated to Germany after the revocation of the Edict of Nantes. His maternal ancestors were of Dutch and Low German origin. After attending a *Realgymnasium*, A. L. Sombart took up the profession of land surveyor in Saxony, a lucrative and interesting job in a period when, as a result of the partial enforcement of the Stein-Hardenberg legislation, there was a great deal of land being divided. Forced to give up his surveying work after 1848 because of failing eyesight, the elder Sombart, who had married in 1842, became active in politics and, about the same time, bought an

---

* This is the focus of Max Weber's early paper "Die Verhältnisse der Landarbeiter in ostelbischen Deutschland," *Schriften des Vereins für Sozialpolitik*, Bd. 55 (Leipzig, 1893), hereafter referred to as *Schriften*. This work is discussed in Reinhard Bendix, *Max Weber, An Intellectual Portrait* (Doubleday, 1960), pp. 38–47 and, more analytically, in Wolfgang Mommsen's *Max Weber und die deutsche Politik* (Tübingen, 1959), pp. 23–38, and Arthur Mitzman, *The Iron Cage* (New York, 1970), Part I.

† Information on A. L. Sombart is taken from his obituary, written by his son, in the *Biographisches Jahrbuch* for 1898, pp. 253–56. The brief description of A. L. Sombart by Gustav Schmoller as a "self-made" man who rose from the profession of surveyor to that of estate-owner is not altogether compatible with Werner Sombart's testimony that his father was born on the "*Rittergut*" of his parents had a private tutor as a child, and attended a *Realgymnasium*. See Schmoller's review of Werner Sombart's *Der Moderne Kapitalismus*, in Schmoller's *Jahrbuch*, 27 (1903), p. 291.

estate in Saxony for sugar-beet cultivation and established a sugar-processing factory. Elected *Bürgermeister* of Ermsleben am Harz in 1848, he became a Bundestag deputy in 1867 and moved to Berlin in 1875, where he remained almost until his death in 1898.

Anton Sombart was elected to the committee of the *Verein* in 1874, and was a regular participant in its annual or biennial meetings. From 1884 on, as oldest member of the *Verein*, he opened and sometimes closed these meetings. He took his role as *Kathedersozialist* seriously. In the mid-eighties, he became sufficiently concerned over the depopulation of the German East to purchase an estate in Pomerania and offer, with no down payment, hereditary leases (*Rentengüter*) to a score or so of settlers. His *Referat* before the *Verein* in 1886 was essentially a report on the economic feasibility of his venture.

What is most interesting in Anton Sombart's paper, and in another one that he presented to the *Verein* in 1890 on the reform of the communal land organization in Prussia, are the social values revealed in them; for the earliest work of Werner Sombart, on very similar themes, displayed a striking sequence of initial affinity and then abrupt rejection of his father's and Schmoller's views that is part of the explanation for the later sudden turns in the younger Sombart's outlook.

In his *Referat* Sombart indicated three grounds for increasing the peasant population of the East Elbian area.[5] By deflecting Germany's growing population from the factory to the farm, it would slow down the unhealthy growth of big industrial cities. By increasing grain production, it would decrease Germany's dependence on foreign food producers. And it would halt the developing depopulation of the eastern agricultural areas. The particular scheme of resettlement Sombart advocated was the division of older, bankrupt or inefficient estates into *Rentengüter*: small tenant farms, whose cultivators would be bound to stay on the land and transmit it whole to one of their descendants, while paying a fixed rent to the owner, a combination of state and private authorities. For Sombart, the virtues of this scheme were two: small farms were economically sounder than, even if not quite as productive as, large estates;[6] and, as opposed to encouraging an influx of day laborers, "It is the best thing when the man is bound with love to his hearth, where, if we create more places, he has a homeland under all conditions, and where he acquires virtues in a political, social and communal sense that the day worker never can attain."[7]

Schmoller, in his following *Referat*, praised the elder Sombart's proposal for more *Rentengüter* as an excellent means of tying important social reform to existing institutions.[8] He argued against any idea of expropriating the East Elbian landowners, whom he considered the backbone of the Prussian state,[9] and stressed the social value of the colonization scheme in encouraging the development of small industrial cities, together with a new, healthy *Mittelstand* of traders and artisans[10] in the eastern territories.

In his *Referat* at the 1890 session of the *Verein*, Sombart indicated an additional virtue in the *Rentengut* idea: it would prevent the spread of socialism in the countryside.

> Consider that when we speak of patriarchal conditions, then the domestic servant still sits at his lord's table, i.e., he receives food and wages. What happens now? The people get cold money, drink brandy mornings, go fairly soberly to work, get nothing regular to eat at noon, and in the evening they become Social Democrats. . . . Liebknecht and Bebel . . . have openly said before great mass meetings in Berlin: The urban and industrial regions we have in our pocket, now we want to try our propaganda on the land. . . . Thus, gentlemen, the danger approaches. Should we not do everything, particularly in the communal area, and while there is still time, throw up a dam, and create conditions which, if not the same as the earlier patriarchal conditions, are yet similar to them. Gentlemen . . . a cottage is very nice for the small man; but if you give him a little piece of land too, then he becomes no Social Democrat.

Werner Sombart was born in 1863 in Ermsleben. Brought by his parents to Berlin in 1875, he grew up there "in the wealth, in the luxury, of the big city."[11] After finishing *Gymnasium* in 1882, Sombart studied economics at the Universities of Berlin and Pisa, and spent the years between 1885 and 1889 doing research on Italian social and economic problems. His earliest publications, written while still in Italy, are on Italian rural problems, and they testify clearly that Sombart was seeing the problems of Italy very much through the eyes of his father and Gustav Schmoller.

In his first article, "Das Familienproblem in Italien,"[12] written at the age of twenty-five, Werner Sombart used the quality of family life as the standard for the level of civilization.* Because of the continued high quality of their family life, Sombart found the Germanic countries to be the cultural leaders of the world. Nevertheless, even in Germany, the weakening of this tie was a serious danger, largely because of the development of new economic relationships, "which have created on the one hand an urban factory proletariat, and on the other a snobbishness [*Protzentum*] decaying in luxury. Where the external development has been fairly healthy [in other words, nonindustrial], there has remained a firm, inherited core of tendencies and interests preserving the family."

In Italy, the quality of family life was much poorer than in Germany. Sombart cited Schmoller, with whom he had studied at the University of Berlin, on the importance of domestic conveniences and kitchen appliances for a healthy family life and "higher cultivation," and argued that "the defective sense of a common domestic existence among the Italians prevents a comfortable outfitting of living quarters."

The only form of Italian social life in which Sombart did not see a disruption of family ties was the *Mezzadria*, a sharecropping system that was probably the closest Italian equivalent to the semifeudal *Rentengüter* which his father was promoting in Germany. (They differed principally in that the tenant in the *Mezzadria* system gave half of his produce to the landlord, while the tenant in the *Rentengut* system gave a fixed money rent.) Werner Sombart was aware that in addition to the "social-political" yardstick, there was another criterion by which one might judge the *Mezzadria*, the

---

* "The condition and consequence of a higher developed civilization is a household organization, grown in freedom, but firmly constructed, a deepening and internalization of family life" ("Das Familienproblem in Italien," Schmoller's *Jahrbuch*, 12 [1888], p. 286).

"technical-economic," and that from the economic standpoint of increasing productivity, the *Mezzadria* could only be condemned. Nevertheless:

> For the adherents of the contractual form in question, the economic-technical disadvantages, to which they are not blind, are outweighed by the social-political advantages which the sharecropping system shows in comparison with other forms of production. Among these advantages is emphasized, with complete justice, the beneficial influence which the Mezzadria exercises on the *preservation of family relations* [Sombart's emphasis]. . . . the whole structure of the contract presupposes a well-constructed family organization. . . . In the microcosm of the settler's economy, every member of the family has his function, from the wife, who is the overseer of domesticity, to the smallest, who shepherds the geese. If the head of the family dies, the obligations and rights go to the heirs, *insofar as they have formed a house community* [*Hausgemeinschaft*] *with the departed.* [Emphasis added.] In brief, the Mezzadria, by its nature, encourages and furthers the spatial and temporal togetherness of the family.

Sombart's conceiving of family existence in terms of "*Hausgemeinschaft*" suggests Tönnies' influence, but that is almost certainly not the case. Tönnies' *Gemeinschaft und Gesellschaft* was not widely read when it first appeared, and it is most unlikely that Sombart, who was in Rome during the year between the publication of Tönnies' work and of his own article, had even heard of Tönnies. In any case, Sombart's reference to Morgan and Bachofen (page 297) strongly suggests that he and Tönnies were merely both reading the same anthropologists. The partial similarity of outlook and categories is nonetheless significant in light of the fact that a dozen years later, Sombart was to come very much under Tönnies' influence, and his later retreat from Marx, industrial civilization, and progress was to be carried out, in effect, from the line of *Gesellschaft* to the line of *Gemeinschaft*.

The occasional ruthlessness in Sombart's advocacy of "cultural progress"[13] strikes a somewhat discordant note in this first article. Though he confesses that poor living quarters are not of such great significance in a country where blue skies and a mild climate allow people to eat and relax outdoors for most of the year, he insists that

> for the state, for the society, these considerations are secondary. For them the foremost question is whether the conditions are at hand which make possible a cultural progress of the whole. The state wants not only satisfied, but useful, active citizens. It certainly cannot, then, be indifferent if a great part of the urban population lives without family and living quarters, even if it is happy and satisfied. The criterion for reform or no reform is not the subjective feeling of the individual, but the conditions for the existence of a civilized nation.

When Sombart sees these conditions from the "technical-economic" rather than the "social-political" standpoint, the "subjective feeling of the individual" who may be in the path of civilization's steamroller will be of even less import to him.

His first major work, "Die Römische Campagna," reveals this ruthlessness yet more clearly, and again in the argument for state intervention. Here there is no juxtaposition of "technical" against "social"; the two are merged, since the measures advocated by Sombart would undoubtedly improve both economic and social conditions. And in raising the need for state intervention, Sombart does not hesitate to call for the expropriation, with compensation, of the present absentee landlords of the *Campagna*, a type of measure condemned by Schmoller in his discussion of the East Elbian agrarian problem.[14]

But these aspects of his thinking, while significant for the future, do not yet dominate his outlook. The focus of his interest in this work testifies that he is still under the influence of the older generation. What he is advocating, after all, is little more than what his father and Schmoller are advocating: the application of a state plan for the establishment of agricultural settlements, in an area where the private interests of the landowners and the interests of society at large are opposed, where the free operation of economic laws and private interests can only continue the tragedy of these malaria-ridden meadows, gone to ruin and usable only as grazing land because of the lack of energy of their absentee landlords.

Both of these earliest writings of the young Sombart indicate, then, that while in Italy he was fundamentally in agreement with the goals of the *Verein für Sozialpolitik*. His dichotomy (in the article on family life) of "technical-economic" and "social-political" criteria for measuring social institutions bears a strong resemblance to Schmoller's distinction of "natural-mechanical" and "spiritual-moral, psychological" causation.* And insofar as his goal is the strengthening or reestablishment, in the name of a traditonal patriarchal social ideal, of a free peasantry, and his attitude to all social forces, whether capitalist or feudal, which prevent this result is one of hostility, he is still in the cocoon of the older tradition. Indeed, if we consider the filial piety implicit in Werner Sombart's conscientious application to Italian circumstances of his father's *Rentengüter* scheme, not to mention his praise of the *Mezzadria* as the last stronghold of the family spirit, it is clear that his repeated emphasis on the value of strong family ties has a more-than-theoretical significance.

This reverence disappeared quickly after the younger Sombart's return from Italy. His first article on a German social problem appeared in the *Archiv für soziale Gesetzgebung und Statistik* of Heinrich Braun, who had established his own journal in 1888 as a left-of-center version of Schmoller's *Jahrbuch*. Braun, who was sym-

---

* Above, p. 138. Sombart's dichotomy bears an even stronger resemblance to a passage in Schmoller's address to the founding meeting of the *Verein für Sozialpolitik* at Eisenach in 1872. Speaking of the recognition by the social reformers who had organized the *Verein* that the contemporary economic system, despite its brilliant progress in the sphere of production, had given rise to serious social problems, Schmoller identified as the "chief cause" of these problems,

> the circumstances that in recent times, with all progress in the division of labor, with all new construction of the factory, of the business institution, of labor contracts, and with all legislation on these things, one has asked only if for the moment production will be increased. One has not posed the equally important question, what effect will this have on men? Does this new organization give sufficient support to the production of moral factors, without which society cannot exist? Does it sufficiently educate the youthful elements? Does it bring about diligence, thrift, honesty, family life among adults so that here too progress besides the economic is probable? They [Schmoller's colleagues] are convinced that the neglect of this psychological connection between forms of economic organization and the whole moral condition of a nation is the core of the evil, and that reform must proceed from the perception of this connection ("Sozialpolitik," *Ausgewählte Lesestücke zum Studium der politischen Ökonomie*, K. P. Diehl and D. Mombert, eds., vol. 14 [Jena, 1922], p. 93).

pathetic to the then-outlawed Social Democrats, complained in his introduction that

> The ruling tendency in political economy has stood until the present under the sway of an attitude which saw the economy principally from the standpoint of production and, in regard to this, let the question of the conditions of the producing class step into the background. Only under the influence of the modern labor movement, of the scientific literature accompanying it, and of the beginnings of a social legislation was the task presented urgently to statistics of researching the position of the working classes and of social conditions generally. The fulfillment of this need found a decided opponent in the state. Only with resistance, under the force of circumstances, and almost always only in reference to the momentary needs and goals of its legislation and administration did it allow to statistics the solution of that task. The scientific viewpoint of a non-party representation of the social conditions of the people, seeking only the truth, thus gave way to political interests.[15]

The journal was, then, to be devoted to this scientific study of social conditions.[16] The phrase "ruling tendency in political economy" ignored, of course, the major work done by the *Verein für Sozialpolitik*, which was far from captive to "an attitude which saw the economy principally from the standpoint of production"; but otherwise the statement indicated clearly the differences with the older social reformers. The state was no longer viewed as a well-meaning apostle of social welfare, requiring only the proper reports to be set on the right track; and the conditions and needs of the new working classes and of the labor movement, rather than of the old *Mittelstand*, were to be emphasized.

Sombart's article conformed to the general outlook advocated by Braun. In discussing the conditions of German cigar workers, Sombart argued that a recent decree of the Bundesrat regulating working conditions in this industry should be extended to cottage outworkers (*Hausindustrie*). Bad as factory conditions were, those in the cottage industries were worse, and failure to include the latter under protective legislation encouraged employers to extend the outwork system as a means of evading the application of the law to their workers, and at little cost to productivity in the technologically backward cigar industry. By implication, then, he was setting himself in opposition to the views of the more conservative social reformers, who at just this time, in the *Schriften* of the *Verein für Sozialpolitik*, were commenting enthusiastically on the social benefits derived from household production.[17]

In 1891 Sombart published a major study on the problem of cottage industry in Germany which made explicit his rejection of the older generation's views in this important question of *Sozialpolitik*.[18]

Early in this article, Sombart contrasted the conceptions of Schmoller and Marx. Schmoller had written in 1869 that cottage industry was "only a special form of artisanry which works for a wholesale market." Thus, in the interpretation of Sombart's teacher, the preservation of cottage industry was a "means of rescuing the artisanry, of providing it with a wholesale market." Schmoller treasured cottage industry for its merit both in preparing the independent artisanry to participate in the new era of world trade and in minimizing the dangerous growth of the proletariat.[19] Marx, on the other hand, two years before Schmoller's book on small industry, had characterized house industry as a form of large-scale capitalist production, which stood in essential opposition to the artisan form of production and had only an accidental relationship to agriculture.[20]

Sombart's own definition of cottage industry was much closer to Marx's than to Schmoller's: "Cottage industry is that form of private capitalist enterprise in which the workers are occupied in their own homes." Sombart added for clarification that in cottage industry the factor of production that was exclusively the possession of the capitalist entrepreneur was "not so much the collectivity of the material means of production, but rather the market, the sale."[21] And some pages further, he again joined Marx in explicitly condemning "the old erroneous conception of our form of enterprise as a sideline":

> The assertion is often made that cottage industry is, as it always has been, a necessary extra job [*Füllarbeit*] for large groups of the rural population. . . . I cannot accept this notion. The sideline theory is just as false for the present as for the past.[22]

Sombart found the basic evil of cottage industry to be low wages. The generally low productivity of house industry set the upper limit of the cottage worker's wage well below that for factory work, and the weak position of the cottage workers vis-à-vis the entrepreneur insured that the actual wage would be underneath even that meager portion to which the cottage worker's productivity might entitle him.[23]

Low wages forced the cottage worker to involve his whole family in a system of merciless exploitation. Even so, they did not allow any more than substandard housing or nourishment. "But workmen who strain themselves physically to excess, and moreover eat badly and live badly, cannot possibly attain any kind of satisfying level in psychic matters. The body badly nourished, the spirit paralyzed, the life of the soul crippled, the moral feelings suffocated if not poisoned in most cases: that is the picture which the majority of cottage workers offer."[24]

This form of production was nonetheless of value to the entrepreneur. For one thing, changes in the business cycle could not injure him, since there was no fixed capital involved on which interest had to be paid and whose inactivity resulted in a loss. For another, the powerlessness of the isolated cottage producer and his general noncoverage by social security measures allowed the entrepreneur to set a very low wage.[25] But Sombart insisted that the system had to be judged by its benefit to the society as a whole. Such benefit, he contended, did not exist. The low wages did not result in cheaper prices, since they signified only that the share of the worker's wage in the market price of his product was smaller, and the entrepreneurial profit higher, than in other forms of production. The alleged elasticity given to the economic existence of the producer was also a fiction, since the agricultural sideline which the cottage worker was supposed to fall back on in times of low demand did not exist in over 80 percent of the cases. And where it did exist, the results of a forced return to heavy farmwork or to road-building could have disastrous effects on the dexterity of skilled cottage workers.[26]

There was one last argument for the preservation of cottage industry—despite all economic disadvantages, cottage work was socially healthy because of its beneficent effects on family relations. These alleged social advantages, as opposed to factory work, included the availability of the father to educate his children, the continued presence of the woman in the home, the direct control and protection of the girls in the family, the latitude available to the worker in fixing his own hours of labor, and several others, such as the possibility of alternating cottage production with agriculture. Sombart methodically destroyed each point in turn, as being either contrary to the facts, or, if real, more injurious than beneficial, or not peculiar to cottage industry.

Sombart finally dealt with the idealization of cottage industry as compared with the evils of the modern factory:

> What has contributed not a little to the perversion of judgment on cottage industry, what has given it this halo which surrounds it, is the fact that one thought to preserve in it all the fancied splendors of the old artisanry. . . . The manufacturing and factory work on the other hand was viewed simply as the presence of the Devil, as the sum total of all distress and all social misery. While one bathed the cottage industry in a golden light, one surrounded the factory with dark night, against which the former stood out all the more brightly. One forgot and still forgets today that both psychologically and materially the position of the factory worker is capable of being raised. Psychologically, through the fact that the workers' right of codetermination, their influence on the course of production, will expand continually and probably quickly. Materially, through the fact that, with increasing productivity of labor, state intervention and the struggle of parties will result in ever more favorable working conditions for the worker. In a hopefully not too distant future, the wife and child of the laborer will be able to stay home and really devote themselves to the household; night- and Sunday-work will disappear. Factory workplaces will be increasingly adapted to the demands of modern hygiene, will become airy and light. The working day of grown men too will not exceed a reasonable limit. If the man comes home at four or five in the afternoon, without being exhausted, *then* he can live in the home of his wife and children—a home not turned upside down by in-

dustrial labor. The factory worker will even be able to indulge in occupation in garden and field, to the degree that industry is decentralized: the introduction of electricity as a moving power opens the widest perspective here.[27]

In this concluding vision, Sombart presents the whole burden of his social *Weltanschauung* for the decade up to 1900: the use of the productivity of modern industry for improvement of proletarian living conditions as the material goal, the right of labor to codetermine with the employer its conditions of labor as the ideal goal; the intervention of the state and the struggles of the workers' organizations as the means to both ends.

Even here, Sombart was not altogether remote from the social perspectives of the older generation. Though he had turned his back on many of their shibboleths and embraced a moderate form of socialism, he had by no means given up the bourgeois ideals of a good family life as one of the criteria of progress. But he was certain that the older school of reformers, falsely reading these social virtues into decrepit institutions, erred because of their attachment to the national past. By 1891 Sombart had broken with that past.

12

Industrialism versus Patriarchalism
1890–1900

THE THEORETICAL BASIS on which Sombart built most of his ideas and proposals over the course of the next decade was his interpretation of Karl Marx. He showed himself a close student of Marx's economic theory in his polemic with Julius Wolf over Wolf's book on socialism and dealt extensively with the third volume of *Capital* in an article of 1894.* I shall not deal with these technical aspects of Sombart's work in economic theory. Of great importance for this study, however, are the social and political conclusions that Sombart drew from Marxian theory.

Basically, there were two conclusions, each corresponding to a distinct sphere of Sombart's activities in the nineties. The first conclusion was that the completion of the capitalist conquest of the old patriarchal order was inevitable and historically progressive. On the basis of this, Sombart joined with a like-minded group of younger economists and reformers within the *Verein für Sozialpolitik* to form a left-wing group opposed to the older school. Working with Sombart in this loose formation were the brothers Max and Alfred Weber, Friedrich Naumann, Heinrich Herkner, and, at times, one of the founders of the *Verein*, Lujo Brentano.[1]

The second conclusion was that the scientific core of Marx's social doctrine lay in the proposition that the growth of capitalism led inevitably toward socialism; therefore, an evolutionary advance into the promised land might come about without upheaval and bloodshed. As a consequence of this theorem, Sombart supported the moderate, revisionist wing of social democracy as a means of avoiding revolution, of bringing the workers into the administration of the economy, and of raising their living standards. Because he advocated this socialist viewpoint, he was trapped in an inferior academic position in Breslau, while his colleague Max Weber, who agreed with him on the obsolescence of the patriarchal order but not on the desirability of socialism, rose quickly to a chair at Heidelberg.† Despite this harassment, Sombart spent a good deal of time

---

* Cf. Sombart's review of Wolf's "Sozialismus und kapitalistische Gesellschaftsordnung," in *Archiv für soziale Gesetzgebung und Statistik*, 5 (1892), pp. 487–98; Wolf's answer to Sombart's criticism, ibid., 6 (1893), pp. 135ff., and Sombart's counterreply, ibid., pp. 147ff. Sombart's article on the third volume of *Capital* appears in ibid., 7 (1894), pp. 555–94.

† According to Schmoller, writing in 1903, "With his strong self-consciousness is correlated the fact that he never made a secret of his Marxism, just as in general he had the energy and courage to express his own opinion, heedless of career. This made it hard for him to rise to the position of an ordinarius" (cited in Plotnik, op. cit., p. 33). Plotnik adds, "It is for this reason that he got his appointment not in Berlin, but in the 'exile' of Breslau, in 1890." It must be added, of course, that Weber did what he could to obtain a better

in the 1890s popularizing his ideas on this subject before a broad public audience of liberal intellectuals, moderate socialists, and trade-unionists.

Sombart did not actually play a major role in the deliberations of the *Verein für Sozialpolitik* until 1899. Before that time, most of his writing that elaborated on his antipatriarchal, proindustrial viewpoint, meant for the audience of social reformers around the *Verein*, appeared either in Braun's *Archiv für soziale Gesetzgebung und Statistik* or in the weekly *Sozialpolitisches Centralblatt* that Braun began publishing in 1892. A comparison of two pairs of articles— one at the beginning of this period on the Silesian cottage weavers, the other at the end of this period on the significance of exports to the national economy—will suffice to show Sombart's abandonment of the last vestiges of his youthful acceptance of the older generation's values. And a recapitulation of the tumultuous debate in the 1899 meeting of the *Verein für Sozialpolitik* over Sombart's justification of the pressure exerted by new department stores on the more traditional retail outlets will reveal the conflict between older and younger generations at fever pitch.

In 1892 the misery of the Silesian cottagers of the 1840s was being presented to the middle-class theater-going public in Gerhart Hauptmann's uncompromising *The Weavers*. In his first article on the subject, Sombart notes with sympathetic irony that the house weavers' desperation has remained unchanged for the half-century since the tragic events depicted by the playwright: "Through this whole long winter, their behavior has been exemplary. They have not annoyed. They have not even complained, as last winter. They have merely starved."[2]

Even the local chambers of commerce have recognized the need to do something and have beseeched the cloth manufacturers to give more work to the impoverished weavers. But to Sombart this is an unreasonable demand, since it asks the manufacturers to use less efficient means of production. The entrepreneur must calculate in terms of profit and loss, and he would be doing no one any good

---

position for Sombart. See Marianne Weber, *Max Weber, Ein Lebensbild* (Heidelberg, 1950), p. 277.

if he used century-old looms when he could establish a factory that would produce at half the cost. For Sombart only the conscious intervention of the state or the society can remedy the situation. Above all, the state should be conscious that "with the house weavers, it is a question of remnants, of dregs, which have remained behind in the transformation of economic life, and can only be artificially removed. The matter is so obvious that the dilatory behavior of our authorities and parliaments is quite inexplicable." In his later article on the subject, Sombart nonetheless implies an explanation for this dilatory behavior: "If only the sentimental preference for old-Frankish industrial forms is completely banned in the circles of authority, the healing of relationships will occur quickly enough."³

In the place of sentimentality, Sombart urges radical surgery. The house weavers must become factory workers.* To achieve this goal the state itself should build textile factories in the house weavers' districts. The Prussian state had already done something similar in the 1840s, and successfully. If the house workers won't go voluntarily into the factories, they should be smoked out by a strict application of factory legislation to their hovels. Sombart closes with another view of the benefits of factory life:

> The factory worker is much better situated; he works ten to eleven hours in the factory and can arrange his cottage and cultivate his cabbage in the same air and the same area as earlier when he was a houseworker. A series of institutions: hospital, orphanage, kindergarten . . . and others too, provide for the workers many conveniences that are beyond the reach of the pitiful house weaver. So no false sentimentality.

Certainly these articles continue the attack on the views and values of his father's generation which Sombart had begun immediately on his return from Italy. But they do not yet reach a complete and explicit reversal of value on the meaning of agriculture to the social and economic life of the nation. Such a reversal occurs in articles that Sombart published in Braun's weekly at the very end

---

* Just as the cottage workers in the cigar industry must become factory workers. Sombart's enthusiasm for the factory, only a few years after his passion for the rural *Mezzadria,* is the first of many hairpin turns his thought was to take.

of the decade.[4] Here Sombart finally approaches the underlying problems whose solution his father had undertaken in the *Rentengüter* scheme—and declares them no problem at all. For the elder Sombart, who saw the soul of the nation in the peasantry, the disintegration of the eastern peasantry was a sign of the social and economic decay of the national culture: social decay because the true values of civilization were embodied in the hardy peasant, and economic decay because the weakening of eastern agriculture forced the nation to import large amounts of food.

In his articles of 1899, Werner Sombart takes up the alleged tendency of Germany to become an *Exportstaat*, a cause of great misgiving to those who, like his father, see value only in the old autarchic, patriarchal, and rural institutions. His argument has two major points: German exports, though increasing in absolute figures, are a decreasing part of the national product; and in any case, there is nothing to fear, because exports and the industrial society that produces them are inseparable from the progress of modern civilization. In this context, his contempt for the agrarian ideal could hardly be more explicit:

> Flowers and delicatessen are the only contributions of agriculture to the refinement of life's pleasures. All civilization is, in this sense too, "urban," i.e., industrial. Thus, increasing wealth, the progress of civilization—obviously only in this incontestable sense of more refined pleasure—is identical with a growing industrial population.

This point is made even more starkly when Sombart, granting the greater economic importance of the internal market, warns against the neglect of exports: "For natural self-sufficiency and semibarbarism, economic interdependence—export—and the progress of civilization are equivalent concepts."

In addition to this explicit antagonism to the values of the older school, Sombart makes an important omission. In his earliest article, "the refinements of life's pleasures" were only associated with civilization insofar as such "refinements" were a precondition for a healthy family life. Here, however, they stand in direct relationship to the progress of civilization, without reference to the family. In other words, a sound family life has dropped out of Sombart's definition of civilization.

Sombart's only major face-to-face encounter in this period with the old school occurred in the 1899 meeting of the *Verein für Sozialpolitik* at Breslau. Here, addressing his father's generation directly for the first time (in a paper on recent trends in retail trade), Sombart argued vigorously against any support by the state for the obsolete selling methods of many older businesses. Dismissing all nostalgic appeals for the retention of the healthy patriarchal spirit embodied in the older firms, Sombart asserted productive efficiency to be the only valid guideline in judging economic phenomena. One should "validate that which is economically higher, that is, economically more productive":

> The final goal in the shaping of economic life can and may only be: to shape the economic forces so that with a given expenditure, a highest possible amount of economic goods is produced. . . . *Trade is a necessary evil.* [Sombart's emphasis.] . . . We do not engage in trade for the sake of trade but in order to procure goods under particular favorable conditions. Today this almost obvious perception is stood on its head. One wants to preserve trade in its stability and its old forms, as though it were an end in itself, and thereby forgets that up to a certain moderate degree, the interest of the consumer too must be respected. . . . In this sense, I think too that if we can create an economic organization which, under similarly favorable conditions, sells the goods without the mediation of trade—and this new creation is seen daily in every newly created consumers' cooperative—then that is the highest form.

Sombart's paper—which, regardless of its value judgments, was an evident masterpiece of economic clarity in analyzing the shifts from older to newer forms of retail trade in the general context of capitalist development—was greeted by the assembly with what the record of the meeting describes as "prolonged, heavy applause."[5]

The discussion the following day revealed differences momentarily concealed by this reception. Attacked repeatedly on economic questions, Sombart spoke again at the close of the discussion and reasserted his position, again amid cheers and applause from the partisans of the *Verein's* left wing, in the strongest conceivable terms:

> And I am of the opinion, of the heretical opinion, as authoritative voices will tell you, *that no approach whatever is significant enough to save a nation from ruin if it makes the preservation of backward classes its policy.* . . . All moral impulses, all feelings of justice will necessarily have to come to terms with the foundation of an economically progressive order of society. Only in this framework can morality strike root. We simply have to accept those forms of economic organization which are most efficient and on the basis of them we can then be moral or anything else. But to want to be moral at the cost of economic progress is the beginning of the end of the whole development of civilization. [Emphasis in text.][6]

It must have been an unpleasant shock to Sombart to discover that the chairman of the meeting, Otto Gierke, one of the "grand old men" of the *Verein*, used his concluding summary to dissociate the prevailing view in the organization from that of Sombart:

> . . . In the whole development of human society economic conditions are supposed to be the sole cause, while legal, spiritual and moral conditions follow from them! If that were correct, then our *Verein* would be superfluous, for all social policy proceeds from another conception. I believe, equally, that a part of the members of the *Verein* is not of the opinion that the goal in the economic sphere is only the highest perfection of production, the greatest economy; but it seems to me that also in the division of consumer goods the most appropriate distribution of produced goods must be at least equally described as the last goal. But in general, for my taste, the speaker lets Man disappear a little too much behind abstract economic concepts and forces. For man as a whole, not merely as an economic, but also as a spiritual and moral creature, is both the cause and the end of the course of development. Therefore a part of the members of the *Verein* also believes that to a higher degree than Professor Sombart accepts, that through economic orders, through legal formations and

psychic interventions one can codetermine, to a degree, the goals of the development, and that therefore the highest community of men, the state, is likewise called and empowered to conscious intervention. . . . Naturally, no one in the *Verein* believes that socially untenable conditions, that irretrievably lost classes should be artificially preserved. But such sinking classes as can still be rescued, to those one can yet offer a hand. From the opposite standpoint, one should have let the peasantry sink in the past century here just as in England. But it has again been raised and brought to flourish through the law on the peasantry. Just because one or another development appears momentarily modern, it does not seem to me necessarily to follow that everything standing on another ground is obsolete and diseased and wherever possible should be the object of a mercy killing so that it ends earlier. The development does not run in such a straight line.

What is of particular interest here is the not very mysterious reference to the peasantry (the only concrete reference Gierke makes), for whose preservation Sombart's father had worked so hard. Indeed, the ghost of the elder Sombart, who had died only the year before, must have hovered embarrassingly over the proceedings. It was quite possibly this inescapable specter that caused Schmoller, who through his personal relationship to both Sombarts could scarcely have entered the conflict without producing a more or less permanent rupture between the young economist and the *Verein*, to give the task of refutation to Gierke, the chairman of the meeting, rather than do it himself.

Gierke's rebuttal by no means ended the dispute. After he had finished, Sombart interrupted the closing of the meeting with a brief statement that Gierke had misunderstood him in all essential points, to which Gierke replied stiffly, "That is an assertion whose evidence I await." Schmoller, who was not chairman, then took it upon himself to close the meeting, both explaining Gierke's unusual rebuttal and flattering Sombart to prevent a rupture:

> Those who were of another opinion than Herr Sombart have purposely kept silent, because our debate on this subject would have gone astray had we attempted simultaneously

to discuss these basic philosophical questions. But just for that reason, those who do not agree with the materialist interpretation of history have had the need to articulate that not all members of the *Verein* stand on this ground. Therefore we have asked Professor Gierke to say that other views exist here. . . .

The speech of Professor Sombart was one of the most brilliant masterpieces of eloquence and spirit that I have ever heard. And I was proud that I can count him among my students . . . even though I find myself on essentially different ground in the question of the materialist interpretation of history and in some of the practical conclusions that he drew from his optimistic consideration of department stores.°

There was a necessary connection between Sombart's defense of industrial capitalism in the circles of academic social reformers and his more public—and notorious—support for social democracy. In an important theoretical article published in 1897, he contended that "the choice of a particular social political ideal is in the last analysis dependent on the individual's whole conception of life and the world and can in its necessity be justified only as a means to an end." The ends which Sombart had in mind, and to which he believed the vast majority of "European-American civilized mankind" would assent, were:

> the preservation and increase of our modern cultural goods [*Kulturgüter*]; preservation and stabilization of our national power position, at least against the inferior East European and Asiatic peoples; natural increase in population; extension of cultural goods to ever broader circles of the population; greatest possible improvement of material existence, i.e., greatest mastery of the powers of nature and greatest relief from economic labor.[7]

° *Schriften*, 88, pp. 259–60. Opposition to the views of the older *Kathedersozialisten* similar to that in the 1899 meeting of the *Verein* appears in Sombart's article of 1897, "Ideale der Sozialpolitik" (*Archiv für soziale Gesetzgebung und Statistik*, 10 [1897], pp. 1–48). His first disparaging remark on the *Verein*'s concept of *Sozialpolitik* appears on p. 4; a polemic against the "ethical" school of political economy occupies pp. 32–35; an attack on Schmoller's view of the goal of *Sozialpolitik* as that of reconciling conflicting social groups within the nation is on pp. 41–42.

Assuming these goals, Sombart then offered two definitions of social policy, the first pertaining to social class, and the second to economic systems:

> (1) A healthy social policy must offer the greatest possible support for the economic class representing economic progress, because only in this way can its ideal, the highest development of the productive forces, be realized; this realization, however, is necessarily required in the interest of cultural progress.
>
> (2) The ideal of social policy is the economically perfect; this is represented at any time by the most highly developed economic system, i.e., the economic system of highest productivity.[8]

Although Sombart failed to mention either capitalist class or proletariat, capitalist system or socialist system, it is not difficult to apply his definition to the problems of his day. In a conflict between the capitalist class and the artisanry, between capitalism and patriarchalism, his policy would be to support the capitalist class and system as the economically more progressive. In a conflict between capitalist class and working class, between capitalism and socialism, his decision would probably lie with the working class and socialism, insofar as these promised to be economically more productive.

The logic that led up to Sombart's socialism, then, embodied a great many "ifs." Sombart's respect for socialism was tied to his respect for industrial capitalism and many of the values on which it is based. If Sombart ceased to see civilization as necessarily "progressing," in proportion to the increase in the productivity of labor and in all the paraphernalia of industrial society that arose from this increased productivity, then he would cease to venerate either capitalism or socialism. Further, if he retained the value on "preservation and stabilization of our national power position, at least against the East European and Asiatic peoples," but came to view the glorification of economic man, whether of the capitalist or socialist variety, as a non-German and unworthy attitude, he would likewise turn his back on this conception of social policy. These possibilities became actual after 1900. But for the decade before, they merely indicate how moderate Sombart's socialism was and how averse he had to be, given his deep appreciation of the progress represented by industrial capitalism, to revolutionary violence.

13

Socialism and the Beginnings of a Voluntarist Ethic

1890–1900

In 1896, WERNER SOMBART gave a series of eight lectures before the Swiss Society for Ethical Culture. It was not the first time that Sombart had given public lectures on socialism. He had done so as early as 1892 and had been immediately honored by a local newspaper with a demand that his superiors dismiss him from his position at Breslau.[1] But in 1896 his lectures had a happier result. They were soon published, in expanded and edited form, by the author, and in the original version, together with the discussion which followed them, by the group which heard them.* The author's version, *Sozialismus und soziale Bewegung im neunzehnten Jahrhundert* (Jena, 1896), was reprinted eight times before 1920, with significant revisions from the fifth edition on. It was translated into numerous languages and thereby provided Sombart with an

---

* Inasmuch as I have been unable to locate the book of 1896, except in translation, the following discussion will be based on Sombart's original lectures, *Sozialismus und soziale Bewegung im neunzehnten Jahrhundert* (Berne, 1897).

international reputation. But even in Germany, it was his first major book.

A good part of Sombart's lectures is devoted to a narrative of the social thinkers and social movements of nineteenth-century Europe. Of greater significance, however, are Sombart's own interpretations. These include an emendation of Marx's concept of history as struggle between classes to cover, in addition, struggle between nations;[2] an analysis of the material and spiritual condition of the proletariat;[3] his assessment of Marx's significance;[4] and his juxtaposition of revolution versus evolution, that is, his insistence on the peaceful character of the struggle[5] and his reconciliation of the economic determinism that allows an *evolutionary* peaceful advance to socialism, with the voluntarism of class struggle which he believes is indispensable to the achievement of socialism.[6] These points can be discussed in the framework of a single large dichotomy, which here clearly emerges in Sombart's work for the first time: historical and economic determinism versus voluntarism as the basic interpretation of human history.

Sombart's reduction of history to the struggles of national and social movements appears at the beginning and end of his lectures on socialism. Mankind evolves in the form of separate communities (*Gemeinschaften*), which struggle among themselves for wealth and power, while within these communities individuals also struggle for the same things. "In history, it is a question on the one hand of the struggle for food-division, and on the other, of that for feeding-place. . . . We are now at the close of a period of vast development of national feeling and stand in the middle of an era of difficult social antagonisms."[7]

From this point of departure, Sombart proceeds to discuss the social movement in terms of class, as the "totality of the strivings of a social class, which seek to transform the existing social order in a way corresponding to the interests of this class." But in his last lecture he returns to the national question, with comments that are heavy with prophecy:

> The socialist movement can be stopped at any moment, if at any time the national antagonisms emerge powerfully. Then the social conflicts must fall silent, because the existence of

both contesting groups is threatened. Even if the civilized states of Western Europe should unite so far that only social oppositions still ruled the field, other elements could intervene, e.g., the Russians or East Asians. The rapid growth of Japan, and the attempt of China, too, to become a civilized state, make such possibilities appear not at all so distant. The moment can come when the society says to itself: all internal conflicts are now meaningless against the threat of the external enemy. Through a threatening inundation with coolies, for example, the labor movement would be cut off at its roots.⁸

In any case, it is apparent that for Sombart the fundamental law of history is struggle, which can take either national or social forms. To see history in terms of struggle is to see it as the result of human will, i.e., voluntaristically. But when one thus raises struggle to the level not of a moral imperative but of a principle of existence, then one is saying that this voluntarism is historically determined, necessary, lawlike. The degree of determinism may remain on this level of a simple assertion of the universality of struggle, or it may take the form of rules of historical development, which predetermine the outcome of the struggle. In the case of national struggle, such rules of historical development cannot be applied, except insofar as the greater economic strength of more advanced countries *may* give them the wherewithal to triumph over less developed countries. (Even this meager principle cannot be applied to contests between equally advanced nations or between an advanced nation of low population and a backward one of high population.) But in the case of social struggle, the principles of economic development virtually assure, for Sombart, eventual victory in any given situation to a particular class, the one representing the more progressive economic system.

Thus, there is a lawlike character in the evolution of the modern social struggle. The bourgeoisie has as its historical mission the development of the material forces of production, and Sombart's enthusiasm for this accomplishment (similar to that of Marx in the *Communist Manifesto*) is clear.* But to attain its end, the

---

* "Impelled by the profit impulse and driven by competition, this class produced that fabulous culture, in whose marvels we rejoice every day and everywhere" (W. Sombart, *Sozialismus und Soziale Bewegung*, p. 8).

bourgeoisie must create masses of propertyless workers. The capitalist system of production tears society into two distinct classes and so creates the justification of the social movement.

Sombart then analyzes the character of the modern proletariat. This analysis fills two long paragraphs. Whether consciously intended or not, the first paragraph provides an objective-determinist view of the phenomenon and the second, a subjective-voluntarist view. Put another way, the first paragraph discusses the way capitalism has determined the objective, more external conditions of the workers, while the second paragraph discusses the difference between the precapitalist artisanry and the proletariat in terms of the personal, subjective feelings and attitudes (Tönnies would have used the word "*Willensbeziehungen*," or relation of wills) that prevail between the members of each group.

Thus, in the first paragraph Sombart connects the misery of the proletariat to the capitalist system of production by reference to "those unhealthy work places in factories, mines, etc., in which dust, heat and noise endanger health and life." Further, women and children are brought into the factory, and the concentration of labor in the cities produces ever poorer living conditions. (Obviously, Sombart's belief in the blessings of factory life has been modified since 1892.) In contrast to this misery, the wealth and splendor of the upper class arouses the hatred of the masses. In addition to all these burdens is the uncertainty of existence in the new working class:

> To be sure, such insecurity is everywhere, caused by nature, but here it is a question of insecurity produced by human economic forms, which is expressed in the impossibility of earning, and in unemployment, and which first brings misery to its full height. If the insecurities produced by nature lead to superstition and bigotry, the insecurity of our proletariat brought forth by the organization of society leads to an increasing moral aversion.[9]

In the next paragraph, Sombart explores the effects of all this on personal views and attitudes of the individual: "Everything that earlier tied them to the homeland, to village, family, and customs, is torn, all earlier ideals are destroyed in this detached horde, crammed together under the command of the capitalist." Yet there is a positive as well as a negative side: "New communities [*Gemeinschaften*] are formed. Through close combination in narrow factory and living rooms, a uniform feeling grows in these masses, class consciousness. And just this makes the movement socialist in its goal."

The economics of capitalism, then, determines the misery of the proletariat. And the will of the proletariat, in response to this misery, forms new *Gemeinschaften*, uses its new conditions to achieve class consciousness, and struggles for socialism. Here, too, the bifurcation of Sombart's social vision into a more deterministically viewed segment (capitalism) and a more voluntaristically viewed segment (the proletariat) is clear; equally clear is the superior value put on the struggling proletariat, partly because it is more progressive, but also because it is struggling. And between the material and the ideal goals of the proletariat, which Sombart has mentioned before and is to mention again, it is the ideal goal, that of the creation of new *Gemeinschaften*, rather than the material one of a higher living standard, which, in the book which is a turning point between this and the next period of Sombart's work,[10] has Sombart's highest approval, once more because it is the least determined by economic laws, and the most dependent on human will.

Sombart's interpretation of Marx sustains this determinism-voluntarism dichotomy. The true significance of Marx and what distinguishes his theory from all revolutionary idealism is twofold. He makes the social movement dependent on, a product of, the previous course of history: "The program for the goal of the whole movement is formulated from the historical development. Not from the head of the thinker, but from the historical conditions of the struggling class is produced the means: the class struggle."[11] And following from this view of history as a moving force comes the argument that the existing institutions, as products of history, cannot be viewed as "errors" and cannot be eliminated merely by the spread of knowledge but in the last analysis only by action:

Previous history is not merely an empty dream or an error, but rather the product of factual power relationships . . . accordingly, all further development cannot rest on the spread of enlightenment, but solely on a shifting of this power relationship in a particular way. In brief, the significance of Marx is to be formulated: With him and his theory socialism ceases to be a problem of *knowledge* and begins to become a problem of *will*. [Sombart's emphasis.][12]

A final point of interest in these lectures is Sombart's support of evolutionary socialism as opposed to the revolutionary variety, and the reconciliation of this determinist notion of evolution with the voluntarist one of class struggle.

It was only consistent with Sombart's view of socialism as historically conditioned that he would reject an ahistorical revolutionary movement such as anarchism. What is noteworthy is that he formulates the opposition between Marx and Bakunin not only in terms of "evolutionary theory" versus "revolutionism," but also in terms of "realistic" world-view (Marx) versus "idealistic" world-view (Bakunin).[13] Within the socialist movement, too, Sombart recognizes the persistence of a "revolutionary" wing. But the trend is "that always new masses are absorbed by the more mature, evolutionist leader-elements."

In a clarification of the evolutionary socialist view, Sombart makes the connection between objective and subjective conditions. This view is based on the facts

> that we are in a continual state of economic and social regrouping; that particular interests and conditions of rule are tied to any given condition; that these are displaced by the development, the ruling classes are slowly dissolved and other classes come to rule; that therefore power can only be displaced to the degree that the subjective conditions, above all, character formation, are displaced.[14]

This is apparently not yet clear enough, for Sombart fears that his evolutionism will be misconstrued as an excuse for inaction, for individuals to fold their hands and wait "until the ripe fruit falls" to them. Nothing could be further from Sombart's mind. The notion that because Marxism posits an objective economic determinism it implies personal quietism is an error that has nothing to do with the true concept of evolution. For this evolution "occurs among living men who themselves complete the development . . . it can therefore never be a lawful one for the living man, but always one made by himself." Ominously, with a touch of pessimism that is rare in this period, he adds, "There can thus be no talk of a natural lawfulness in the strict sense, and we can confidently add: not even the resolves which aim at particular goals are a necessary natural law. For why should the development lead to socialism, and not to a decline of West European civilization?"[15]

Thus, the class struggle plays an indispensable role in the slow wresting of power from the ruling classes, even in this revolutionary conception. In the expanded version of these lectures, Sombart indicates most clearly the voluntarist bias embedded in his notion of the class struggle. Completely apart from any social function served by it, he prizes and glories in the struggle itself. Answering the fears of his contemporaries that class strife will destroy civilization, he says:

> And it seems to me that such internal struggle, such conflict of different interests and ideas, is not only without danger to our civilization, but on the contrary will be the source of much that is desirable. . . . It is only through struggle that the most beautiful flowers of human existence bloom. It is only struggle that raises the great masses of the common people to a higher level of humanity. Whatever of culture is now forced upon the masses comes to them through struggle; the only warrant for the hope that they can be developed into new and higher forms of culture lies in the fact that they must rise through their efforts, that step by step they must fight for their rights. It is struggle alone that builds character and enthusiasm, for nations as for classes. . . . I rejoice in this law of the history of the world; that is a happy view of life which makes struggle as the central point of existence.[16]

Sombart is aware, however, that if uncontrolled, conflict may destroy rather than regenerate civilization. So he imposes on it two limitations: the legal order (which, again, is an obstacle to pure revolutionism) and the principles of honorable conduct. These limitations slightly inhibit but in no way negate the grand status of this aggressive voluntarism, which, in future years, will emerge from its determinist framework like a butterfly from its cocoon, and will establish undisputed sway over Sombart's values and interpretations.

14

Sombart's Voluntarism

An Overview

IN SOMBART'S ARTICLE of 1897,[1] he revealed the theoretical basis for his voluntarism, and its relation to politics as a science. In his view, social and political ideas were chosen by the individual to fulfill the demands of his "whole conception of life and the world." Apparently, the choice of this conception was not bound by any logical necessity but was made freely by the individual. By this he did not mean an "arbitrary ... pursuit of randomly posited goals," but rather "that politics, as all effective action, is incompatible with the thought of a natural necessity of events not subject to the influence of the individual will." The social theoretician could study only this "natural necessity"; he could have nothing to say about the validity of the goals chosen by politically active persons, because, although these goals were chosen largely within a framework of social evolution that was historically determined, the goals themselves were, as indicated, freely chosen.*

To be sure, aspects of these ideas, not related to their validity, could be subjected to the deterministic analysis of the social scientist. He might examine them genetically, that is, in terms of the causal

---

* Sombart quoted from J. S. Mill's logic a passage roughly to the effect that, though the laws of nature were even more rigid than the laws of social evolution, human will could exploit these laws to its own ends, and that the degree to which it did this characterized civilized, as opposed to savage, man.

conditions that surrounded their origin,* or critically, in terms of inner contradictions. But what he could not do was to posit an ideal as scientifically correct, to the exclusion of all others. For Sombart, who saw here the great mistake of Rudolf Stammler's *Wirtschaft und Recht*, this was an indefensible intrusion of science, which had no right to go beyond the sphere of perception, into indiscussable questions of teleology and metaphysical belief.

> The essence of social "lawfulness" has been discovered by Stammler in the (teleological) relation of the individual social event to the single objective goal of all social events, which [goal] scientific thought has the task of establishing as an apriority. I hold this standpoint to be wrong . . . because it gives to the sphere of perception an area of human existence which mainly does not fall to it. All political striving has its ultimate foundation in the whole conception of world and life of the individual. But this extends with its final goal into the metaphysical sphere of life, into which perception is incapable of following it. The often-emphasized contradiction of the Kantian ethic, that in the end it cancels the life's work of its great creator, in that it oversteps the bounds drawn to human perception in the *Critique of Reason*, and reintroduces ontological evidence for Ethics that had been excised from scientific knowledge for religion, this very contradiction is what runs through Stammler's line of argument.[2]

Lawfulness of perception thus rested in the uniformity of human thought. But lawfulness was nonexistent for political action because there was no equivalent objective uniformity in final goals.† Was, then, the man of science to be excluded from any role in the creation or promotion of political ideals? By no means!

> The bearer of science—it may never be forgotten—is himself a living man, and if not completely dried out, a man with living ideals, in whose direction progress seems, for him,

---

* An example of such analysis, Sombart wrote (in "Ideale der Sozialpolitik"), was his interpretation of the socialist ideal as a result of the conditions caused by capitalism, in *Sozialismus und soziale Bewegung*.
† It is to be noted that Sombart's brief critique of Stammler preceded by ten years the major work of Max Weber on the same subject ("Stammler's 'Überwindung' der materialistischen Geschichtsauffassung," *Archiv für Sozialwissenschaft und Sozialpolitik*, 24 [1907], pp. 94–151).

to lie. And as no one will renounce convincing others of the advantages of his own ideal, of subjecting the other to his will, neither will the scholar who rejoices in life and striving. He shall not be despoiled of the hope that the very clarification of the situation as he is capable of undertaking it with the means only he possesses can contribute to influencing the direction of political action. But just for that reason he should draw the line between science and action so much the sharper. He should openly and honestly admit where he ceases to lead the reader and listener through the compelling force of his logical deductions, where he resorts no longer to his perception but to his will. Then he may employ his whole personality, his own *Weltanschauung* and experience of life, the weight of his own eloquence—if his temperament so inclines him—to guide the will of the other into the path of his own striving.[3]

With this peroration, which points directly to Sombart's future activities as man and scholar, the presentation of Sombart's first period may be closed. Sombart has made clear the importance with which he views the power of the human will in history in his lectures on socialism; this importance is to become even more marked in his subsequent work. To anticipate schematically the significance of Sombart's notion of voluntarism for his work after 1900, and the relation of this notion to other theoretical relationships between science and values that were then current, I offer the following propositions:

1. The radical separation between scientific philosophy and the voluntarism of value-setting means that this voluntarism, and the philosophy of will and struggle that it implies, will remain completely unaffected, indeed will gain in stature, as Sombart's esteem for scientific philosophy and the civilization that produces it sinks. Voluntarism will remain as the center of Sombart's value scheme, and he may either build a new interpretation of history around it (the spirit of capitalism as the moving force that, through the will of the capitalist, creates modern society), or he may let it stand alone as the sole criterion of civilization (the apotheosis of the hero in *Händler und Helden*).

2. The freedom of science from values thus has, as its sometimes-forgotten corollary, the freedom of values from science. The

freedom of goal-setting from any *necessary* social or economic framework allows for the fairly abrupt shifts in values which occur in Sombart's life and career. Some comparisons will clarify this question. The system of Marx so ties social ideas to an economic substructure, and changes in these ideals to changes in that substructure, that such rapid shifts of ideals would be impossible to anyone who accepted this side of Marxian doctrine. Sombart, who accepts much of Marx, is nevertheless compelled by his neo-Kantian epistemology to maintain the independence of the will from socially conditioned perceptions of the world, and the impossibility of *necessarily* linking ideals—creations of the will—to prevailing economic systems, which the individual perceives through his senses. Weber maintained a position similar to Sombart, but, thanks to a strongly ingrained set of ethical values, avoided the very sudden changes in outlook and values to which Sombart was subject.* Tönnies, on the other hand, acknowledged a polarity of antagonistic social systems—*Gemeinschaft* and *Gesellschaft*—each of which had a "natural law," an ethic firmly connected to it. In this sense of an ethic determined by a social system rather than free-floating, Tönnies was closer to Marx, although in the sense of giving great importance to the human will as the basis of his system he had obvious affinities to Sombart as well, especially the Sombart of the "capitalist spirit."

3. The difference between the theories of Tönnies and Sombart as regards the lawlike relationship between values and social systems may be explicable in terms of their different social backgrounds. Tönnies was the descendant of generations of peasants in Schleswig. He did not leave his *Heimat* until he began university studies, and after some years of student migration, he returned to the area of his forefathers for good. In his sociology, he dealt with,

---

* On Weber's value relativism, see W. Mommsen, *Max Weber und die deutsche Politik* (Tübingen, 1959), p. 70. For him it was not only not the task of sociology (or any other discipline) to discuss the validity of values; it was completely impossible. The cost of this position was, of course, that values became independent powers whose constructive and destructive characters could extend so much the more easily into the irrational. On the stability of Weber's own moral code, see Leo Strauss, *Natural Right and History*, Chicago, 1953, p. 43: "What he said about the moral commands is not much more than the residue of a tradition in which he was brought up and which, indeed, never ceased to determine him as a human being."

and perhaps solved, one of the most vexing problems of nineteenth-century philosophy—the erosion of a natural moral law by modern science. The rootedness of his theoretical value structures corresponded to the rootedness and lack of ambiguity of his own value system, which was clearly cut from the mold of the *Gemeinschaft* that was his origin. This value system remained basically unchanged from the time he created his youthful masterwork until his death.

Sombart, on the other hand, had no such solidity of background. His father had made a great deal of money in a wide variety of roles that characterized both the old and the new Germany: surveyor, estate owner, factory owner, Reichstag deputy, and sponsor of land-resettlement projects. Werner Sombart spent his first twelve years on a rural estate, and then was abruptly plunged into the splendors of Berlin. Superficially a docile disciple, in his first work, of his father's septuagenarian championing of the old patriarchal order, he quickly reversed himself and stridently demanded of the older generation unconditional surrender to the advance of industrialism. Thus, the lack of any solid social heritage, as compared with Tönnies, allowed, perhaps encouraged, Sombart to seriously entertain a variety of values and this, in turn, precluded the kind of strict dependence of value on social system that we find in Tönnies.

4. Nevertheless, the choice was not unlimited even for Sombart. Apart from the common voluntarist denominator (which only became apparent in 1896), his social ideals (until 1910, when he began another new phase coincidental with his acquaintance with Max Scheler) were hinged on the polarity of patriarchal and industrial social systems. Initially captive to the patriarchal leanings of his father, he switched to a strong defense of industrialism in his first major period. In his second period, beginning roughly in 1900, he returned, slowly, to another version of the patriarchal vision; but this time it was not Schmoller's but Tönnies', and it came to be as uncompromisingly antagonistic to the modern industrial order and associated notions of progress as his previous vision of progress through productivity was to the remnants of the guild system.

5. One must distinguish, then, between two related elements in Sombart's thought: his social ideal, and his conception of the func-

tion of will in achieving that ideal. The framework of his social ideal changed around 1900, as noted, from that of Marx (industrialism and the advance of the working class) to that of Tönnies (the patriarchal *Gemeinschaft* and the old artisanry). The framework of his concept of will and its relation to social action altered with the social ideal he was defending at any given time. Very roughly, there seem to have been three permanent influences.

The first was Kant, in Sombart's Marxian period. He used one aspect of Kant—the critical aspect that, to him, implied the denial of any scientific validity to social ideals, and which he therefore believed to be compatible with Marx—against another aspect, the side which "reintroduces ontological evidence for Ethics," and which therefore was used by Stammler *against* Marx. But in this period there is also evident in Sombart's book on socialism a glorification of will which went beyond the needs of a defense of Marx. This was an anticipation of the central role that human will was to play in Sombart's conception of capitalism which appears in the period after 1900.

In this second period, while the dissociation of science and values, founded on Sombart's understanding of Kant, was by no means abandoned, it was less important. Apparently under Tönnies' influence, Sombart broadened his idea of the historical role of human will, which in his earlier work had been no more than the source of social ideals, in order to make it the foundation of economic systems. Though rarely explicitly, Sombart based his thought increasingly on a Diltheyan distinction of *Geisteswissenschaften* and *Naturwissenschaften*. Indeed, he clearly used the dichotomy in his radical reinterpretation of Marx (1908)* to give him the best possible foundation for an antiprogressist philosophy of history. But although at the time of the latter study he had completely turned away from the political scene, he was to return to it in a few years (1911–13) with new theories of the responsibility for the modern capitalism he had come to detest: theories which placed primary responsibility on the Jews and absolved Germany completely.†

In this third phase of his work, with the value placed on the

---
* See below, pp. 234–38.
† See below, pp. 251–54.

heroic will of the adventurer entrepreneur and the disdain for the calculating will of the merchant, Sombart, though not disavowing either Kant or Dilthey, was clearly working in the shadow of Nietzsche's *Herrenmoral*. While Sombart's notion of the will, however, seemed to be merely recapitulating three of the nodal points in the German evolution of a conceptual opposition between spirit and nature (Kant, Dilthey, Nietzsche),* he used this opposition in an increasingly independent way. In his earliest phase, his theory was barely distinguishable from that of a moderate Marxist such as Bernstein. In the second, though he used the basic categories of Tönnies, he concentrated on a somewhat different problem; the actual economics of the victory of capitalist *Gesellschaft* over patriarchal *Gemeinschaft*. In his work after 1910, with his bifurcation of the capitalist spirit into active and calculating halves, he broke away from antecedent thought almost entirely, and it was in this phase, in which the voluntarist tendency in German thought became fused to a systematic sociological analysis of and reaction against modern capitalism, that Sombart's thought became most important for the development of social theory.

The importance of this last phase is evident if one considers the twofold meaning of the term "voluntarism." On the one hand, "voluntarism" can refer to an explanatory device: the assumption that intelligent will, spirit, or mind is the creator of history. This was the emphasis of nineteenth-century German academic thought on history and society. On the other hand, it can be a normative postulate: the placing of value on the will. This was the emphasis of social philosophers like Nietzsche, whose work lies for the most part outside the sphere of academic disciplines. Both of these meanings can be discerned in all three of Sombart's phases. But in the first two, Sombart primarily saw the will as an explanatory device. In the third, the heuristic function is still present, but of greater importance is the implicit recognition of the heroic will as an ideal. In general, it is fair to say that this distinction of will as explanation from will as ideal or ethic is what separates Kant and Dilthey from Nietzsche. What distinguishes Sombart from Nietzsche, however, is

---

* For an excellent general statement of the development of this opposition, see Talcott Parsons, *The Structure of Social Action*, Glencoe, Ill., 1949, pp. 473–87.

his application of Nietzsche's ideal to the phenomenon of modern capitalism. Nietzsche's insights, brilliant as they may have been, did not merit consideration by the scientifically oriented academy. But when applied in the analysis of an important and respectable economist, they did.

In a sense, through the work of Sombart, the philosophy of Nietzsche was becoming academically respectable and socially relevant, a combination of qualities which was to have most dangerous implications for the future.

15

Dennoch!

The Trade Unions and Community

SOMBART'S WORK *Dennoch!*, based on four lectures given before largely trade-union audiences in the early months of 1900, brilliantly illuminates his mind at a decisive turning point in the evolution of his social ideals. Although still adhering to the cause of labor and of industrial civilization, he was trying to reconcile these causes with a new value on the restoration of *Gemeinschaft*; and through the whole, the will of the social actor continued to play a major role.

Apparently under the influence of some of the same anthropologists read by Tönnies, Sombart had, in his first published article of 1888, placed great weight on the retention of family community (*Hausgemeinschaft*). In later works, he continued to use the term *Gemeinschaft*, and with a positive significance, but in a way that either indicated ignorance of Tönnies' theory or indifference to it. In his "Ideale der Sozialpolitik," he used *Gemeinschaft* to describe the nation-state, as it stood united in conflict with other nation-states;[1] in his lectures on socialism, when describing the disruption of traditional communal ties, he used it to refer to the new ties represented by the unions, but *not* to refer to the old ones.*

In 1900, however, he not only revealed close acquaintance with Tönnies' theory, but used it, with minor distortions, as the basic framework for a visionary reconciliation of the labor movement and industrial society. For the time being, the goal to which Sombart aspired was harmony rather than conflict, and although he continued to value will, he no longer suggested that it might be an end in itself, but rather viewed it as an indispensable means of attaining social harmony. Thus, he mentioned national conflicts only fleetingly; once at the beginning (p. 1), and once in a passage that asserted the strength of unions to be just as much a deterrent to social war as the strength of the army was to war between nations (p. 12).

In his first lecture Sombart saw the trade-unions as "only the last link in a long chain of community structures." Man was a herd animal who decayed in isolation, and only a few great souls were capable of living alone. The rest had an inherent need and tendency to associate with their fellows:

> Thus, from the beginnings of civilization until our own day, those natural associations prevail which rest on blood relationship or neighborhood: tribe, enlarged family, village community, those organic structures, as a genial scholar has named them, in which the individual grows and thrives, as it were, only as a member of an inseparable whole. Now the old native communities are in a state of progressive decay. Individuals are torn from the earth in which they had been rooted, and are cast helter-skelter into the modern state, and particularly the modern metropolis. At first without cohesion, without any more structure than that produced by state or

* *Sozialismus und soziale Bewegung*, p. 9. Interestingly enough, in the debate over Sombart's paper on retail trade (1899), Gierke mentioned the function of the cooperatives as sources of a new *Gemeinschaft*, but Sombart, a fervent supporter of the cooperatives in his paper, never once used the term. It is almost as if in this year, in which Sombart, both here and in his articles on exports, made his most extreme defense of the industrial order, the very word *Gemeinschaft*, suggesting as it did the old order, was an embarrassment to him.

communal authorities, they turn up again in new surroundings, with no more organic unity than a row of garments in a closet, or than the individual grains in a sandpile. Thus could arise the fitting talk of the barrenness of metropolitan life.

But the natural striving of humanity for organic structure was reasserting itself. "Artificial community structures, or societal structures, which have their common mother in the community of interests of particular groups of persons, arise."* Associations (*Verbände*) for the pursuit of common goals in art, or charity, or for the furtherance of certain leisure activities were emerging. To such groups belonged those which stemmed from the interests of a common profession. Trade-unions, then, were a species of the genus "professional interest group."

But for Sombart, trade-unions were associated with *Gemeinschaft*, not only as "artificial community structures" in an age when the advance of industry was destroying the original, natural communities, but also as the potential regenerator of community and social harmony on the large scale. Although he was not to develop this notion fully until his last lecture, it is clear from earlier lectures dealing with the correct relationship of trade-unionism to both capitalism and socialism, and from his glorification of English social relations, that this harmony was his main goal.

The principal function of the trade-union was to protect the interest of the worker, both on the job, in terms of better pay and working conditions, and when he had lost it, in terms of financial support and help in finding another one. This function was to be exercised within the framework of the capitalist economic system.[2] Sombart was not, however, implying that the trade-unions posed no threat to the absolute control of the capitalist over his factory. Indeed, if they were properly to fulfill their function, they had to pose such a threat, and it was this threat—which Sombart saw as "the innermost core of all union strivings"—rather than any possible shrinkage of entrepreneurial profit, that the capitalist feared most.[3] But apparently the scholar saw in this shifting of power relations

---

* It is at this point that Sombart strays from Tönnies' theory. Tönnies would no more have referred to "*künstliche Gemeinschaftsgebilde*" than to "mechanical organisms." It would have been a contradiction in terms.

nothing more than that henceforth the entrepreneur would have to "prevail as born leader of the administration among free men, rather than rule over slaves," and he advised him "to adapt himself with dignity to the inevitable." Apart from this weakening of the absolute power of the entrepreneur, Sombart saw definite advantages accruing to him from a hypothetical victory of the union movement. Once a contract was signed with the union and it obtained some power over working conditions, strikes over trivial issues were less likely to occur, and cut-throat competition was eliminated by industry-wide wage contracts.[4] It was on the basis of such notions that Sombart could say "that capitalism and socialism are no mutually exclusive oppositions, that rather up to a certain degree their ideals can be very well realized in one and the same society."[5]

What, then, was Sombart's view of socialism? In *Dennoch!* it seems to have varied according to whether he was talking about the socialist movement and its leaders, which, by 1900, he was consigning completely to the sphere of social-political utopianism,[6] or about the socialist ideal, which he believed the trade-unions would realize, with some secondary assistance from a properly oriented political labor movement. Thus, immediately after asserting that trade-unions were designed to function within the framework of capitalism, he sharply distinguished them from the socialist movement on the ground that though both aimed to uphold the interests of the workers, the socialist movement wanted to do so by replacing the capitalist system with a socialist system.[7] The hope of accomplishing this, he contended, rested on the childish, utopian belief in the imminent "end of the bourgeois world," and people who thought this way would be much too busy looking around every corner for the new world of milk and honey to take part in the slow and difficult construction of the trade-union movement.

He found this lack of understanding in the founders of the German socialist movement, too. Lassalle had no use for trade-unions because the iron law of wages precluded for him any possibility of the workers' economic advancement.[8] Marx was willing to accept the union movement, but only as a means of strengthening the workers for the final struggle with capitalism.[9] And the contemporary leadership of the socialist movement seemed to be beneath contempt. He called on the trade unions

> to liberate the working class from the superficial, brainless gabblers who now set the tone in the press, in mass meetings and in organizations, from those lazy fellows who are good for nothing but repeating like a parrot or bellowing like a bull, a couple of memorized misunderstood phrases from the party literature, who are no good for any work outside of party agitation—to liberate the working class from the caricatures of political agitators.[10]

Sombart was nonetheless convinced of the permanence of the Social Democratic party, and he hurled his favorite epithet, "utopian," at anyone who would hope to eliminate it by strengthening the unions: "And every friend of a peaceful, organic development of our state of life will have to wish not that the Social Democrats should vanish, for that would remain a pious hope, but rather that they become civilized."

What Sombart recognized as the "civilized" function of a workers' party was its legitimate interest in any legislation affecting the welfare of the working class. This included social security measures, laws governing the conduct of trade-unions, and any other questions of internal or external politics which may affect the workers' fate.

As opposed to his denigration of the existing socialist movement, Sombart's support for the socialist ideal, and his conception of how it could be realized, emerges from the following passage, again in condemnation of revolutionary utopianism:

> Whoever still believes in the effectiveness of political action without corresponding economic presuppositions, whoever still lets himself be led by the nose with the old Robespierre talk of the dictatorship of the proletariat, whoever is incapable of seeing that under the changed political conditions of the present only a quite gradual organic transformation of our legal order will be capable of leading the Socialist ideal to its realization, whoever does not yet discern that we are in the middle of an advance to a Socialist order of society, that there will never be more fundamental innovations to lead us to the new world than the first workers' protection law, the first city

purchase of a street-car line resulting from a conscious social policy, or the granting of a state subsidy for the pension of an invalid: such a person is hopelessly lost for this world; he will also never learn to understand the deeper meaning of the union movement: that this too is one of the innumerable bridges from the realm of birth and property to the realm of talent and labor.[11]

Consciously borrowing from Marx's use of England as a model for the international—and the German—development of capitalism, Sombart saw in that country[12] the wave of the future, as far as the integration of labor into the national community is concerned. He seemed to worship England at this juncture, and in his praise we see clearly the continued prominence in his value scheme of economic development: "Still today, England predominates over all other nations as a colossus in the external development of civilization; still today, its economic prosperity has not been even approached by any other land."[13] It was because of England's advanced economic development, moreover, that Sombart saw in the English example "the real essence of the trade union of the future" and "a stage of our own future development."[14] Accompanying this older value of economic progress was the new one of social harmony. What Sombart prized most of all in England was that the unions, having adopted a realistic view of their function, had won the frequent appreciation of the employers by striving, not for class war, but for mutually acceptable, industry-wide agreements with the employers. Dragging out his old comparison of social with national conflicts, he rejoiced that "the open war—the strike—is replaced as far as possible by the armed peace and a series of institutions which aim at quickly settling threatened, and, in the worst of cases, already-begun strikes."

For the scholar, weary of conflict in his personal as well as his public condition, there was no antagonism between this state of affairs and the goal of socialism. In his concluding remarks on the English example, he characterized it, "not as the grave of socialism, not as the end of independent labor politics, as one has so often opined, but rather, as we shall see, as the ally of all these strivings of the proletariat."

Nonetheless, we note that the path to the good society is still described in terms of strivings. Though it is undeniable that for Sombart the goal of the social movement had by 1900 become one of harmonious integration with the existing social structure, the will of the social actor, rather than any economic law or social determinism, remained the only vehicle that could reach that goal.

Thus, Sombart argued against the iron law of wages, taken over by Lassalle from the English classical economists, seizing on the word "customarily" in Lassalle's formulation "that the average wage always remains reduced at the standard of living which is customarily required in a people for the prolongation of existence and for reproduction." In acknowledging the "customary" character of the standard of living, Lassalle, said Sombart, negated his whole theory. For the level of the workers' wages was thereby made dependent only on their ability—or inability—"to make a higher living standard a customary one":

> "To make." In these words is to be expressed, against the conception of a mechanical wage formation, the correct manner of social observation . . . which sees in the division of national income the result of a struggle between different interest groups, a struggle whose outcome is to be thought of as dependent not on the externally visible and numerically expressible positions of the commodity and labor market, but precisely from the determining factors altering the power position of the parties. We saw how organization is one of these factors. If, therefore, it would be first placed beyond doubt that the workers can, in reality, conquer for themselves a better living standard, indeed, a greater share in the collective yield of production, then must come the further insight that they must conquer it. All that follows from the correct conception of economic processes, which are the result of innumerable contacts and frictions between living men, and not the mechanical play of lifeless, automatically moved bodies.[15]

Nevertheless, as mentioned, this voluntaristic element in Sombart's *Weltanschauung* was now no longer an end in itself, but was temporarily, at least, reduced to the status of a means to the end of social harmony. His fundamental problem at this point was the reconciliation of new values connected with this social harmony—to a degree, the values of *Gemeinschaft*—with the values of industrial progress, which he had by no means surrendered.

The unions were, of course, the key. But in the very terms that Sombart used to describe how the unions are to effect this reconciliation, its instability becomes evident. He studied the unions' significance from the standpoint of

> a *Gemeinschaft* condemned to living and striving together . . . the prospering of the national culture. . . . We ask whether it [the union movement] is qualified to lead our social [*gesellschaftliches*] life to higher forms, and thereby to make our social organization more efficient for the development of power and *Kultur*;* of power, that means power of resistance to attacks from without; of *Kultur*, that means individual freedom, wealth, and internal beauty.[16]

Though in his first lecture Sombart appeared to accept the distinction of Tönnies (the "genial scholar" can be no one else) between *Gemeinschaft* and *Gesellschaft*, even there he tended to confuse the two concepts. But here the confusion is much more obvious. He was using both terms to characterize modern culture, and in the same paragraph. True, he gave to *"Gemeinschaft"* something of the character of aspiration, while *"gesellschaftliches"* was more an attribute of the real *"Zusammenleben."* But in listing the attributes of *"Kultur,"* he again made "wealth," which implies the most technically progressive operation of modern industrial society, coexistent with "individual freedom" and "internal beauty." In terms of the thesis of Tönnies' book, which in two years Sombart was to explicitly call "epoch-making"[17] and which he later asserted to be the basic framework of his studies on capitalism,[18] internal beauty and individual freedom (in the sense that Sombart meant it) were attributes of *Gemeinschaft*, while wealth and the military power which had become a by-product of wealth in the modern world were attributes of *Gesellschaft*.

---

* *"Kultur"* means both culture, in the broader sense, and civilization. Usually one sense or the other predominates, but this usage seems to imply both equally. I have therefore left it in the original, rather than lose half the meaning by an inadequate translation.

It was easy for Sombart to show how trade-unions were encouraging technical progress (which he casually equated with social progress). By forcing up wage rates, they were compelling the capitalists to install labor-saving machinery in order to avoid an increase in labor costs. And this machinery increased productivity. The unions thus aided in "the great historical mission of capitalism: to develop the forces of production." They also contributed no little to ironing out the imperfections of this same capitalist system by expanding the consumer base and so lessening the severity of economic crises, and by helping the worker to a better standard of living. But Sombart's theorizing again became tenuous when he attempted to argue that the unions contributed involuntarily "to leading the capitalist economic system in organic transformation to higher social forms."[19]

Here he was evidently thinking of the way the unions could overcome the loss of independence of the worker in a capitalist enterprise. This is the point where Sombart tried to reconcile "individual freedom" and "internal beauty," his *Gemeinschaft* values, with the technical progress and wealth of capitalism.

Sombart admitted that the material poverty the trade unions were trying to overcome did not originate with capitalism. For him, rather, the evil peculiar to capitalism was the "growing economic dependence of the great majority of men on the capitalist entrepreneur."

> The *Mittelstandspolitiker* are not wrong if they point to this increasing loss of independence of ever-growing circles as an inner failure and injury of the capitalist development. And what sharpens the painfulness of the case is that the growing dependence of economic existence follows in step with the awakening of the self-consciousness of the individual—the increasing strengthening of the personality. Thus, a conflict, one of the many of our times, and, as it seems, one of the most insoluble. For there may be no doubt about it. A halt in that development to the capitalist organization of society, perhaps in the sense that the *Mittelstandspolitiker* conceive of it, would mean the suicide of the nation. Under the threat of impoverishment and misery, of economic and thereby

general ruin, the old "independence" of the artisan's existence must give way to capitalist relations of dependence. But here the union movement again appears as a helper. It makes it possible to soften the too-great harshness of the increasing loss of independence of the workers, insofar as it promises to create for us a new form of industrial and labor organization: the constitutional. Everything that we have learned to recognize as its accomplishments . . . amounts to nothing else than a limitation of the sovereignty of the entrepreneur, who therewith ceases to be an autocratic ruler, and becomes a constitutional ruler. . . . *The innermost core of the conflict around the union problem is the struggle for industrial constitutionalism against industrial absolutism or feudalism.* [Sombart's emphasis.]*

Sombart's concession to the *Mittelstandspolitiker*, modest though it was, was a significant retreat from his unswerving defense of capitalism before the *Verein für Sozialpolitik* less than a year before. What seemed to be the keystone of Sombart's logical edifice, however, and what, because of its fragility, threatened the structure with collapse, was not the view of capitalism as a destroyer of independence, but the view of the workers' dependence as aggravated by "the awakening of the self-consciousness of the individual, the increasing strengthening of the personality." This sounds suspiciously like a projection by the intellectual of his own psychic condition onto the masses.† But if it was, if what Sombart called "the hot yearning of the laborer for self-determination" was a myth, then in what sense could the unions remain any longer an instrument for the attainment of "individual freedom" and "internal beauty?" Thus, when Sombart said that the cultural mission of the unions was to

---

* Werner Sombart, *Dennoch!* (Jena, 1900), p. 88. This is a shift from his position in *Sozialismus und soziale Bewegung*, where, after similarly admitting that poverty was not an invention of capitalism, he said that the general unhealthiness of living and working conditions was. The distinguishing mark of capitalist misery has shifted from the material to the spiritual sphere, a shift corresponding to the general change in Sombart's concerns beginning around 1900.

† For an analysis of the way Max Weber's similar identification with the workers' desire to be free of patriarchal despotism affected his analysis of demographic movements in East Elbian agriculture, see A. Mitzman, *The Iron Cage*, pp. 75–147.

create an organization of industrial society "in which the human being in the worker will again achieve full recognition," he was planting the seeds of future disillusion. As soon as he came to realize that he had been reading ideals into the union movement and capacities and strivings into the worker which did not exist in reality, as soon as he concluded, as he would by 1906, that the position of the proletarian destroyed him as a human being and extinguished all "hot yearnings," he would have to choose between the "efficiency" values of industrial progress and his other values, for it would no longer be possible to reconcile them by means of the proletarian's need for freedom and economic community. These other values fell into two groups: those connected with *Gemeinschaft,* in Tönnies' strict sense of a natural communal life absolutely antagonistic to industrial capitalism, and those which exalted the individual and his striving.* It was to one or the other of these *anti*-progressist value schemes that Sombart was to lean in the years to come.

---

* Ibid. Apart from the voluntarism in *Dennoch!* and earlier works, there are two passages in *Dennoch!* which suggest an embryonic *Herrenmoral.* One is the reference at the beginning to "the few great natures" capable of being "solitary men." The other comes at the end, where, without any preparation, Sombart begins to talk, in a manner reminiscent of Tocqueville, of the aristocratic character of all previous culture, of the awareness, especially present in "aristocratic natures," of the need for educating the masses then entering political life to responsible participation in public affairs, and of the danger of a decline of civilization if this is not done (p. 90).

16

Modern Capitalism
The Origins of the Capitalist Spirit

SOMBART'S LONGEST work in the years before World War I was his two-volume *Der Moderne Kapitalismus,* which appeared in 1902.* There is little assertion in the body of this work of its author's values. The main theme is the victory of early industrial capitalism over the handicraft system that preceded it. In general, the first volume deals with an historical survey of *how* this victory occurred;[1] the second volume, with a theoretical analysis of *why* it occurred.[2] In both volumes, the major part of the work is devoted to economic history and the theoretical establishment of tendencies leading to the rise of capitalism; but while Sombart argues for the material superiority of capitalist over handicraft production, in cheapness, soundness of workmanship, and even aesthetic quality,[3] he nowhere attempts to argue that this economic superiority is any sort of ultimate value or is a condition of progress. Indeed, at the beginning of his section on "the theory of industrial competition," he excludes such argument from consideration:

> In the following the question of whether the victor in the competitive struggle is, economically or any other way, the "higher," "more perfect," whether with its victory, then, a "progress" is or is not bound, is not at all broached; but our task is exhausted if we have *established* the fact of a particular development.[4]

* Sombart published a new edition, in four volumes, in 1916, and a further two volumes, on high capitalism (*Hochkapitalismus*), in 1927.

There are, of course, indications of where Sombart's sympathies lie. But owing to the fact that the work was written over a period of several years, during which Sombart's values were changing significantly, these indications are inconsistent.

Thus, major sections of the work fully support Schmoller's view of it:

> One could characterize the material content in two words as the glorification of capitalism. . . . To it we owe the higher civilization and prosperity of today, while we Germans were still in 1849 a pretty crude, uncultivated barbarian people. Something like that is the leitmotiv which varies in the two volumes, but is brought forth in all details.[5]

In general, the latter part of the second volume, where Sombart describes the reasons for capitalism's victory over the artisanry, indicates, as Schmoller noted,[6] a warm admiration for all technical advances, from the newest equipment in barber shops to the overnight bag of the Parisian coquette. Nevertheless, it is noteworthy that just here Sombart explicitly refuses to discuss the question of progress, a question he has never before been reticent to raise and answer.

In the part of the work dealing with the genesis of the capitalist spirit, however, a more skeptical stance emerges, at least toward the mental attributes of the modern age. Thus, at one point, after describing the stormy element of fantasy that accompanied the search for precious metals in the Middle Ages, Sombart confesses,

> It is a wonderful charm which adorns those times, and puts everyone who has preserved any sense for poetry and romanticism under its spell. To us, who have been stunted in the barrenness of economic rationalism,* it will hardly seem believable that generations let themselves be misled by fantastic fairy tales, that the best of their time could hunt phantoms for centuries, and all because that sinister yearning for the golden metal had seized their childlike believing souls.[7]

---

* Note the continuing shift from material to spiritual concerns: before, in *Dennoch!* (p. 3), it was the "barrenness of metropolitan life" that bothered Sombart.

As against this appreciation for the medieval imagination, Sombart's comments on the mind of modern economic man suggest aversion. He seems to give ethical sanction to the patriarchal style of business where the business was merely a means of making a decent living. In the modern period, however, he sees a slow reversal of means and ends, such that economic activity becomes an end in itself; "but now in the new form, as calculation, speculation, as business":

> Slowly the Moloch of business sense extends its talons, to embrace generation upon generation with growing success. If at first objective property became a person, now slowly, the person became an object, an involuntary gear in the giant works of business dealings. So it is that long after the greed for money has died, the entrepreneur shunted into the mechanism of business life continues just as before, restlessly to make money until at last he conceives this as the real goal of all activity and all existence. The whole world becomes in his mind a giant business enterprise, in which there are just as many accounts as there are states, cities, classes, or even single individuals. Valuation in money, numerical calculation of service given and service received, debit and credit become the categories of his view of the world. And over the whole structure there flames forth in letters of gold the motto:
> Assets and Liabilities![8]

It is most significant that the area of modern capitalism that Sombart refuses any longer explicitly to evaluate, though his implied admiration for it appears undiminished, is the area of actual production, while the area in which his values seem most directly involved, and in which he does not hesitate to use pejorative terms (such as "Moloch") is the area of the mind: the kind of capitalist mind or spirit he sees as the root cause of modern capitalism.

By 1902 Sombart had come to view historical causation no longer in terms of economic processes, but in terms of the mind that creates and continues these processes. And just as he previously measured civilization in terms of the material culture produced by economic processes, now he is inclined to evaluate it in terms of the mental life created by the capitalist mentality or *Geist*.

Sombart gives us the theoretical basis of this great emphasis on the mind of the economic actor in a twenty-four page foreword, which not only provides the key to the entire work, but also places it in the general evolution of Sombart's thought and values. Indeed, the line of continuity from *Dennoch!* to *Der Moderne Kapitalismus* becomes quite clear. On the one hand, the effort of *Dennoch!* to establish harmony between opposing social classes is now extended to the intellectual realm, to the establishment of harmony between opposing ideas. Four pairs of ideas are harmonized, each pair constituting diametrically opposed ways of interpreting the world: the empirical and the theoretical, the causal and the teleological, the psychological and the material, and the historicist and the Marxist are all reconciled with their opposite numbers and then fused into one system of interpretation. On the other hand, the importance of will in relation to economic determinism is further magnified: the economic system itself is now viewed as the product, in the last analysis, of a particular type of mentality or spirit that wills it into being.

Sombart begins by noting in contemporary social science a major conflict between empiricists who have no use for general ideas and grand theoreticians who have no use for the individual fact.[9] On the basis of the Kantian theory of perception ("There is no doubt that all our perception begins with experience") Sombart rejects all grand theories not based on observation of the facts.[10] But he also rejects the lack of an organizing theory. His own work, which he says has a wealth of facts as its foundation, will contribute "to the resolution of that painful antagonism," by ordering its factual material "under the viewpoint of a unified principle of explanation."[11]

This principle of explanation in history can be either causal of teleological. But Sombart does not believe that the choice of either one can be made on the basis of abstract principle. The choice should rather depend on the character of the historical period under observation. For instance, the character of economic life in the bureaucratic states of the sixteenth to eighteenth centuries naturally suggested to theoretical observers the teleological principle of explanation and direction, since "the economic life presented itself to the observer as a structure essentially created, or at least molded, by conscious organs of the collectivity. . . . It is the essence of this first period of modern state life, and of modern capitalist economy, that it remains completely captive to the thought processes of medieval community life."[12] The determining role that Sombart here gives to "thought processes" anticipates the main burden of his theory.

Naturally, the theoretical observer uses a teleological principle in explaining such a system.

> But to the degree that economic freedom is established in economic life; to the degree that the so-called "individualistic" shaping of the society becomes the truth; or, more correctly, to the degree that the economic process withdraws from regulation by any consciously ordering organs, and that the individual economy falls ever more into sole dependence on the market, whose laws work on the analogy of natural law, uninfluenced by any kind of ordering social force, blind, iron, pitiless, to the same degree, the causal method of observation presses forward with compelling necessity as that principle of explanation which can alone do justice to the course of economic processes, apparently evolving according to natural law. Economic life no longer appears as a structure, which is formed according to goals, but as a process which runs according to particular moving causes. Thereupon the time has come to help the causal principle of explanation to the leading principle in the social sciences which is its due.

To be sure, Sombart will still have recourse, on occasion, to teleological explanation: "How should I, for example, describe a capitalist enterprise other than under the teleological viewpoint? Or a factory? Or a department store?" But the last, highest principle of explanation for the modern period is the causal one.

What *kind* of a causal explanation does Sombart seek? He first tells us what kind he does not mean. He does not mean that which relates a phenomenon to the lawlike repetition of events: for example, statistical laws (for every hundred x, there are so many y), or economic laws governing numerical relationships ("the saleability of a good grows in quadratic relation to its transportability," most of Marx's work on surplus value, Sombart's own work on the formation of cities, etc.).[13] He does not mean any kind of "[natural] lawfulness in the strict Kantian sense, i.e., with the requisites of universality and necessity," because such lawfulness, except for trivialities, is inapplicable to the subject matter of the social sciences. What he does mean is "to view as the ultimate cause to which we want to lead back social events, nothing else than the motivations of living men."

For various reasons, Sombart believes it inadvisable to try to go beyond this motivational origin to *its* causes: he sees these as occurring in as-yet-unfathomed depths of individual psychology and small-group relations, and wants to stop the causal regression while he is still in well-charted territory. In further defining his goal, he argues that he cannot, by virtue of his demand for a unified explanation, deal with the relation between the will and the economic phenomena resulting from it on the basis of individual events.[14] Rather, he must find a series of motives which explain the pattern of economic activity as a whole[15] (thus leaving aside accidental motives, such as the desire to satisfy the whim of a loved one),[16] and moreover, since the pattern of economic activity is clearly different in different epochs, that series of motives which accounts for the pattern of economic activity prevailing in some particular historical period. Thus, Sombart offers a final definition of his goal as a "homogeneous ordered explanation from the ruling series of motives of the leading economic subjects prevalent in the economic life of a particular epoch."

Sombart is aware that other factors than the motives of economic subjects must be taken into account in explaining the economic phenomena of a period, but he does not give them the dignity of being causes: they are "objective *conditions*."[17]

In his extensive analysis of these conditions, Sombart reveals a striving for a harmonious ramification of methodological differences in the social sciences which is complex, poorly presented, and largely barren of result. For the most part he is simply switching sides on substantive issues while stubbornly clinging to old labels.*

Only when Sombart expands his notion of harmony to an aesthetic principle governing all the sciences of man do we find a perspective which transcends the confines of his methodological hairsplitting and prepares us for his future evolution. Behind the antagonism of fact and theory, Sombart says, stands the eternal hostility between life and perception. The theoretician seeks unity, but life creates only multiplicity: "May the scholar above all keep in view the fact that he is basically a pitiful wretch who can do nothing better than cover the thousandfold life with a barren formula; a fearful creature in whose hand what formerly had a living breath must wither." The only remedy is for the scholar

> himself to breathe a kind of life into the dead construction by artistic shaping. . . . The offense which every science commits against life can only be expiated if it itself kindles a new life in its creations, in that it strives to shape them as works of art. Whereby I am thinking primarily not of the art of external presentation, but of the artistic construction of the thought itself. That a scientific system as such should be beautiful— that, it seems to me, is what we should strive for.[18]

Given the contemporary insensitivity to such matters, Sombart believes it will be generations before "the ethical political economy will be replaced by an *aesthetic political economy* [Sombart's emphasis]." He finds it shameful that most scholarly books bear no

---

* Schmoller, in his review of Sombart's book, perceived the illusory character of the most important synthesis claimed by Sombart, the unification of Marx and the German historical school:

> Sombart has taken the basic concept to which the book is dedicated, capitalism, from Marx and the socialist literature. . . . With Marx it had a good meaning. Marx denies all psychological, ethical, institutional causes; he knows only mechanical-technical economic processes; capital accumulation and capital use in modern production are for him the sole cause of the contemporary economic and social condition, of the division of wealth and income, of the impoverishment of the masses. Sombart no longer shares this viewpoint. He perceives, quite correctly, what Marx had no idea of, indeed believed the opposite of, that psychic causes alone explain all economic events. . . . But he still calls the result of this historic psychic cause "capitalism," as if it were a consequence of capital per se, and not of the psychic factors that he himself depicts as the direct cause.[19]

imprint of the man who wrote them, and declares "that it is the highest goal of my scholarly striving to live on in it as a living man."

Apart from Sombart's extension of the principle of harmony to the demand for an aesthetic political economy—a demand which is to play an increasing part in his values—two other important developments in his thought merit emphasis. Underlying the quest for harmony in methodological matters is a growing reconciliation with the methods and spiritual outlook of the older generation of theorists. And, related to this reconciliation, Sombart's conception of economic causation has changed in a way that both reflects and furthers a fundamental shift in his judgment on modern industrial society.

Sombart has been led to the whole idea of the capitalist spirit as the moving force of the modern age, as the determinant of modern capitalism, by the increasing value and importance he has placed on the will of the individual or class. Ever since his 1896 lectures on socialism, the idea of will and struggle has competed with economic laws as a cause or, more correctly in the case of the proletariat, a potential cause, of social change. By basing his whole concept of capitalism on the notion of a typical capitalist spirit or mind, he removes this vital function of the will from the doubtful future to the certain past and advances it from the status of competitor with economic laws to that of master over economic destiny. It is perfectly understandable why Sombart should do this, given his past glorification of the will.

But what a dilemma he has got into! In assigning the key role in the evolution of society to the will, he cannot fail to give it an even greater stature than he formerly did in his hierarchy of values. Until now, when he was conceiving of the economic process primarily as a machine following fairly mechanical laws, the principal yardstick he used in judging it was that of productivity, or the machine's efficiency in reproducing itself on an ever greater scale. But now that he sees the heart of all economic process not as a machine, but as a human will, he is all too prone to pose the question: To what extent does this will, this unfathomable, struggling, living will to act and shape the world in accord with its desires, to what extent does such a will reproduce itself in the world it has created? And he finds to his dismay that in the world created by the capitalist spirit the living person is becoming merely "an object, an involuntary gear in the giant works of business dealings."

This discovery, that the ultimate result of the capitalist spirit is the murder of spirit by capitalism, is to destroy permanently Sombart's belief in industrial civilization as the agent of progress. And with the new critical view of this civilization, he is to develop an increasing distaste for its most advanced social product—the once-glorified proletariat.

17

The German Economy

Nostalgia for the Whole Man

IN HIS STUDY of German economic life in the nineteenth century (*Die deutsche Volkswirtschaft im neunzehnten Jahrhundert*), published only a year after *Der Moderne Kapitalismus*, Sombart began to work out in more detail his new view of capitalism. He made unambiguous his increasing alienation from modern industrial society, from Germany, which provided the most fertile soil for its growth, and from the working class, its unpretty flower. Corresponding to this coolness toward those former objects of his admiration was warmth for the economic life of the Middle Ages, in particular the medieval artisan, whom Sombart was coming to view as the norm by which to judge his modern counterpart.

The chief characteristics of the medieval artisan, according to Sombart, were three: the full absorption and development of the personality of the producer in his work; limited goals; and the shaping of the productive units on the model of the family community.

By full development of personality, Sombart meant that in handicraft production, the single artisan, possibly with some assistance from apprentices, was responsible for the production of an entire article, and he therefore had to be "a kind of industrial 'Mr. Microcosm.'" Technical abilities which were later divided among many individuals with separate skills were here united in one man. Joined to this technical omnicompetence of the producer was an indispensable artistic sensitivity and sense of the whole, a talent for organizing the work of his assistants around his conception, and the capacity to be his own merchant, for he and no one else sold the products of his labor to the public.[1]

This well-roundedness of the artisan's personality to some extent accounted for the limited character of his goals. He did not strive to be anything else than what he was, or to have any more than he had, or to take responsibility for any work that would require of his economic personality more or less ability than it possessed. What the *Werkmeister* was was independent, and he wished to remain that way. (If he was an apprentice or journeyman, of course, he strove for the independence of the master—but for no more.) What he had was a customary standard of living, and he wanted no more than that—a characteristic he shared with both the peasant and the *grand seigneur* of his age.[2] As for the limit on the kind of work he would do:

> What the dexterity of his hands can perform, what the breadth of his arms can embrace, that is the sphere of his action, which thus appears as a direct outflow of his personality. . . . To this idea of labor as an activation of the entire personality corresponds the occupational organization characteristic of handicrafts. This is such that the individuality of a man can and should stretch its power over a certain sphere of activity, which is held together by a spiritual bond, by the ideal of a whole. An expansion of this sphere must burst his powers, while if these powers are activated in too narrow a sphere, or only a single direction, the worker sinks into the dullness of purely mechanical industry.[3]

Finally, the economic unit was built around the family community.[4] The master artisan was like a father to his apprentices and journeymen, who together with him and his actual family formed "an organic whole." None of the parts were there for the sake of the others, but they were together a *Selbstzweck* (goal in itself), and functioned "as an organ in the service of a common whole."

As compared with this idyllic picture, modern economic society has, in Sombart's analysis, serious defects. The old communities of blood and neighborhood are being dissolved; "the population is thrown together like grains of sand and in the new great commonwealth where no bond any longer ties one to the other."[5] The unaesthetic quality of modern life Sombart characterized by invoking the image of electric street cars and factory whistles—an image in stark contrast to the serenity of the old world which he sums up in the figure of the town night watchman who, armed with spear and horn, sang to mark the passage of the hours: "Expression of childlike helplessness and backwardness in technical things. But nevertheless full of primitive originality and naturalness, such as we no longer see today. Today one whistles a shrill signal on a pipe, where formerly one sang! Do you comprehend what that means?"[6]

Sombart is further skeptical about the contribution of modern technology to the security of the person. He grants that physical security may be increased by advances in medicine and by the increased safety of transportation and housing. But he finds the *social* security of the person badly undermined by the unsteady character of modern economic life:

> The path from the peasant, who fulfills all his needs on his own land, to the factory owner, who only produces iron wheels for mine-wagons, leads to ever greater insecurity of the economic result. . . . A hundred years ago perhaps already the Silesian linen producers or the wool exporters in the seaports may have come to know the caprices of the market. . . . But the great majority of economic subjects still lived in secure relationships; most landowners, peasants, artisans, tradesmen pushed their carts on the same tracks in which they had run for centuries. Now, the phantom of "economic ruin" enters the most hidden Alpine valleys, it hovers over the small tradesman behind the counter, sits on the planing-

bench of the artisan, and frightens the East Elbian landowner when he rides out to his hunt.[7]

Tied to the universality of economic fate in the modern world, which is the cause of this ubiquitous anxiety, is the leveling of all regional cultural differences. Local dress, folk songs, and customs vanish. What is obvious in the cities spreads to the countryside as well: "In the place of the rooted, concrete, regional man steps more and more the rootless, abstract man of the world."[8]

Sombart has not forgotten that alongside of all these defects, the modern world has produced tremendous wealth and has also presented man with a wonderful increase in the variety and quantity of cultural goods; he finds this most striking in the production of books, in education, in scientific knowledge, and in the visual arts. But as indicated, his primary interest has shifted from the material results of capitalism to the spiritual results of the capitalist spirit. Most of the critique just recounted relates to the spiritual side of modern life, and to it, as the most damning indictments of the modern world, Sombart adds his view of the relationships in that world of producer to product, of individual to mass, and of the living person to dead matter. It becomes clear from all of these that he is now posing more seriously than ever the question of what the capitalist spirit does to the spirit, and that it is *the* criterion by which he is judging capitalist society.

From his view of the capitalist's relation to his work, it emerges that Sombart sees his relationship to his own work as opposed to that of the capitalist and similar to that of the artisan:

> Completely alien to the essence of capitalist organization is the highly personal, individually isolated work activity of the lone worker. It is the characteristic of artistic or scientific accomplishment that it flees from men. And the artisan has still preserved a good part of this leaning towards isolation on the part of all creativity. In the last analysis his best accomplishment rests in the imparting of his personality to the dead matter. While contrariwise the capitalist entrepreneur would have to wither in isolation, because he lives on commerce. In this tendency [Angewiesensein] to the continual

tying of people to one another lies the specific social-constructive power of the capitalist enterprise.⁹

We need only recall Sombart's remarks in *Der Moderne Kapitalismus,* that the scholar has an obligation "to breathe a kind of life into the dead construction by artistic shaping" and that "it is the highest goal of my scholarly striving to live on in it as a living man," to see the personal identification in the above statement.

When Sombart seeks out the connection between the altered living conditions produced by modern society and the "inner essence of the new culture," he seizes on just this subordination of the individual to the mass, which he had opposed to the artisan's way of life. As literary points of reference, he compares Schiller's *Wallenstein* with Hauptmann's *Weavers:* "In the former, the unbounded dominating single personality, who is subject only to destiny; in the latter, the collective personality, united in feeling and acting, in which the individual is only one member dependent on all others: the social class as hero!"¹⁰

But this is not the most significant effect of the economic transformation on spiritual life. Sombart rather sees this effect in

> ... the victory—not of the mass over the individual—but in that of dead matter over mass and individual equally, hence over living men. ... What we have ourselves created only with such a great expenditure of spirit and energy forces us unconditionally, it seems, under its rule ... it seems to be a psychological law that through the increase of sensual pleasures, which the use of commodities affords us, barrenness develops inside us, which we initially (until the great reversal, which leads to the desert) try to fill by multiplication of those pleasures. Thus wealth produces from itself that underlying mood which we have become accustomed to call materialistic. In the abundance of pleasures which grow around us, the ideal impulses of the heart find their natural grave.¹¹

A problem arises in connection with this notion of the modern enslavement of will. From everything that Sombart has so far said, we might assume that the net result of capitalism has been to destroy the will of the individual, to force him to slavish dependence on forces beyond his control. Yet he asserts to the contrary that "where formerly there was internal peace, today there is struggle . . . the gentler impulses of the heart have receded, the functions of the will have developed more sharply."[12] This apparent contradiction is resolved if we realize that Sombart has adopted as the basis of his theory of action a voluntaristic dualism very similar to Tönnies' *Wesenwille–Willkür* distinction. This similarity comes closest to view when Sombart, comparing the Latin mentality with the German, says:

> The artistically disposed man sees the world from the viewpoint of beautiful appearance, harmonious shaping, the internal repose of all things: the inartistic man under the viewpoint of goal. For the former, every phenomenon of the external as well as the internal world is an end in itself [*Selbstzweck*]; for the latter, it is a means to an end.[13]

There are, then, two "human natures," for Sombart as for Tönnies. But the first, the *Wesenwille* type, is unquestionably the more "natural" of the two. In this sense the will of the individual in *Gemeinschaft—Wesenwille—*actually is much more a product of what both men might call the living essence of the individual and of the original, equally natural communities that produced him. Insofar as this will is active it creates a world harmonious with and true to itself, and it uses all the "natural" experience within it to do so. The *Willkür* type, on the other hand, emerges after the disintegration of "natural" community into "conventional" society. Though the ruthlessness of this society may well force it to be more active than that of the *Wesenwille* type, it is actually very remote from the natural living basis of *Wesenwille,* and unlike *Wesenwille* may at the height of its activity be under the control of institutions alien to itself. Put somewhat crudely, one might say that just as with everything else in industrial society, the quantity of will increases while its quality decreases.*

---

* Another contradiction appears in the closing pages of Sombart's work on the German economy when he argues that the German bourgeoisie completely lacks a will to power (*Die deutsche Volkswirtschaft im neunzehnten Jahrhundert,* Berlin, 1913, p. 470). But this is understandable in terms of the context of the passage, which talks about political power, and probably has a Nietzschean, as opposed to a Tönniesian, frame of reference.

The same dour outlook appears now in Sombart's view of the proletariat. In 1896 Sombart interpreted the characteristic misery of the proletariat to signify principally its wretched living and working conditions, the improvement of which was a principal task of socialism. In 1900 the most characteristic misery was in the breakdown of the old folk community and the loss of personal independence, which the trade-unions were to make good by introducing the era of "industrial constitutionalism." Now, in 1903, the misery of the proletariat encompasses not only "the unconditional subjection of the legally free to the will of another: economic slavery," but in addition, "*die Entgeistung der Arbeit,*" the despiritualization of labor. And there is no remedy for this despiritualization of labor within the framework of modern industrial society; it is a process of the factory itself, with its extreme division of labor:

> The maintenance of mechanical handles under hygienic or aesthetically objectionable working conditions was the opposite of what the living man needed for the activation of his whole personality. And therewith it became a terrible certainty that technical labor in the context of the society lost its ethically and aesthetically beneficent effects, that the labor of the proletariat ceased to be for him the most holy and precious thing that a man can possess on earth. I would like to describe it as the most powerful and consequential of all effects of capitalism on the working class that it has taken from this class labor as the highest good. Against which even that dependency, that unfreedom of which I spoke, loses significance.[14]

In view of the helplessness of the worker's spiritual condition it is only understandable that Sombart should show disenchantment with both the trade-union movement and the socialist goal. The magic of the early heroic days of the movement is past. From the elite of passionate revolutionaries has developed a mass reform party: "Here too, quantity has replaced quality." The social movement has become boring. "Whether 'orthodox' or 'revisionist,' from the old sect of utopians, revolutionaries, and espousers of principles has come the great party of opportunists and accommodationists."[15]

Precisely because the older revolutionaries were not yoked to the tide of history, precisely because they were those "utopians" whose reliance on their own will to the exclusion of economic laws he had formerly scorned, Sombart now prizes them as heroes. To be sure, his understanding of the historical current is unchanged. He sees as the "wave of the future" the same amalgam of the socialist ideal with capitalism that he predicted in *Dennoch!* But now aversion has replaced enthusiasm: he emphasizes that in the *Sozialkapitalismus*, to come, "capitalism" will be the noun and "social" the modifier.[16] And he is most skeptical about the possibility of even a fully socialist system removing the basic misery of the proletariat: "Whether such an economic system would quiet the yearning of the proletarian, whether in particular labor and freedom, on whose reconquest his striving is directed, might be granted to him by it, may encounter justified doubts in all nonbelievers."[17]

When Sombart begins to describe the close connection between the capitalist spirit and the national character of the German people, he shows the extent of his disenchantment with the land of his fathers. He also shows us, unintentionally, his future escape route from this particular disillusionment.

The initial remarks on the German disposition for capitalism are positive: they deal with the physiological freshness, strength, and fertility of the Nordic peoples. But as soon as he begins speaking of mental characteristics, this mild enthusiasm fades into—again— aversion. I have mentioned above his comparison of Southern versus Northern peoples in terms of the *Wesenwille-Willkür* distinction. Tied to this dichotomy of viewing the world as an end in itself or as a means to an end is, on the one hand, the quest for *"piacere,"* which Sombart holds to have no equivalent in the German language, and, on the other, the pursuit of one's *Pflicht*, or duty, which he equally holds to be incomprehensible to Latin peoples. Both of the German characteristics—seeing objects as means to ends and a strong sense of duty—Sombart finds indispensable to the forming of the capitalist spirit.[18]

Sombart further discerns in his countrymen a bent for specialization, to an extent a product of the strong sense of duty, which is again necessary for the development of capitalism, and again missing in the southern European:

> The latter, with his sensual-artistic nonethical nature, has the tendency to group the world around himself and thus to preserve it for himself as a whole. We, on the other hand, dissolve individuality into a number of parts, which we adapt and subordinate to objective ends. Since we have only a meager sense for form, we also have only little sensitivity for the organic quality of a living personality, at peace with itself. . . . And thus we achieve the important capacity to activate ourselves in any desired direction, to develop only a small particle of our essence, and, supported by the above-mentioned *perseveranza*, to evolve into virtuoso specialists.[19]

In the old days, when science and philosophy were one, the Latin sense of the whole could produce universal geniuses who worked on the basis of "creative intuition and genial combination."[20] And in the founding generations of natural science, there were just as many Latins as Germans represented. But, Sombart argues, when the advancement of science depends on "diligent and conscientious specialization," the Nordic lands become the unquestionable leaders. This talent for specialization in science has had the most favorable results for those German industries (especially the chemical) which are largely dependent on technological cleverness.

An equally important by-product of the German's gift for specialization is the social *Teilmensch*,

> our capacity to subordinate ourselves in a great whole, so that we function as a gear in a mechanism, and so that from the cooperation of many springs a great increase in the power effect. To it belongs, more exactly seen, above all, once again a renunciation of personality, of wholeness, of characteristic individuality, belongs again the devotion to an objective goal.[21]

The result, he adds, is the factory discipline so indispensable to the growth of industry.

Once more, everything Sombart detests appears in this dissection of the national character most advantageous to the rise of capitalism. Where, however, are the roots of this character? Sombart toys momentarily with climatic explanations[22] and suggests a correlation between the German sense of discipline and the military drill imposed for centuries by the Prussian state on its subjects.[23] But his real interest is in a racial explanation.

Sombart finds it fortunate for the development of capitalism that Germany has an unusual admixture of races. His analysis of the contributions of these races shows the beginnings of distinctions that later, in *Der Bourgeois* (1913), enabled him to reattach himself both to Germany and, in a way, to capitalism.

He credits Swabians and Saxons for "the two sides of capitalist organization: speculation and calculation, initiative and execution, synthesis and analysis." This is a little ambiguous. Sombart has given us three pairs, and at first sight the "two sides" are not apparent. What he probably means is a side of calculation and speculation, representing analysis, versus a side of initiative and execution, representing synthesis. Though in this period of his waning ardor for modern society there are only weak indications of preference for one side or the other, in *Der Bourgeois*, ten years later, the polarity will recur: one side, that of action, as the entrepreneurial spirit; the other, that of calculation, as the bourgeois spirit—the first with a positive, the second a negative, connotation.

The main objects of Sombart's discussion of racial contributions to Germany's propensity for the capitalist spirit are the Huguenots, of whom he is himself a descendant, and more—much more—the Jews. This emphasis represents a marked shift from his warning only a year before, in *Der Moderne Kapitalismus*, that the importance of the Jews for his subject should not be overestimated;[24] but consistency was clearly not one of Sombart's virtues.

Sombart singles out as important for the modern economy three alleged character traits of the Jews: "the predominance of the will, selfishness, and the abstractness of their mental constitution." The Jew's willpower, understood of course in the pejorative sense of *Willkür*, equips him for the singleminded pursuit of any goal he decides to achieve. For the most part, of course, this goal is economic advancement. In this context, social phenomena previously valued by Sombart become suspect: the Jew's strong family sense, for example, allows him to hand on his economic attainments from one generation to another. Another trait that greatly helps the Jew to accumulate capital has never been very high in Sombart's personal value hierarchy: "great sobriety in the manner of living."

Sombart's evidence for the prominence of selfishness in the Jewish character is a good example of the Catch-22 logic usually found in racist arguments:

> If we find so many Jews with just the opposite manner of thinking, with what one might almost call an extravagant altruistic sense, a rigorous selflessness and a zealousness against all selfishness, we may then deduce just from these reaction phenomena the existence of the indicated national characteristic.[25]

In any case, the unscrupulousness that flows from this selfishness makes the Jew "a virtuoso in advertising."

But all this, without the Jew's capacity for abstract thought, is insufficient to explain his role in the modern economy. For Sombart, this manner of thought "is synonymous with indifference to all qualitative values, with the inability to appreciate the concrete, individual, personal, living." The symbolic expression of this capacity for abstraction is money, which dissolves all use-values into their quantitative equivalents. In this way Sombart relates the abstract Jewish intellect to the Jews' inordinate desire for and overestimation of money.[26]

Historical as well as racial factors are of course involved in the Jew's economic prominence. Sombart sees these in the Jew's exclusion from all traditional means of advancement: the offices and dignities of Christian society being closed to them, their only means of advancement was through wealth.[27] But these historical conditions seem to do little more than further the inherent racial tendencies.

In general, Sombart's valuation of the historical factors in the history of German capitalism gives them a role inferior to that of racial characteristics, both Jewish and German. Essentially, Sombart reduced these historical factors to the lack of any state role in the encouragement of the economy. He sees the positive results of this in the necessity of the unprotected German trader to adapt himself to the needs of foreign cultures, which gave strength to German exporters in competition with those of other lands;* and the necessity of this same unprotected trader to become more aggressive in selling on the world market. Sombart also sees negative advantages in Germany's retention of a semiabsolutist state structure, which kept the bourgeois elite out of politics and so strengthened the economic development of the nation.

There are two significant and complementary tendencies in Sombart's chapter on national characteristics which, after the lapse of some years, were to allow him to absolve his compatriots of responsibility for capitalism and to reattach himself to the fatherland. One was the large role played by non-Germans in the development of capitalism. Although in 1902 these were the Jews, in 1915 the foreign seedbed of capitalism was to be temporarily transplanted to England.

At the same time, we note that the German state has apparently kept clear of any contamination with the development of capitalism and has even kept its ruling elite free from bourgeois infiltration. In his remarks on this elite, the Prussian Junkers, Sombart repeatedly mentions, besides their political prowess, their scorn for everything to do with capitalism and modern economic life.[28] He also notes that the relationship of the Junker to his farm workers had retained "a qualitative coloring" which was opposed to "the purely quantitative relationship of the proletarian-capitalist work dispensation [*Arbeitsverfassung*]."[29] These half-bows in the direction of Germany's traditional ruling caste anticipate Sombart's later reconciliation with his *Volk*.†

But for the time being, the predominant feeling aroused in

---

* Of considerable significance is the fact that Sombart associates this malleability with his father and calls it a "*Sklavensinn*" (*Die deutsche Volkswirtschaft*, pp. 118–19).
† In this celebration of Junker virtue, Sombart reveals his ignorance of the work of the man with whom he was shortly to cooperate in editing Germany's principal journal in the social sciences: Max Weber. A decade earlier, Weber had mercilessly attacked precisely these self-advertised advantages of Junker agriculture and had argued that the Junkers' need for cheap labor had led them to import legions of migrant workers from Poland, thus undermining both the traditional social relationships and Germany's ethnic majority in the East Elbian lands. See A. Mitzman, *The Iron Cage*, pp. 75–147.

Sombart by the social, economic, and political scene was aversion. The old communities had dissolved. The capacity for social or political idealism had vanished. "An unprincipled, barren opportunism, a passionless, businesslike attitude" dominated German politics. The topics of political discussion—freedom of trade, workers' legislation—had become cold and uninteresting to him. A major cause of his disinterest was the role played in political affairs by the proletariat:

> The mass, which appears as subject, has flattened the discussion: the mass, which is to be administered as an object and has produced a hitherto unheard-of complication of legislation and administration, has made of politics a difficult profession, which the schooled specialist with the least possible spirit is best capable of exercising. And if one adds that the content of this despiritualized activity is for the most part the conflict over material advantages, one will no longer be surprised when one sees how far the level of political life at the end of the nineteenth century has sunk below that of all earlier decades.[30]

Concluding his book with an obviously autobiographical paragraph, Sombart wrote:

> A consequence of this desolation of our politics, which one might say has degenerated into a guerilla war of classes, is that the educated, more than at any time in the past generation, are drawing back from public life and are losing interest in political events, which naturally results in a further lowering of the level of politics. And in fact, it is not to be demanded that someone who is not personally concerned, or who does not make a profession out of it, should interest himself in the raising of the cotton tariff, or the reform of the brandy tax or the sick fund law, or the enactment of the Brussels sugar convention. Whether the times will return in which the struggle for great ideals, for great political principles, arouses the passions and also draws the educated, the economically impartial into its spell, who can tell?[31]

18

The Estrangement of a Modernist

"A Man of Culture, He Who Hates All Culture"

THE WRITING of *Die deutsche Volkswirtschaft im neunzehnten Jahrhundert* marked the end of a period of intense literary activity for Sombart. After the publication of *Der Moderne Kapitalismus* in 1902 and *Die deutsche Volkswirtschaft* in 1903, another work of similar size did not appear until 1911 (*Die Juden und das Wirtschaftsleben*), and of similar scope, not until 1913 (*Der Bourgeois*). Although Sombart the man was never particularly remote from his scholarly creations, this would seem to be an appropriate point to take a closer look at that man and his milieu.

Paul Honigsheim, the inveterate chronicler of German sociology's early days, once described Werner Sombart as "this Proteus of the German social scientists, who had as many *Weltanschauungen* as women (and that's saying a lot)." Despite the scandalous tone, one must grant the juxtaposition, if not necessarily statistical accuracy, at least a certain insight into the moving forces of Sombart's life. For the same sense of desolate aridity and lovelessness that continually estranged Sombart from the academic world and his successes in it also played a major role in estranging him from his wife and family and leading him into what appear to be at least two extramarital affairs.

The phases of Sombart's work before World War I all reflect

his unsuccessful attempts to find satisfaction through his career for the wild *Sturm und Drang* personality developed during his student days. He was a man of unusual ambition, unusual gifts, and also of an unusual temperament, aesthetically and emotionally set at fever pitch. He restlessly abandoned one clearly defined position after another. His earliest work, based on his doctoral research of 1887 into the agrarian problems of the Roman Campagna, was generally in harmony with the conservative economics of his teacher, Gustav Schmoller, and his father. The decade of the nineties encompasses Sombart's work as a reformist interpreter of Marxism, who could ardently support capitalist progress at the expense of the old *Mittelstand*. Though new editions of Sombart's famous work on socialism and the social movement kept appearing with no overtly antisocialist bias until the twenties, Sombart fundamentally rejected his earlier stand for economic progress and moderate socialism between 1900 and 1903. *Der Moderne Kapitalismus* suggests a fundamental ambivalence about the nature of the capitalist spirit; his study two years later of the German economy in the nineteenth century reveals an increasing estrangement from modern Germany and everything remotely connected with industrial society; and his articles in the journal *Morgen* in 1906 and 1907 openly confess a total rejection of the values he had held a decade earlier. Though not nearly as productive in this period of bitter rejection as in the decade before or after, what Sombart did write in this period—for example, the brief sketch of the proletariat that he wrote for Martin Buber's series *Die Gesellschaft*—shows considerable influence of Tönnies' historical dichotomy of *Gemeinschaft* and *Gesellschaft*.

Sombart's last change occurred about 1909, when he began to perceive a dual character in the capitalist spirit: an older adventurer spirit of enterprise, which was disappearing, and an increasingly dominant spirit of commerce and cold calculation. By gradually coming to perceive in Germany the spirit of enterprise and in its enemies the spirit of commercial greed, Sombart reidentified with his homeland, though his attitude to modernity remained at best ambivalent. This is the Sombart of *Die Juden und das Wirtschaftsleben*, *Der Bourgeois*, and that notorious piece of wartime Anglophobia, *Händler und Helden*. The dominant influences on Sombart's value system in this period were probably Scheler and Nietzsche.

There is no common denominator in these positions outside of Sombart's own psychology. But what does emerge clearly from Sombart's letters to his close friend Otto Lang* is that his numerous changes in *Weltanschauung* were the result of an unceasing conflict between his desire to perpetuate the excitement and passion—intellectual, aesthetic, and emotional—of his student years, and the grimly arid demands, the social straitjacket, if you will, of the German academy to which he committed himself, and from which he initially expected not only the fame he did soon receive, but far more personal satisfaction than it could give. Thus, Sombart bore in his psyche and gradually revealed through his work the unusual tension between the personal development allowed a son of the high bourgeoisie in his student life and the dry uncompromising formalism, the overinstitutionalized paternalism, of the social structure he had then to enter, a tension typical of his generation of the German middle class, a generation characterized by Max Weber as "epigones."

In his first letter to Lang, in September of 1886, Sombart made clear both his personal ambition and the profound dissatisfaction with his age that was ultimately to undermine his successes. Significantly, he expressed his great hopes for success in a metaphor that anticipated one of his most important subsequent scholarly accomplishments: the analysis of the spirit of capitalism. After telling Lang (then a fellow student and apparently like himself on vacation) that five years earlier he had used his letters as a savings bank in which he, like any good proletarian in spirit, invested his ideas to receive them back with interest from his friends, he confessed that "in time" (Sombart turned twenty-three that year) "one becomes 'capitalist' in spirit, and the great productive enterprise for which one is headed swallows up instantly all free

---

* Otto Lang was a leader of the Swiss Socialist party in the early twentieth century. The unpublished correspondence between Sombart and Lang is in the archives of the International Institute for Social History in Amsterdam. References will be indicated by the letters S-L followed by the date.

surplus." Yet the length and warmth of the letter belie the anality one might read into such a passage, and the contempt with which he looks on the bulk of his fellow students, on the prospect of someday teaching their successors, and on the whole society of which they are a part seems hardly consistent with his worldly ambitions. Responding to Lang's disillusionment with student life in Heidelberg, Sombart says:

> I am nauseated at this dance around the golden calf which an internally rotten society increasingly displays, and I cannot conceive of you in the midst of the colorful bands of beer-drinking students. As is well known, the much-praised bourgeois idealism finds its lowest expression in German student life. Every arch-philistine feels obliged once in his life to be revolutionary, anticonventional, free, inspired . . . but when the philistine wants to be inspired, a disaster is the inevitable result. As evidence we have the wretched miscarriage of student life. "Freedom" consists in coming home late at night—ideal impulses in early drinking and dueling—and needs of the heart are overabundantly satisfied with waitresses and street girls. I am sometimes fearful when I contemplate my future profession, which is to consist in shortening their tedium, and whose triumph is to be received by a stale bourgeois plebs with abundant applause.[1]

Three years later Sombart was to write that he had been a "blood-red Social Democrat" in his student days, had then been repelled by the crude tone of the party, but had returned to his earlier beliefs on discovering through Lang "that someone could be enlightened, tolerant and decent and still be a Social Democrat."[2] His bitter denunciation in 1886 of German society and student life dates then from Sombart's second flirtation with socialism. After spending the winter semester of 1886–87 at Berlin, again with Lang, he moved to Pisa and Rome to do six months of field research for his doctoral thesis on the *Campagna*. His letter of May 1887 gave vent to a suddenly sharp hostility towards the Social Democrats alongside of a euphoric description of his professional activities and prospects, and one cannot help but speculate on the connection between the two.

As if the spectacle of the "dance around the golden calf" had never even occurred to him, much less upset his stomach, Sombart wrote of the socialists: "The foolish, exaggerated ridiculing and scorning of our whole 'bourgeois civilization' enrages the thinker who is based on this same civilization and feels supported by it." Sombart then proceeded to list his intellectual grievances against Lang's party. As one might suspect from the conservative tone of his earliest publications, which he was working on at just this time, his views were hardly distinguishable from those of his mentor, Schmoller, and many others of the older school of *Kathedersozialisten*, such as his father: The Social Democrats were to be condemned first for their materialism, which was a carry-over from the dominance of English and French thought in the earlier part of the century. In addition, their doctrine was antihistorical and rationalistic: "It constructs . . . instead of developing," Sombart charged, borrowing from the fashionable dichotomy of "mechanical" versus "organic." By its antihistorical outlook, social democracy ignored "the greatest spiritual and political current of our century" —nationalism—an oversight Sombart viewed as leading to the absurd attempt to apply the same political stereotype to such completely different political cultures as Prussia and Switzerland. But the most important argument against Lang's party was that despite its name and its verbiage, it was individualistic. Its desire merely to improve the well-being of individuals ignored the concern of genuine socialists—state socialists such as himself—for the prosperity of the society as a whole and for the use of the power of the state and the existing economic system to promote this prosperity.

Though this last point about the material benefits to be derived from the further development of capitalism may serve as a plausible fulcrum around which Sombart's swing to moderate Marxism in the nineties becomes comprehensible, there is no mistaking the hostility with which Sombart viewed the forces of subversion in May 1887. Nor is there any doubt as to the immense professional aspirations he was developing at just this time.

A latter part of this letter is devoted to a description of Sombart's social life and research and, most importantly, of his attendance at an international meeting of statisticians in Rome.

Clearly a favorite of the gods, the twenty-three-year-old doctoral candidate radiates professional euphoria. He was permitted to attend the meeting as a reporter for Schmoller's *Jahrbuch* and to mingle socially with Germany's leading economists. Of Adolf Wagner, a *Kathedersozialist* as important and as conservative as Schmoller, and moreover Sombart's seminar teacher at Berlin, he writes:

> We reveled naturally in friendship—he met my fiancée etc. ... Seeing and hearing so many well-known persons is indeed very valuable. I also met personally the whole set of "significant men." The next day we had ourselves photographed together—a pretty memento—and on the following day an excursion went to Terni and Siena, the women, too. That was really nice.

Despite Sombart's jubilance in being so close to the academic establishment, despite his proximity to connubial bliss and to the completion of his preprofessional labors, there is a slightly discordant note in his description of his everyday life, which vaguely echoes his Bohemian scorn of the previous year for bourgeois society and his bourgeois peers: he never mentions associating ordinarily with like-minded scholars, but "at noon, I either eat alone or in the company of some German artists"; a "mysterious Knochenhauer" whose apparatus is enormously complicated—probably a photographer—is his close companion.

Sombart returned to Berlin in October 1887[3] to prepare for his doctoral exams and to finish his thesis. A long letter to Lang expressed a sense of boredom with his work, despite obvious encouragement from Schmoller, and pangs of nostalgia for his carefree student days with Lang. "Is it anything more than a respectable decline," he writes, comparing his present sober (twenty-four-year-old) existence with his and Lang's earlier forays into "the grottoes of subterranean Berlin, with their charms and torments." Lang, too, in Sombart's view, was "burning all his youthful enthusiasm in archival dust"; a life of philistinism confronted them both. Probably looking back to his earlier phase as a believing socialist, Sombart lamented the disappearance of "all the courageous striving and struggling for a fixed goal—the dear precious one-sidedness of the first phase of development." Indeed, there was a grudging envy in Sombart's recognition that Lang, by retaining his social democratic convictions, had preserved "at least some fragments of innocent belief from the shipwreck of the period of youth."

Of the exciting prospects of Sombart's spring in Rome, only his engagement still maintained its charm. Though he recurred again to the festivities accompanying the professional gathering and the value of meeting so many people, his comments on Schmoller, Wagner, and his immediate career prospects betrayed a considerable sense of disappointment. The Roman friendship with Adolf Wagner had turned into something close to enmity in Berlin. Ostensibly because Sombart was too advanced, Wagner had excluded him from his seminar (Sombart was sure it was because Wagner disliked his quarrelsomeness). Apart from its impact on Sombart's ego, the exclusion cut short his hopes of using his momentary intimacy to obtain professional favors: "If Wagner weren't such a dried-up philistine, his acquaintance could save me perhaps half a year as a *Privatdocent*."[4] Nonetheless, Sombart was clearly the favorite of the faculty, particularly Schmoller, who wanted him to become a *Privatdocent* right away at Berlin: "They all overestimate my knowledge—why, I don't know. At the doctoral exam there's going to be a tremendous scene. Even Wagner judges me much too favorably."[5]

Apart from the professional unease Sombart felt in being pushed by Schmoller, disliked by Wagner, and overestimated by both, he wanted to get married, and he knew that the income of a *Privatdocent* at Berlin would not support a wife. To solve his problems, he took a decently paid position as *Syndicus* (adviser) to the Bremen Chamber of Commerce, where he remained from 1888 to 1890. By September of 1888, he had passed his doctoral examination, married, and moved to Bremen.[6] The University of Berlin accepted his thesis on the *Campagna*, and in November he received his degree.[7]

Sombart's move to Bremen, despite his excellent connections and prospects in Berlin, supports the note of inner desolation in his letter to Lang after his return to his home city. And his four letters to Lang from Bremen in 1889 suggest strongly that he was searching for some medium of generational revolt which could link his career to the passionate enthusiasm of his student days and his tenuous, yet very important, friendship with Lang.

At the beginning of the year, although Sombart had by no means severed his relations with Schmoller's *Jahrbuch*, in which he was still publishing, he had serious hopes of using Heinrich Braun's new *Archiv für soziale Gesetzgebung und Statistik* as "the organ of the tendency of our new younger generation," a tendency in which he included, besides Lang and himself, Heinrich Herkner and Karl Lamprecht.[8] The three basic assumptions of this new school were to be: "historical interpretation" (unelaborated); a "Zolaist-realistic grasp of the present"; and "state-socialist or social-economical (i.e., antiindividualist) thought—Rodbertus-Lassalle variety as opposed to Social Democratic (anti-Prussian) party leadership." Sombart did not think that Lang's rejection of the last point excluded his cooperation in the venture. Apparently he considered the common enthusiasm for Zola[9] a sufficient bond.

By June he had discovered it was not, and the result was two more long, occasionally abusive letters attempting to convince Lang of the sterility and folly of his socialist position. Much of Sombart's polemic was a repetition of his earlier accusations of materialism, individualism, and cosmopolitanism. But in several ways, these letters signaled the turn toward a more tolerant and interested position that Sombart's thought was to take by the end of the year.

Perhaps the key to this softening in Sombart's attitude was his expressed need to retain Lang's friendship. Despite all the angry reproaches, this need for reconciliation dominated the tone of these letters; indeed, the medium by which Sombart came to grudging acknowledgment that social democracy amounted to more than a league of dogmatic bomb-throwers was his linking of Marx and Engels to the historical *Sturm und Drang*, whose echo he and Lang had recently lived through in their student adventures. And this *Sturm und Drang* was in turn profoundly rooted in a "modern conception of the world ['*Moderner Weltauffassung*']," which Sombart saw as linking himself and Lang to the mainstream of Western culture since the Renaissance.

Before he began his detailed critique of Lang's socialism in his letter of June 1889, Sombart conceded that he was willing to maintain intimate friendship with even "an extreme agitator" provided he was not involved in bomb-throwing, and provided the agitator maintained a minimum of tolerance and philosophical concern. Sombart would in fact rejoice in finding a friend with such a *"frische, fröhliche Oppositionsstimmung"* as the old Lang represented, and particularly now. For his only other close friend from his student days had recently died of typhus, and Lang thus represented "the last vestige of my earlier youth, my mad boyish bachelor days with their mistakes and errors and strivings . . . it would be a heartfelt joy if I could preserve another true comrade from my study years."

In analyzing the character of the various groups that composed the Social Democratic party, Sombart recurred again to the excitement of his and Lang's student years when he described

> a group of high-minded enthusiastic youth, for whom it is appropriate to go through a transitional phase of radicalism in their *Sturm und Drang* period. . . . Every man of eminence lives through four or five centuries in four or five years. Who among us did not revel in the raptures of Werther; who did not enthuse with Rousseau for pure nature; who did not feel infinite development in Byronic romanticism; who was not a devotee of Schopenhauer, a republican, and a Social Democrat?[10]

But, Sombart argued in his letter of June 1889, this group had no business remaining in socialist politics, since the party as a whole—a combination of uneducated proletarians and half-educated petty bourgeois—was mired in obsolete dogmas that had little to do with the vaguely socialist sympathies of youth. Although prepared to accept the term "socialism" to describe "the great cultural and ideal power, the modern world-outlook," Sombart saw this *Weltanschauung* as represented only by groups that were too scattered to form a party. In contrast with his earlier denunciation of the party from Rome, however, Sombart's critique had partially left the secure framework provided by his elders and was focusing on separating social democracy not so much from Schmoller's style of historicist state socialism as from the modernist ideology Sombart was trying to work out.

Lang apparently replied quickly and heatedly, for less than a month later Sombart wrote again, to lament in his opening lines "the disappearance of the last common views and goals." Sombart rejected completely the notion that the existing social order was evil incarnate or the result of evil and irrationality. He argued that its basic character was sound and that peaceful, constitutional progress was a genuine possibility. Nonetheless, by the end of this letter, Sombart acknowledged that socialism, if not the exclusive representative of the "modern world-view," was at least one contemporary manifestation of it.

There are two separate and somewhat contradictory definitions of the modern world-view in this letter: a teleological and a methodological one. Sombart thought Lang would agree with him on the teleological view, which was something of a compromise between the collectivism of the state socialists and the alleged individualism of the Marxists: "The goal of human development must be the freest and fullest development of all the capacities of individuals and all the functions of the total organisms. The individual should enjoy life to the full and so should mankind." Beyond this, Sombart could only quote from Faust: "'May the trace of my earthly days vanish as little through the ages as the trace of mankind.'" The notion of modernity in terms of methodology was largely a reflection of the neo-Kantianism of the age, expressed perfectly for him, he wrote, by the philosopher Staudinger—to distinguish free spirits from philistines, one must ask not *what* a man thinks, but *how* he thinks: "To be modern means to be led by reason alone." This is the spirit which had guided apostles of true enlightenment since the Renaissance, among whom Sombart names Descartes, Spinoza, Rousseau, Kant, Darwin, Lassalle, and Paulsen. (One can only assume that Paulsen, so important in Tönnies' development, had also influenced Sombart.)

In the latter part of this letter, Sombart discussed in some detail the place of Marx and Engels in the history of thought, and elucidated their line of descent from the individualism of the *Stürmer und Dränger* before the French Revolution: "There was a passionate yearning to escape from the corrupt and evil world into the world of harmony and nature. Rousseau! The Stolbergs!" The

Sturm und Drang led directly, Sombart argued, to the "*Freiheitsschwärmerei*" of the early-nineteenth-century democrats, and Marx and Engels were simply specimens of the 1848 counterparts of these democrats. Apart from the democratic side of Marx's theory, everything else, such as the theory of surplus value and the socialization of the means of production, was secondary, according to Sombart.

From all the complex verbiage of these two letters of mid-1889 a certain pattern of ambivalence emerged, a forerunner of Sombart's future erratic shifts of *Weltanschauung*. On the one hand, Sombart was emotionally drawn to the *Sturm und Drang*, the unleashed rebelliousness which he saw as the basic meaning of socialism and which seems to have made his student days with Lang the high point of his life; on the other, his professional superego, based on his training under Schmoller, was historicist, and from this historicism flowed his accusations that socialism was antihistorical, antinationalist, and individualist. If, however, Sombart could perceive in socialism an evolutionary movement of social reform, which acknowledged the contribution of the historical bourgeoisie in the creation of modern civilization and sought not to destroy but merely to improve that world, then he could reconcile his factious impulses with his theoretical conscience. The lapsing of the antisocialist laws in 1890 brought such a reformist position to the surface of social democratic politics.

Historians of German Social Democracy have come to recognize the great significance of Bismarck's antisocialist laws in obscuring the evolutionary side of Marxian socialism and thus delaying the appearance of German revisionism until the lapsing of those laws in 1890. Thus, it should not surprise us that Sombart, whose knowledge of Marx was in any case rather shallow before 1890, was ignorant of the reformist and historicist implications of Marxist theory. What is most noteworthy, however, is that even before the abandonment of the antisocialist laws, Sombart, on the basis of the first meeting of the Socialist International in 1889, was excitedly inquiring of Lang, who had been elected to the executive committee of the International Congress in Paris, about the possibilities of reformism in Germany. Only a few months after his ambivalent assaults on Lang's party, Sombart was grasping at the as-yet-unproffered straw of revisionism:

> Everything depends on the way the agitation for the demands raised [i.e., the eight-hour day] is put into action—whether it is in a generous style, unrevolutionary and practical like the English trade-union movement, or both dynamite and phantasies, indiscussable until now, in Russia and Germany. If your paper, "The Eight-Hour Day," could really become a reformist organ of a healthy, powerful, practical labor movement, which has stepped out of the baby shoes of revolutionism. . . . In any event, I ask you urgently to let me know more than previously of the factual development in your party.

Sombart's work in the nineties clearly reflected the reformist socialism he was moving toward at the end of 1889, and which has been discussed above (pp. 151–53). It is of cardinal importance here to recall that, like Tönnies (though not so drastically), Sombart paid a price for upholding his convictions—in his case, by the sacrifice of any chance of professional advancement for almost two decades. And it is also useful to remember that, although he had made clear his enmity to the surviving precapitalist industrial order and its academic advocates in an article of 1891,[11] Sombart's notoriety as an academic radical apparently began with his publication in 1892 of articles sympathetic to the impoverished Silesian weavers[12] and his arguing in an off-campus speech that, given the existence of a revolutionary party, he "saw the best guarantee against revolution in the acceptance of a Marxian theoretical evolutionism."[13]

By the fall of 1893, Sombart had probably reached his point of maximum commitment to the socialist cause. He was critical of the way the party leadership had treated the *Jungen*, a revolutionary anarchist faction within the party, but only because the orthodox Marxists did not openly embrace a reformist, antirevolutionary position. He was apparently deeply impressed by the practical outlook of the younger party leaders, such as Bruno Schoenlank, then an organizer in Breslau. Sombart saw in Lang too an example of the "promising young generation of proletarian leaders" and assured him and the party of the support of a significant group of bourgeois academicians. Sombart spoke of his friends and himself—who wrote primarily for the two journals published by Heinrich Braun—as a fifth column in the universities, and offered some valuable insights into the attitudes of this group:

> We stand behind you, more than you think. And what keeps us at the lectern is for one thing a matter of predisposition —I, for example, would make a very poor party man—and in part a healthy, practical opportunism (a matter of taste, of course, it's not so in my case). I recently encountered this in the amiable Schulze-Gävernitz, whom I met here in the mountains. He said to me: what use would it be to the labor movement, if you or Herkner or I or another of us younger men became a "comrade," wrote in the *Neue Zeit* and worked for the *Vorwärts*. None at all. For the Social Democratic party has more than enough intelligence. But it can be of great use if the German universities are by and by filled with a new spirit. . . . In a certain sense, we writers and teachers are the most advanced posts of the great proletarian army and the most distrusted by the enemy.[14]

As Sombart assumed the role of secret agent for Vollmar and Bernstein, his sense of estrangement from most of his colleagues grew. He described his vacation as idyllic, because he had not seen "a living soul with a reputation, and above all no professors, which is the main thing."[15]

Two months later Sombart wrote another of his extravagantly nostalgic letters to Lang, suggesting again an inner estrangement from his profession. Almost obsessively he recurred to their wild, impulsive student days, contrasting them to the continual reflection and calculation that had to underlie their every move as professional men:

> It is the greatest jump that a man makes in his life: from the vestibule of life, where the mystical dawn is dreaming, into the harshly lit main hall, where one can no longer cower in a corner and moan with bliss or sorrow but where—at least in our sober age of exchange balances and stamp taxes—the carefully considered action, the correct posture, the cool reflec-

tiveness are alone permissible, apart from the few hours when we indulge ourselves in the memory of that dreamlike age, secretly, behind a wall, so that no one can see. That the roots of our friendship are planted here is the wonderful thing. . . . Do I deceive myself that the best friendships originate in that time of life? I sense the differences between our friendship and on the one hand the earlier school friendships and on the other the subsequent friendships of profession and discipline.

The chasm between Sombart's inner life and the demands of his professional milieu, and the fecklessness of his attempt to bridge that chasm by espousing a "respectable" Marxism, appeared clearly in this and subsequent letters to Lang. But what made his position totally untenable was that he was unable either to obtain the conventional rewards of outstanding scholarship or ultimately even to retain his closeness to Lang.

He looked forward, in December 1893, to obtaining an *Ordinarius* through a major work on "the social movement"—his first reference to *Sozialismus und soziale Bewegung*, which appeared three years later and was revised and republished in ten later editions and translated into more than fifteen foreign languages. Yet even his preliminary research for this work brought him professional embarrassment. His colleagues were horrified that, through Heinrich Braun's mediation, he had obtained from August Bebel letters of introduction to leading Italian socialists. Indeed, a sympathetic critique of the third volume of Marx's *Capital* that Sombart wrote at this time earned him the praise of Friedrich Engels.[16] But even though Sombart quickly became very critical of certain aspects of Marxism, such as its treatment of the agrarian question,[17] and even though his publications were distinguished by a passionate brilliance unmatched by his contemporaries, the nature of his work condemned him to professional stagnation. By 1896 the ambitious and prolific Sombart finally realized that he was doomed to an indefinite exile in his provincial purgatory at Breslau. After mentioning a visit to his father, aged but still lively, in Berlin, he wrote, "And we are still in Breslau. . . . Yes, still in Breslau. And yet one is really no idiot. But Allah is great—and Stumm is his prophet! . . . For despite my tameness, so very suspicious to you, I am a thorn in the eye of my colleagues."

To be sure, Sombart continued, academic freedom prevented his dismissal.* But given the denunciations of him by various officials of the state, neither was there any chance of advancement. Sombart professed indifference, satisfaction with his income, and pleasure in his well-attended lectures. But the note of frustration and bitterness was unmistakable.

At the same time, his criticism of both Marxism and the Social Democratic party was increasing. Though he retained his "high respect" for Marx, he now saw more holes in the theory than earlier, and his reason for not joining the party was somewhat more serious than his distaste two years earlier for party discipline. True, he still saw the party as the indispensable vehicle of social progress, but attendance at a rally in Breslau had reawakened his sensitivity to its narrow-mindedness and dogmatism. Only a handful of people, reformists such as Schoenlank, stood out from the "Philistine and pitiful quality" of the gathering.

Thus do illusions crumble. Throughout the nineties, Sombart's prosocialist position was premised on the notion that he could combine academic respectability, the cause of human progress, and the only half-repressed *Sturm und Drang* that his friendship with Lang represented, by supporting socialist reformism. The historical background of this effort was the apparently favorable conjuncture represented by the practical side of the Erfurt Program of 1891, the sudden appearance of reformists like Von Vollmar, and the "new course" that Wilhelm II and Caprivi settled on about 1890. With Caprivi's dismissal, with the growing authority of Baron von Stumm, and with the refusal of the old Marxist leadership of the Social Democratic party openly to accept the reformist position, Sombart's ideological perch became as insecure as his prospects for advancement became dim. Perhaps his final disillusionment was the discovery, about 1900, that Lang too sided with the old Marxists

---

* Academic freedom would not, however, have protected Sombart from administrative sacking had he actually been a member of the Socialist party, as the cases of Leo Arons and Robert Michels were shortly to show.

against Bernstein's revisionism.[18] The middle ground that Sombart had sought between his private self and his public ambitions had been swallowed up in the larger and irreconcilable antagonisms within Imperial Germany.

The ugly, irreducible fact remained that the modern world to which he had tried to accommodate the spirit of his inner fury was intractably opposed to that spirit, and as if in belated recognition of this fact, Sombart projected his earlier awareness of an incompatibility between the dreamlike visions of his late adolescence and the harsh, calculating reality of his professional existence into the contrast of precapitalist and capitalist imaginations. He condemned modernity itself in *Der Moderne Kapitalismus*.

Thus, the bleak confrontation between the Faustian will of economic man and the capitalist machinery he has created, a confrontation in which the person becomes "an involuntary gear in the giant works of business dealings," mirrors Sombart's realization of the impotence of his own ambitious will in the power machine of Imperial Germany.

Though this hypercritical posture was obscured in much of *Der Moderne Kapitalismus*, written over the course of a decade, it was uniformly clear in *Die deutsche Volkswirtschaft*, written in a few months, in 1901 or 1902. From these years on, until roughly 1910, Sombart's work was infused with a Tönnies-like reverence for the communal man of the Middle Ages, and particularly for the aesthetically inclined artisan, with whom Sombart identified himself.*

---

* Certainly Sombart's description of the artisan in *Die deutsche Volkswirtschaft* seems very close to Tönnies' *Wesenwille*: "The artistically disposed man sees the world from the viewpoint of beautiful appearance, harmonious shaping, the internal repose of all things: the unartistic man under the viewpoint of goal. For the former, every phenomenon of the external as well as the internal world is an end in itself; for the latter it is a means to an end" (p. 107, 1913 ed.). In *Das Proletariat* (Frankfurt, 1906), Sombart laments the disintegration of community (pp. 59, 80). Sombart's awareness of Tönnies goes back at least to Tönnies' review of a book on socialism by Julius Wolf (1892), a conservative with whom Sombart conducted a running feud for half a decade (S-L, 21/12/93). Tönnies was the only other academic speaker at the same meeting of the Zurich Ethical Society where Sombart gave his famous lectures on Socialism and the social movement (S-L, 14/6/96). Further, after meeting Sombart accidentally while vacationing in 1905, Tönnies wrote Paulsen that he always enjoyed talking with him (T-P, 30/9/05). The first clear sign of

Sombart's personal estrangement from the social roles available to him in Imperial Germany was total. In the late nineties, he began to give up hope not only in modern German society, in the academy, in radical politics, and in his old friend Lang, but in his relationship to his wife as well. He had become engaged in 1887 while still the favorite of Schmoller and Wagner, and married the following year.[19] In 1897, Sombart pleaded with his influential father to intercede for him with the Prussian authorities who were blocking his advancement to *Ordinarius*.* Shortly after the failure of this plea, the first oblique references to an extramarital affair appear in the correspondence with Lang.[20] In the fall of 1901, following years of family bickering and increasing loneliness, Sombart met a woman whose relationship with him, he wrote Lang in 1904, was "the most significant event of my life."[21] She remained his companion for most of the decade. He had written *Die deutsche Volkswirtschaft*, with its profound nostalgia for a more aesthetically harmonious age, during the first months of their encounter, and for that reason, this book, which he dedicated to her in spirit, was his favorite.[22] In 1906, when Sombart finally obtained an appointment in Berlin, at the business college, he separated from his family for a period of three years.[23] His reuniting with it in 1909[24] coincided with his rediscovery of the virtues of German adventurer-capitalism. But he summarized his estrangement from modernity after the turn of the century in his laconic inscription on a postcard of Wall Street that he mailed from New York in 1904: "*Götterdämmerung der Kultur.*"[25]

The picture given us by one of Sombart's students at this time (around 1900) is an attractive one. Physically, he was "tall and very dark." He was reputed to be a Don Juan as well as a socialist, which "made him an object of curiosity to the students, of holy

---

Tönnies' influence on Sombart is in his *Dennoch!* (1900, first lecture). Two years later, in *Der Moderne Kapitalismus*, Sombart refers to Tönnies' typology as "epoch-making" (II, p. 142). In the second edition of this work (1916), Sombart suggests that he took the whole framework of his analysis of capitalism from Tönnies (II, p. 1081).

* The important letter to his father of 1897 is reproduced at the end of the recent republication of *Sozialismus und soziale Bewegung* (Vienna, 1966), pp. 121–24.

terror to the citizens, and of distressful emotions to the faculty." He appeared to be "a new type of the combination of man of the world and artist, for undoubtedly he was both; and though not supposed to be a poet, he went driving in Byronic fashion with the handsomest opera singer, sat lolling in his seat at concerts and passing his delicate hands through his long black hair." His classroom impression was one of eloquent mastery of his subject matter: "This was the man whose definitions had a classical lucidity, and who could always, without wearying his audience, bring home the most complicated economic statistics, both to mind and imagination. He was the best teacher I have ever come across in my life." Furthermore, there was "not a trace" of "professional pomposity."[26]

Shortly after this student's encounter with Sombart, the latter was to undergo the important shift in *Weltanschauung* described earlier. In these years he also began a most significant friendship with Carl Hauptmann, the poet, dramatist, and elder brother of Gerhart Hauptmann. This relationship probably accelerated Sombart's retreat from the area of public concerns, indeed from the modern world, and provided a secure haven with a kindred spirit.

The friendship of Sombart and Hauptmann is documented in Hauptmann's letters.* Of eighty-five communications which Carl Hauptmann sent to friends and acquaintances between April 1902 and July 1912, more than half bear Sombart's address. Hauptmann's biographer, Walter Goldstein, testifies that Sombart was Carl Hauptmann's closest friend in these years.[27] It is likely that Hauptmann meant as much to Sombart.† Indeed, by 1905, after a series of

---

* Carl Hauptmann, *Leben mit Freunden, gesammelte Briefe* (Berlin, 1929). Hereafter referred to as Hauptmann, *Briefe*. Unfortunately, the Sombart side of the correspondence has never been published.
† Leopold von Wiese, in his article on Sombart in the *Zeitschrift für die gesamte Staatswissenschaft*, 101 (1941), pp. 597–605, mentions Hauptmann as one of the two friends of Sombart. The other was the writer Wilhelm Bölsche. Bölsche, in an essay on Carl Hauptmann, depicts Sombart at Hauptmann's home in Schreiberhau, reading aloud from Goethe's *Faust*, and then debating with Hauptmann and others on the inheritance of acquired characteristics (Wilhelm Bölsche, *Ausgewählte Werke* [Bad Pyrmont, 1931], vol. 5, p. 357). And Tönnies, in the only reference to Sombart in his published letters to Paulsen, mentions encountering Sombart and Hauptmann on a joint vacation trip in 1905 (*Tönnies-Paulsen Briefwechsel*, p. 391, letter of Sept. 30, 1905).

visits to the poet's home in Schreiberhau, some sixty miles West of Breslau, Sombart seemed to be seeking out Hauptmann. Hauptmann's letter of February 20, 1905 is a regretful refusal of a joint trip suggested by Sombart. And on August 20, 1905, Hauptmann refers again to "your desire for a joint stay somewhere," which he is now happy to fulfill.

The Hauptmann-Sombart friendship seems to have flourished in the five years following Sombart's completion of *Der Moderne Kapitalismus* (that is, about 1902–1907). Only a few years earlier Hauptmann had gone through much the same "revaluation of values" that Sombart was now experiencing, and so was in an excellent position to accelerate this revaluation on the part of his friend. Carl Hauptmann had begun his career as a scientist, devoted entirely to the understanding of the world by means of natural laws of physics and biology, and mathematical formulae. But in the course of the nineties, he became increasingly unhappy with this way of viewing the world, which he found spiritually crippling, and changed his field of work altogether, to literary pursuits. In so doing, he developed a *Weltanschauung* more critical of modern life than anything either Tönnies or Sombart might have accepted, but which nevertheless must have been a sharp spur to the growing disenchantment of his friend.

This *Weltanschauung* emerges clearly from one of the few essays written by Hauptmann: "Unsere Wirklichkeit."[28] The theme of the work is that the charm of the primitive, the naïve, the naturally and directly emotional, has disappeared from modern life. The implication is that the sensual animality in man is superior to anything that any civilization can make of him. Though it is unlikely that Hauptmann had read Tönnies, a dichotomy similar to that of *Wesenwille–Willkür* pervades this work, and an emphasis on the living personality, on nature, and on the qualitative as opposed to the quantitative anticipates similar strains which in the next few years will evolve in Sombart's thought.

Hauptmann uses personal experiences and literary examples to make his point clear. Perhaps the best of these is the story he relates of an engineer supervising the construction of a railroad in the Caucasus. The man noticed that one of his workers, a young Circassian, would disappear from the job for hours at a time. Overcome with curiosity, the engineer followed him one day, and found him dancing in a broad summery meadow—alone:

> This aimless love of beautiful movement. This holiness of the freedom of dancing in beautiful lonely nature. And now think of the compulsory social affairs and compulsory dances which are drilled in like popular songs, which everyone only keeps on dancing because it belongs to the tone and custom of our balls and parties. Do you not suspect here too why I see modern man in a heavy armament, which ever more separates him from natural life, and kills and withers the living source of beautiful free activity, which only runs in flesh and blood?[29]

This juxtaposition of primitive versus modern permeates a great deal of "Unsere Wirklichkeit," and towards the end of it, Hauptmann has recourse to one of the common themes of romanticism: the exalted comparison of the primitive with the child:

> The childlike man [*Kindheitsmensch*] still felt directly that in the peace and greatness of the ancient harmony, great and free feelings were released in him. The understanding had not yet pushed the societal concepts of things separatingly into his reality, nor torn his experience into a so-called dead world of matter and an ideal inner world. He therefore held not to a single meaningful mode of communication, that of speech, and did not believe in the exclusive channeling of men and things and experiences in word and doctrine from the outside inward: But he observed with wonderment in all real things, in sun and spring and air, in the whispering of forests, as in the breath of the mouth or in the voices and visions of one's own breast, the marvel-working, life-awakening call, the eternal secret of all communication.

That Sombart found such views of Hauptmann's most attractive in his period of growing disenchantment, and that they hastened his own evolution, seems reasonable. Indeed, in his brief *Das Proletariat*, which he wrote in 1906 for the series *Die Gesellschaft* (edited by Martin Buber), he uses that same romantic image of the natural child to show his outrage at the contemporary abomination of child labor:

> Thus, everything perverted to the unnatural! The child who flits in his butterfly way from flower to flower, whose whole existence is a fluttering "play," who painfully feels any compulsion to continuing occupation as a burdensome shackle; the child, who is supposed to dally laughingly, carelessly through life, who in our petrified world of goals is supposed to embody the healthy aimlessness of all natural existence, who, with his lack of restraint, with his primitiveness, with his harmlessness, should focus all sunshine into our ordered, sober life; the child, forced into the lifeless mechanism of a factory, sacrificed to a system of goals; the child, chained to a machine, which pitilessly demands a given amount of continual labor! The playgrounds, withered! The cheerful laughing and singing, silenced![30]

But in all likelihood the predominant intellectual influence on *Das Proletariat* was that of Tönnies, whose very strict opposition of old and new and whose sharp cultural pessimism about the new recurs continually throughout this work. The picture of the modern worker, one of unrelieved darkness, thus continues, perhaps completes, Sombart's trend away from socialism, which had its roots in the *Gemeinschaft* conception of *Dennoch!* and was already far advanced in his study of the German economy.

In *Dennoch!* Sombart had seen the characteristic misery of the proletariat in the disintegration of the communal bonds of the older society, and the loss of their independence in the mechanism of capitalist industry. Sombart was, however, completely confident that it was the nature of the proletariat to regroup itself into new *Gemeinschaften*, via the trade-unions. In the work on the German economy, this possibility was neither affirmed nor denied, but the main burden of the proletariat's abasement was laid, in addition to the loss of independence, to the "despiritualization of labor," which was incapable of solution within the framework of the factory system. In *Das Proletariat*, Sombart returned more strongly to his earlier theoretical borrowing from Tönnies and approached again the problem of new proletarian communities. Here, however, he reached about the level of pessimism displayed by Tönnies in the original writing of *Gemeinschaft und Gesellschaft* and saw not the slightest possibility of the trade-unions functioning as agents of a new *Gemeinschaft*. After describing the continuance into the capitalist era of a community of labor based on the survival of certain precapitalist forms of trade and industry, he added:

> The pure proletarian work relationship knows nothing more of all those ethical and patriarchal accessories. The basic characteristics of capitalism have completely permeated it. Even the modern labor contract is not supposed to be anything more or less than a business which the single, independent worker concludes with the entrepreneur over a particular performance of labor. Bare payment is the only bond which ties the contracting parties together.° Every community of interest is dissolved, just like every community of labor.[31]

In another place, Sombart emphasized again the lonely fate of the worker: "No community intercedes for him, thinks or acts for him."[32] When he did mention the unions by name, it was with the neutral, casual connotation of something the proletarian might go to if he could overcome his weariness at the end of the day,[33] or as "consciously formed goal organizations" whose character is the direct opposite of the "old, traditional, original *Gemeinschaften*" whose place they are taking.[34] "The single light in this dark night" was "the comfort which religion affords, the hope in a better hereafter";[35] but he added that capitalism, with its Enlightenment, had destroyed this hope too.

In the last section of *Das Proletariat*, Sombart discussed the psyche of the modern worker, from the standpoints of morality and intellect.[36] In both areas, Sombart's terminology and concepts revealed once more the strong influence of Tönnies' ironclad opposition of old and new.

The disintegration of the old, honorable customs and morality did not surprise Sombart; it was a natural consequence of the

---

° Werner Sombart here seems to be echoing his father's lament, uttered at the 1890 meeting of the *Verein für Sozialpolitik*, over the fate of the East Elbian landworker. See above, p. 142.

destruction of former community groups and their replacement by a war of all against all. Instead of the sanctified usages and moral outlooks of an earlier day, he saw the coming of a "ruthless cynicism" and an "impious impudence." For Sombart, it was "only a wonder that the proletarian brood, growing up in complete neglect, is not more depraved than was or is the case, that the mass of this poor race is not much more brutalized in the midst of the inhuman living conditions in which we have met them."

As for the intellect of the proletariat, Sombart found it either stupefied by the monotony of working-class life[37] or, where a "ray of culture" had fallen on it, enlightened in the worst sense of the term, remote from nature and from fantasy, abstract, rational, and utilitarian:

> Like all city people, he too distinguishes himself from the earthbound, rooted, child of the land through the predominance of the understanding over the feeling and instinctual faculties.[38]

> It is not the intuition of things that stimulates these men; what they strive for is not the emotional-instinctual grasp of reality; and acting and creating are to them not heartfelt needs; but what is such a need is perception, the elaboration of a conceptual system. The world and men no longer stimulate, but the "theory" of the origin of the world and of men does; not flowers, but botany, not animals, but zoology, not the soul of man, but psychology.[39]

It is clear from the above how close Sombart still was, in this period, to Tönnies' categories. Indeed, any revival of *Gemeinschaft*, particularly in the proletariat, was now excluded; and the working class was held to be completely divorced from any "natural" (*Wesenwille*) way of viewing the world. This was completely in keeping with the historical pessimism of Tönnies' theory (although Tönnies himself was just about this time contradicting his theory by allowing for the possibility of new *Gemeinschaften* in the cooperative movement). But when he came to consider the educated classes, Sombart departed from Tönnies' strict relationship between social psychology and social system by allowing to those classes and to himself, simply as a choice of will, the option of turning away from the modern world and cultivating a frame of mind that was close to, if not identical with, *Wesenwille*. He seems to have personally drawn a group of literary and artist friends around him with whom he probably tried to cultivate this relationship. Besides Carl Hauptmann, this circle must also have included Richard Muther,* the art critic, and Wilhelm Bölsche, the essayist, and may have extended to Robert Michels, whom Sombart accompanied to the Stuttgart Socialist Congress in 1907.†

The literary outlet of Sombart and his friends, a weekly journal called *Morgen*, first appeared in June 1907. The question of Sombart's control over this periodical is clouded. The editor-in-chief, Arthur Landsberger, apparently gave Sombart the first place in the masthead as founder and as editor of *Kulturphilosophie*. But Landsberger insisted that the magazine publish political articles of a more general and popular nature, which may have been inconsistent with Sombart's own views. In an early number Sombart disclaimed all responsibility for such articles. About a year later, over a similar question of editorial control, Sombart broke his connection with *Morgen* altogether.[40] But in the meantime, his friends Muther, Bölsche, and Hauptmann had done a good share of the writing for *Morgen*, and Sombart had also printed articles by Robert Michels and David Koigen, socialist eccentrics whose views held definite affinities with his own.

Although in the year of his association with *Morgen* Sombart gave extensive coverage to the ideas of the new syndicalist movement, and discussed the aesthetic fruits of capitalism as well—advertising and the decorative arts—his principal contributions centered around the sterility of German political life and the proper concerns of a truly cultured person in the face of this sterility. Three of these contributions ("Unsere Interesse an der Politik," "Politik und Bildung," and "Wien") offer autobiographical intimations of past sins and present aspirations which are of great help in establishing Sombart's mood at the time.

---

* Hauptmann mentions an ocean voyage undertaken jointly by Muther and Sombart (Hauptmann, *Briefe*, p. 119).
† See below, p. 306.

The Estrangement of a Modernist

Sombart characterizes the "political man" of his day as someone who places great importance on the public intervention of the state, whether he is for it or against it:

> He walks in the forest and thinks of the injury done to trees, of poaching, of hunting rights, wood-gathering rights and fiscal forest policies. He travels in Italy, and thinks of the poor administration of railroads, of the wrong of begging, of the draining of the Pontine marshes, of the latifundia in the Roman *Campagna* or perhaps even of the Triple Alliance. And in the gay halls of the Alhambra, when the white fog climbs from the valley of the Guadalquivir; and on the cliffs of Heligoland, when the sun sinks below the red rocks into the sea; then he pulls the evening paper out of his pocket to see how the vote came out in the second reading of the agreement with Austria-Hungary on hoof-and-mouth disease. The poor living conditions of the broad masses pain him, and he resolves to intercede "in speech and writing" for the improvement of workers' protection laws, for the abolition of tariffs on victuals, and also for the broadening of the political rights of the workers, so that they might themselves gain influence over legislation and administration.[41]

Opposed to this dried-out, aesthetically insensitive political man is the man of culture, whose total estrangement from the society that has produced him Sombart sums up in the paradox: "A man of education is he who keeps himself distant from all education; a man of culture, he who hates all culture."[42] For such a man what is important is the personal and the individual, in whose unfolding lies the meaning of life. Anything coming from the outside, from the state, the society, the objective culture, is of value only insofar as it encourages this unfolding "of our personality, our living soul."[43] If it threatens this unfolding, if it dries up the soul, then the man of real education and culture must hate it.

Hence, isolation and life in nature, both of which allow for inner development, are dear to this man. He treasures the muses, who beautify his life. And—a familiar reference—"he loves meaningful labor at a work which itself breathes or produces life." Finally, "he loves association with the simple and with children, who show him the originality, the essentiality [*Wesenhafte*] of humanity; he loves association with genuine women, who let him experience the whole person, because they are not yet crippled by any straitjacket of professional or similar part-activity [*beruflicher oder ähnlicher Teiltätigkeiten*]."[44]

This crippling of personal value by specialization is just what the man of culture hates, as he does everything that usually goes by the name of education, for it is "all mere knowing, unsupported by experience."[45] He is eager for quality, rather than quantity, of experience, so he reads little, and does not often attend theaters, concerts, or museums. Considering Sombart's earlier veneration for the material prosperity of modern culture it is most noteworthy that "he hates the external attainments of modern civilization, above all, technology, because they crush and kill the spirit; he hates bustle, swarm, mass, and commercialism because in them the individual is cut up, rubbed away, specialized, and thus loses the characteristic, the personal."[46]

What he seeks for himself—"the harmonious development of his substance to its own noble shape"[47]—Sombart's man of culture looks for in others. "He judges man according to what he is as a whole: how he behaves with high and low, how he plays with his children, how he buries his mother, how he helps friends in need, how he rejoices in sun and sea, how he loves and suffers. He does not go through life as a strict judge."

Nonetheless Sombart's view of the pleasures of life is a far cry from the eroticism and Epicureanism of his earlier days:

> We may by no means think of our friend as a man of pleasure, or as one of those supermen who kill time in the cafés, and view playing with art and liaisons with dear sweet girls as the content of life, and call themselves free and a personality because they are impudent and immoral. Our friend knows that the basis of everything personal is the control of the instinctual life; he knows that "enjoyment makes things common," and that the man without deep, serious life content is hollow. Because he sets personal freedom above everything, he always remains conscious: from the despotism which binds all creatures, man liberates himself by overcoming himself.[48]

In "Wien" (July 19, 1907), the antagonism toward progress implicit in all of Sombart's work since 1903 becomes explicit. Discussing the slow change in the traditional character of the Austrian capital, Sombart writes:

> "Vienna does not progress." To that, one ought to answer not: It does, but: Alas, and much too much! If only, finally, the whole emptiness of this idol "progress" would be recognized, before which capitalism brings us to our knees! Whereas we ought to admit with all violence: We no longer want to pray to your "progress," which makes us neglect our old saints, which is a destroyer of the best values. Because—led only by thoughts of utility—it mixes with a crude hand into an organic structure of pure humanity, which has grown for us through the centuries. Vienna too is threatened by progress, like Florence, like Rome, like Paris.[49]

Sombart admits that ten years earlier he felt differently. But "In these ten years (I think) has occurred my development as a man of culture, and therefore I now love—Vienna."[50]*

---

* As mentioned above, Sombart's articles in this period also included a number of articles on the contemporary syndicalist movement. These articles were incorporated into the sixth edition of his *Sozialismus und soziale Bewegung* (1908). I have not discussed them in the text, because they add little to an understanding of Sombart's evolution. He admires the syndicalists to the extent that their voluntarist emphasis and their critique of contemporary culture correspond to his own. But he has no more hope that they will transform society than he does that the orthodox Marxists will do so. For Sombart's relationship to Michels in the context of his passing interest in syndicalism, see p. 306.

19

Voluntarism and the Theory of Antiprogress

THE YEAR 1908 marked the beginning of a new phase in Sombart's theoretical development. In that year appeared his first work of a clearly theoretical nature since *Der Moderne Kapitalismus*: his article on Marx and the social sciences.

The two works were not entirely dissimilar. Just as the foreword to *Der Moderne Kapitalismus* had transferred Sombart's impulse toward harmony from the reconciliation of social antagonisms to the reconciliation of methodological ones, so "Karl Marx und die Sozialwissenschaft" (1908)* transferred his open hostility to the idea of progress from a sentiment applied to social history to a theory applied to academic disciplines. Also like the foreword to *Der Moderne Kapitalismus*, the 1908 work had the significance of a transitional piece, summing up past views and pointing toward future ones. This was particularly the case insofar as Sombart's ethical assumptions were changing from a Tönnies-like preference for natural understanding (*Wesenwille*), in opposition to calculating utilitarianism (*Willkür*), as the proper psychological disposition for a student of man, to a Nietzschean *Herrenmoral*, which sharply distinguished between drudge craftsmen (formerly not drudges but symbols of

---

* This article, originally published in the *Archiv für Sozialwissenschaft, etc.*, 21 (1908), pp. 429–50, was reprinted with minor changes as Chapter III of *Das Lebenswerk von Karl Marx* (Jena, 1909), pp. 30–59. Unless otherwise indicated, references will be to this version.

Gemeinschaft and models for the true scholar), and the rare geniuses who tower above them, the true bearers of culture.

In "Karl Marx und die Sozialwissenschaft" Sombart establishes as the foil against which he will construct his own theory, Engels' comparison between Marx and the great synthesizing geniuses of the natural sciences. He argues for a clear distinction between natural and social sciences, on the basis of the difference between the objects of these sciences and on the basis of the different psychological capabilities each requires on the part of the scholar.

The different objects that separate the natural sciences from the social sciences are nature and man; or, more precisely, since the purely physiological side of man is eminently subject to scientific study, phenomena that have as their origin the action of bodies and those that have as their origin the action of minds. His distinction is "in essence coincidental with the traditional one of natural and mental sciences [*Natur- und Geisteswissenschaften*]."[1]

The different natures of these objects require different ways of perceiving them. And again, these different ways are not very far from the kinds of perception Tönnies would associate with *Wesenwille* and *Willkür*. "To perceive nature means to describe it, means to reduce the observed processes to a formula, means to hypostasize causes of whose essence we know nothing. To perceive man and his actions means to explain, means to interpret from one's own experience, means to indicate reasons of which we have information from within ourselves, which we thereby know."[2] In other words, our real knowledge is confined to our understanding of human actions; our knowledge of science is merely "a description of external processes of whose inner connection we know nothing":

> I do not know the ultimate cause that brings the stone to fall; for if I call it gravity, I substitute a word without penetrating any deeper into the question. If, however, somebody beats someone else over the head with a stick, I am able to explain the action which led to the head-beating from my own soul. Who can say why the earth circles around the sun? But why Romeo circles around Juliet, Napoleon around England, and

> the jobber around the stock exchange; that I know, for, again, I have experienced it.³

Thus, we see a further tightening of Sombart's voluntarism: the only knowledge worth having is knowledge of purposes. And in his scorn for the natural sciences and their study of causes without purpose there emerges again the antagonism of quality and quantity:

> What modern natural science strives for is just the unbroken substitution of quantity for quality, which finds its last and most complete expression in a mathematical formula. What it all aims at is, so to speak, the despiritualization [*Entseelung*] of nature. Where there once was assumed to be living essence and living action, is now supposed to rule an interplay of dead bodies.⁴

In natural science alone is progress—the building of one man's knowledge on another's—conceivable. In the human sciences it is not. In history, for example, Sombart sees progress neither evident nor possible from Thucydides to Mommsen.⁵ What makes for greatness in the student of the human spirit is

> always the new view of the world and of men. He too is great as a discoverer. But not as discoverer [i.e., formulator] of laws, but rather as the discoverer of men and of human substance. What we treasure in him is the power to bring men to life, to put them bodily before our eyes in their thought and feeling and action.

So that the only discernible course followed by the human sciences is a circular one, in which great visionaries alternate with narrow specialists who destroy their visions.

> All "development" of the knowledge of man . . . exhausts itself in the recurring process: that with a great paroxysm, men are discovered and displayed, that then slowly the picture is covered over by the scholarly spinning of all kinds of specialists until it has become quite unrecognizable and must be replaced by a new creative achievement. When the paroxysm fails, then the cobblers take over. And their work it is to cover the living with the dead rubbish of learning, to replace man and his action with all kinds of abstractions.

What is most noteworthy here, apart from the denial of even the possibility of progress in the cultural sciences, is the juxtaposition of the cultural hero versus the cultural cobbler. In Hauptmann's letters to Sombart, the image of the cobbler appeared as the model for his own cultural labors.[6] In Sombart's use of this image in a wholly derogatory sense, was there an unconscious desire to shake off the milieu of his friend as perhaps not sufficiently elevated? Indeed, Sombart's own work from 1903 on was full of laudatory comparisons of the true scholar to an artisan. Apparently the positive emphasis on the artisan was on the point of vanishing and, perhaps with it, the whole glorification of *Gemeinschaft* culture on which it was based. What new social models Sombart was to hallow in the years to come, and what they would signify, clearly emerged in the sketch of Marx's greatness which, in this work, he drew to refute Engels:

> What Marx discovered was not so much a sum of legal institutions and economic methods, as they form an economic system, but rather the living men hidden behind these institutions and processes. He discovered the subjects of capitalism, the capitalist entrepreneurs, and from their psyche was able to explain the whole great workings of a market economy.[7]

Whatever one may think of this view of Marx, the fact is that Sombart, when he renewed his studies of the capitalist entrepreneur during the next four years, would see himself continuing in the line of Marx's greatest work. The difference between the two men, which Sombart did not choose to mention, was that whereas Marx's purpose in analyzing the psyche of the entrepreneur had been to expose him as historically obsolete, Sombart's was to exalt him as the living source of economic activity. Thus, Sombart's work from 1909 to 1913 reexamined the spirit of capitalism with the aim, conscious or unconscious, of somehow overcoming the estrangement and disenchantment with the contemporary world which flowed from his earlier view of that spirit as the destroyer of *Gemeinschaft* and the creator of the spiritless mechanism. Sombart would reach his goal by tacitly abandoning his *Gemeinschaft* values, replacing them with something akin to a Nietzschean *Herrenmoral*, and dividing the once indivisible capitalist spirit into an adventurous, entrepreneurial element, which he identified with Germany, and a calculating bourgeois spirit, which he associated with outsiders. But underlying the old and the new Sombart, as the continuing basis of his life's work, was the ever-increasing dominance of the vital will, which remained as the supreme value and the creative force of history.

20

The Celebration of the Entrepreneur
1909

In "Der Kapitalistische Unternehmer" (1909),[1] Sombart anticipated much of his major work, *Der Bourgeois,* which appeared four years later. In particular, he outlined that separation of the capitalist spirit into commercial and entrepreneurial components which was to be the main subject of the later work. Despite the new perspective it revealed, however, this study contained major links to its author's earlier work. For on the one hand, this very separation of entrepreneurial and commercial functions (*Unternehmer und Händler*), had already been suggested in *Die deutsche Volkswirtschaft.* On the other, we can illuminate his description of entrepreneurial intellect and morality in 1909, by comparing it with his description of proletarian intellect and morality in 1906. In both cases, Sombart showed the extent of his reconciliation to the driving forces of his society.

In his study of the German economy, Sombart had made a division—similar to that between *Unternehmer* and *Händler,* though not as severe—between the organizing and the rationalizing functions of the capitalist. The entrepreneurial organizer was at that time compared unfavorably with the handworker, who in isolation "imparted his personality to the dead matter," and who was a complete master of all the techniques required by his work. The entrepreneurial rationalizer, on the other hand, who corresponded roughly to the *Händler* of 1909, received surprisingly favorable mention, considering the general drift of Sombart's thought at the time. To succeed, he required not only a "sharp understanding" but "abundant fantasy" as well. In this sense, Sombart spoke of a "creative entrepreneur." This relatively favorable attitude probably had as its source a respect for certain great business "personalities" (he names Krupp and Siemens) whom Sombart, in accord with an earlier tendency to except a few heroic individuals from the fate of the masses, seems to have been willing to place outside the value bias he then had for *Gemeinschaft*.

In any case, by 1909 a sharp reversal had occurred. The *Händler* had become a man "whose whole intellectual and emotional world is directed to the money value of conditions and dealings, who therefore continually calculates everything in terms of money," not a particularly flattering picture, with no more talk of "fantasy."[2] The entrepreneur, on the other hand, was stoutly defended for a trait that would have been severely negative six years earlier—the limitation of his function to organizing the work of others. Sombart denounced the idea that he should himself be able to carry out all the technical process of his enterprise as "monstrous nonsense . . . born of the idea-world of the artisan" and advanced "by representatives of the *Mittelstand*."[3]

As for the entrepreneurial intellect and morality, the contrast with the proletariat, that other product of the capitalist spirit, which Sombart had described only three years earlier in the blackest of terms, is also striking. *Das Proletariat* had depicted the worker's mind as stupefied when undeveloped, and mechanical and abstract when developed; his morality was dog-eat-dog. The standard of comparison Sombart used for this characterization was the value structure of *Gemeinschaft*, and Sombart's picture was so gloomy that it seems to have cost him a publishing opportunity.* But in 1909

---

* Letter of Eugen Diederichs to Carl Hauptmann, July 6, 1906, in *Eugen Diederichs' Leben und Werk* (Jena, 1936), p. 140. Hauptmann had ap-

Sombart was quietly withdrawing from his patriarchal Tönniesian *Heimat*, and he indicated the later direction of his thought by giving to moral attributes of the entrepreneurial class, similar to those of the proletariat, a modest halo, while making its intellectual characteristics less abstract and more imaginative.

Intellectually, the entrepreneur had to have a quick perception, a sharp judgment on men and conditions, a keen sense of what is essential, and a good memory. He had also to be "ingenious: thus rich in ideas, insights, rich in a particular kind of fantasy that Wundt calls the combining."[4]

In terms of character, the entrepreneur had to be energetic, cold-blooded, and disciplined. By energetic, Sombart meant "quick of decision, steady in execution, persevering, diligent, restless, goal oriented, tenacious, boldly adventurous." Cold-bloodedness (Sombart began by using the word *nüchtern*, "sober," but his explanation showed that he meant cold-blooded) signified the lack of any impediments of sentimentality or moral scruple. This characteristic, to which Sombart devoted almost four full pages of explanation, had been damning in the case of the proletariat, but was now almost a virtue: "It would be completely mistaken to take the modern entrepreneur for a morally decadent [*moralisch verlumpten*] man. His amorality is an expression of his power, and this expresses itself in another form as strength of character, as discipline, as solidity." This notion of discipline or solidity, Sombart filled out as "reliable in business, true to duty, loving order, and thrifty."[5] And these traits, too, were "virtues," another major shift from Sombart's former scorn for the German sense of duty.[6]

In all, Sombart saw the entrepreneur as

> equipped with an extraordinary vitality, from which flow an overnormal yen for activity, a passionate joy in work, an unbounded drive for power. . . . [They are] men with pro-

---

parently suggested Sombart's name to Diederichs, a publisher, as someone to be included in a series he was preparing. Diederichs' answer was that he did intend to speak with Sombart to see if his views were compatible with the approach Diederichs desired, but that "I heard last week that his piece in the new monograph collection *Die Gesellschaft*, on the proletariat, insofar as it saw only the losses in the new development but not the new beginnings, was not so good." Sombart never did publish anything with Diederichs.

nounced intellectual-voluntaristic talent, with weakly developed emotional and spiritual life; robust natures in the double sense: robust for the mastering of great tasks and the crushing of hindrances, but robust too in the observation and valuation of life; men carved with an axe; smart men.[7]

The key words "vitality," "joy in work," "drive for power," and "voluntaristic" show the extent to which Sombart was associating long-held values with the entrepreneur. But there still remained a good deal of reserve for the prime mover of capitalism. Apparently, there were too many bourgeois traits in the modern entrepreneur for him to fit neatly into Sombart's growing admiration for the hero-adventurer. And of course he remained remote from the *Gemeinschaft* value scheme which Sombart had not quite abandoned entirely. Thus, at one point Sombart noted sourly that the general course of entrepreneurial history starts with the *condottiere* (whose adventurousness he admired) but ended with the corporation officer (whose morning dress suit he did not).[8] At another, he sharply distinguished entrepreneurial psychologies (*Willkür*) from artistic ones (*Wesenwille*).*

> The former are goal-striving, the latter are goal-hostile; the former intellectual-voluntaristic, the latter affectionate; the former hard, the latter soft; the former sober, the latter drunken; the former men of the world, the latter alien to the world. . . . Our entrepreneurial natures are just as little related to artisans, rentiers, aesthetes, scholars, hedonists [*Geniessern*], moralists, and such like.[9]

Despite this reserve, a number of passages reinforce the impression that Sombart was at least beginning to identify with the entrepreneur. For example, after describing some of the mechanisms of the capitalist enterprise, he proposes "to return to the living core of the capitalist enterprise, the entrepreneur, so as to determine how he acts inside the framework of objectified goals imposed on him (profit-seeking) and forced means (rationalization of the economy): *how he fills the dead model with living spirit.*"[10] (My emphasis.) And quoting extensively from Walther Rathenau's description of the

---

* Sombart does not use these terms, but they are useful reference points.

entrepreneur, he cited a passage that may have had a very personal meaning for him:

> But he who had believed he had created a living organism of men, capital and laws, which would move and defend itself, must henceforth, again an isolated man, hang on the spokes of the exhausted flywheel, and, with newly kindled energy, begin the work anew. The second time, it succeeds; the work is ended; but success does not yet arrive. The construction requires a decade, the working in, a second, often more tiring, for now the details exhaust the aging man.

Could Sombart have seen in these sentences an economic parallel to his own efforts to achieve recognition for his social theory, which had only appeared in 1902, and which he was now "beginning anew"?

In perhaps the most revealing line in this essay, Sombart placed his own father among the ranks of the great German entrepreneurs.[11] In 1903 when Sombart mentioned the names of a few heroic entrepreneurs, his father was not among them.[12] The only reference at that time to A. L. Sombart was in connection with the "slavish sense" of obedience to the business customs of foreign lands, which the son accused his father of spreading. And before 1900 Sombart seems to have grown in mortal combat with the "patriarchal" notions of his father and the elder generation. But a decade after the father's death, the son was finally mentioning him for the first time in a favorable light, and, moreover, in his sometime role of entrepreneur.

21

The Two Faces of the Bourgeois
1913

Der Bourgeois (1913) was perhaps Sombart's most important work as a sociologist of capitalism, certainly his most important of the prewar period.[1] Even *Der Moderne Kapitalismus*, though twice the size of *Der Bourgeois*, was of lesser importance, because the bulk of it, devoted as it was to the transition from pre- to early-capitalist economic systems, did not stand in any necessary relation to the author's truly original contribution at the time, which was his perception of the *Geist* behind this transition.

In *Der Moderne Kapitalismus*, Sombart really had very little to say about the capitalist spirit. Its *manifestation* was the economic development he portrayed; but this portrayal merely presented a large, well-organized chunk of history in relation to which the stated origin in the will of economic man appeared as an appendage that the author could have omitted without much change in the body of the work. To have given his thesis of a "capitalist spirit" the solidity necessary to serve as a foundation for the history of capitalist society, Sombart would have had to show precisely what changes in the prevailing economic ethos of the Western world were necessary to produce the characteristic features of modern capitalism, and what caused these changes. But Sombart was at that time loath to broach the question of the origins of the capitalist spirit at all, arguing that he would be forced to enter the *terra incognita* of individual psychology and small-group behavior.[2] By 1913 this reluctance to explore the question had disappeared, and we may, with fairness, call *Der Bourgeois* the third and most important volume of *Der Moderne Kapitalismus*.

Why Sombart should have undertaken in 1913 a task he had evaded in 1902 is understandable both in terms of his personal development and of the evolution of the intellectual world around him. In 1902 Sombart's personal disenchantment with materialism and progress had only begun to affect his work. By 1913 he had been through the worst phases of alienation and failing productivity, and was resuming, on the basis of mostly new intellectual and emotional loyalties, both his creative work and his ties to the society around him. Scrutiny of *Der Bourgeois* shows how important these loyalties were to his work.

At least as important as Sombart's personal evolution was the changed intellectual environment of 1913, as compared with 1902. In the earlier year, Schmoller's historicism was still the prevalent pattern in economic theory. For Schmoller too there was a *Geist* behind economic activity, and it was to a large degree historically determined, but this *Geist* was normative, a moral force, shaped according to the precapitalist ethics of the German *Mittelstand*, and if in reality its morality was blemished, the task of the economist was to restore to it its ideal purity by public activity. On the basis of his early separation of science from values, Sombart, when he recognized *Geist* as the source of economic activity, stripped it of all normative qualities, making it exclusively a tool of analysis. Furthermore, following Marx, he insisted upon using the concept "capitalism" to describe the totality of the economic system; and again, this was a major error in the eyes of Schmoller and the older school, for by characterizing the economic system in terms of capital, Sombart had made the entire noncapitalist *Mittelstand* appear something close to historically obsolete. Thus, Sombart's earlier definition of the capitalist spirit, meager though it seems from our present vantage point, was a major innovation and a challenge to the older school.

In 1913, however, a much more extensive discussion was necessary. Sombart's own work had by then been followed by Max Weber's rigorous inquiry into the sources of the capitalist spirit, and a new generation of scholars, including in particular Ernst

Troeltsch and Max Scheler, had thrown important light on the general connections between Christianity and bourgeois society. Indeed, Scheler, after moving to Berlin in 1910, became a close friend of Sombart, and Sombart revealed his intellectual indebtedness by using the notion of Ressentiment, which he took from Scheler's essay of that name (1912), as an important explanatory device in *Der Bourgeois*. It was on the basis, then, of this new body of ideas that Sombart found it possible and, in a sense, necessary to write his major study of the origins and evolution of the capitalist spirit.

Der Bourgeois is one of the most important works in the history of ideas to appear in the twentieth century. As with almost all of Sombart's work, it has an inner structure of values, loyalties, perhaps prejudices, around which, to an uncertain degree, much of the work is built. My method will be: first, to establish the objective structure of the capitalist spirit as Sombart sees it in *Der Bourgeois*; second, to show the role of the evaluative inner structure in shaping the outer structure; and third, to relate this structure to the main body of Sombart's work and values.

In this work of 1913, Sombart conceives of three stages of Western economic history, each with its own characteristic spirit: precapitalism, early capitalism, and high capitalism. In all three of these stages, he distinguishes two elements that together compose the characteristic spirit of each stage. One of these elements has the character of a power relationship between men; that is, it is based on the use or the threat of force to attain economic ends. The other has the character of an exchange relationship between men; the rules of this relationship are that the attainment of economic ends is based on some sort of market mechanism.

The power relationship appears in all three stages as the spirit of enterprise. Sombart's definition of enterprise is "any realization of a far-sighted plan whose execution requires the continuing co-operation of many persons under a single will."[3] In the precapitalist stage, the spirit of enterprise may take the form of outright seizure of land or goods through conquest and thus have nothing to do with any exchange relationship. In the early capitalist stage, the spirit of enterprise may join with the "exchange" side of the economic spirit by giving the organizing impetus to long-distance commerce, or to the slave trade. Though tied to exchange activity in this stage, the aggressive, entrepreneurial side of economic life nonetheless may still be more important than the calculating, marketing side. In the last stage, the spirit of enterprise is tamed. Though remaining important, it is definitely subordinated to the needs of the exchange economy.

The economic relationship changes its fundamental character from one stage to the next. In the precapitalist stage, the economic needs of the individual are fixed by tradition; the model is the *seigneur*, who, remote from any desire for profit, seeks only a customary income largely determined by his customary expenses. Indeed, his real interest is in the using of wealth, and he has no interest in acquiring it except as he needs it.

The early-capitalist economic type is the *Bürger*. Sombart uses the same word to describe the high-capitalist economic type, but the difference between them is so vast that he should have used two different terms. The *Bürger* is distinguished from the *seigneur* in that, instead of using his expenses as the standard to which his income must be adjusted, he uses his income as the standard to which his expenses must be adjusted. His economic activity, furthermore, is governed by certain principles of rationality (bookkeeping) and sound business conduct which are absent in the *seigneur*. And the *Bürger*, once again as opposed to the *seigneur*, definitely has the desire for profit, "*Erwerbslust*," which is the prime characteristic of the capitalist spirit. But the early capitalist *Bürger* still has one all-important quality in common with the *seigneur*: his economic activity is still centered around and determined by the needs of individual men. The pre-nineteenth-century *Bürger* may, perhaps, seek to accumulate wealth beyond what is allotted to him by custom, but he does so only to satisfy his or his family's desires for a comfortable life. And, yet more important, he recognizes the legitimacy of these desires on the part of others and will refrain from any business practice likely to cause economic hardship to his fellow *Bürgers* or their workers. If, for instance, a merchant sees a possibility of eliminating middlemen and so increasing his profit margin, he will not do so because of the unemployment he would cause; nor will he advertise to entice customers from another *Bürger*.

In the high-capitalist economic type, these restraints are removed, for the center of economic interest has shifted from human needs to business needs, and the appetite of the Business, unlike that of man, is insatiable. There is no longer a moral brake on either rationalization or cutthroat competition. In this phase, the business mechanism seems to be governing the men who created it.

Sombart's presentation of his material in the first half of *Der Bourgeois* is disconcerting. The sharp distinction between the spirit of the *Bürger* and the entrepreneur seems to have become clear to him only after he had written over a hundred pages, and he did not bother to rewrite. Nevertheless the above broad outline constitutes the objective structure of his argument in that part.

The second half is an inquiry into "the sources of the capitalist spirit." It examines a series of causal complexes and determines the extent to which each was responsible for developing the capitalist spirit in either its entrepreneurial or *"bürgerlich"* aspects. These causal complexes are: different racial characteristics; moral forces, including philosophy and religion; and social conditions, under which Sombart discusses the state, migrations, discoveries of precious metals, technological development, the precapitalist occupational structure, and capitalism itself.

To introduce "the biological foundations" of the capitalist spirit, Sombart offers a chapter on *"Bourgeoisnaturen"* (pp. 253–65) in which, using some of the passages from his article "Der Kapitalistische Unternehmer," he recapitulates his definition of the bourgeois as a fusion of *Unternehmergeist* and *Bürgergeist*, and poses the problem of how different racial groups accelerate or slow down the formation of the bourgeois character. The chapter on "the talents of the peoples" then discusses this problem in detail.

Sombart initially distinguishes two groups: the under- and the overtalented. The Celtic peoples are the main undertalented group: Wherever they form a majority of the population, "the upper layer, the nobility, lives in great seigneurial style, without any sense for thrift and the bourgeois virtues; the middle layers persevere in traditionalism, and prefer the smallest secure post to restless moneymaking." To their Celtic stock, Sombart ascribes the noncapitalist character of the Scottish Highlanders, the Irish, part of the French, and most of the Spanish and Portuguese. Among the overtalented peoples, Sombart distinguishes between "those peoples who had a special talent for large-scale power enterprise, for piracy, and those whose capacity lay rather in a successful peaceful trading activity."[4] The first group—the entrepreneurial—includes Romans, Venetians, and Genoese in Italy, and the English and Germans. The racial origins of these peoples, except for the Romans, are the Norman, Langobard, Saxon, and Frankish tribes. The second group—the *bürgerlich*—includes the lowland Scotch (Frisian), the Florentines (Greek and Etruscan), and the Jews.

The influence of "moral forces," both philosophical and religious, seems to have been exercised almost exclusively on the development of the *Bürgergeist*. Sombart sees the main contribution of philosophy to have been the early Renaissance revival of ancient Stoicism, which, he believes, was an important stimulus for the business-oriented utilitarianism of the Florentines. The role of religion, however, seems to have been of greater significance for Sombart than that of philosophy: to his study of the economic teachings and influence of Catholicism, Protestantism, and Judaism, he devotes over five times the space he gives to philosophy. In part, his stress on the religious influence is because he attempts in this section to answer Weber's thesis on the derivation of the capitalist spirit from Calvinism; in part because he recognizes that, in general, the overwhelming moral influence on the men of the early capitalist era came from religion.

Two features stand out when we look at the significance of this section on religion for the work as a whole. In the first place, following the pattern he established in *Der Moderne Kapitalismus*, Sombart is locating the true "cause" of the capitalist spirit in psychological phenomena, i.e., the moral force of religion, which tends to derogate the social conditions he will discuss further on to *mere* conditions that may encourage or discourage the spread of attitudes inspired by religion. Secondly, this section bears out the impression given us by the first half of the book: the entrepreneurial side of the capitalist spirit is essentially constant, while the *Bürger* side is variable, entering into varying relations with the entrepreneurial side and so really responsible for *changes* in the capitalist spirit. For as I have mentioned, the "moral forces," the real causes of the birth and evolution of the capitalist spirit, exercise their influence almost exclusively on the formation of the *bürgerliche* character.

In outlining the influence of Catholicism Sombart used the bifurcation of Christianity established by Troeltsch,[5] and also used by Scheler,[6] into an other-worldly religion of love and grace, stemming from Paul and Augustine, and a this-worldly religion of law. Thomism, which merged these two systems into a higher unity, was of vital importance for Sombart insofar as its this-worldly ethic provided the main ingredients of the *Bürgergeist*.

The goal of this ethic was the "rationalization of life," the application of a rational natural law to the "natural . . . instinctual world," and the consequent transformation of the latter to a "moral, rational world, born of freedom":[7]

> From this basic idea of rationalization had to spring an essential furthering of capitalist thought, which, as we know, is itself rational and goal oriented. The idea of profit, as well as economic rationalism, signifies nothing but application of general rules of life, given by religion, to economic life. In order that capitalism could develop, the natural, instinctive man first had to have every bone in his body broken; a specifically rational mechanism of the soul had to take the place of the primitive, original life; a kind of reversal of all life values had to occur. The *homo capitalisticus* is the artificial and artful creation which finally resulted from this reversal.[8]

Thus, the rationally maintained household avoiding the extremes of avarice and extravagance became the economic ideal. The "expense economy" of the *seigneur* was replaced by the "income economy" of the *Bürger*. Many ingredients of what Sombart calls "shopkeeper solidity" also owed their existence to the Church, and as a result of the Church's influence on the conscience of the merchant, long-distance trade, remote from the watchful eye of neighbor and guild, also became subject, to a degree, to the principles of "solidity."[9]

In some ways, Thomistic doctrine encouraged entrepreneurial activity too. Thomas, recognizing the menace offered by uncontrolled eroticism to the virtues of moderation, urged the inhibition of the erotic instinct. In Sombart's opinion, this encouraged in the economic sphere not only the frugality of the *Bürger*, but also the activity of the entrepreneur, who by husbanding his sexual powers had more energy for his work.[10] The prohibition of interest was a further stimulus to enterprise. Although in its original formulation this prohibition was maintained not only against usury, but against any form of capital investment as well, in the fourteenth and fifteenth centuries—under the pressure of the economic advances of the age—it was lifted from such investments with the single proviso that

> the capitalist must be directly involved—through profit and loss—in the enterprise. If he holds himself back, if he lacks the daring, the "spirit of enterprise," if he is unwilling to risk his money, then he should not make any profit either.[11]

For Sombart this stimulus had its source in Thomism's general prohibition on idleness. Thomism did not, however, change anything in the nature of enterprise, which it simply took over in one piece from its precapitalist, noneconomic status and endowed with some religiously sanctioned or conditioned economic outlets; whereas the Thomistic ethic virtually creates the early capitalist *Bürger*.

Nota bene: *early* capitalist. The background of Sombart's section on religion was Max Weber's masterly derivation of the capitalist spirit from Calvinism. Sombart's early-capitalist *Bürger* type corresponds perfectly to Weber's patriarchal type. Did Sombart, then, follow Weber in accepting Protestantism as the principal agent for the transformation of the early capitalist mentality into the high capitalist one (which for Weber was where the capitalist spirit really started)?

Sombart began his section on Protestantism as a refutation of Weber's thesis: "All along the line, Protestantism signifies first of all a serious danger for capitalism and in particular for the capitalist economic mind." He reasoned that the Reformation, as a "deepening of religious feeling," necessarily produced "indifference to all economic things," which in turn, signified a "weakening and decomposition of the capitalist spirit."[12]

Sombart quickly modified his position, which was applicable in its extreme form only to Lutheranism. He acknowledged that non-Lutheran Protestantism in general demanded a suppression of instincts and a rationalizing and methodizing of life which led to an intensification of most aspects of the Thomistic economic ethic: industriousness, useful occupation, moderation, and thrift.[13] In one area alone did Protestantism significantly alter the Catholic ethic: by intensifying the demand for thrift, it destroyed "all traces of an aesthetic need for observable greatness and splendour," which Sombart held to be the source of "the incomparable beauty of the Thomistic world of thought." The prime virtue of Puritanism became niggardliness, the opposite of Catholic *magnificentia*, and a sin to the Scholastics.

But this was merely a slight twist in the pattern of *"bürgerliche"* virtues accepted whole from Catholicism. Unlike Weber, Sombart denied that Protestantism was responsible for inculcating those virtues into economic life. Nor was it responsible for the major change in them that appears in the high capitalist epoch. It was not the source of the unlimited activities of the profit motive, of the "business idiosyncrasy," for all the old prohibitions against money-making as an end in itself were retained by the Protestant ethic. Nor was it the source of ruthless business practices; here too the old restraints, such as the just price, still prevailed. Finally, Protestantism was in no way responsible for the development of entrepreneurial activity, whose appearance in certain Protestant lands Sombart declares to be nothing but coincidence.

Having absolved Protestantism of responsibility for the birth of high capitalism, Sombart placed this responsibility squarely on the shoulders of Judaism. To be sure, in many respects the economic ethic of Judaism resembled that of Catholicism and Protestantism. Judaism had a *Bürger* code similar to the Thomistic one. And its severe rationalism, its extreme repression of sexual instincts, and its antagonism to the visual arts were very close to the Protestant ethic.[14] But in one vital respect, Judaism produced a fundamental change in business practices that became the basis of the high capitalist spirit: its moral law distinguished sharply between behavior permissible toward Jews and that toward non-Jews. While the treatment of coreligionists was governed by an early capitalist *"Bürger"* spirit, practically anything was allowed, even encouraged, in the case of outsiders.[15]

Sombart saw the most significant feature of the Jewish "foreign law" (*Fremdenrecht*) as the permission to collect interest on loans, which Jewish law forbade in dealings among Jews.[16] Thus did the Jews become the usurers of the medieval world. The importance of this profession for the development from early to high capitalism was enormous, for it occurred, as Sombart pointedly remarked in a later chapter, "in a time when natural economic relationships, standing under the category of quality, still ruled everywhere."[17] In such an environment, Jewish moneylenders served as a "drill school" for the inculcation of a high capitalist mentality:

> In moneylending, all quality is completely extinguished and the economic process is determined exclusively by quantity. In moneylending, the contractual side of business has become the essential: negotiating over service and counterservice, promise for the future, the idea of delivery, form its content. In moneylending, everything to do with sustenance has vanished. In moneylending, everything physical (technical) has been definitively wiped out: the economic act has taken on a purely mental character. In moneylending, economic activity as such has lost all meaning: activity with moneylending has altogether ceased to be a meaningful activation of the body or the mind; thereby its value has been torn from itself into its result; the result alone still has meaning. Moneylending is an especially fruitful field for the development of accounting skills [*Rechenhaftigkeit*]; a man actually sits out his whole life with pen and paper at a table. In moneylending appears quite clearly for the first time the possibility of earning money without one's own sweat, through economic dealing. Quite clearly appears the further possibility: to make other people work for one without acts of violence. What the professional moneylender, the usurer, *lacks* . . . is the spirit of enterprise, daring.[18]

In general, quite apart from such specific phenomena as moneylending, the separate code for "outsiders" had two major effects on the Jews' mentality. The ruthlessness of dealings with non-Jews led to an over-all weakening of business morality.[19] And it also led to the conception of free trade, in which a new, completely amoral code wiped out any notion of a just price, of strictures against advertising, of guild regulation and monopoly.[20] Thus, the "earthshaking changes" which led into the age of high capitalism, conceivable only with the disappearance of all Christian moral restraints, "are to be brought in harmony with one ethic alone: the Jewish."[21]

Sombart was by no means willing to place the entire responsibility for the development of high capitalism at the feet of the Jews. I have already mentioned the great importance for him of biological characteristics, which determined the extent to which any people was *capable* of a capitalist development. In addition to this qualification, he devoted approximately the last quarter of *Der Bourgeois* to an exposition of the social conditions necessary for the growth of the capitalist mentality. An examination of this section, however, reveals that, first, these had the character of conditions and not causes; second, many of them were related only to the emergence of an *early* capitalist mentality; third, of those which did affect the emergence of a high-capitalist economic ethic, two of the most important, moneylending and migrations, were again closely connected with the Jews,* fourth, the type of high capitalist Sombart was trying, in part, to explain remained essentially that which the Jewish "foreign law" had produced; and finally, once again, the entrepreneurial side of the development was not qualitatively changed by any of these conditions, as was the *Bürgergeist*, but was simply brought more closely into the framework of economic life (as when Sombart says, "The new form of commodity production, as it is conditioned by the new technique, *enables* the activation of the entrepreneurial spirit.").[22] Nevertheless, for one facet of the high capitalist spirit Sombart gave prime responsibility, not to the Jews, but to the "feedback" effect of what the capitalist spirit had created. The technology and methods of capitalism itself were the cause of that objectification of the capitalist spirit which for Sombart was one

---

* Sombart also explains the connection of Protestantism with capitalism as a result of the forced migration of persecuted sects, a point which Weber refuted in the notes to the final version of his own work on the subject. See *The Protestant Ethic and the Spirit of Capitalism*, Talcott Parsons, trans. (New York, 1948), p. 190.

of the most unpleasant aspects of his subject: the transformation of the business from a means of sustenance to an end in itself, with no limits to its striving for growth and profit.[23]

Despite Sombart's disclaimer, however, the original and most active ingredient in Sombart's high capitalist spirit was still the "foreign law" ethic of Judaism. And this function of the Jews had great significance not only for Sombart's historical scheme, but for his value structure as well.

22

Sombart's Values and *Der Bourgeois*
The Hero and the Merchant

SINCE THE ENTREPRENEUR represents the union of will and force, while the Bürger symbolizes a rational decomposition of quality into quantity, Sombart identifies with the spirit of enterprise, but detests the spirit of the *Bürger*. Since he sees the entrepreneur as originating in the military or landed aristocracy, while the *Bürger* has his origins in the middle-class man of *Ressentiment*, Sombart identifies more strongly than ever with the aristocracy and despises the middle class. Since he finds the Germanic peoples the most disposed for enterprise, and the Jews, by race and religion, the most disposed for trade, he identifies with Germany and despises the Jews. Since early capitalism is characterized by the predominance of the Nordic entrepreneurial spirit, and high capitalism by that of the Jewish trader spirit, the past, both pre- and early capitalist, has his sympathy, and the present his hatred.

Insofar as he is antiprogressist, he continues a trend which was explicit in 1907. But whereas then his hostility to progress was emotional, and a year later ("Karl Marx und die Sozialwissenschaft") it was methodological, now it is a philosophy of history.

A composite picture of these traits shows us that in *Der Bourgeois* Sombart favors and closely associates aggressive enterprise, the aristocracy, Germany, and the past, while he abhors trade, the middle class, the Jews, and the present. If we consider that all of the things Sombart favors are associated with permanence and a more or less natural order of things, while all the things he condemns are associated with change and artificiality, we can see the deeply conservative character that his thought has assumed. True, one might have said the same of his ideas from 1902 on, when the values of *Gemeinschaft* came to dominate his outlook, but the great contribution of Tönnies' *Gemeinschaft* theory was to show clearly that the past was irretrievably lost. Since in Sombart's present *Weltanschauung*, the German nation represents the spirit of the "heroic" past, and the major guilt for the "trading" present has been shifted to the Jews, his new reactionary philosophy has dangerously activist implications.

We may infer Sombart's admiration for the entrepreneur, as a man of will and force, from his description of the entrepreneur's precapitalist ancestors, the warlords:

> There we see the classically pure type of a warrior enterprise, which is free from all profit-seeking. The necessary presupposition for it is . . . that the "heroic age" in the development of a people should have already begun, i.e., that strong men desirous of "enterprise" should have separated themselves from the great mass of the indolent, and should now be in a position to impose their will on the others. For this differentiation between leader and led . . . between subject and object, between spirit and body, makes the life element of any enterprise.[1]

In the early capitalist era, the freebooter becomes the link between the warlord and the capitalist entrepreneur. Sombart's description again shows his value bias:

> They are conquerors of very great caliber, abounding in power, adventurous, accustomed to victory, brutal, avaricious.

... These genial and ruthless sea robbers ... men in whom an adventurous fantasy is joined to the greatest energy; men of complete romanticism and yet with a sharp eye for reality; men who today command a pirate fleet and tomorrow administer a high office in the state, who today dig for treasures with a covetous hand and tomorrow begin to write a history of the world; men with passionate joy in life, with strong sense for splendor and luxury and yet in a position to bear for months the deprivations of a long sea journey into the unknown; men with the highest capacities for organization and full of childish superstition. In a word, Renaissance men.[2]

Sombart's dislike for the *Bürger* type and its reduction of quality to quantity should be clear from his characterization of the moneylender. Moreover, even in the early capitalist stage, Catholicism could only create the *Bürger* by breaking every bone in the body of natural man, a creature for whom Sombart did, after all, have a certain affection.

In view of the strong participation of the nobility in freebooting, which was often an international outlet for a martial impulse that Renaissance princes sought to suffocate within their borders,[3] Sombart's general identification of the original capitalist entrepreneur with the nobility was logical, if nothing else. His acceptance of a biological distinction between nobility and third estate, however, together with his conviction that low blood alone could produce the *Bürger*, led him into a remarkably circular argument concerning the origins of the Florentine *Bürger* type.

Florence, as I have noted, was to Sombart one of the seedbeds of the *Bürgergeist*. One reason, he argued, was that the nobility, which had German blood in its veins, and which gave the city its early warlike character in the thirteenth century, was forced out of power, expelled, and killed off by the middle class (Greek and Etruscan stock). This explanation is, however, only a partial truth for Sombart. He went on to theorize that even to the extent that the nobility remained and intermarried with the middle class, it was destroyed owing to the "law whereby in the mixing of seigneurial and common blood, the latter proves itself the stronger." As evidence for the existence of this law, Sombart cited his favorite Florentine source, Leon Battista Alberti. The Albertis were in early generations a noble family of German origin famous throughout Tuscany for its military enterprises. Forced in the thirteenth century by the loss of their party (presumably the Ghibellines) to move into the city of Florence, their descendants soon took up middle-class professions, and one of them, Leon Battista, wrote a book which anticipated the bourgeois Philistinism of Benjamin Franklin by four centuries:

> What streams of peddler blood must have flown into the noble blood of this noble family before such a thing could have happened. In Leon Battista himself, we can show this "*Verpantschung*" on good authority. *He was born out of wedlock in Venice* [Sombart's emphasis]. Thus a completely *bürgerliche* woman with merchant blood in her veins from God knows what stock must have been his mother.[4]

"Must have been," because of a Gresham's law of blood-mixing, which had as its sole supporting evidence the unknown, but to Sombart incontestably middle-class, mother of Leon Battista Alberti.[*]

Apart from the inferior blood that Sombart was convinced filled the veins of commoners, he attributed to them one particularly unsavory psychological trait: *Ressentiment*. Applying this label of Nietzsche and Scheler to the *Bürger*, Sombart saw him as filled with a "comical and childish hatred against the *Signori* . . . from whose ranks he was excluded . . . against the seigneurial pleasures of the hunt, against the morality of the followers [*Klientelei*]." Thus, Sombart saw in *Ressentiment* and the hostile reversal of all noble values that flowed from it "perhaps the strongest motive" for the bourgeois virtues he had earlier traced to Thomism.

This rigid, biological distinction between the spirits of *Bürger* and entrepreneur enabled Sombart to overcome his estrangement from modern German society. For the Germans, together with the other European peoples whose aptitude for bold enterprise was

[*] For a sharp criticism of Sombart's effort to establish Alberti's ethic as indistinguishable from the middle-class business ethic of the seventeenth and eighteenth centuries (as epitomized in Benjamin Franklin), see Weber, *Protestant Ethic*, pp. 194–97.

great, were now absolved from the sin of commercialism: they were *Heldenvölker*—hero-nations—while only alien races, such as the Jews, the Scots, and the Florentines, bore the stigma of *Händlervölker*—merchant nations.[5]

Finally, within this framework of *Heldenvölker* and *Händlervölker*, Sombart's hostility to progress, an emotional bias in 1907, a methodological precept in 1908, became in 1913 a philosophy of history. The Europe-wide predominance of the spirit of daring and enterprise was characteristic of the early capitalist period,[6] but in the high capitalist epoch, heroism had slowly vanished, to be replaced by the mean visage of the trader.[7] Whether this was to be explained by reference, ultimately, to the evil genius of the Jews, or to the feedback effects of capitalism itself, Sombart's scorn for life in the postheroic age was unmistakable.

In his characterization of modern economic man, he saw the primary contrast with the older bourgeois type in the shifting of concern from "the living man" as the measure of all things, to the abstractions "profit" and "business." Corresponding to the infinite needs of the Business was the infinite expenditure of economic energy required to satisfy those needs.

> With this goal [the welfare of the business] . . . the end-point of the striving of an entrepreneur is pushed into infinity. Earlier, incomes were limited by custom, but this natural limit no longer applies either to the accumulation of profit or the prospering of a business. At no point, no matter how far off, can the total profit rise so high that one could say: it is enough.[8]

Sombart compared the mentality that arose from such conditions, fixated on giant figures in production and sales, to the child's. But it was no longer the romantic child, the *Kindheitsmensch* of Carl Hauptmann, or even the natural child that Sombart himself had used as a point of comparison in *Das Proletariat*. Even the child had lost his charm. The four ideals by which Sombart now identified him were visual magnitude (*sinnliche Grösse*), fast movement, newness, and the feeling of power. Idealization of modern technical advances, based as they were in the childish lust for the new and the quick, was thus unworthy of "a really great generation [*Geschlecht*], which struggles with the great problems of the human soul." And with the striving for unlimited profit came a Pandora's box of social disasters: advertising to entice customers from other dealers, price-cutting, total unscrupulousness. Furthermore, the virtues of the *Bürger* were transplanted from the person to the business: "They have ceased to be qualities of living men and have instead become objective principles of administration [*Wirtschaftsführung*]." For instance, where once a father built the principle of diligence into his son by constant admonition and example, now "the tempo of industry decides over his own tempo. He can no more be lazy than a worker at a machine," and the same objectification holds true for thrift and "solidity."[9]

The full force of Sombart's antipathy to the effects of modern technology on the spirit of man only appears in the chapter devoted to "Die Technik" itself. With melancholy contempt, Sombart writes:

> To the great advances of technology, we owe yet another characteristic of the spirit of our time: the heavy overvaluing of material things. We have quickly become rich, we have accustomed ourselves to peace, technology has brought security from plague and cholera: no wonder that the lower instincts in man, his delight in unhindered pleasure, his sense for comfort and good living, have stifled every ideal impulse. The herd grazes peacefully on the fertile meadow.[10]

And in Sombart's concluding words on the direct social effects of modern technology, we find a number of familiar phrases that have branded the objects of his desire and aversion for a decade:

> The natural, living world is beaten into ruins, so that on these ruins an artful world made of human inventiveness and dead matter may be raised: it is valid for both economy and technology. And, most undoubtedly, this shift in technical methods has substantially influenced the shift in our whole evaluation of the world. To the degree that technology pushed man from the center of the economic process, man vanished from the center of economic as of general cultural valuation.[11]

The extent to which Sombart's loves and hates determined important theses in *Der Bourgeois* is difficult to assess. On the one hand, it seems likely that his acceptance of a racial distinction of *Helden-* and *Händlervölker* resulted to a large degree from his desire to shift the blame for high capitalism onto the Jews. The categories of this theory were certainly flexible enough, for when the First World War broke out, Sombart blithely purged the English from the ranks of the hero-nations. Ignoring the Jews, he made England the very symbol of a *Händlervolk* and the chief antagonist of the manly German *Heldenvolk*.[12] On the other hand, major sections of the work cannot be dismissed without more serious argument: the distinction of entrepreneur and *Bürger*; the characterizations of early and high capitalism; the significance of Catholicism for the development of the *Bürger* type.*

In any case, apart from the close definition of the capitalist spirit, which made his work of 1913 the climactic volume of *Der Moderne Kapitalismus*, the underlying value structure of *Der Bourgeois* represented an integral stage in Sombart's evolving personal *Weltanschauung*. His glorification of the heroic will had now found an object worthy of honor: the entrepreneur, who still lived on in a part of capitalism and, most importantly, in the German nation. The sharp distinction between *Gemeinschaft* and *Gesellschaft*, and the adherence to *Gemeinschaft* values, which had served as the framework for Sombart's turning away from the productivity ideals of industrial capitalism, and for his reversion to the patriarchal outlook of the older school of economists, had finally been overshadowed by that aggressive voluntarism, that joy in struggle, which he had first proclaimed in 1896.

On the last page of *Der Bourgeois*, Sombart prophesied with eerie accuracy the course that both his own thought and the spirit of German hero-enterprise, yoked though it may have been to capitalist commercialism, were to take.

> What will happen, once the capitalist spirit will have ceased to possess its present elasticity, does not concern us here. Perhaps once the giant is blind, he will be trained to draw a democratic culture-cart. Perhaps also it will be the Twilight of the Gods. The gold will be given back to the Rhine.

* For an excellent commentary, see Max Scheler's "Der Bourgeois und die religiosen Mächte," in his *Umsturz der Werte* (Bern, 1955), pp. 362–81.

Sombart here anticipated what he and others like him would see in the Weimar Republic as well as what they would revere in the Nazi movement; for the latter would signify to many of its intellectually inclined followers the forces of anti-Mammon, the returners of the gold that has corrupted mankind. Indeed, in his love for aggressive enterprise, aristocracy, Germany, and the past, and his abhorrence for trade, the middle class, the Jews, and the present, we find the raw materials of a mood common to many middle-class Germans in the early 1930s.

Sombart's clearest anticipation of that mood was his brief *Händler und Helden*, which, appearing in 1915, used against England the same invidious comparisons that he used against the Jews before and after the Great War.[13] The idea of "hero-nations" and "trading-nations" reappeared, of course, but in a considerably less subtle form.

The opposition of *Held* and *Händler* was expanded to the fundamental opposition between Germany and all the degenerative Western ideals that sprang from the French Revolution, including both capitalism and socialism.* The hero-nations, and the spirit of enterprise that they had represented in *Der Bourgeois*, were absolutely divorced from capitalism, which was made identical with the merchant spirit. The prophet of industrial utilitarianism for the merchant nation was Herbert Spencer. War for the English was a capitalist enterprise; for the Germans it was a last defense against the onslaught of commercialism on the soul of modern man.

Before the war, Germany too had been in the thrall of this evil spirit.

> Everything that we did seemed to have become meaningless. We heaped riches on riches, though we knew that no blessing flowed from them. We created wonders of technique, and did not know why. We played politics, feuded, and dirtied ourselves: Why? We wrote and read newspapers; mountains of paper towered before us daily and suffocated us with worthless news and worthless opinion: no one knew what for. We

---

* Werner Sombart, *Händler und Helden* (Munich and Leipzig, 1915), pp. 4–5, 55, 113, 116. An exception is allowed for the early "heroic" generation of European and Russian revolutionaries (p. 111).

wrote books and plays and hordes of critics did nothing their whole lives but criticize, and cliques formed and feuded: and no one knew what for. We enthused for "progress," for the furtherance of meaningless life: more wealth, more records, more advertising, more papers, more books, more plays, more education, more technology, more comfort. And the thoughtful had to ask ever again: What for, what for? Life had really . . . become a treadmill. A life without ideals . . . a rotting, a stench, when all mankind was entering a state of corruption from which idealism had vanished, like a body whose soul had departed.[14]

The response of the German nation to the war had ended this "*Kulturpessimismus.*" The old German hero-spirit, whose embers had been concealed, but not extinguished, by the ashes of prewar German culture, was flaming forth anew. In this consuming spiritual fire, all petty differences were being burned away and "we have placed ourselves, all purified and, so to speak, newborn, in the service of the totality."[15] It had taken the war to spread an "idealistic *Weltanschauung*" through the nation and to make easily understandable to every German "the idea of the state *Gemeinschaft*, to which he is associated as a serving member."

This idealization of *Gemeinschaft* was, of course, altogether different from Tönnies' conception. If there had still been a trace of Tönnies' influence in *Der Bourgeois*, in *Händler und Helden* it was finally eliminated; in his work of 1915, Sombart wrote of *Gemeinschaft* in the transcendent terms of German romanticism:

> The *conviction* that we are called on to live and die for this totality which lives over us, which is *there*, even without us and against our will, that only its life is genuine life, because it is a life in God and in the spirit: this moral consciousness forms the content of the fatherland idea and has nothing to do with the sentimental adherence to homeland and soil.

Starting from the twisted idealism of the state *Gemeinschaft*, Sombart established an imperialist mission for Germany which was not without similarities to that of the Nazis before 1940. This mission, Sombart wrote, was the reverse of the English ideal of empire.

The English tried to impose their own civilization and cultural ideals on barbarian peoples. They could probably do this because their ideal was the merchant and, Sombart argued, it was no great feat to make a man into a merchant. But German civilization could not be so easily transplanted to other peoples, for its ideal was heroism and "heroism cannot be installed like gas pipes just anywhere on earth."[16] Thus, the German imperialist mission is not that of commercial expansion or of granting the blessings of German culture to other peoples, but of obtaining living space for the German state:

> We want to be and remain a strong German nation and thus a strong German state, and thus also to grow in the limits of the organic. And if it is necessary that we expand our territory so that the larger national body should receive space for its development, we shall take as much land for ourselves as appears necessary. We shall also set foot anywhere that it seems necessary for us to do so from strategic grounds for the preservation of our untouchable power. We shall therefore, if it behooves our power position on earth, perhaps establish naval stations in Dover, Malta, or Suez.[17]

But all this has, of course, nothing to do with expansion for its own sake. For Germany's true mission is an internal one: the development of a pure German spirit, a "heroic *Weltanschauung*," the preservation of Germany as "the last dam against the muddy flood of commercialism."[18]

The sequence of historical experiences that characterized German history for the postwar period—humiliating peace, inflation, and depression—produced, in the mass of Sombart's lower-middle-class compatriots, the same mood of primitive exultation that we find in *Händler und Helden*: the atavistic glorification of a heroic national community (*Volksgemeinschaft*). One might say that the fierce atomization of bourgeois existence, coming about as rapidly as it did in late nineteenth-century Germany, and without any concomitant and counteracting sense of belonging to a political class that was a power in society, bred a longing for the former closed, secure, noncommercial social condition (roughly, *Gemeinschaft*), and that this longing, when catalyzed by the catastrophic events of 1918–30, led to widespread acceptance of what Fritz Stern has aptly called "the politics of cultural despair": the rejection of all the values of "enlightened" Western civilization, the reversion to a quest for a harmonious union of the nation *against* all outsiders.

It was only to be expected that this quest for *Gemeinschaft* should twist the actual sociological significance of the term as established by Tönnies out of recognition. Tönnies was, of course, correct in asserting that the epoch of *Gemeinschaft* was closed. The ideal pursued by Sombart and his postwar compatriots was a myth rooted in resentment of the new commercial world by individuals trapped within it, fear of isolation in this world, and desire to overcome the feeling of social impotence by submerging one's useless individuality in a total order. And all of these roots characterize the twentieth-century myth of the state community as an illness of bourgeois society itself, which only the diseased mind produced by that society could view as a solution to all its problems.

Thus, Sombart's achievement must be viewed in the context of German social and political history as well as of his own personal development. If this study has consistently stressed the personal development—Sombart's relation to his family and friends and the growing voluntarist emphasis in his analysis of society which is probably a by-product of this relationship—there can be little doubt that the uninspiring Philistinism of bourgeois life and the bureaucratization of socialism formed the "objective conditions" within which Sombart's fevered groping toward a heroic *Weltanschauung* occurred. In brief, Sombart's special sensitivity to the spiritual malaise of the German bourgeoisie, and his total disillusionment with the regenerative power of socialism, led him to a proto-fascist mentality two decades before the collapse of the bourgeois economic order spread such an attitude among the masses of his compatriots.

PART IV

Robert Michels (1875–1936)

Petermann had no understanding for the brown-shirt, but when he inveighed against the bosses, the old shopkeeper felt secretly good. When you heard the speeches and saw the faces of the Secretaries and Deputies there was nothing left of the old fighting spirit, and instead of pouring fire into hearts as they once did, they now drew statistics from their pockets and read them out. Petermann often looked at the portrait of Bebel. "What they have made of your cause, August . . . offices, nothing but offices"; he sighed, and thought with great sadness of the pride and defiance of the May Days in the nineties.

ERNST GLAESER, *Der Letzte Zivilist*

23

Introduction

The Iron Law
and Its Legislator

THE ONLY ONE of Robert Michels' major works still in print is his *Zur Soziologie des Parteiwesens in der modernen Demokratie*, published originally in 1911, and, within four years after, translated into French, Italian, and English (*Political Parties*). The author summarizes his argument in a section titled "The Oligarchical Tendencies of Organization":

> The fundamental sociological law of political parties (the term "political" being here used in its most comprehensive sense) may be formulated in the following terms: "It is organization which gives birth to the dominion of the elected over the electors, of the mandataries over the mandators, of the delegates over the delegators. Who says organization, says oligarchy.[1]

Michels terms this law the "psychology of organization itself," and he mentions two secondary psychological principles that harmonize with it: "the tendency of the leaders to organize themselves and to consolidate their interests," and "the gratitude of the led toward the leaders, and the general immobility and passivity of the masses."

The importance of Michels' thesis in the history of social theory lies not so much in its uniqueness (for others, before Michels, have elaborated the idea of the oligarchical substance of government) as in the living, concrete experience behind its formulation. Michels' logical foundation is sound. His ready familiarity with the theories of bourgeois radicalism and socialism that support his position is obvious. But what convinces, and what Michels intended to be convincing, is the enormous wealth of empirical detail that leads like an arrow to his theoretical conclusion.[2]

Perhaps it is this union of the empirical and the theoretical that raises this work sufficiently high above the large bulk of Michels' writings to merit its stature as a classic and its numerous reprintings. However, the peculiar position of *Political Parties* as the only one on which Michels' fame rests leaves open several problems. Chief of these is that this man, surely one of the most complex social theorists of this century, is known, through the single dimension of this one book, merely as a Machiavellian, or at best, a disillusioned disciple of the Enlightenment. His many articles and essays are buried in obscure periodicals, placing formidable obstacles in the path of a more just analysis. Therefore treatments of him have been rare and usually restrict themselves to his single major work.*

---

* The reasons for this lack of interest vary. For one thing, Michels has been overshadowed by his better-known contemporaries, Sorel, Mosca, and Pareto, all of whom dealt with similar problems and emerged with similar answers. For another, there is a live political problem in the core of Michels' book. For conservatives it confirms long-held beliefs, but they are prone to center their social pessimism in more orthodox elite theorists like Mosca and Burckhardt. Michels' total absorption in European social democracy, even from the standpoint of flaying it alive, makes him, perhaps, suspect in their eyes. Those from the opposite political camp seem not to want to understand him. Conze's treatment (in the recent German edition of *Political Parties*), for instance, turns a theoretical argument into a semantic one, by saying, in effect, that democracy is to be measured by democratic institutions (elections, parliaments, etc.) and since we have all these, it is absurd to say that democracy is impossible. A variation on this approach is John D. May's "Democracy, Organization, Michels," in the *American Political Science Review*, 1965, pp. 417–29. Thus, I have been unable to discover a single book that is exclusively concerned with Michels.

He is treated briefly as a disciple of both Sorel and Mosca in the two works by James Meisel on these men. He rates a chapter in James Burnham's *The Machiavellians* (New York, 1943), but as usual, the author seems to have read only *Political Parties*, and thus disseminates a number of misleading evaluations of his subject. (It is interesting, of course, that Burnham wrote on Michels when he stood in an intellectual position skeptical of democracy very similar to that of his subject.) In H. Stuart Hughes' book, again Michels is discussed only in his relation to Pareto and Mosca. Guenther Roth deals with him primarily as a disciple of Weber in *The Social Democrats in Imperial*

Is this obscurity deserved? Perhaps, if one is looking for lasting contributions to social theory. Apart from the analysis of democracy in his *Political Parties*, Michels has said little of striking importance. But a proper understanding of Michels' intellectual evolution before World War I may be of great importance to the historian of ideas and the sociologist of knowledge, for it casts a brilliant light on one of the central phenomena of thought in the modern epoch: the death of the idea of progress.

Michels' work, in the period up to the end of World War I, may be grouped in three chronological sections. From 1902 to 1905, he wrote as a socialist of broad interests, thoroughly imbued with, and propagating through his writings, ideas of the perfectibility of man, the injustice and coming abolition of war, the rights of women, the immorality of most of the institutions of bourgeois society, the right of every people to national self-determination, and, fundamental to all the rest, the class struggle of the international proletariat as the means of ending the iniquities of society. The assumption, unstated to be sure, seemed to be that there was a natural law, based on the welfare of peoples, which *should be* the foundation of society and therefore—with the help of Michels and the class whose self-liberation was to mean the liberation of mankind—would be.

In the second period, beginning in 1905 and ending in the years 1908–12, Michels, during the course of a prolonged campaign against the opportunist politics of the German Social Democratic party, engaged in a tortuous revaluation of his early beliefs, centering almost exclusively on his view of the proletariat and culminating in *Political Parties*. In place of natural law as his basic presupposition, Michels came to accept historical law as the principle that dominated society. Concomitantly, the sharpness of his social ideals was dulled by moral relativism. What *was* dominated what *should be*.

Germany (Totowa, N.J., 1963). Perhaps the most intensive recent analysis of Michels is the article on him by Juan Linz, in the *International Encyclopedia of the Social Sciences*.

In the final period, Michels wearily turned his back on political strife and settled into the academic vocation. In many of the writings of this time, such as those published in 1914 under the title *Probleme der Sozialphilosophie*, his method of defining his problem is basically historical and descriptive, rather than normative. The clear perception of morality as relative, and of the tendency of social development as hostile to his own personal morality, the acknowledgment that the rational and the moral may be antagonistic, are the characteristics of these writings.

The theses of this section are: (1) certain of Michels' personal values provide a common denominator for the differing, and even opposed, views in these three periods; (2) the great changes that occurred in Robert Michels' thought all were prepared well in advance by subsidiary elements in the thought of previous periods; (3) the intellectual influences to which Michels submitted were accepted only because, in providing a new theoretical framework for his values, they helped him to abandon views that his own experience had shattered; and (4) in the ten-year period from 1900 to 1910, Michels underwent a change from Condorcet-like optimism to a pessimistic rejection of progress and reason characteristic of the totalitarian epoch. In short, he serves as a microcosmic mirror for one of the major developments in Western thought since the eighteenth century.

24

Michels' Youth

The Destruction of the Cologne Patriciate

IN 1930 ROBERT MICHELS devoted a hundred-page essay to the life of his paternal grandfather.[1] From this biography comes information about Cologne and Michels' family tradition—at least as he himself understood it—that has great value for an understanding of his thought. The relevant material from this essay may be grouped under two closely related headings: a French cultural heritage in both the city and the family background; and, also present in both backgrounds, an antimilitarist tradition.

The French tradition rested on three props: geographical proximity, which allowed for much interpenetration of German- and French-speaking people; the Napoleonic epoch, during which, from 1794 to 1814, Cologne was a part of the French Empire; and a social structure that was more French than German in its retention of a large and independent middle class.

Apparently the closeness to the French border resulted in a large influx of French traders as early as the sixteenth century.[2] But the principal French influence came from the Napoleonic epoch. According to Michels, the reverence for Napoleon as a great genius was common in the older generation even in the 1860s and was transferred to the younger generation by such customs as the use of French words for household objects. Indeed, many German words were unknown.[3] Also dating from the Napoleonic era was a considerable cultural flow toward Paris, manifested in the migration of a number of Cologne artists, architects, and musicians, among whom Jacques Offenbach is perhaps the best known, to the French capital in the first half of the nineteenth century. Further, the Cologne jurist Daniels was one of the leading figures in the preparation of the Napoleonic Code.[4]

The social and class structure of the city probably strengthened these Gallic cultural bonds, since it seems to have been more characteristic of France than of Germany. The basic difference between the two countries, at least for the century prior to World War II, was the survival in France of a huge precapitalist middle class of merchants and artisans, which coexisted peaceably with the development of a highly concentrated heavy industrial sector that seemed in no way inclined to destroy the "*petits.*"[5] The reasons for this strange reluctance of the large firms to wipe out their smaller competitors, unparalleled in any of the other advanced industrial countries, and especially in Germany, are too complex to discuss here, but there can be little doubt that an important factor was the firm tradition of Catholic patriarchalism that prevailed, among the wealthy entrepreneurs as well as the little men, in business conduct; the vision of one's business as a family inheritance, not to be risked in dangerous speculation, but rather to be used as the means for the accumulation of a "safe" fortune, adequate for an early retirement, and then to be handed down intact to the next generation: in short, the stubborn resistance to any "capitalist spirit" that might dictate accumulation for its own sake.[6] The similarity of the Cologne economic and social structure to the French model is implied in Michels' description of his native city as a place "where the middle layers withstood the accumulation tendency of the machine age better than elsewhere,"[7] and is even more clearly indicated in a passage cited by Michels from a history of Cologne written in 1916:

> Characteristic of the Cologne economic development, as opposed to the general tendency in Germany, is the fact that, though the smallest concerns are declining (their complete disappearance even so is excluded), the medium-sized concerns have developed very powerfully, and show absolutely no sign of being devoured by big business. In other words,

next to the great enterprise, a powerful middle class still maintains itself successfully.[8]

Although the relative economic aggressiveness of the middle layers in relation to the smaller firms distorts the similarity to France, the general character remains closer to France than to the rest of Germany. And in any case, the apparent economic traditionalism of the Catholic patriciate is what is most relevant, since this is the class into which Michels was born, and which, until the Franco-Prussian War at any rate, seemed particularly close culturally to France.

The Michels family had good reason to feel pro-French. The Continental blockade had made the family fortune, through Robert Michels' great-grandfather: he was in the wool trade and in the years that English competition disappeared, business soared.[9] This gentleman's son, Peter Michels (Robert's grandfather), was born a French citizen in 1801; he spoke and wrote French as well as German,[10] and married a woman of mixed French-and-Flemish descent, Constance van Halens, whose native tongue was French.

Three aspects of Peter Michels' life are particularly interesting in light of his grandson's career: his political activities before 1848, his social idealism in the years after '48, and some of his personal moral and political attitudes.

Before 1848 the older Michels was a member of the Cologne chamber of commerce. According to Michels, the goal of the men in this trade group was "the struggle against the absolutist Prussian bureaucratism, which wanted to curtail the rights of this old French institution, and to subject it to the regime . . . in order to reduce it to complete insignificance."[11]

This position seems to have been retained by Peter Michels well into his later years, when he is portrayed as sharing an antipathy for Prussia widespread in the Rhineland at the outbreak of the Austro-Prussian War.[12]

In the years after 1848, however, Peter Michels' political activity dwindled as he became involved in the nonpolitical Catholic journeyman's movement. Peter Michels had always run his business by patriarchal principles. His salesmen lived in his house and ate at his table. He took pride in his business honesty, opposed any kind of speculation, and was satisfied with a modest profit. In the period after 1848, at the same time that Prussian hegemony seemed unalterably firm, the precipitous decline of the guilds presented Peter Michels with a new challenge: the preservation of the way of life he held dear. Although, as a result of the continued survival of small and especially medium-sized concerns in Cologne, the journeyman in the third quarter of the nineteenth century "was in no sense a mere survival from the past," he was being sundered from his traditional living community with his employer by rationalization of the work process and rising real-estate prices which made the living together of master and journeyman uneconomical. Under the influence of Eduard Kolping, Peter Michels helped to establish a Catholic journeymen's association whose goal was "the reawakening of pleasure in one's profession," and through that the fashioning of a counterweight "against the tendencies of the large factory, against capitalism and socialism." It appears that some sort of cooperative living quarters were established for unmarried or traveling journeymen, where perhaps they could also meet socially with their masters.[13]

Noteworthy in this picture of the elder Michels' social and business ethic are the traditionalism on the one hand and the interest in work for its own sake on the other. It is interesting to note that Max Weber also had a merchant grandfather who served him as the model for a traditional, early capitalist existence distinct from, and even opposed to, the demonic creature serving the capitalist spirit.[14] Both of those analysts of bureaucracy and capitalist society, then, may well have approached these phenomena on the basis of this same early patriarchal image, whose force we have already noted in the work of Tönnies and Sombart.

Other elements in the background of Cologne and the Michels family probably influenced Michels' intellectual development. Most important was the antimilitarist spirit that went hand in hand with the businesslike character of a trading patriciate and its history of resistance to Prussian domination.[15] In 1870 the letters of Peter Michels to his son Julius revealed "honest and unconcealed fear" before the prospect of war, despite the fact that the war would certainly be good for his textile business. Peter's words to his son were "filled with genuine pacifist spirit."[16] In 1880 the four-year-old Robert Michels found a box of wooden soldiers representing the Prussian and Austrian armies in his grandmother's storeroom, and was informed by his aunts that such playthings were wicked and had been hidden on that account. "That was the mood which, some fourteen years after the end of the '66 war, still ruled in the house of Michels."[17]

Altruism was another quality of the old man noted by his grandson. In a letter to his wife written in 1864, we read, "In my life, I have found that the greatest egoism, the greatest happiness that one is capable of providing oneself, consists in making *others* happy."[18]

Yet another noteworthy characteristic, and one easily understood in view of the family's cosmopolitan background, was an apparent lack of any feeling of racial or national superiority. Peter Michels described the workers on a Polish property he had acquired for sheep-breeding as "honest, diligent people. When you see them work, our wage-earners look like loafers and idlers."[19] His wife is alleged to be equally free of any feelings of national hatred. Their grandson explains a momentary lapse into Italophobia at the time of the Austro-Prussian War by the fact that the Italians had just destroyed the papal dominion and separated Church and state in the new nation, which outraged the old woman's strong Catholic faith.[20] But in general, the frequent presence of Italian terms of endearment and sayings in her letters to Peter Michels belie any cultural hostility to Italy.[21]

This whole little world of the Catholic, cosmopolitan, pacifistic, anti-Prussian Cologne patriciate was crumbling at the time of Robert Michels' birth in 1876. The origin of the decay seems to have been both political and religious: on the one hand, the crushing of the local liberal bourgeoisie in the aftermath of 1848, on the other, the gradual dominance in the upper-middle class of Protestants whose whole way of life was opposed, in the Weberian sense, to their Catholic counterparts.

The growing power of Prussia after 1848 is perhaps the more important element. Robert Michels sees the Prussian social psychology as founded on the outlook of the bureaucracy, the military, and the landed nobility. There was no manufacturing element except for Huguenot emigrants, always somewhat alien, and trade was largely in the hands of the despised Jews. In Cologne, on the other hand, it was the patrician-patriarchal bourgeoisie that put its stamp on the area's social outlook. "Powerful, self-conscious,[22] and convinced of its cultural superiority," the cheerful, bantering upper-middle class held the military in low esteem and was particularly uncomfortable in the presence of the "domineering" and "arrogant" Prussians. But gradually, through the military spirit engendered by universal military service and the war of 1866, the Prussian outlook came to dominate social life on the Rhine too. From being a city where, in 1799, Michels' great-grandfather was almost prevented from marrying into a goldsmith's family because he was the son of the lowly commander of the harbor artillery, Cologne became a place where it was considered "improper" and "socially unacceptable" for a reserve officer of the Prussian army, in his civilian life, to stand behind a counter and serve customers. In time, a command of the military authorities even made this taboo official.[23]

Robert Michels was born into this declining patriciate in 1876, but as we have noted, hostility to the military was still strong in his childhood. Other aspects of the older way of life must also have been present. His mother, for instance, was a granddaughter of another member of the pro-French chamber of commerce of 1833 (which also included Peter Michels), and she taught him the three R's until he was nine, when he left home to attend a "Franco-Gallic" *Gymnasium* in Berlin.[24]

This sudden shift in locale at the age of nine was the beginning of a marked geographic mobility that was to characterize the whole of Michels' life, and especially the schooling years from 1885 to 1900. After three years in Berlin, he transferred to an Eisenach *Gymnasium,* left that before receiving his diploma (*Reifezeugnis*) to join a regiment in Weimar, after a year in the army spent some months in England, studied in Paris, Munich, Leipzig, and Halle, in that order (picking up his *Reifezeugnis* at some point during these years), and finally obtained his doctorate in Halle in his twenty-fourth year (1900).[25] During that same year he married Gisela Lindner, daughter of a Halle history professor with whom he had studied, moved to Turin, and there joined the Italian Socialist party.[26]

Michels' motives in joining the forces of subversion are difficult to establish, since he never discussed them explicitly in any of his published works. But by piecing together some of the general things he did later say about the motives and costs of adhesion to socialism for a bourgeois, and also using our knowledge of his background and of the kind of ideology he displayed in his earliest socialist writings, we can hazard an informed guess.

For one thing, the decision must have been painful:

> The wealthier the family to which the bourgeois belongs, the more strongly it is attached to its family traditions, the higher the social position that it occupies, the more difficult is it for him, and the more painful, to break with his surroundings and to adhere to the labor movement. . . . As soon as he displays the intention of becoming an active member of the Socialist party, of undertaking public work on its behalf, of enrolling himself as an actual member of the "rebel" army, the deserter from the [upper] bourgeoisie is regarded by his own class as either a knave or a fool. His social prestige falls below zero, and so great is the hostility displayed towards him that he is obliged to break off all relations with his family. The most intimate ties are abruptly severed. His relatives turn their backs upon him. He has burned his boats and broken with the past.[27]

Thus, the circumstances attending the decision to convert to the new faith steels the conviction of the novice:

> The violent internal and external struggles, the days of bitterness and the nights without sleep during which his socialist faith has ripened, have combined to produce in the socialist of bourgeois origin, especially if he be derived from the higher circles of the bourgeoisie, an ardor and a tenacity which are rarely encountered among proletarian socialists.[28]

The force that compels the proletariat to turn to socialism is economic necessity; but among the bourgeois renegades, it will be idealism, which may be either of two types, scientific or sentimental.

There is good reason to believe that Michels saw his own motivation as being more of the sentimental than of the scientific variety. Not only did he associate the sentimental motive with youth and the scientific with maturity, but another, much more important dichotomy leads to our ascribing the sentimental motive to Michels: an egoistic-altruistic dichotomy. On the one hand,

> The stimulus which drives [the man of science] is idealistic in this sense, that he is capable of sacrificing all other goods to science and its gains. In thus acting, he obeys the powerful impulse of his egoism, though it is an egoism ennobled. Scientific coherency is an inborn need of his nature. Psychology teaches us that in human beings every free exercise of faculty produces a sentiment of pleasure. Consequently the sacrifices which the socialist man of science makes for the party serve to increase the sum of his personal satisfaction.[29]

On the other hand, for "those who are inspired with an intense sentimental attachment to socialism," the motives are "a noble disdain for injustice and a love for the weak and the poor, a delight in self-sacrifice [N.B.] for the realization of great ideas."[30]

This dichotomy of egoistic versus unselfish or self-sacrificing behavior runs throughout Michels' work. Altruistic behavior invariably has a strong attraction for Michels' ethical impulses, already revealed in his laudatory description of Peter Michels' humble equation of egoism with the happiness that stems from making other people happy. It comes through even more clearly in a passage of an early article on Italian rural socialism (1902), where Michels reveals that the basis of his admiration for the proletariat is precisely its capacity of sacrificing for the common good: "Rarely in the history of economic struggles has the proletariat showed itself so self-conscious, but at the same time so self-sacrificing and unselfish."[31] These two factors of self-consciousness and self-sacrifice emerge four years later as a causal sequence in an article criticizing the German Social Democratic leadership's faint-hearted fear for the party treasury:

> Only the force conscious of itself is a decisive historical factor. But the preliminary condition for all force conscious of itself

is the spirit of sacrifice. . . . A movement which pursues the emancipation of the working class loses not only its efficacy but its *raison d'etre*, when it begins to weigh sacrifices and to fear them.[32]

It seems likely that in the discovery of these virtues in the proletariat, Michels was really projecting his own idealistic renunciation onto the movement with which he identified.* Certainly, Michels must have seen his devotion to socialism in terms of self-sacrifice for the sake of self-consciousness (that is, consciousness of his historical role as leader and educator of the oppressed). And even more certainly, though he accepted the Marxist formula that traced class conflict to the worker's lack of property in the scheme of production,[33] Michels had a very high opinion of the extent of idealism in the proletarian movement. In an article published in 1904, Michels said that the economic struggle was not an end in itself, but rather was "only supposed to provide the basis for the development of all spiritual and physical powers in common peaceful work in all cultural areas."[34] The innermost desire inspiring the masses, according to Michels, was the wish for the equal participation of all men in the fruits of culture. Providing an oblique confirmation of my hypothesis that in his youth, Michels was projecting his ethical values onto the proletariat, Michels later ascribed to "the socialist enthusiast of bourgeois origin . . . a tendency to overestimate the significance of the moral forces of the movement and sometimes an excessive faith in his own self-abnegation."[35]

Returning to this odd formula of sacrifice and consciousness, we may find another dimension to Michels' motivation if we recall that not only was unselfishness a prime characteristic of Michels' grandfather, but "self-consciousness" was characteristic of the Cologne patriciate as a group.

I have already pointed out that in Michels' school days, the patriarchal local culture of the "self-conscious" upper-middle class was rapidly giving way to the Prussian military ethos. Michels tells

---

* Michels later defended himself against Sombart's charge that he had become a socialist through resentment by asserting that at the time of his adherence, he had been "a young man with the best of hopes, to whom, through birth, rank and marriage, all doors stood open" (*Bedeutende Männer* [Leipzig, 1927] p. 148).

us almost nothing about his father, but we do learn that one of his uncles became an officer. For the author of *Political Parties* this was not an isolated event, but was part of a social pattern—the absorption of the best talents of the bourgeoisie into the machinery of the Prussian state—which he later came to view in terms of his own modification of Pareto's theory of the circulation of elites. In one of his early critiques of German socialism, Michels noted the "alienation" of many sons of the bourgeoisie from their own class. They "assume the thought patterns of their feudal environment."[36] And in a passage of obvious autobiographical significance, published shortly before World War I, he wrote:

> In contemporary Germany, there is no socially independent bourgeoisie, proud of itself. The German bourgeoisie is in its summit only a first step to the nobility. Its highest aspiration is first to be accepted by the nobility, then to enter. That goes above all for the so-called patrician families, which look back on a past which if principally mercantile, is venerable, and can support themselves with considerable means. On the Rhine, the ennobling process has already set in powerfully.[37]

If we hypothesize for a moment the permeation of the young Robert Michels with the spirit of his grandfather's society, then we are forced to ask, Where could he go with his values? The traditional world was dying, and the new one was antagonistic in every respect to the old. With Prussianism sweeping the land and Michels clutching to his soul the old family virtues of cooperative endeavor, devotion to the welfare of others, and proud consciousness of class, conversion to socialism, much as it may have brought down social and family ostracism, nevertheless takes on, in a sense, the very substance of conservatism. To be sure, there is no indication that Michels himself was ever conscious of this transference, and it would be extremely imprudent to forget that what is in question here is not at all a love for the old patriarchal institutions, but rather the involuntary internalization of the psychology, the value scheme that was imbedded in them.

For it is incontestable that a great many of the specific liberal beliefs of the old Cologne society reappeared in the garb of revolutionary doctrine in the early writings of Robert Michels.

The hostility to militarism and war of any sort, indeed a pacifist opposition to any act of violence, was one such belief.[38] The cosmopolitanism of the family tradition merged with the proletarian internationalism of the young socialist to form another. At the same time, united in a state of tension with the pacifism and internationalism was a liberal insistence on the right of all nations to self-determination. Michels most clearly reveals this tense union in the following lines written in 1904:

> In short, socialism recognizes that there are natural differences between peoples, and, though it wants to take from the earth the arbitrary diplomatic boundary divisions, it is still quite clear about the continued survival of speech and racial boundaries as far as such exist in sharply delimited form. But it does not recognize that these natural racial differences must lead to mutual hatred and homicidal blood-spilling, and wants that every people and every tribe should have the inalienable right to determine its adherence to this or that land according to its own free judgment, and therefore looks with disgust on all . . . germanization of the world.[39]

The relationship of these elements to one another, since their compatibility was maintained only by Michels' faith in the proletariat's ethical powers to handle all three without contradiction, serves as a useful guide precisely to this faith of Michels' in the proletariat.

Another very characteristic element in Michels' early credo was a strong pro-French and pro-Italian bias, which equally bespoke no revolutionary rupture with his family heritage. The young scholar lived in Italy from 1900 to 1901. In 1900 he helped found a small art magazine, *La Commedia*, in Turin. Several of his earliest articles glorify the Italian proletariat. His first major scholarly work was a study of Italian socialism in the *Archiv für Sozialwissenschaft* (1905 and 1906) in which he favorably compared the Italian movement to the German (1906, pp. 12–14). Michels' French sympathies are revealed in his adherence to the *Mouvement Socialiste* group from 1904 on, in his selecting Louis Blanc's national workshop idea as the subject of his first historical study in nineteenth-century socialism (in *Ethische Kultur* for 1903), in his assertion, at one point in his quixotic struggle with the German socialist bureaucracy, that the French party had replaced the German as the international socialist model,[40] and in the poverty of references to German theorists compared with the long list of French social theorists to whom he acknowledges his indebtedness in the very important "Oligarchischen Tendenzen der Gesellschaft": Rousseau, Tocqueville, Proudhon, Considérant, St.-Simon, Fourier, and Ledru-Rollin. The existence of this Latin alternative in his cultural background and scheme of values very likely hardened his critical attitude toward the authoritarian and chauvinist aspects of German socialism during his years of activity within it.

25

The Path to Syndicalism and Back
1901–1907

MICHELS LEFT GERMANY for Turin in 1900. He came back in 1901, but returned to Italy in 1907. His efforts during those six years to realize his social ideals within the framework of German socialism constitute the major political experience of his life. Indeed, his analysis of what happened in those years is the basis for *Zur Soziologie des Parteiwesens in der modernen Demokratie* (*Political Parties*). Consequently, a sketch of Michels' views and experiences during this period can be of much value in revealing the stages of his disillusionment and developing critique of both democracy and the notion of progress.

Michels returned to Germany around the fall of 1901, in the expectation of being able to teach history at the University of Marburg.¹ His membership in the Socialist party, however, made it impossible for him to do so.* What Michels' sources of income were during the years that followed is difficult to say. He was almost certainly cut off from his family's wealth. His wife may have worked. He did give lectures in Paris and Brussels in 1905 and 1906. But probably his income came largely from the heavy flow of articles that streamed from his pen in the years after his return to Germany,† an output which initially seemed to espouse a quite moderate form of socialism.

Among these articles were two that clearly revealed his bitterness toward the academic profession. A four-page piece in *Das Freie Wort* of February 20, 1902, "Die Voraussetzungslosigkeit der Geschichtswissenschaft auf den deutschen Hochschulen," mocked the claim to impartiality in the academic profession, pointing to the crude nationalism that permitted the professor to advocate the annexation of Holland and Belgium because of their alleged Germanic population but forbade him to suggest that because the Poles were *not* Germanic, the Reich should relinquish its Polish provinces. Michels insisted that by comparison the outlawed socialist approach was "at least as scientific and *certainly much more idealistic*" (emphasis in original). In the following year, Michels published a three-page piece in *Ethische Kultur*, "Kapitalismus in der Wissenschaft." In this stinging, ironical attack the author compared the scholar's field of specialization to capital, which the owner jealously protects. He also accused older scholars of cultivating the toadying

---

* Michels later referred to a "ministerial ordinance" forbidding professors to join the Socialist party under pain of immediate dismissal (MS, 13 [1904], p. 195, and 14 [1905], p. 241). Michels either did not know of this directive or thought that it would only apply to members of the German party, and that his Italian party membership would not affect his academic status. Whatever the case, his exclusion must have been an unexpected and cruel blow. For a discussion of the antisocialist ordinance, see Fritz K. Ringer, *The Decline of the German Mandarins* (Cambridge, 1969), pp. 141–42.

† Michels published close to two hundred articles between 1901 and 1907. Some of the articles that did not appear in *Das Freie Wort* and *Ethische Kultur* are listed in Chapter 25, footnotes 8–12. A complete bibliography of Michels' work may be found in *Studi in memoria di Roberto Michels* (Padova, 1937), R. Universita degli Studi di Perugia, *Annali della Facolta di Giurisprudenza*, pp. 39–76.

of younger scholars to spread their own fame, especially through dissertations.

These brief articles take on added significance when compared with their author's remarks on the academic vocation in his entrance speech at the University of Turin in 1908.[2] For the moment, examination of them will serve to highlight what was most characteristic of the early Michels, and scrutiny of the changed emphasis from the one article to the other will suggest the ideological development of their author from tepid social-reformism to revolutionary intransigence in the years from 1901 to 1905.

The major note of the first piece is indignant insistence on the right of national self-determination, and directly behind this, a liberal idealism—embittered, to be sure, but idealism nonetheless. If the university were to be true to its philosophical precepts instead of hypocritical about them, it would *prefer* socialists because they are "more idealistic" than the aggressive nationalists who have *carte blanche*. Probably, at the time of writing this, Michels would have *liked* to teach in a German university.

In the second piece, we can seriously doubt this desire. The accusation made against academic life rises from hypocrisy to total and necessary corruption. We see here the first glimmerings of the type of analysis that produced the iron law of oligarchy. As the latter in good measure presupposed a Marxist identification of economic base and ideological superstructure in the dissection of the socialist functionary, so Michels' acid criticism of academia also thrust the professor into the implacable grip of capitalist society. The professor concerned himself primarily only with the material value of his position; his ideas were so much abstract "capital" whose worth depended not on their usefulness but on the absence of any competition in his narrow field. Hence, the command: Specialize! This second article thus reveals a considerably more antagonistic attitude towards society, though Michels had not yet discovered his own party to be as obedient to the laws of that society as the academic institution. The relative moderation of the first article is, however, more characteristic of the social-reform phase of Michels' writings.

Certainly, in the first years after his Italian sojourn, the ardent revolutionary syndicalism for which he later became known was nowhere evident in his writings. In his first article, on Italian socialism, Michels argued that the vision of the future state was less important in Italy than in Germany, probably because of the long association of such ideas with the Church. The Italians wanted tangible results. This coincided in Michels' view with the general European tendency for the age of utopian visionary socialism to give way to an age of practical reform. The three immediate struggles in Italy were for the eight-hour day, for women's rights, and against militarism ("the sharpest struggle . . . is directed against the army").[3]

This piece reveals two important value judgments on the Italian national character that help to explain not only Michels' fondness for Italy and distaste for Germany, but also his early closeness to the revisionist position. Owing to the "democratic character of the entire people,"[4] all layers of the population were represented in the Italian Socialist party, and the left-liberal parties presented a united front with the socialists, instead of fighting them as they did in Germany. Closely related to this "democratic character" was "the inborn tolerance of the Italians in differences of opinion," which permitted the socialist in Italy to express his opinions without fear of social ostracism. Thus, a great many leading academicians were supporters or members of the Socialist party, which allowed Michels to establish friendships among the Italian academicians that were very significant for him in retaining a link to the *Italian* bourgeois academic world.

A final sign of moderation, so strange from the pen of one who was soon to deny categorically any identification with German national interest, was a warning to his German audience that the recent German tariff measures against Italy "are hardly appropriate for making the left parties in Italy friendly to *us*. Even in the ruling circles of *our old ally*, a sharp turn toward the entente is in the making."[5] (Emphasis added.)

In his next article on Italian socialism, in addition to the value placed on the self-sacrifice and self-consciousness of the proletariat (mentioned above in connection with the influence of Michels' personal values on his ideology) there was also praise of the Italian socialists for directing the movement "into quiet, worthy, legal paths. . . . This is its great service, for which state and society cannot be sufficiently thankful."[6] A stronger contrast to the sarcastic blasts that Michels was later to heap on the "legalitarian cowards" of social democracy is unimaginable.[7]

A quick survey of the journals for which Michels wrote in the years from 1901 to 1904 gives another indication of the moderate temper of his opinions. The bulk of those articles appearing in the German socialist press were either historical studies or journalistic reports of developments in the Italian labor movement; the historical pieces were printed in Eduard Bernstein's *Dokumente des Socialismus*.[8] Only two articles appeared in the *Leipziger Volkszeitung*, principal organ of German socialism's extreme left, one of them on divorce in Italy, the other on Italian politics.[9] A large number of short, generally unimportant pieces appeared in the journals of the movement for women's rights: *Dokumente der Frauen*,[10] *Die Frau*, and *Neues Frauenleben*. A few pieces discussing drama or art in Italy also appeared in the strictly cultural journals, *Südwestdeutsche Rundschau* and *Lotse*.[11] Also in these years appeared Michels' first articles in a scholarly journal, the *Politischanthropologisch Revue*. In the first of these he discussed Italian claims on the Austrian Tyrol. In the second, dealing with the importance of English civilization, he denied, largely on the basis of England's suppression of the Boers, the value of English society as a model for Germany.[12] This view of English society was to be of great significance in keeping Michels from getting too close to Bernsteinian revisionism or to the anti-Prussian *Kathedersozialismus* of Lujo Brentano. But his most important pieces before 1905—on the relation of nationalism, socialist internationalism, and pacifism—appeared in the liberal journals *Das Freie Wort* and *Ethische Kultur*.

Only in 1903, the same year that saw his hardened criticism of academia, did Michels write his first condemnation of revisionism. Writing against an ethical culturist who showed obvious distaste for the socialists' conception of suppressing violence in society by greater violence, Michels argued that precisely from the ethical standpoint, socialism must preserve its purity against any accommodation with the *status quo.*

> The haggling with principles, the exchanging of peoples' rights for cannons, the *Real-Politik* which, to gain a bagatelle for today, forgets or postpones the great ideal of tomorrow —no ethicist can sanction all that. A world-view such as socialism, which is inseparably tied with the belief in the progress of mankind, to be attained in determined paths, may have as its representatives no tit-for-tat diplomats [*Do-ut-Des Diplomaten*]. . . . If the seizure of power through the proletariat is not to degenerate into the dictatorship of a proletarian sect, the socialist agitation, until the time when it is completed, must create as many socialist consciences as it requires to be able to act as a successful counterweight against the other unsure elements who will then join their action. But socialist consciences are not made through rising in struggle over petty ordinances, useful as such propaganda may sometimes be, but through raising the great perspectives which lead the socialist movement, and the powerful goals which it follows. *Only through a class struggle that is tightly bound to intransigent unspoiled [unverkümmert] mental goals can the socialism of the ethicist be brought about.*[13] (Emphasis in original.)

What was the motive behind this altered viewpoint? Not enough is known about Michels in these years to say with certainty, but he himself provides us with a probable answer. In an autobiographical reminiscence on these years, published in 1932, he refers to an incident in the university city of Marburg, where he lived from 1901 to 1907.[14] The socialist candidate in the 1903 Reichstag election had been soundly trounced but, since no one had received a majority, a run-off election between the two leading candidates—a Conservative and a National-Social—gave the socialists a second, indirect opportunity for electoral activity. The local socialist group, in which Michels was a leading member, urged its members to abstain, basing itself on the decision of a party congress only to support run-off election candidates who pledged themselves to vote against any increases in the military budget.

Much to the chagrin of the Marburg socialist group, just before the election, the Berlin *Vorwärts*, claiming that the Conservative grain-tariff line must be opposed at all costs, urged the socialist electorate in Marburg to vote for the National-Social. And the revisionist Social Democratic deputy, Wolfgang Heine, a personal friend of the National-Social candidate, cabled him the news of the *Vorwärts* article in time to prepare a last-minute leaflet giving the paper's stand, and thus to gain enough socialist votes to secure the election.*

The Marburg socialist group was furious. In an exchange of letters between Michels and August Bebel, the veteran party leader, Bebel took the Marburger side completely, told them to send someone to the coming Dresden party congress "with hair on his teeth," and promised to give his unconcealed support.

The denouement of the incident was anticlimactic. On the first day of the congress, Bebel made a powerful speech against the revisionists. Michels, as the next speaker, was expected to bring in a motion of censure against Heine. For this step, he had the strong urging of the left wing around Luxembourg and Ledebour and, after the denunciations of the revered Bebel had cleared the way, very likely the support of a majority of the delegates. And this move might very possibly have led to a splitting off of the revisionists. Michels had fully intended to bring forward the motion for censure at the close of his speech. But at the last moment, oppressed by the atmosphere that Bebel's speech had produced, he decided to end with an appeal for unity and brotherhood.

For one thing, he felt that the responsibility of his intended move was too great for someone of his youth (he was twenty-seven). For another, he felt "the lack of generosity that would have lain in exploiting, even for higher goals, the hatred, not always free from personal motives, with which the so-called radicals opposed the revisionists, generally so superior in intelligence and education."[15] Finally, he stood aghast before the unthinking passion of the crowd before him. "The mass of delegates, after Bebel's

---

*It is ironic that this same Wolfgang Heine, whose bureaucratic maneuvering Michels so bitterly opposed in 1903, later became one of Michels' favorite sources for trenchant attacks on the party bureaucracy (see *Political Parties*, pp. 33, 105, 129, 229, 230, 264, 322, 398).

speech, were completely in tumult, incapable of any serious reflection. It was in a position to become the booty of the first one who, with heightened wrath, would have agreed with the great agitator. Michels' conscience forbade him to be this first one."[16]

Though there is, in the above account, evident dissatisfaction with the revolutionary wing of German social democracy, it was probably Michels' original wrath against Wolfgang Heine and his betrayal of principle that provoked the antirevisionist comments in the *Ethische Kultur* article.

In the following year, Michels' general antipathy to things German, his particular search for a theoretical position with none of the disadvantages he saw among revisionists and revolutionaries, and, perhaps, pure chance brought him in fruitful contact with the French syndicalist group around Hubert Lagardelle and Eduard Berth. At about the same time that Michels himself was being convinced by the arguments of this group, centered around the journal *Le Mouvement Socialiste*, Georges Sorel too was on the point of adopting this periodical as his major literary vehicle. I shall discuss below Michels' evolving critique of German social democracy, and the political activities, hopes, and disappointments which resulted from that critique during the period of his collaboration with *Le Mouvement Socialiste*. In order to view more clearly, however, the development of Michels' thought that leads into the *Mouvement Socialiste* period, it may be profitable to consider one of the main themes that emerge from his earlier writings, the last of which overlap by almost a year his first articles in the French journal. (Michels' first article in *Le Mouvement Socialiste* was in the December 1904 issue. His last in *Ethische Kultur* were in November 1905.)

Michels' principal theoretical concern in the years 1902 to 1905 was the discovery of a single ideological framework for the three principal components of his social morality: pacifism, internationalism, and the right of all peoples to national self-determination.[17] The main problem that he confronted was how the right to national self-determination—an integral part of his anti-Prussianism—could be kept from turning into narrow-minded nationalism, which then would strive to oppress other nations' rights, start wars, and destroy international brotherhood. A corollary problem that occurred to him[18] was how to prevent socialist internationalism from passing over in silence the fate of oppressed nationalities.

In his first article on the subject, in 1902,[19] he established a shaky distinction between *Nationalismus* and *Nationalbewusstsein*. *Nationalismus* may be relatively harmless where, as in the English and French variety, it is directed only against people living beyond the borders, who cannot be touched in peacetime. But in the German, Russian, and Hungarian forms, where it is directed against foreign nationalities within state boundaries, "its goal is assimilation, its innermost essence is arrogance and ignorance, and its weapons are intolerance and hatred, which easily degenerate into cruelty."

Nationalbewusstsein, according to Michels, "exists only with peoples who are pressed much too much into the defensive to be able themselves to proceed offensively with success. It is the struggle for success of small and oppressed minorities." Nevertheless, once successful, *Nationalbewusstsein* must gradually develop into *Nationalismus*, "to be sure not by virtue of its inherent nature, but from basic causes that are ubiquitous in the present social circumstances." (The single exception Michels allows to this development is Italy, which although free, has no desire to oppress other nations.) We may assume, then, that Michels has in mind this "inherent nature" of *Nationalbewusstsein* and not its existing social conditioning when he says, a moment later, "*Nationalbewusstsein* is therefore something thoroughly healthy, insofar as a . . . group formation through nationalities must be the indispensable transition to a higher form of world order." Although unstated, the agent that can lead nationalities in the direction of their own "inherent nature," which is the direction of Michels' social idealism, and away from the corruption of existing social conditions, can be no other than the social revolution.

Thus, the presuppositions of Michels' idealistic social philosophy, which is the real underpinning of his critique of social democracy, begin to emerge.

There is an ideal nature inherent in human groups and their thought processes. This nature is, in general, healthy and moral. But in the hard, material context of bourgeois society, this inherent nature is overwhelmed, corrupted, and destroyed. Thus, Michels' struggle against bourgeois society is a struggle for the moral ideal, which even possesses a shadowy ontological structure, against the immoral corruption of the material. It should not surprise us, then, that Michels sees the masses as the historical embodiment of social morality,[20] and the "innermost wish" of the masses as "the self-evident equal right of all people to participation in the goods of culture." Granting the necessity of the violent struggle that the proletariat carries on against the ruling class for economic advancement, Michels insists that this struggle is no end in itself, but is "only supposed to provide the basis for the development of all spiritual and mental powers, in peaceful work on all spheres of culture."[21]

What happened to Michels' idealism, his readiness to view the world according to "inherent natures," was that as he struggled against the materialistic evils of the world, he discovered more and more the extent of the corruption, and his idealistic view tended more and more to give way to an analytic, empirical view which, in place of inherent natures, discovered iron social laws. The key words he used to divide the groups still seen in a hopeful, idealistic light from those seen in a pragmatic, materialistic light all reflected his personal values: on the one hand, self-sacrifice and self-consciousness; on the other, egoism.

One faint example of this tendency exists in Michels' changed view of the university between 1902 and 1903. The very titles, not to mention the content, of his two last articles on nationalism, pacifism, and socialist internationalism in *Ethische Kultur* (1905) provide a much better case. The title of the penultimate article, "Die Formen des Patriotismus," suggests an abstract treatment of the subject, and to a great extent, this is so. Although he roundly denounces the "pseudo-ethical patriotism" of German imperialism as a mask for the suppression of other nations, the "interested patriotism" of the bourgeoisie as a mask for the suppression of the working class, and the "atavistic patriotism" of the majority as a totally inadmissible glorification of brute force, he nevertheless insists on "the right of national self-determination" as "the cardinal principle of international ethics."[22] Rebuking abstract internationalism, Michels calls for "the reconciliation of oppositions between love of fatherland and love of the world" in national and social internationalism.[23]

Two points of view in this study distinguish it from Michels' previous articles on the same subject and point toward his future work, both political and intellectual. For one thing, though the dominant tone of the analysis is still idealistic, the justification of valid nationalism is at least partly in terms of historical factors, race, climate, language, rather than purely abstract "natures." for another, Michels, in asserting the "atavistic patriotism of the majority," has for the first time seen the masses as trapped in the immorality of the world.

In his last major article in *Ethische Kultur*, "Rasse und Entwicklung,"[24] Michels dissects the historical development (*Entwicklung*) of the idea of race (*Rasse*) to show the invalidity of the latter. Here he abandons his precarious juggling act and makes no defense of any kind of nationalism. Written at the height of his revolutionary fervor, this article shows two clear qualities: a proletarian internationalist standpoint and a strictly historical approach to his subject.

The very first paragraph sets the tone of the historical treatment, at the same time that it casts a slight shadow on the author's previously bright picture of human progress:

> Each of the historical epochs previously experienced by Europe has left the world something lasting. Each has enriched civilization and thereby human progress with a permanent possession. And each has bequeathed to the period after it a chaotic mass of prejudices and injuries which, to be sure, is impermanent but which nonetheless, burdening progress in the worst possible way, must be carried quite some distance further, until new attainments finally do away with it.[25]

While the earlier article carefully distinguished between bad and good patriotism, strongly upheld the right of self-determination of peoples, and castigated an abstract internationalism that only served to perpetuate national oppression, this article neither distinguishes, nor upholds, nor castigates, but rather, continually warns against the validity of national or racial characteristics. Great pains are taken to demonstrate the silliness of the distinction between "*Romanen*" and "*Germanen*," by showing historically the lack of any such distinction until recent times. National characteristics, too, are condemned as being only projections of individual qualities such as honesty, cleanliness, aloofness, and so forth.

The principal cause for this change in Michels' view of patriotism is apparently the growing belief on his part that any kind of patriotism, even that which only wants the independent cultivation of a national culture, is used by the powers that be to destroy proletarian internationalism:

> Chauvinism, this gruesome inversion of the beautiful and proud thought "I am I" into the mad boast, "I am more than you," and the consequent demand, "because I am more than you, you must become like me and obey me," sticks deeply, in the present generation, like a stake in the flesh of the working class of all nations, and all the strivings of healthy-thinking doctors . . . have not yet been able to pull it out.[26]

Hence, faced with the inevitability of the "beautiful and proud thought" turning sour and corrupting the proletariat, Michels must choose between nationalism on the one side and proletarian internationalism and pacifism on the other. The choice, again couched in an historical framework, is clear:

> The most important argument against the misuse in the attribution of national characteristics consists in the fact that another collective factor is beginning to replace the nation. Already one can assert, without fear of serious contradiction, that the workers of all civilized lands show more points of contact among themselves than with the possessing strata of the different nations to which they "belong." And this is true not only in political things, where they are frequently bound together by the uniting ideological bond of socialism, but also in their whole immanent thought and feeling, in all their morals and customs. The German worker undoubtedly stands closer to the French worker than to the German bourgeois. Just for this reason would a war between France and Germany be a war of brothers, a crime which we must use every means to prevent.[27]

Thus, the focus of Michels' intellectual concern has altered from the now hopeless salvation of idealistic nationalism to the struggle for idealistic socialism. And the fight for the latter, unlike that for the former, is to involve Michels in day-to-day political agitation and frequent activity in socialist congresses.

What is the basis of this idealistic socialism? Perhaps if one were to say *socialist* consciousness as opposed to pure *class* consciousness, one would be close to the heart of the matter. Certainly the "beautiful and proud thought 'I am I,' " correctly understood, is the crucial component. In the nationalist sense it meant an understanding of one's national character, at the same time that it was automatically supposed to imply understanding of the national character of others. In its socialist context it no longer has any national quality; it assumes a character of universal humanism which sees the struggle of the proletariat as absolutely necessary for the elimination of injustice and war, but at the same time is opposed to proletarian consciousness per se, i.e., the limited consciousness of only "egoistic" and materialistic class interests as distinguished from universal human interests. Left to its own devices, the proletariat would never rise above this limited materialistic perspective.* To reach a truly socialist consciousness, a consciousness of the ultimate human goals of their struggle, the proletariat must have the aid of renegade bourgeois intellectuals (such as himself).[28]

This crucial role given to the leadership of the socialist movement distinguishes Michels' interpretation of the social struggle from the more mechanically Marxist one of orthodox German socialists. The latter saw the universal human goal—abolition of all classes, including the proletariat—as springing directly from the economic class struggle. But for Michels, the bread would not rise without the yeast of the intellectuals.

In his very first article in Le Mouvement Socialiste, Michels opposed the German Social Democrat Eduard David's demand for strict adherence to legality, because for Michels exclusive concern with increasing the parliamentary strength and the number of votes

---

* It was from this standpoint that Michels, in the 1904 *Dokumente des Sozialismus,* analyzed an exclusively proletarian party in nineteenth-century Italy. For reference, see note 8 of this chapter.

of the party would cripple the development of socialist consciousness.[29] Michels saw German social democracy, despite its huge numbers, as incapable of effecting the slightest improvement in the German political structure. He found many reasons for this impotence. One was the united opposition of the bourgeoisie and the feudal regime; another the weakness of the German revolutionary tradition; yet another the character of the German masses, "rather passive than active, and indecisive, heavy, slave to tradition and to milieu, little enterprising and of a desperate slowness."[30] But none of these was the most important cause: "Our masses are slothful and unready for action because the education which the Socialist party has given them is rather political, and even diplomatic, than socialist and moral."[31] This defective education bore the main responsibility for the fact that "the German proletariat lacks one essential quality: the courageous will for action, the revolutionary ferment."[32]

Michels probed the failure of leadership in terms that went beyond the personal coefficient. The good faith and sense of sacrifice of the leaders were to him above suspicion. He attributed their failure rather to their parliamentary outlook and the blackmail of the 3,000,000 socialist voters over the activities of the 400,000 party members. As an example, he offered the complete surrender of the party's antireligious posture: fearing the loss of religious voters in the more backward parts of Germany, the party had adopted the slogan "religion is a private affair," and had completely stopped its antireligious propaganda. Another result of the party's sacrifice of daily mass agitation for a moderate, inactive, legal position: when the Saxon government arbitrarily suspended the right to vote, the Saxon proletariat was so lethargic that it was impossible for the leadership itself to organize protest demonstrations.

The core of Michels' criticism was

> that the supposed radicalism of German socialism is no longer occupied in creating socialist personalities, socialist consciousness. It is so everywhere, in France and in Italy, as well as in Germany. Parliamentarism kills socialism, seen in its most profound aspects, by substituting for it a one-sided political socialism. Men of heart and of mind in our ranks

view with sadness the disappearance of the whole idealistic side of our system of ideas. Socialism used to be a faith, a sentiment which took hold of a man completely and determined every act of his life. . . . Today this spirit takes refuge only in those countries where the socialists have not yet reported electoral successes. Everywhere that we have triumphed—sometimes thanks to our absolute silence on theoretical questions—the masses are filled with coldness. . . . As a result of preaching every day the strict dependence of the sentiments and ideas of men on economic fatality, we have arrived, in fact, at denying the eternal truth that will and energy can also exercise a strong influence on our actions and sometimes even in contradiction with the material demands of life.[33]

In addition to criticizing socialist parliamentarism from the standpoint of its narcotic effect on the will of the masses, Michels also took it to task for its tactical naïveté:

In a country where the power of the state rests on three pillars, of which two, the Bundesrat and the Emperor, cannot legally be touched, a party which would want to take *seriously* the coin of legality, would be quickly dead and buried, as a socialist workers' party: it would be only one more bourgeois party like all the others.[34]

The author's conclusion: "German socialism cannot attain its end without breaking the law."

His next article in *Le Mouvement Socialiste* continued the advocacy of antireligious propaganda and revealed for the first time a German socialist faction with which Michels' antiparliamentarism could identify.[35] At the Prussian Socialist Congress in Berlin, a proposal for party members to withdraw from membership in the churches was enthusiastically hailed by Michels (although, of course, not approved by the congress). Michels hoped such a measure would "unify the family into small groups entirely socialist" (here Michels possibly shows the influence of Sorel), "purge the party of all the half-conscious ones and petty-bourgeois who infect it," and permit the clearer emergence of the party's "scientific essence."[36]

For Michels, however, the most important event of the congress was the coming together of elements of both the right and the extreme left of the party in support of Bernstein's proposal for street protests against the Prussian three-class voting system. Though among Bernstein's declared adversaries, Michels hailed with joy his insistence on the party's duty *"to do everything possible to inspire the German proletariat with the feeling of revolt."*[37] Bernstein had reproached the German workers for "cowardice in the face of . . . town policemen,"[38] and denounced the party's propaganda as lacking the force of specific demands: "Our propaganda does not frighten a cat."[39] The response of the orthodox left-wingers in the party congress was hostility to the very idea of single-aim demonstrations. Zubeil and Adler even made chauvinistic attacks on such demonstrations in France and Italy.

With a pen dipped in vitriol, Michels commented:

> What an ironic spectacle! The saviors of the "old traditions" of the party, the mortal enemies of opportunist revisionism, rising as protectors of the *quieto vivere*! . . . These comrades give us the most lamentable caricature of revolutionary socialism. Behind the pseudo-Marxism which serves as a screen for this party current is hidden a singularly harmful state of mind: a beatific contentment with the state of affairs within the party, an immobilizing satisfaction in regard to everything, a force of inertia that is sometimes reactionary, a manifest hostility in regard to all new ideas, a Teutonic arrogance towards the comrades in *"Ausland,"* towards everything not their own, and a Buddhist conception of political life, through which, draping themselves in big words, they cry: "We do not move for trifles."[40]

Similarly disgusted by the attitude of the orthodox Marxists, three important men of the extreme left—Karl Liebknecht, Haenisch, and Meist—supported Bernstein's resolution. Naturally, through the combination of non-Bernstein revisionists and orthodox left, the proposal was easily voted down. Nevertheless, Michels hoped that in the future the new Bernstein-Liebknecht grouping might move the party to action. In general he wanted action in order to "accustom the proletariat to make use of its will," to train it for the revolution through partial conquests. In particular his enthusiasm for Bernstein's motion proposing demonstrations against the three-class voting system stemmed from his conviction that the most pressing need in Germany was the creation of a democratic republic, in which the workers could move more freely toward the social revolution.

Thus, the significance of the Berlin Congress for Michels lay in the affirmation, even though confused, of "a neorevolutionary current, *a revolutionary revisionism basing itself on two fundamental points:* on the clearest rigidity of principles (anti-revisionist), and on the courageous will for revolutionary action (anti-revolutionary old style)." (Michels' emphasis.)

At the end of March 1905 Michels continued his attack on German social democracy with an angry roar at the management of the Ruhr miners' strike.[41] Michels denounced the bureaucratic leadership for having long blocked the desire of the rank and file to call the strike. He assailed the timidity of the socialists in concealing their socialist viewpoint from the strikers, for fear of offending the many Catholic and liberal trade-unionists among them. He heaped scorn on the peaceful and legal straitjacket the leaders imposed on the strike, and imposed with such success that a patriotic Berlin paper could take pride in "this discipline of our workers." But most significant, for the evolution of Michels' political critique, were his attacks on the socialists' proposal for nationalizing the mines and on what he saw as the narrow materialism of the unionists in ending the strike as soon as the strike fund was exhausted.

Accusing the orthodox Marxists of "statism" and an "absolute lack of Marxist spirit," Michels cited as "the most essential insight" of Marxism, the notion that the state is an interlocking directorate of the capitalist classes and rulers:

> Now look at the official socialists of Germany, the Bebels and Ledebours, going to ask shelter against capitalism from its own business agent. To deliver the workers from the exploitation of capitalism, they want . . . to deliver them to the exploitation of the boss of the feudal state. . . . All the police and military forces set against the workers by the crushing state employer, whose despotism would no longer even be veiled or attenuated by competition, this is what we are offered.[42]

For ending the strike as soon as the strike fund was exhausted without consulting the mass of strikers, the 170 union delegates received this comment from Michels:

> We grant that well-filled treasuries are good allies. But only allies. To want to combat the capital of the capitalists with the capital of some poor devils is absurd. It is not by force of ready cash that the strikers can win, but by means much stronger and of a more moral order: solidarity, socialist class sentiment, and the absolute economic necessity of the proletariat.

In his next piece in *Le Mouvement Socialiste,* Michels continued his attack on the union chiefs.[43] Supporting his thesis on the example of the French and Italian union movements, Michels demanded the rejuvenation of socialism through revolutionary syndicalism. Instead of generating "a basely utilitarian sentiment in the hearts of the workers," the German union movement had to embody "the idealism of class solidarity," to incarnate the class struggle. It had to be "the organizer of the social war, against all peace, all compromise, all diplomacy."[44]

But there was little hope of that. Assailing the "bureaucratic marvel" that the German unionists had created, and their view of the union treasury as their only means of combat, Michels admitted, "They dream only of peace and tranquility, for only peace and tranquility allow them to amass this famous collection of silver pieces, which to them is the *ne plus ultra* of the workers' movement."[45]

It was then with understandable hostility that Michels viewed the principal decisions of the Union Congress of Cologne, to emasculate the May Day celebration by reducing it to an evening holiday and to condemn the general strike. He appealed to the party "to combat vigorously the pacifist spirit of the unions," and closed by once again juxtaposing the loss of energy and virility in the German unions to "the revolutionary, antilegal, even antistatist conceptions" of French and Italian syndicalism.

Michels' report on the Social Democratic Congress at Jena showed a flicker of optimism over the general direction of German

socialism that was absent from his other writings after 1904.*
Apparently the failure of the Ruhr miners' strike had produced a
hardened attitude on the part of the orthodox party Marxists, as
well as a wave of disaffection among rank-and-file unionists
which, together, compelled a retreat by the union chiefs on such
issues as the May Day celebration and the general strike. The congress reinstated May Day as a proletarian holiday and, by approving a motion made by Bebel himself, it accepted the general strike as a legitimate means of proletarian defense (though not of offense).

At the same time, however, that Michels noted this improvement in the over-all position of the party, his hopes for the tendencies with which he personally identified were crumbling. The only syndicalist union in Germany, the thirteen-thousand-member Berlin "localist" union, saw its ideological leader, Raphael Friedeberg, vehemently attacked by August Bebel and then forbidden to reply because he was not a delegate. Michels, whose own activity seems to have reached a peak at this congress, replied to this attack on Friedeberg by denouncing Bebel's "socialist patriotism" as indistinguishable from bourgeois patriotism.

Bebel had said he would defend the smallest piece of German territory. Michels raised the question of those parts of the Polish, French, and Danish nations that had been incorporated into the Reich. Michels' speech nonetheless showed his continued belief in the right of national self-determination. Though a distinctly subordinate element of Michels' thought in his syndicalist phase, this conception seems never to have been completely eliminated and, after the years 1905 and 1906, it returned again, stronger than ever, because unfettered by any real hope for proletarian internationalism.

Two further setbacks for Michels' point of view were the voting down of a motion sponsored by himself, together with Haenisch (one of the "revolutionary revisionists" of the Berlin Congress) and two other delegates, to revoke the right of socialist Reichstag depu-

* Robert Michels, "Le socialisme allemand et le congrès de Iena," MS, 17 (1905), pp. 281–307. Hendrik de Man, in his autobiography *Gegen den Strom* (Stuttgart, 1953), p. 70, mentions making Michels' acquaintance at the Jena congress, and lists him, with Karl Liebknecht, Rosa Luxemburg, and Konrad Haenisch, as one of the representatives of the young radical left.

ties to sit as delegates without local mandate at a party congress, and the rejection by the congress, after a furious denunciation by Bebel, of Karl Liebknecht's motion for antimilitary agitation among young men about to be called into the army.

Michels' closing remarks on the Congress of Jena were little more than an obituary for revolutionary revisionism:

> The men who seemed destined to be the champions of this movement, tired of preaching without being heard, are letting go. Some, like Friedeberg, tend to detach themselves from the party. Others are content to slip into the ranks of the extreme left, with the *Leipziger Volkszeitung*. Others, again, become simple antireformists. The rest compose a *Fronde* without soldiers and without consequence.[46]

Thus, despite his happiness over the improvement in the party's position on the general strike and some whistling in the dark over the increasing number of antiparliamentarians in the party, Michels left his readers with a clear feeling of desolation regarding the prospects of the "revolutionary revisionist" coalition of the Berlin Congress.

His halfhearted optimism regarding the party's course was quickly shattered by the absolute refusal of the German socialists even to discuss international antiwar demonstrations at the time of the Moroccan crisis of 1905, though repeatedly approached by leading foreign socialists.[47] According to Michels, the best foreign socialists could hope for from their German comrades, in case of hostilities, was a vote in parliament against the war. Even the "defeatist" approach of the German socialists' left wing—centered around Kautsky—hoped only that after a defeat of German militarism by France and England, the German revolution could rise from the ruins. Venting the anger and sarcasm of disillusioned idealism, Michels wrote:

> Our "internationalist" Germans, then, do not dream of keeping the sons of the proletariat from the capitalist army: they are given to it with the burlesque hope that these socialist workers, after having been conquered, killed, crushed, will revive in the shape of revolutionaries.[48]

His previous articles had established two of the motives for this new betrayal of the international socialist cause. Fear of jeopardizing party and union treasuries, "meticulously accumulated with the care of an economical petty bourgeois,"[49] was one. Parliamentarism, the abandonment of the field of class struggle, was another. A new theme, however, of great significance as one of the germs from which the iron law of oligarchy was to develop, linked the socialist functionary's political quietism to his economic position: "An innumerable army of employees lives today from the party and the unions and . . . this mass of functionaries does not resolve easily upon risking, by a bold action, the secure positions which are its own."[50]

If Michels' report on the Congress of Jena had been an obituary for revolutionary revisionism, his next article, on the Mannheim Socialist Congress, was as much for socialism itself.[51] At the congress, Raphael Friedeberg's anarchosyndicalist union was given a year to dissolve into the regular union organization or see its members expelled from the party. Bebel had reversed his earlier stand for the general strike and aligned himself with the revisionists. With an eloquence forged in despair, Michels wrote,

> The field of glory of the Congress of Mannheim is sown with corpses and wounded. Dead, killed, assassinated, that poor embryo of the general strike for which there was some hope at the Congress of Jena; mortally wounded, German unionism; seriously hurt, the remnants of Marxism! And socialism itself, debased, outraged, degraded to the life of an idler and a clown.[52]

Although Michels closed this piece, like so many of his others, with a prophecy that rank-and-file militants would soon see the errors of the party leadership and revive German socialism, his despair over the obstacles to reform had brought him very close to the end of his tether. This became evident a few months later in a polemical essay inspired by Eduard Berth's review of his book on Italian socialism.[53] Yet the very manner in which Michels showed his growing disillusion also revealed how necessary it was for him to cast off his syndicalist baggage before he could broaden his analysis of social democracy and build on it a sociological theorem.

Berth had contended that representation was the curse of the party system, breeding treason and embourgeoisement. The only hope for the salvation of socialism lay in the direct, autonomous, unrepresented action of the working class. But to Michels' mind there was a fly in this ointment too. Why, he asked, did Berth apply his theory to the party alone? The direct action of the proletariat had still to be mediated through the syndicalist union, and unions, too, suffered the curse of representation. Michels corrected his old friend: "Instead of saying: the party engenders embourgeoisement, he should have said, 'organization engenders embourgeoisement and deviation.' But the principle of organization embraces equally the party and the union."[54]

As a solution, Michels sought "a means of reacting against the imminent defects of all organization, of all representation." Yet, in palpable contradiction to what he had just said about organization dominating the union as well as the party, in his closing words on the subject he still saw syndicalism as this "means of reacting."

In his critique of German social democracy, Michels had profited much from his association with the French syndicalists. Having developed from a quasireformist position to one that criticized any compromise of principles as a betrayal of the party's task of creating "socialist consciousness," he had come to accept the syndicalists' proposition that the only way this consciousness could be created was by steeling the will of the proletariat through revolutionary skirmishing (the general strike). He had further adopted their thesis that social democratic parliamentarism, in direct contradiction to this view, was sapping the revolutionary will of the masses and destroying the idealistic side of socialism, and that only revolutionary syndicalism, free from the parliamentary taint, could liberate the proletariat.

For the motive behind parliamentarism, he found the refusal by the leadership to risk the dissolution of the enormous party organization through any move outside of the legal, parliamentary arena. This refusal, in turn, he traced to the metamorphosis of the worker, once absorbed by the party machine, into a salaried petty bourgeois, whose vested interest in his job, and in the preservation of the *status quo* that guaranteed him that job, outweighed any lip service he might still pay to socialist ideology.

But all this was still criticism of the German Social Democratic party, not of organization itself. To rise from political analysis to sociology, which seeks universal social laws or tendencies, Michels had to dissociate himself from syndicalism. Only to the extent that he did so was he able to develop the theorem of his friend Berth into a general critique of organization.

The reply to Berth was the last article that Michels wrote in *Le Mouvement Socialiste* as a syndicalist. A few months later he left his German residence in Marburg and returned to the University of Turin, which he had left in 1901. The shift from revolutionary syndicalist to academician appeared abrupt, but this impression is dissipated by a consideration of Michels' close friendship, during the years he wrote for *Le Mouvement Socialiste*, with Italian socialist academicians such as Arturo Labriola and Ivanoe Bonomi, and also by a cursory review of his life outside of the *Mouvement Socialiste* context from 1904 to his departure for Italy.

Since 1905 he had been giving a course at the *Université Nouvelle* in Brussels, where he taught alongside Emile Vandervelde and Enrico Ferri,[55] and occasional lectures at the Parisian *Collège Libre des Sciences Sociales*. In 1906 he also gave a lecture before the *Gesellschaft für ethische Kultur* in Wiesbaden and Berlin on his old hobbyhorse, patriotism and ethics.[56] Michels was most active, however, in the small circle of socialist intellectuals in Marburg.

Two successive groups seem to have formed around Michels in Marburg. The first was composed of Michels and his wife Gisela, Ernst Thesing (a young interne), Thesing's wife, and Otto Buek, a German-Russian student of the neo-Kantian Hermann Cohen and translator of Tolstoi. In general, Michels tells us, the basically Marxist philosophy of history in this group was well mixed with Kantian and Tolstoian ethical elements. Here we have the intellectual core of the Marburg socialist section that sent Michels to Dresden in 1903 to slay the revisionist dragons.

By the end of 1906, Buek and the Thesings had left Marburg.

They were replaced in Michels' circle by Adolf Köster, a theology student who had just finished a study of Pascal's ethics and was later to cooperate with Michels in translating from the Italian a book of Niceforo's on the anthropology of the lower classes; Rudolf Franz, a friend of Köster's; and Hans Teschemacher, a student who joined the party in Marburg and, in 1912, published a study on the income tax and the revolution in Prussia.

Köster and Franz agreed with Michels in their emphasis on a living socialist idealism, in their rejection of any compromise or alliance with the bourgeois parties, indeed, their rejection of parliamentarism in general, and finally "in the passionate appeal to the youth."

It was to the youth in particular that Michels turned as his hopes for a healthy development within German social democracy faded. The high point of his efforts to win the university students for socialism was a public debate in February 1907 between, on one side, Köster and himself, and on the other, a National Liberal librarian and a Catholic Center party schoolteacher. The debate and ensuing discussion lasted six hours and were attended by an overflow audience of students, workers, and townspeople. Only a few professors were present, but among them was the neo-Kantian Paul Natorp.[57] Michels valued this debate highly for the intellectual stimulation it gave the university community, and he agreed to repeat it a few weeks later in the nearby university town of Giessen.

In summarizing these years, Michels emphasized the elements of political romanticism in the thought of the Marburg group.

> Even where much reflection was present, instinctive impulsiveness [*das Triebsmässige*] frequently predominated, which is not necessarily politically harmful.* It was a youthful reaction

---

* We find a graphic illustration of the romantic side of Michels' personality in the following remarks, coming just after a passage analyzing the lack of public lovemaking in Italy, written in 1906 ("Erotische Streifzüge," *Mutterschutz* [1906], p. 366):

> Every time that we—my wife and I—return from Italy, we greet—and we are nothing less than what is commonly called patriotic—the first love-pair with a genuine German shout of joy, through which, to be sure, this pair is sometimes unpleasantly shocked. When we traveled, some years ago, directly from Rome to Eisenach and, in the course of a nocturnal walk around the quiet wooded slopes of the Matilstein, found bench after bench in the

not only against the bourgeois world, the regime, but in the last analysis also against the labor movement, such as it had become. It was, as Platon has said of French syndicalism, an organic reaction from disgust with party politics and its consequences, a rebellion against the mediocrity of the professional party leadership which was not conscious of its responsibility either to the nation or, above all, to the idea, a struggle of ideology against organization for its own sake.[58]

Michels attributed to this critical attitude toward the labor movement, the interest of Max Weber and Werner Sombart in the Marburg group. Weber, in his sharp criticism of the "petty-bourgeois physiognomy" of the party leadership, certainly shared many of Michels' opinions on the subject, and became a good friend of Michels, defending him before other academicians and exchanging visits with him.[59] Sombart, in line with his surviving interest, if not sympathy, for socialism, was also interested in the Marburg group, and in 1907 Michels was able to prevail on him to attend the international socialist congress at Stuttgart where, in addition to meeting Michels' syndicalist friends from Italy and France, Sombart resisted a determined attempt to convert him to the syndicalist point of view. As a result of these warm contacts with Weber and Sombart, the pages of the journal they jointly edited, *Archiv für Sozialwissenschaft und Sozialpolitik*, were opened to Michels and other representatives of international syndicalism.

Michels himself published most of his scholarly studies from 1905 on in the *Archiv*, and in 1913 and 1914 he jointly edited the journal with Weber and Sombart. During his syndicalist period he wrote a study of the class composition of the Italian socialist movement, of which only the last section, published in 1906, is important;[60] a similar, though briefer study of Socialist party members and elec-

---

service of love, of an open love, which didn't even stop kissing and whispering when the walker observed them, then we had a warm, comforting sensation of something grandiose. It was not only that we were pleasantly touched by the pull of romanticism that surrounded this species of lovemaking with a warm breath of the artistic and beautiful. No, it was, in addition, that the open, unashamed sensuality, almost proud of itself, and presented to the public gaze, appeared to us as something primitive, healthy, powerful, promising the future in defiance of all the grey on grey of the social relations of Germany.

torate in Germany;[61] and an analysis of the role of the German party in the Second International.[62] These scholarly pieces, quite moderate compared with his fire-eating performances in *Le Mouvement Socialiste*, were still definitely radical in tone. Though they added little that was new to the analysis Michels was making in his hot blasts to Paris, they did sometimes deepen this analysis and by adding detail, they always made it more convincing from a scholarly point of view.

In the long article on Italian socialism (1905 and 1906), the only thing of significance for his later critique of organization was a comparison of the Italian and German socialist leadership. Michels pointed out that in Germany, the Socialist party put its Reichstag deputies on the party payroll, since they received no salary from the state. In addition, the paid labor secretaries and editors of party papers composed a powerful army of officials. Finally, in the lower ranks of the socialist bureaucracy, especially on the newspaper staffs, the party employed many political workers who had been blacklisted from their trades.

The Italian party, not nearly so tightly organized, had very few paid positions to offer the worker-revolutionary. Consequently, most of the leadership positions tended to be filled by independent professionals, writers, and academic intellectuals who sacrificed their bourgeois connections, and much of their time and money, to serve the proletarian cause. Michels commented:

> This has the disadvantage that the workers' party is sometimes commanded by a general staff of lawyers. Such a disadvantage however, is, for the most part, compensated by the fact that this system does not experience the serious harm of a stable, necessarily ossifying, professional officialdom. In this way, not only does the party preserve its mental elasticity, and the fresh-pulsing individual differentiation of its components, but the party work, too, insofar as it is deprived of all, or nearly all, material privileges, is put on the basis of service purely in the name of love for the cause.[63]

His next article in the *Archiv*, on the composition of electorate and party members in German socialism, continued this theme. Most strikingly, Michels discussed the broader significance of the function of the party bureaucracy as a status escalator (*"Klassenerhöhungs-maschine"*—in typical detestation of anything Teutonic, he immediately labeled the word *"monstruöse"*).⁶⁴ Just as the party payroll created petty bourgeois out of proletarians, the Catholic Church offered a hierarchy of social ascent for petty bourgeois and peasants, and the Prussian army served as a bridge for the upper-middle class to enter the nobility.*

Though Michels' next study in the *Archiv*, on the relation of the German party to the Socialist International, also had a brief glimmering of a universal sociological approach, it was still primarily concerned with analyzing the specifically German aspects of the party's corruption. Perhaps the best general statement of Michels' view of the party-nation connection was in a lecture given in Paris at roughly the same time he was working on the *Archiv* article:

> In a country where initiative doesn't count, but where one can be marvelously disciplined, where the great masses form vast, mechanical, and rigid organizations, where everything is bureaucratic and militarized, the workers have followed the same road and taken the same form as the other classes. . . . Modern Germany is a mold, in the imprint of which are formed all its component parts; everywhere is the same accomplished regularity, the same stubborn labor for the work to which one is attached, the same fidelity, the same discipline. In truth, one understands how our workers' organization has become, from the means it was supposed to be, an end in itself, a machine that one perfects for its embellishment, and not for the services it could have rendered.⁶⁵

Continuing this line of thought, Michels wrote in the *Archiv*:

> To overcome the centralized power of the state, it [German socialism] has centralized itself, and since it uses only one means for the overcoming of this power, namely, the single democratic element in the German constitution, the right to vote, its whole organism is tailored merely for the attainment

---

* Having served for a year as a junior officer in a regiment whose officers were almost all Prussian noblemen, and having seen an uncle take this path into the upper class, Michels was well familiar with this bridge. (His own army experience is mentioned in "Le Socialisme Allemand et le Congrès d'Iena," MS, 17 [1905], p. 294 (fn.); his uncle is discussed in "Peter Michels.")

of electoral successes. . . . Therefore, everything is repugnant to it that could interfere in the spokes of its wheels, its organism, or could at least threaten its external form, the organization. . . . It does not educate men, but strives to cast little machine parts for its complicated machinery, disciplined party comrades whose highest characteristic consists in the great plus—or minus?—of the German national character: the capacity for herd organization, the ability to obey, the quality of subordination in an administrative subdivision.[66]

Thus, criticism of the bureaucratic rigidity and parliamentarism of the German party led Michels back to a consideration of the character of German society as a whole. In general, his criticism stopped there, but at one point in this study he did go further. In explaining the decline in the internationalist sentiment of German socialism, he briefly blamed the division of labor for the slow death of internationalism. As the party evolved from its early illegal stage to close contact with the workings of social and economic legislation (local gas rates, factory inspection, etc.), it came to be less and less concerned with any problems outside of its increasingly narrow scope. Michels quoted Ladislaus Gumplowicz: "That is not to be altered, any more than it is to be altered that with the progressive growth of scientific research materials, the polyhistor has died out and the universal zoologist has given way to the ornithologist and the myrmecologist."[67] He then returned to his specifically national level of analysis, pointing out that because German Social Democracy was the party most immersed in specialized and practical work, it was also the least sensitive to pleas for international solidarity.

There were, then, three levels of motivation and analysis discernible at this stage of Michels' political thought. As a syndicalist, the object of his attack was parliamentarism, and the stultifying effects on the socialist ideal of a centralized party bureaucracy. As a son of the old Cologne patriciate, he was very quick to find the cause of parliamentarism and party bureaucracy in the stiff mechanical mold of a Prussianized Germany. But as a young sociologist, he was also becoming aware that the mechanization of society, though it may have risen to unprecedented heights in Germany through its marriage with the Prussian feudality, was a universal phenomenon, visible in the historical *Drang* of the division of labor, and that the curse of representation, which so quickly transformed organization from a means of social change to an end in itself, was an inescapable consequence of any form of political organization.

26

Scholarly Retreat, Social Pedagogy, or Elitism?

IN 1903, when he was just beginning to take a position critical of orthodox socialism, Michels had written,

> To yield to the sadness which comes over a serious person when he discovers major flaws in an institution, movement, or party with which he is closely tied, would be unjustified sentimentality. For such an institution must give in to the powerful critique which one makes of the discovered flaws. Only through continual struggle against evil, wherever it may be, does mankind come closer to its final goals.[1]

In the spring of 1907 a disillusioned syndicalist, weary of the struggle against evil, returned to his beloved Italy and settled into the academic vocation whose venality he had so proudly scorned four years earlier. A few months later, Michels withdrew from membership in the Italian Socialist party to concentrate on his lectures and on an article for the *Archiv*, which was to appear in the latter part of 1908, entitled "Die Oligarchischen Tendenzen der Gesellschaft."[2]

Here, for the first time, he emphasized, not the iniquities of German socialism or of socialist parliamentarism, but the sociological analysis of political organization per se. He directed his analysis primarily to the organization of mass democratic parties (i.e., parties whose professed goal is the organization of the masses to prepare for the rule of the masses), and the Marxian solution to the ruling class problem, the socialist state.

Michels' criticism of the Socialist party as a status elevator, which he had begun to generalize when he pointed out similarities between the party, the Church hierarchy, and the Prussian army, was being broadened, through his contact in Turin with the mainstream of sociological thought, into a modification of Pareto's theory of the circulation of elites. Pareto agreed with his contemporary, Mosca, that history revealed a political elite to be a constant factor in political life; a ruling class, which would always be present, whether the outward form of the regime were democratic, aristocratic, or monarchic. But Pareto's particular contribution to elite theory was to point out the abrupt, catastrophic character of the change from one elite to another, as a result of the inevitable physical and moral exhaustion and decline of any particular ruling group. Michels saw this process of change in the elite, on the contrary, "less as a real succession than . . . a continual amalgamation of new elements with the old."[3] This was the framework in which Michels placed his critique of popular democratic movements. Instead of destroying the ruling class, they give it new life.

> No popular movement, no matter how powerful and energetic, is capable of producing lasting and organic changes in the social structure of human civilization, because the leading elements of this popular movement itself, the men who once led and inspired it, little by little separate themselves from the masses, in order to be absorbed by the "political class," to which they bring perhaps few new ideas, but so much the more youthful creative power and practical intelligence and which they thereby conserve in a kind of continually renewed process of rejuvenation. . . . Eternally immature, the majority of men seem to be compelled, through a cruel fatality of history, to endure the rule of a small minority from their midst, and only to serve as a pedestal for the weight of oligarchy.[4]

This modification of Pareto's theory—based on Michels' personal experience of the mode of absorption of the upper bourgeoisie into the Prussian army and of the function of socialism as a status escalator*—was to constitute the Cologne idealist's major contribution to sociological theory and to provide the theoretical basis for at least two major studies after *Political Parties*.⁵

Michels' critique of the Marxian solution to the problem of elitism relied largely on Mosca. Michels began by recognizing Marx as the author of the only scientific doctrine capable of opposing the elitist thesis that ruling classes were an inevitable feature of human society. For Marx, capitalism created, in the proletariat, its own gravedigger. As soon as the proletariat was sufficiently mature, it would seize power and nationalize all property. In doing so, it would abolish class distinctions and antagonisms and, consequently, any possibility of class rule. Michels replied:

> The administration of society's wealth can only proceed satisfactorily through the creation of an extended officialdom. In this point, however, doubts are again raised which lead to an outright denial of the possibility of a classless society. The administration of an immeasurable capital, above all when it is a question of capital belonging to the state, puts into the hands of the administrators just as much power as would the possession of their own capital, of private ownership. Does not the possibility then arise, say the critics of the Marxian society, that the same instinct which leads the present property owners to leave their accumulated riches as a legacy to

---

* French socialism, though not the target of Michels' attack, was the best example of his "status escalator" analysis. From Millerand to Robert Lacoste, the leaders of the French working class showed a remarkable agility in entering the house of power and leaving their troops on the street. But these were usually instances of bourgeois climbing, since the leadership was usually thoroughly bourgeois in origin. In the analysis of German social democracy that he made in his syndicalist days, it was the corruption of the proletariat, through the entrance of its most conscious elements into a petty-bourgeois stratum of party bureaucrats, that aroused Michels' ire. Of course, under the Weimar Republic, the German party leadership, purged of its left wing but including some ex-workers like Ebert, climbed en masse into the seat of power. It is true that, unlike their French colleagues, the German leadership never cut their ties to the party once they had arrived. Whether this was because their power was still rooted in the party or because German workers are more tolerant than French of their leaders remains an open question.

Scholarly Retreat, Social Pedagogy, or Elitism? 313

their children will cause the administrators of public wealth and property under a socialistic constitution to use their immense power to have their sons named as successors in office?[6]

Michels' own attitude toward this analysis was divided. The somewhat different positions he adopted clearly reflected his recognition that the tendency of all organization to oligarchical control did away with both the ethical, redemptive effects which, in his youthful fervor, he had hoped would result from the entrance of the proletariat on the stage of world politics,[7] and also the possibility of any control by the masses over their own organizations and over that of the state.[8] But this recognition produced a threefold reaction.

As a disillusioned socialist, tired of fruitless polemics, he sometimes appeared ready to abandon all hope for political improvement and retreat behind ivied walls of scholarly relativism:

> For the idealist, every penetrating analysis of the forms of democracy, such as is offered to us today, must release feelings of the bitterest disillusionment and discouragement. Perhaps only a world-view which, without indulging in sentimental dilettantism, recognizes the relativism of all scientific and political ideals, is capable of delivering a just judgment on democracy.[9]

This view, if consistently followed, would have brought Michels close to the detached position of his colleague and fellow elitist, Mosca. But he had sacrificed too much of his life, his career, his youth to the proletarian cause to surrender completely his old idealism. The tendency to oligarchy, while inescapable, could at least be mitigated through the criticism and control of the leadership by the masses. And the degree of this mass control depended to a great extent on the level of material well-being and education in the proletariat: "The leader of the rich has much less unlimited power over the circle of his class comrades than the leader of the poor, who, taken as a whole, stand mostly in a relation of complete helplessness to their leader, because their low formal education does not enable them to judge him and his dealings correctly."[10] Therefore, it was still possible for an intellectual idealist to fight against the oligarchical tendency in the labor movement through what Michels called "social pedagogy."

Yet a third position appeared in this essay: acknowledging the weakness of democracy and the inevitability of a ruling class, discarding democracy as an ideal, and simply favoring the cultivation of the best possible elite. In discussing the antecedents of Mosca, whom he acknowledged as the leading contemporary representative of elitist thought, Michels referred to an essay by Barrault, a follower of Saint-Simon, entitled "La Hierarchie." Barrault contrasted the society of the future, "the political transformation of the love which unites all men in God," to the society of the present, "this sad *independence* which today isolates feelings, opinions, and efforts, and which, under a pompous name, is nothing but egoism, accompanied by all the evils to which it gives birth." The Saint-Simonian proposed a ruling class of "the most loving, the most intelligent and the most strong men, living personification of the triple progress of society, capable of directing it in a greater development [*dans une plus vaste carrière*]."[11] Michels presented Barrault's ideas sympathetically, and if we recall that the "egoism" against which Barrault preached invariably had a similar negative connotation in Michels' writings, we can perceive the attractiveness that this line of thought must have had for Michels.*

---

* In *Political Parties* (Glencoe, Ill., 1949), where this passage from Michels' article was copied over, the author added three insertions, which largely undercut the earlier sympathetic treatment of the hierarchical conceptions of the Saint-Simonists and Fourierists. These insertions appear to have been primarily inspired by Sorel's view of the utopians, since, like Sorel, Michels in his additions deprecated the acceptance by the utopians of absolutist, Napoleonic, and Caesarist conceptions. Nevertheless, three other minor passages in *Political Parties* reveal Michels' continued attraction to the elitist position. At the end of footnote 25, p. 178: "Among those who voted against the resolution were such men as Antonio Graziadei and Alessandro Tasca di Cuto, belonging to the old aristocracy of birth, and perhaps for this reason inclined to take a more elevated view of human dignity"; and "There are a few theorists of syndicalism who already speak unreservedly of socialism as an evolution based upon the action of working class elites" (p. 353); and "The ideal government would doubtless be that of an aristocracy of persons at once morally good and technically efficient" (p. 407). The latter passage, it is true, appears in the context of a paragraph arguing for democracy as a lesser evil, since the "good aristocracy" was so rarely attainable. But the point is not that Michels was an elitist in 1911, merely that the position had its attractions for him.

Thus, alongside of Michels the disenchanted scholarly relativist and Michels the social pedagogist, there appeared the first anticipation of Michels the supporter of fascist elitism.

27

From International Socialism to Italian Nationalism

THE WAY THESE THREE ELEMENTS in Michels' thought worked themselves out in future years was largely a function of how he adjusted his value system to his altered view of the world.

As a young man, impelled by a communitarian ethic that emphasized self-sacrifice and condemned egoism, Michels rebelled against German bourgeois society. The philosophical value of self-consciousness, drummed into him, as into so many of his compatriots, by the traditional philosophical idealism of the German university, meant to him, above all, consciousness of one's social self: pride in one's class and in its historical role might be the closest interpretation of what the phrase meant to him. But Michels' class of origin—the Cologne merchant patriciate—was at the time of his birth fast crumbling before the encroachments and attractions of Prussian military bureaucratism. In the face of this destruction of his hereditary ethos, Michels could identify neither with the German bourgeoisie nor with the Prussianized Germany that was reducing it to a servile condition. As an uprooted idealist, an alienated intellectual, he could have resolved his need for identification by identifying with another class, or with another nation.

Michels first identified with the proletariat. The outlines of this identification are clear. In his earliest works[1] he depicted the proletariat as achieving self-consciousness, by which he meant not only pride of class, but consciousness of its universal human value as well through the spirit of self-sacrifice as developed in economic and political struggles. The social ethic that he saw as resulting from the proletarian achievement of self-consciousness consisted basically in pacifism, international solidarity, and recognition of the right of every nation to self-determination. For Michels too, self-consciousness, that is, consciousness of true human interests and values, was only attainable through sacrifice and renunciation, the surrendering of his class position, his family ties, his inherited wealth, and his career. For Michels too the social ethic that emerged from his achieved consciousness consisted in pacifism, international solidarity, and recognition of the rights of weaker nations. That these values were smuggled by Michels himself from his family heritage and only then discovered as a part of the natural law and the proletarian's consciousness is immaterial. What is crucial is the parallelism imposed in Michels' mind on his own value scheme and that of the proletariat. The only point where the two outlines conflicted —and here, dramatically—was in the original motive for sacrifice and renunciation. For the proletariat, it was economic necessity, arising from the workers' position in the process of production.[2] For the intellectual, it was social idealism.[3]

As Michels' criticism of the workers' organization developed, he was gradually driven to conclude that the difference in motives produced different desires, capacities, and moral codes. The distinction between socialist consciousness and proletarian class consciousness, mentioned above,[4] evolved. The workers, without the idealistic intellectuals, could never rise to a universal human conception of their political task, but would merely sink into the materialism of class egoism. The conception of the working class as an historical agent of moral regeneration gave way to one in which the leadership alone played the really active role in the mass movement. The leaders could take the path of least resistance, accommodate themselves to the materialism of the masses, and establish themselves within the workers' movement as a new oligarchy.

Or they could follow the path of idealism, raise the masses to their own creative, ethical level, by continually steeling them, through revolutionary strikes, for the final struggle.

In his important *Archiv* article of 1908, Michels abolished this choice. The iron law of oligarchy guaranteed the historical obsolescence of the idealistic motive. This article established the fundamental theoretical basis of *Zur Soziologie des Parteiwesens in der modernen Demokratie (Political Parties)*, published three years later. But having established the inescapable tendency of the leadership to oligarchy, Michels was still faced with the problem of recasting, in sociological terms, his definition of the proletariat itself. This recasting emerged in three studies written during the years 1908 to 1912 and published, along with some half-dozen other essays, in *Probleme der Sozialphilosophie* (1913). Accompanying it was a fundamental transformation of his idealist presuppositions.

The first, and perhaps most important, of Michels' sociological studies of the proletariat, was his inaugural speech as a professor in Turin, delivered in December 1908, and printed in the *Archiv* of 1909.[5] "Zum Problem der Kooperation" was an attempt at a sociological analysis. Though Michels clearly valued cooperation, he was apparently uncertain of his conceptual ground in approaching the phenomenon. To the extent that he fell back on an idealistic framework, a framework of essences and natural laws, he was inclined to view favorably the prospects of human cooperation on any level, from the trade-union to the entire development of human society. Viewing cooperation in its empirical historical development, however, he found it little more than a mask for the egotism and antagonism of one group against the other.

Thus, he continued to reveal the split mode of analysis that I have referred to in his two early articles on the academic vocation and in his two articles of 1905 on the relationship of nationalism and internationalism. But now a circle has been completed.

In Michels' first article on academic freedom, though he mocked it in practice, he appeared to accept the principle of it. In his second, the idealistic principle was ignored in favor of a view that emphasized the total corruption of the institution by bourgeois society. Michels' idealism retreated to the political arena, to the struggles of the weaker peoples and the oppressed classes. In 1905 he ceded the area of national liberation too to the depravity of the pragmatic, real world, and his idealism retreated again, to the working class. It almost simultaneously surrendered a part of the soul of the working class—the strictly material class interest—and withdrew to the embattled beachhead of revolutionary syndicalism to carry on its struggle for a moral world. And here, Michels' radical idealism was quite destroyed. In his admission of the iron law of oligarchy he handed over his last position to the enemy. Vanquished on the political battlefield, Michels' idealism, impelled partly no doubt by his own material needs, partly by his many friendships among academicians, but surely also by his need to grasp intellectually what he could not politically conquer, took refuge in the territory it had years earlier surrendered to the enemy: the university.

Much of this development is unwittingly recapitulated in Michels' essay on cooperation. The first page and a half of this study, with its total abstraction from actual historical development and its presupposition of a simple pleasure-pain calculus as the mainspring of human behavior, might have been written by an eighteenth-century *philosophe*:

> In order to grasp the immanent tendency to cooperation in the Homo Oeconomicus, the indispensable precondition is to comprehend the essence of the general aspirations of mankind in an isolated economy. . . . Man labors not so much for the goal of producing goods, but he is rather driven to labor and suffers it patiently—for work has never lost completely its initial character of pain—only because he hopes through it to escape a yet more intensive feeling of pain, which would necessarily originate through the failure to satisfy his needs.

The essence of the operations of economic man, Michels went on, was summed up in the question: "How can the most usefulness be attained with the least expenditure of energy or, in other words, with the least amount of displeasure?" Since human needs could not be satisfied by individuals working in isolation without an enormous amount of trouble and strain, "We may therefore assert that the principle of cooperation stems from the law [N.B.] of the least expenditure of energy."

Immediately following these introductory paragraphs, Michels offered a purely *historical* account of the medieval dominance, French revolutionary dissolution, and then renewed dominance in the modern period of cooperative institutions.[6] But here "cooperation" received a different economic connotation. In the first paragraphs, cooperation merely meant the purely objective division of labor that prevails in any society beyond the most primitive. It could easily include the unrestrained competition of laissez-faire capitalism. In the main part of the essay, cooperation described only the conscious, willing, working together of economic men (though it also comprehended compulsory working together, under a mercantilist system). By thus altering his conceptual framework in these first pages, Michels reduced the scope of cooperation from a universal and necessary phenomenon, independent of subjective wills, to a product of specific historical conditions, largely dependent on the group will of the cooperators.

The source of cooperation in the modern period was the helplessness of the isolated propertyless worker in capitalist society, driven to cooperation for self-defense.[7] His organs of cooperation were the trade-union, the Socialist party, the consumers' cooperative, and the producers' cooperative.[8] As an answer to the workers' cooperation, both the capitalists and the petty bourgeoisie had seen fit to break with their individualist ideology and organize their own forms of countercooperation: price-fixing cartels, trusts, etc.[9]

Thus, cooperation was the result of social antagonism. It bound together, but it also bound against. It produced social harmony within a group at the same time that it confirmed the antagonistic relationship of this group to another in the society:

> The presupposition of cooperation is opposition, struggle. An eternal Janus Bifrons, cooperation is surely, by its essence, directed toward striving for the solidarity of mankind (teleological cooperativism). Nevertheless, insofar as it only maintains its capacity for life through the quarrels and differing interests of different groups of the social aggregate, it owes its origins and its growth principally to the negation of human solidarity (practical cooperativism).[10]

Was there a quiet irony, perhaps self-irony, in this juxtaposition of the teleological and the practical? of cooperation viewed positively, on the one hand, as solidarity and defined by "essence," and viewed negatively on the other, as antagonism, defined by the historical causes of "origin and growth"?

Michels' sociological analysis of working-class cooperation was further darkened by his realization that social antagonism also existed between different groups of workers: between workers and unemployed, between city and land workers, between skilled and unskilled labor, between workers and worker-officials of socialist parties, and, perhaps worst of all, between workers and worker-managers in a cooperative. He commented bitterly, "The organized workers, who tend to be so sensitive to the exploitation they are themselves subjected to, are often completely void of the same sensitivity, as soon as it is a question of comrades to whom they stand as employers."*

To Michels, then, "It is easily understandable if, among men of science, there are not lacking those who, in the face of the inextricable mass of social conflicts, are beset by pessimistic weariness, and formulate this weariness in the theoretical formula that the word 'cooperation' is only a euphemism, behind which hides the hateful egoism of small groups of economic men, and that it is incapable of ever developing to the representative of the general interest."[11] Nevertheless,

> there is still one ground on which cooperation is capable of thriving, regardless of all differences of a social, national, and confessional nature. This ground is science. The god of science is no Janus Bifrons. Scientific cooperation . . . undoubtedly represents the purest and most elevated form of cooperation. Theoretically outside of the struggles of the day, to which the other forms of cooperation owe their origin, and raised above

---

* In one of his earliest articles, "Ein Kinderstreik" (*Die Frau*, October, 1902, pp. 16–19), Michels had acknowledged that a strike of Milanese girls against their petty-bourgeois employers was in many cases a struggle of proletarian against proletarian, since their employers were often themselves only a higher layer of the proletariat. But unlike his later view in the essay on cooperation, he had decided that the *real* conflict was nevertheless the one between capital and labor, since even the proletaroid element was only exploitative because the big capitalists were so niggardly in paying them.

every prejudice, science, international according to its innermost essence [N.B.], feels no interested hatred against any of the social classes, since its only and indivisible goal consists in the serious and strict, but unprejudiced and just, search for the truth.[12]

In the case of economic and social cooperation, Michels had looked behind the formal and abstract essence—the striving for human solidarity—to the practical origin in social antagonism. In the matter of scientific cooperation, he takes the "essence" at face value. What a contrast to his earlier article, "Kapitalismus in der Wissenschaft," where the academic world itself was depicted as an arena of competing egoists!

In the brief essay "Solidarität und Kastenwesen," Michels again took up the motives of cooperation. Here, altruism and selfishness are jointly listed as necessary ingredients of class solidarity. But "the most significant motive" is hatred.

He viewed the proletariat in somewhat different terms in an essay published the following year.[13] The earlier study had essentially been an attempt to trace the historical development of cooperation, and especially working-class cooperation, analyze its motives, and measure them against Michels' accustomed value categories: egoism and altruism. In the later piece, Michels' own values were not so obvious. The study rather represented an attempt to locate the correct conceptual treatment of the proletariat amidst the conflicting approaches of those who would like to apply the maxims of natural biology directly to the analysis of society (social Darwinists), and those who would like to establish limits on the applicability of natural science to the social sciences.

In a manner typical of his scholarly writings in this period, his first section was an historical narration of the changing view of the proletariat since the eighteenth century. He adumbrated the admiration of the *philosophes* for the man of the people, whose physical endowments and moral character were seen as a healthy contrast to the softened, degenerate upper classes. He traced the decline of this view, beginning with the actual contact between middle and lower classes in the French Revolution, to the point where the modern age, as attested by quotes from Tocqueville and

Sombart, had come to believe that the more a worker perfected himself as a worker, the more he degenerated as a human being.

Thus, in general, the modern world viewed the proletariat with hostility. Social Darwinism was the scientific form of this hostility: "The natural scientists justify the miserable position of the proletariat through the law of selection. The poor have deserved their poverty, because they are mentally, spiritually, morally and physically destitute. Their destitution . . . lies in the very interest of human civilization."[14]

The political scientists and economists—and Michels sided with them—though they did not deny the wretched physical and spiritual status of the proletariat, refused to give it any moral justification, such as an appeal to the law of selection. Arguing against the social Darwinist Otto Ammon, Michels distinguished the sphere of human society from nature by pointing to man's economic and social institutions, and the social and psychological laws that arose from these institutions.[15] The law of natural selection could not apply to a society where, in the wealthier classes, the weak were artificially preserved and, among the poor, poverty killed off even the strong. A second distinction, according to Michels, was that between nature and human economy. Citing Eduard Bernstein, and speaking once more in terms of essences, Michels characterized the inherent tendency of nature as the greatest conceivable waste, while that of human economy was toward husbanding, the preservation of goods: "Its whole art consists in taming and restraining, as far as possible, the beast of nature. It is the greatest possible emancipation of men from natural forces."[16] The only jurisdiction that Michels would unreservedly concede to natural science was over the physical condition of the individual. Only in rare cases could it govern groups of men, and then not at all insofar as their "higher functions" were concerned. Political economy, on the other hand, was not at all concerned with the individual.* It rather in-

---

* This view of the task of political science probably explains Michels' insensitivity to the *verstehen* philosophy of history, which emphasized understanding the individual and renounced the possibility of historical laws. Only once in Michels' writings does one encounter any appreciation for *verstehen* methodology. This was in a 1904 review, in *Ethische Kultur*, of a book on Pietro d'Abano: "Sante Ferrari has become to him [d'Abano] an extremely

vestigated the mass phenomena of social and economic institutions, unlocked the secrets of their existence and development, and deduced from them social laws governing past, present, and future. This Michels named "descriptive and normative economy."[17]

Michels continued here the double level of analysis that characterized his essay on cooperation. In rebutting social Darwinism on the historical, descriptive, empirical ground of existing human society, he was objecting to its applicability to social classes, but he was not really denying its ultimate validity. He was not denying, for instance, that if the class differences could be leveled, there might be a natural tendency for the stronger to survive and the weaker to perish, and that efforts to encourage this tendency might be morally unobjectionable. Nor was he denying that *within* existing social classes, unjustifiable as the social division might be, the law of selection perpetuated the stronger individuals. Only through the second, normative argument, proceeding from the different "inherent tendencies" of nature and human economy, did he categorically refute the scientific and ethical viability of social Darwinism: it denied the essence of man.

In his conclusion, Michels recognized Niceforo's thesis of the physical inferiority of the poor compared with the rich "as the anthropological-anthropometric proof of a proposition long recognized by social science, and logically derived directly from the basic concepts of historical materialism." Michels' closing question, in echoing his previous call for social pedagogy, revealed the lingering shadow of his old idealistic hopes for human betterment: "Is this spiritually and physically defective proletariat, as it appears in the studies of political-social anthropology, ripe for its emancipation as

---

diligent and conscientious biographer, more, an understanding *Nachfühler* and *Nachdenker*." The basis of Michels' indifference to this then very important approach to history can only be surmised, since he never discussed it. Perhaps it is that even when he was concerned, as a syndicalist, with the willing, feeling, acting proletariat, his interest was in the class, not the individual. And at this stage, he was in any case much too politically committed to interest himself in this kind of theoretical problem. Later, when his disillusion led him into sociology, he was only concerned with establishing the laws of the system that defeated him. By the time of his enthusiasm for fascism in the 1920s his theoretical framework had been set for life.

a class, and, if we must answer no to this question, what have we to do to make it ripe?"[18]

Three years later, Michels had come much closer to the social Darwinist position. He no longer attacked it on any level, but simply raised the question of whether the physiological inferiority of the proletariat was a biologically permanent fact of heredity or a function of the low living standards of proletarian families.* Reflecting this uncertainty was the dual task of eugenics which Michels set forth to raise the level of the lower classes:

> No Nietzschean art production of supermen, but an anthropological improvement of the race through the elimination of completely unfit and morally inferior elements from the reproductive cycle and, what we would perhaps value even more, the initiation of a reform work improving the economic and social relations of men.[19]

Alongside of this partial acceptance of biological techniques—with their social Darwinist overtones—as one valid method of raising the level of the lower class, emerged another significant feature of Michels' development. Michels had originally conceived the masses as the subject, or moving force, of history. In his syndicalist phase, he imposed the responsibility for bringing out this subjective capacity of the masses on an idealistic leadership. In his social pedagogy phase, though acknowledging the inevitability of oligarchy—shifting the center of action still more towards the leadership—he preserved a role for the masses and their idealistic friends, as a democratic countercurrent. Even in the last lines of his introduction to Niceforo's book (1909), he implied that, with the help of the social pedagogist, the proletariat might yet become ripe for its own emancipation. In the paper on eugenics, he removed from the proletariat even a potential role as a subjective power and placed the entire responsibility for its healthy development in the

---

* Robert Michels, "Zum Problem der Eugenetik," in *Probleme der Sozialphilosophie* (Leipzig and Berlin, 1913), pp. 44–53. This study was written after August 1912, since it refers to the eugenics congress of that month, and is probably the German version of Michels' "Sociology and Eugenics," which appeared in *Problems in Eugenics*, papers communicated to the First International Eugenics Congress, University of London, 1912. Page references will be to *Probleme der Sozialphilosophie*.

hands of the intellectuals. They alone were capable of transforming the world.

Michels' negative reference to Nietzsche ought not to obscure for us how close he had come to accepting the philosopher as respectable company. The drastic evolution that this near-acceptance symbolized in the development of Michels' value system appears clearly in the light of an earlier evaluation of Nietzsche. In 1904, Michels had written:

> What an absolute difference between Nietzsche and de-Amicis. There the crassest egoism and individualism; here the noblest altruism and socialism! Artists though they both are, the one tears down tradition only to replace it with an ideal of self-satisfaction, while the other, though equally destructive of tradition, demands, with a prophetic view of humanity, a better and more secure future, which he declares not only humanly, but aesthetically, more beautiful than the barren present.[20]

Further evidence of the weakening of Michels' original value system appeared wherever his values interacted with his social theory. Two conspicuous cases were his attitude toward human progress and his studies of sexual morality.

The attitude Michels ascribed to de-Amicis—"the prophetic view of humanity"—characterized his own early view of progress. Elsewhere, Michels accepted progress as a given rather than a problem.[21] Only once did he present a brief analysis of the concept of progress. In his first publication in a scholarly journal (1904) he wrote that there were many notions of progress, and each was conditioned by the world-view in which it appears: "For, as Antonio Labriola says, we express nothing with the word 'progress' but that, according to an empirically ascertainable tendency, 'the successive acts and labors are constituted, so to speak, in reference to a goal, the attainment of which is only gradually possible by means of intermediary steps.'"[22]

The equation of progress with the idea that "successive acts ... are constituted ... in reference to a goal" signified that Michels adhered to a teleological conception of history. He did not consider the question of nonteleological conceptions of history. Since the teleological view was part of Michels' idealistic socialism and the argument from "essences," it should not surprise us to find a drastic revision of his notion of progress in the period when Michels' idealism crumbles.

Having, in effect, abandoned as impractical his teleological conception of social phenomena (such as cooperation), Michels became concerned with destroying the assumption that had been implicit in this teleology: that progress was manifested in the actual course of history.[23]

He began where he had stopped in 1904: The concept of progress depended on the values of the viewer.[24] He then divided the problem into manageable areas where certain lines of development might or might not be viewed as progressive, depending on the point of view: economy, demography, aesthetics, progressive social movements, and international understanding. In each case, wrote Michels, the appearance of improvement, the form, was undermined after a close inspection of the content. (This "form" turns out to be the more quantitative material aspect of the evolution, while the "content" usually refers to the more qualitative, or spiritual, aspect.)

Thus, in literature, a quantitative spread of learning produced more scholars and more dissertations, but fewer and less important geniuses. He pointed to a life of decadence in all the major European literatures: from Dante to d'Annunzio, from Molière to Rostand, from Goethe to Sudermann, and from Shakespeare to Shaw. And, paradoxically, most of the great poets and authors emerged precisely in "epochs of political stagnation, tyranny, and economic crises."[25]

In demography, urbanization had brought progress in prolonging life, but only at the price of over-all physical degeneration in the increased population (the result of foul air, urban diseases, poor living conditions, etc.).[26]

A cursory glance at the techniques of production revealed "the only unambiguously established progress."[27] But this progress, too, was questionable if one considers the social evils that accompanied nineteenth-century industrialism. "The future will decide on the reality of economic progress." Prophetically connecting the social instability of German economic success with a world war that was still in the future, Michels feared that perhaps "the most magnificent and remarkable economic development which modern history knows, is only the prelude to a symphony of Hell."[28]

In the case of social movements aiming at the transformation of society—the problem at the base of Michels' whole intellectual development—the "duplicity of progress"[29] was no less clear. Once again, the health of the flesh concealed the decay of the spirit. Progress in the enlarging of party treasuries, membership lists, and voters was indisputable. "But at the same time, with the growth and predominance of an independent leadership, viewing the party increasingly as an end in itself, the party is alienated from the goals for which it originated. . . ."[30]

On the question of internationalism, Michels saw the same dichotomy of external progress (the institutions) and internal regression (the sentiment). But here his own values were ambiguous, because he could not decide whether internationalism, which preserved the peace, or nationalism, which might disturb the peace but manifested the will to a national existence, was the more important. The old triad, internationalism, pacifism, nationalism, was again present. Michels, having exhausted his internationalist sympathies in the syndicalist movement, had recultivated his nationalist sentiments, but he had not yet abandoned his pacifist inclinations, and his old internationalist beliefs still lingered beneath the surface of his desire for world peace. He was, however, aware that if peace were to be permanently secured, without a plebiscite among all peoples, it would only preserve injustice (e.g., the suppressed nationalities of the Austro-Hungarian Empire). This awareness brought him to the following tortured conclusion: "War is irrational, but not immoral, at least not absolutely. War can be unjust, but it is not so in itself. It can even fulfill a mission of justice."[31] Thus, Michels presented us with a separation of reason and ethics, whose significance for his later sympathy towards fascism cannot be underestimated.

In Michels' conclusion, he opted for an arbitrary, or at best cyclical rather than progressist, conception of most aspects of history, and invoked Vico, as the theorist of historical *corsi* and *ricorsi*.* His final decision on the subject was clear and hard: "It would be appropriate to ban the word progress, at least as an absolute, from the terminology of the scholar, and at most permit the discussion of definable, limited progress in definable, limited spheres."³²

Another area in which we can see a relaxing of Michels' value system was his approach to sexual morality. From 1903 to 1905, his writings on the subject revealed little more than a detestation of bourgeois sexual ethics and a corresponding elevation of proletarian morality. Articles in 1906 and 1909 showed a progressive softening in his approach. His study of coquetry (written between 1909 and 1913) was a masterly analysis of the motives and function of the phenomenon, without a trace of moral indignation.

His "Beitrag zum Problem der Moral" (1903) was a glorification of proletarian morality over bourgeois. Proletarian women were chaste in their clothing, bourgeois women were crudely coquettish. Proletarian sexual relations were more natural than bourgeois. And bourgeois men did not respect the honor of proletarian women.

In *Brautstandsmoral* (1904) he condemned as emotionally unhealthy the essentially bourgeois custom of keeping the betrothed couple strictly separated before the wedding night.

In "Die Dirne als die alte Jungfer des Proletariats und die Prostitution" (*Mutterschutz,* 1905, pp. 58–65), he compared the middle-class old maid with the working-class woman of the streets, viewing the forced prudishness of the one and the forced sexuality of the other as two sides of the evil effects of capitalist morality on unmarried women. Prostitution was condemned without qualification as aesthetically nauseating and ethically degrading. Society itself was the archvillain: "So long as it is still possible for a woman's body to be bought for a shabby gold, silver, or nickel coin, our much praised civilization is nothing but a pretty façade behind which are concealed filth and crime."

---

* "The political, mental, and artistic history of peoples consists in an incalculable series of small progresses and small regressions, joined to one another without any harmony and method, and with no other lawfulness than that capricious tendency, which Vico described as the *corsi* and *ricorsi* of history." *Probleme der Sozialphilosophie,* p. 84.

Michels wrote this piece at the height of his syndicalist fervor against bourgeois society. A year later, his hatred for *German* society was just as strong, but it was softening as far as France was concerned. "Erotische Streifzüge" (*Mutterschutz*, 1906, pp. 362–374) maintained the condemnation of German prostitution, but made the distinction, in the Parisian variety, between the really degraded playthings of the wealthy on the Right Bank, and the sophisticated streetwalkers, frequently sensitive to intellectual and aesthetic matters, of the Latin Quarter, who often had platonic relationships among the students, or nonpaying lovers, who were unaware of their profession.

A few years later, Michels further modified his once absolute condemnation of prostitution and the society that produced it in "Die Zwischenstufen der Ehrbarkeit" (*Mutterschutz*, 1909, pp. 351–59). Analyzing sexual behavior in Italian cities, he found it difficult in many cases to say who is a prostitute and who not. There was, apparently, a whole stratum of single girls who would take both sewing work and men in the same room for pay. The ground, of course, for accepting this kind of supplementary income was the low wage for sewing piecework. How, then, were these girls to be economically classed: as dressmakers or prostitutes? And how were they to be morally judged? Clearly, no unambiguous solution was possible. Michels held the same relaxed view of young married middle-class women, who, bored with a purposeless existence, might frequent dance halls and flirt with young men while their husbands were at work.

Finally, in "Zum Problem der Koketterie" (*Probleme der Sozialphilosophie*, pp. 94–98), he subjected coquetry to a purely sociological analysis. The principal theses were: that the motives of coquetry were more often the desire to be admired than sexual licentiousness; that one must distinguish three motives of coquetry: a) the simple sensuous love of beautiful clothing, b) sexual desire, and c) antisexuality, or the use of coquetry by sexually cold women to gain control over men; and that the function of coquetry was to serve as a socially sanctioned lightning rod for polygamous sex drives that monogamous society is incapable of eliminating. Characteristic for the evolution of Michels' values is the shifting of responsibility for coquetry between the first article and the last, from "bourgeois society," which was an object of attack, to "monogamous society," at most an object of investigation.

Underlying all these changes in Michels' moral stance is a crucial problem in the history of Western thought since the French Revolution. How, if one rejects idealistic categories, traditionally bound to natural law, such as inherent tendencies and essences, can one retain the secular social ethic that is also bound to natural law? In his early years, through the idealist and socialist doctrines he accepted, Michels had been a philosophical descendant of eighteenth-century proponents of natural law. His absolutist ethics were also derived from that tradition. Now, his faith in socialism shattered, he veered ever closer toward the moral relativism of social Darwinism and the historical school of law. How, in this new framework, was he to maintain any kind of philosophical basis for the strong ethical impulse that had so far guided him?

Now it is most unlikely that Michels' value system was fundamentally determined by purely theoretical considerations. Michels' difficulties in maintaining a theoretical basis for his moral presuppositions can be traced to his gradual weaning, under the impact of harsh political reality, from idealistic socialism, or—and this is the psychological aspect of that weaning—to the breakdown of his identification with the proletariat. I have asserted above that, as a result of total alienation from both his native land and his class of origin, Michels had to identify either with a different class or a different nation. His efforts to identify his romantic idealism with the proletariat having failed, he very quickly began to find a haven for his personality and values in the Italian national character.

One of the grounds for this new identification appeared in a sociological study of the international bourgeoisie written between 1910 and 1913.[33] Mosca had pointed to three bases for the power of a ruling class: physical power (the warrior class), economic power (the wealthy class), and mental power (the religious and the intellectual class). In terms of historical development, the warrior class was the most primitive, and the intellectual—often developing from the religious—the most advanced. In *Political Parties*, this triad is presented nonhistorically as "factors which secure the domination of minorities over majorities," with two minor changes: the religious factor is ignored, and the warrior factor is presented as the factor to which it has been reduced since the Middle Ages, i.e., "tradition and hereditary transmission (historical superiority)." In his piece on the international bourgeoisie, Michels assumes that all three of these factors are at hand in every ruling bourgeoisie, but that the predominance of one factor or the other produces a fundamental difference between the characters of the national bourgeoisie. Thus, in Germany the power of custom is uppermost, in America the power of money, and in Italy the power of education and culture.[34] We need only reflect a moment on what these different factors symbolized to Michels' mind to see why his view of the Italian ruling class as imbued with the spirit of culture made Italy so attractive to him. The power of custom was associated with the "brutal egoism" of the Prussian feudality. The predominance of the money factor represented everything Michels hated apart from the Prussian state: the crude materialism of the trade-union bureaucrat and the smug bourgeois. But a bourgeoisie of intelligence, of culture, of education was another matter. Culture and quality as characteristics of a bourgeoisie must have offered great attraction to Michels.

Apparently as a result of his early impressions as a student in Turin (1900–1901), Michels was, even in his first publications, full of praise for the social and political life of Italy.* As noted above,

* In addition to what I have mentioned above on pp. 281–85, there are, for example, the following references:
"From the tree of recent political freedom [in Italy] have grown, continually, social fruits . . ." ("Kampf um eine Arbeiterinnenschutzgesetzgebung in Italien," *Die Frau*, June–July 1902, p. 618).
"Italy is distinguished in other respects essentially from Germany. It has democratic institutions, and possesses no industrial monstre-établissements" ("Zum Problem der Arbeiterhäuser," *Deutschland*, #2, 1903, p. 740).
"Italy has far surpassed Germany in some things. This is so in the sphere of criminology, that is, in the area of the penal code, and also in the effecting of true academic freedom, as well as in many aspects of the so-called woman's question" (book review, *EK*, XI, 1903, p. 248).
Further, Michels found a complete absence of militarism in Italy. The reasons were the lack of a military tradition; the Italian sense of justice, which cultivated a love of peace; the forty-year war of liberation, which strongly impressed on the national consciousness the idea that the army was only in existence for the liberation of one's own land from foreign servitude, and not for the seizure of foreign territories ("Die Friedensbewegung in Italien," *Die Frau*, May 1903, p. 461).

when he was analyzing the perilous tendency of *Nationalbewusstsein*, once national independence was achieved, to pass into aggressive *Nationalismus*, Michels specifically exempted Italy from this course. Nevertheless, his transfer of allegiance from the proletariat to the Italian nation was no more abrupt than his occupational development from revolutionary syndicalist to academician. Just as the latter change had been prepared by numerous friendships among German and Italian scholars, as well as a series of scholarly studies of German and Italian socialism, so his change in personal identification similarly occurred through intermediary steps.

The initial stage was his revulsion against German socialism's failure, as embodied in Bebel's patriotism, to recognize the right to self-determination of national minorities within the boundaries of the Reich.[35] This revulsion, apparent in 1906, suggests the brevity of Michels' rejection of any kind of national sentiment, which appeared in only one article of late 1905.[36] But as yet, Michels' renewed acknowledgment of the right to national self-determination was abstract, unspecific, and mainly directed against the patriotism of some of the German socialists.

In 1908 we find the first signs of a new identification. In a report on the German Socialist Congress at Essen, Michels expressed great concern over the increased patriotic fervor of the party chiefs, especially Bebel.[37] As "the most serious danger" which might result from this patriotism, Michels feared that precisely the internationalists in the socialist movement, who had rejected patriotism as a prop to the state, might be forced into a patriotism of their own.

> If it is no difference to us whether we are French or German, it is not a matter of indifference to us whether we live in a democracy or in an autocratic empire. And then, in face of the reactionary moves of German socialists, the question is posed for us: Before the dangerous patriotism of the most menacing state in Europe, ought we not to prepare ourselves to shelter from its attacks the milieus which offer to civilization and to culture the guarantees which are necessary to them? This reawakening of a democratic patriotism, which would be comprised of a union of all the free forces of Europe, is the

extreme consequence which is implied by the patriotic action of the socialists of the Germany of William II.³⁸

It seems likely that around this period Michels saw his ideals at least partially represented in French democracy in general* and in French socialism, which he claimed had superseded German social democracy as the model for other movements to emulate.³⁹

In 1909 Michels' democratic patriotism took a new turn. He castigated not only German social democracy, but socialism in general, for its feeble defense of oppressed minorities. Pacifism too was condemned, insofar as it would perpetuate their subjection by preventing wars of national liberation. Nevertheless, Michels was moving toward his future nationalist position without any illusions. He was as aware as ever that even movements of national liberation, once they attained their goal, invariably turned into movements for the suppression of other nationalities. Michels had once exempted Italy from this tendency.⁴⁰ In view of Italy's bellicose threats on the Austrial Tyrol, he no longer did.⁴¹

In the same year, Michels showed greater attachment than ever to the Italian character in "Der ethische Faktor in der Parteipolitik Italiens."⁴² In large measure, this attachment took the form of admiration for Italian socialism, which he declared to be at least partially superior to the French.⁴³ Working-class solidarity, he wrote, "frequently assumes forms of sacrifice, of idealism which the *Realpolitikers* of the North are not only incapable of emulating, but even of feeling, of mentally reconstructing."⁴⁴ Moral demands that the Germans scorned as utopian were written into the party program in Italy: "Morality is one of the first postulates of the Italian worker. Corresponding to this is the demand for the personal integrity of the socialist, in which all representatives of Italian socialism are united."⁴⁵

Praise of the Italian proletariat, however, had been present from the beginning of Michels' literary career. More interesting was

---

* Unlike Sorel, Michels insisted upon the value of a democratic milieu as the framework for revolutionary agitation. See Michels, "Le Syndicalisme et la Socialisme en Allemagne," in *Syndicalisme et Socialisme,* Hubert Lagardelle, ed. (Paris, 1908), p. 24; Georges Sorel, *La decomposition du Marxisme* (Paris, 1908), p. 61.

another form of admiration, which appeared for the first time in this article: the discovery of ethical principles in the hearts of the Italian bourgeois. This could take the shape of true academic freedom—hiring of professors without respect to political or religious beliefs—with the result that some sixty university teachers were members of the Socialist party.[46] It could take the shape of sympathy and admiration for the struggles of the lower classes.* It could also take the form of a very understanding, human relationship based on common conceptions of the national good between bourgeois and socialist parliamentarians. In this context Michels' characterization of the Italian bourgeoisie as a bourgeoisie of culture is easy to grasp.

A study of patriotism, four years later, shows further development of Michels' thought on the decline of socialist internationalism and the growth of patriotic feeling in the working class.[47] It is noteworthy that he copied several pages directly from one of his own early studies on patriotism, in which he juxtaposed the position of the worker in production against that of the capitalist, to show how the worker was forced to think along class rather than national lines, and how the patriotism of the capitalist was a mere mask for interest.[48] But Michels presented this earlier view only to show how obsolete it had become.

In probing the decline of socialist internationalism, Michels cited five factors in particular.[49] The character of democracy was one. To gain the favor of the masses, the rulers, or contenders for rule, had to flatter the crowd and its national characteristics. Thus, democracies were always more patriotic than aristocracies. The reduction of socialist tactics to parliamentary activity was another such ground. Parliamentarism also dictated the abandonment of internationalism to avoid the charge of being "unpatriotic" and a consequent loss of votes among marginal supporters. A third and very significant reason was increasing prosperity and more educa-

---

*"When the Internationalists wanted to hold a regional conference in March 1873, in Mirandola . . . the enthusiasm in that city was so powerful that even the innkeepers were captured by it, and offered to lodge the participants of the congress, without cost, in their houses" (p. 87). Michels uses here, for the first time, the word *Opferfreudigkeit* (self-sacrifice) to describe the actions of a specifically bourgeois grouping.

tion. With the decline of illiteracy, Michels argued, the workers were tied closer to the national culture through the national literature.[50] Thus, an ironic result of the social pedagogy Michels had previously championed to help the workers resist the betrayals of their leaders was to increase the patriotism of the proletariat. A fourth ground was the development of economic conflicts between the national working classes through proletarian migrations. The working classes of many countries became inaccessible to international solidarity by the competition in the job market from imported foreign laborers. Finally, imperialism, too, bred patriotism in the working class. The worker was dependent, in many cases, on the position of his branch of industry in the world market: imperialism secured old markets and seized new ones for the products of the land. To the extent that the workers' organizations were strong enough to extort a share of the booty for him, the worker too profited by imperialism.

But the rising tide of patriotic socialism was not only inevitable; it was also preferable to a purely internationalist socialism. The Austrian party, through its espousal of abstract internationalism, only served the cause of national oppression, because it weakened the parties for national independence within the Austro-Hungarian Empire.

Perhaps most significant of all was Michels' separation of patriotism from logic and ethics: "We are dealing here partly with a sentimental impulse, partly with a juridical concept, both of which, however, defy any logical or ethical description."[51] Wars of national liberation may also have been irrational phenomena to Michels, but his theoretical support for them was certainly based on ethical grounds. Some sort of ethical justification had always been crucial for Michels, no matter what he did. It was his own "inherent nature." Was he now abandoning all his old ethical standards in his growing cultivation of Italian patriotism?

A more plausible explanation is that Michels' value system was undergoing a change of which he himself was perhaps unaware. He was not abandoning his old values of self-sacrifice and self-consciousness, but neither was he ready to recognize that the meaning he was giving to these terms was changing radically. In pursuing his socialist ideal of a society of morally pure human beings, conscious of their dignity, and all sacrificing for the common good, Michels had accepted the syndicalist ideology of will—the will of an elite—as the element that would shake the workers from their lethargy and lead them to act for the new social order. As everything else faded from his socialist ideal, he retained this notion of will; it played a vital role both in his general Italian patriotism, and in his later sympathy for fascism. But though the notion of a national will was inseparable from the patriotism which Michels was coming to accept, it was too much in opposition to his traditional detestation of egoism for him to accept it as an ethic. He was forced to play a game of hide-and-seek with his values, with the result that, at one point, he could accept the attraction of patriotism on his sentiments while denying it any conscious sanction from his value system.

Michels' final number in a series of epitaphs for international socialism which he had been writing since 1907, appeared in 1916.[52] Here Michels analyzed the disintegration of the Second International as a result of the war. Though he generally condemned the workers' movements for submitting without resistance to the demands of their governments for aid in the war effort, he placed the real responsibility on the shoulders of German social democracy. The other parties, he wrote, merely came to the defense of their attacked fatherlands. But the Germans actually helped their government in preparing a war of conquest and plunder.

Wherever the blame lay, however, Michels considered it impossible that international socialism, after the war, should see a renewal of the ideals of fraternity and justice of prewar years:

> Alas! Socialism had promised to become a noble path against every kind of oppression: and it has not understood that the Serbs of Austria thrilled with the desire to be united to their brothers of the Serbian Kingdom; and it has allowed the crushing of Belgium, as if it were the most logical and natural thing, in closest conformity with socialist dogma. The socialists had guaranteed that they would do everything to prevent an offensive war; and they have acclaimed it, on the contrary, with an arrogant joy. The socialists had maintained they did

not know the meaning of racial hatred; and they began, on the contrary, as soon as the war had broken out, to speak of inferior and superior races. Today, millions of socialists . . . disparage, insult, hate and massacre one another. Socialist virginity no longer exists, and there is nothing that can bring it back again.

Nevertheless, socialism, if not of an idealistic hue, was sure to revive again, once the workers felt in a position to press their material claims of recompense for their wartime suffering:

> After the war will rise a working class certainly forgetful of its old goals of international justice, but more than ever penetrated with its egoistic rights, and firmly resolved to make them prevail without too many agreements. The class struggle will not cease to persist, but it will be deprived of all idealism; it will be base in its ends, but implacable in its means. It will be led according to a method full of ruses, deceptions and villainous ambushes, like this infamous war in which the submarines excel. And it will be precisely those states whose submarines are now doing, in this war, the most destructive work, where—if signs do not deceive—"the workers' revival" will be most palpably manifested.

By 1916, then, socialism had become associated for Michels with the antitheses of morality. His old identification with the proletariat was irrevocably broken. Soon after, the new identification, not yet centered exclusively on Italy, emerged more clearly than ever. In a speech delivered in Turin in 1917, Michels revealed his deep attachment to the values of Latin—especially French and Italian—culture.[53]

The characteristics of Latin civilization which, in Michels' eyes, distinguish it from and raise it above other civilizations are notably familiar. They include (1) aesthetic aptitudes, "infinitely more developed among the Latin peoples than among all others";[54] (2) natural intelligence: "There is some truth in the sarcastic phrase of Enrico Ferri that the peasant of Calabria, though unable to read or write, is more intelligent than half of the German university professors."[55] (3) "the spirit of moral rebellion against all oppression and every offense to human dignity"; and (4) "a great force of moral attraction and a capacity for assimilation, which one must attribute to a characteristic quality of their mode of civilization, artistically and humanly superior, though technically less evolved."

In his conclusion to this essay, which pointed as much to the future of his thought as his previous work had pointed to the past, Michels emphatically reasserted his new fusion of morality with the cause of Latin culture:

> The vitality of a people is determined neither by its antiquity nor by its youth, but only by its moral forces. France and Italy have proven that they are not deprived of them, and have demonstrated also by deeds that they can still fulfill a considerable moral and political function. Even today, the Latin heritage extends its light over the ancient historical sphere of Rome.

Conclusion

THE FIRST WORLD WAR marked a turning point in the history of the psyche as well as the polity of the West. The apprehensions of cultural disaster that governed the basic assumptions of the earlier and most creative work of Tönnies, Sombart, and Michels were echoed and distorted on a massive scale by the militant antiliberal *Ressentiment* of the lower-middle class in Germany and Italy. Moreover, the fall of the Wilhelmian Empire had deprived the bureaucratically oriented Mandarins of the German academy of much of their institutional support, with the result that the dominant group of conservative antimodernists, who had looked disdainfully on the questioning, antitraditional aspect of the sociologists' work, suddenly found their traditions—not to mention their status—threatened by imminent destruction. Conservative protectors of the regime under the empire, they became vehement opponents of the socialist-supported republic in the 1920s. Their opponents, the heirs of the modernist social scientists of the *fin de siècle*, men such as Ernst von Aster, Leopold von Wiese, and Karl Mannheim, were in a situation where at long last modernism had a tangible regime to defend. In this new context, the antimodernist cultural criticism of the prewar Tönnies and Sombart, even if undulled by age, was bound to be barely distinguishable from that of the postwar epigones of sociological antimodernism, men such as Hans Freyer, Carl Schmitt, and Othmar Spann.

Thus, the First World War signaled a major change in the intellectual milieu as well as the perspective of my subjects, a change so great as to make extensive consideration of the later careers of the two of my subjects who remained in Germany the concern of a book dealing in depth with the cultural and social history of the Weimar Republic. In the context of this change, both Tönnies and Sombart found themselves largely conforming to the line of development set by their earlier work. For Tönnies, the full realization of what had happened to Europe, of the destructive forces latent in the social development of *all* the nations of Europe, aborted his growing reconciliation with the German nation-state. His later reflections on the question of progress, while they maintain some hope for a temporary reprieve from barbarism through the rise of the working class, envisage the same fate of ultimate decline that had obsessed his earlier years:

> Even if these hopes should be fulfilled more completely than I think probable, such fulfillment would not shake me in my judgment of the final destiny toward which our civilization proceeds. It is a tragic destiny, which insightful and decisive will (which is, alas, so rare) may long delay, but without conquering it, a destiny which yet may be raised and transfigured for centuries through all the flames of a burning civilization, but which approaches as unavoidably as the Ragnarök of the Asians. It is not far wrong to see in the experiences of the seven years 1914–21 and in the victories of Panslavism a prelude to the tragedy.[1]

Tönnies' philosophical consolation vis-à-vis this approaching doom was a circular notion of history similar to Vico's *corsi* and *ricorsi* and Nietzsche's eternal return, and a pantheistic conception of human civilization as merely one minor expression of the infinite and eternal forces of nature.[2]

Werner Sombart obtained from the war a nationalist fervor and a confirmed hatred of Western European culture which enabled him, despite certain reservations, to become one of National Socialism's leading intellectual fellow travelers from the early 1930s until his death in 1941.[3] The work of Tönnies had, in a sense, more decisively refuted the nostalgic hopes of the historical school of political economy, with its preindustrial values, than any of the direct polemics with its representatives in which Sombart had engaged. When Sombart suddenly sickened of his early ideals of progress and industrialization, he quickly realized that the door to the past, which Schmoller and Gierke had thought to be open, was proven by Tönnies to be irrevocably shut. As for the class of the future, the proletariat, Sombart had associated it too closely with the now-rejected values of industrial society to see any hope in socialism. Too energetic a man to maintain for long the complete withdrawal from social commitment of the years 1903–1908, Sombart discovered within the capitalist spirit the spirit of heroic enterprise, and, by identifying the latter with the German nation, found a new basis for the passionate commitment to a living ideal which his nature seems always to have craved.

For Michels, of course, the war signaled the complete collapse of any surviving hopes for a socialist world, the horrible fulfillment of all his expectations. He had, in any case, for some time before its outbreak considered himself an Italian, and the war signified only the ultimate rupture between himself and the land and class he had rejected. Michels seems to have, in a way, mirrored the political evolution of Sombart, with the difference between them being more geographical than anything else. But this is illusory. Sombart had made many commitments to causes. For Michels, there was only one, and when that was wrecked by his own experiences and then obliterated by the war, a part of his spirit died with it.

Certainly, none of his postwar works even approaches the stature of *Political Parties*. The reason for this, I believe, lies in the complicated kind of social idealism, stemming perhaps from the old guild ethics of his grandfather and possibly furthered by his contact with Georges Sorel, which led Michels to his fervent advocacy of socialism in the years before his disillusionment. According to James Meisel, Sorel agreed with Durkheim's belief that, "By breaking up the old professional associations which held the individual wills together we have destroyed with our own hands the chosen instrument of our moral reorganization."[4] Was there not some relation to this view of Sorel's and also a spark of Peter Michels' heritage present when Robert Michels described the type of the "half-educated and arrogant" American labor leader in the words of *Le Neveu de Rameau:* "I will be like all the dressed-up beggars. I will be the most insolent scoundrel you have ever seen."[5] In thus citing Diderot as having a premonition of the amoral opportunist of the nineteenth century, Michels simultaneously bared the soul of Diderot's work and his own as well. But there was one important difference. Diderot could explore the dialectic in his own personality—the coexisting elements of, on the one side, the good eighteenth-century burgher, filled with most wholesome and enlightened moral ideas, but just a bit of a Philistine, and, on the other, the wild Bohemian, cynical and romantic, never viewing a human relationship as valuable in itself but only as a means of satisfying the ego—in a spirit of play, because the opposition of the two elements in the social order would only emerge in the future. Life in the prerevolutionary regime was so well organized into groups—guilds, estates, salons—that there was no danger of the asocial beast being really unleashed as a social phenomenon (individual cases were, of course, always possible). But in the fractured society of Michels' day, this unleashing becomes an ever greater possibility. It is particularly easy for it to occur in the workers' movement. Not only on the part of proletarian leaders who have become alienated from their original class, but equally among leaders of bourgeois origin who have become alienated from their faith:

> For those who have been thus disillusioned, no backward path is open. They are enchained by their own past. They have a family, and this family must be fed. Moreover, regard for their political good name makes them feel it essential to persevere in the old round. They thus remain outwardly faithful to the cause to which they have sacrificed the best years of their life. But, renouncing idealism, they have become opportunists. These former believers, these sometime altruists, whose fervent hearts aspired only to give themselves freely, have been transformed into skeptics and egoists, whose acts are guided solely by cold calculation.[6]

Michels' early intellectual model seems to have been the *philosophe*, who could face the future serenely and could trust his intellectual and spiritual milieu for a conservative, healthy, personal development outside the framework of the corrupt and outmoded institutions of society. But as his education in the ways of his party became fuller, Michels saw that not only was socialism turning into another bureaucratic institution of society; it was turning into the most advanced institution—the most asocial, opportunistic, egoistic institution—that society could offer. His reaction to this discovery took the form of a retreat from the arena of the political *neveux* to a private intellectual life within the academic institution. Here he was able to retain a thin scrap of his former idealism, but as a result of the suicide of the *neveu-daemon* within, he was unable to prevent the extinction of that spark of genius that the safely internalized anarchist-rebel-Bohemian had lent to Diderot and, in his younger years, himself.

At the cost of his own soul, then, Michels closed the door to the future just as surely as Tönnies had closed it to the past.

But the social commitment of these men not only caused them spiritual travail, it also severely handicapped their careers. As a socialist, Michels was barred from teaching in Germany. Tönnies had to wait until twenty years after the publication of his *magnum opus* before obtaining a permanent position at Kiel. And Sombart, though permitted to teach in Breslau and, after 1907, in the commercial college in Berlin, did not receive a position commensurate with his stature until 1917.

What is the contemporary value of the sociological insights bought with such sacrifices? For the most part, a set of negative propositions: human community is *not* compatible with contemporary institutions; the victory of the capitalist spirit ends in the murder of the autonomous spirit by capitalism; and the movement that intended to transcend capitalism and reestablish community became a mirror image of what it opposed and hence incapable of changing anything fundamental. Under the conditions of half a century ago, these propositions led their authors to a blind alley of despair, to the "iron cage" lamented by Max Weber in his work on the Protestant ethic. Today they can have a different meaning.

In the first place, we need reminding that such ideals as Tönnies' community, Sombart's autonomous creative spirit, and Michels' altruistic socialism were considered by these sociologists of Imperial Germany to be worth the sacrifice of potentially magnificent academic careers. In the second, the possibility of implementing these ideals must be reexamined. For industrial centralization, alienated labor, and economic scarcity, which were more or less presupposed by these men, and on which their despair was at least partially contingent, need no longer be viewed as the inexorable destiny of mankind. The re-creation of a decentralized communal life becomes conceivable when the urban complexes which the factory system required are rendered unnecessary by automation. The same automation may so reduce the necessary labor time as to liberate individual personality from subjugation and manipulation by the economic apparatus. And if the increased education and vastly increased leisure time made possible by the new industrial revolution permit the replacement of professional political bureaucracies by rotating committees of unpaid citizens, then the iron law of oligarchy may prove to be made of inferior tin.

I am not attempting to assert the "objective" desirability of these goals, though I make no secret of my personal sympathy for them. Nor am I asserting the inevitability or even the probability of their attainment. But it does seem to me that if the tormented communities of mankind can avoid their self-destruction by ecological or nuclear apocalypse, they may soon be in a position to break out of the cage of bureaucratic and industrial modernity in whatever directions appear most consonant with their values, happiness, and mutual welfare. In such circumstances, it seems to me of great value for the social scientist and the humanist to return to the obscured origins of contemporary sociology, where they may find not only perspectives for the delineation of new critical approaches to the analysis of society, but also examples of the courage that they will need to face their responsibilities.

Abbreviations Used

ASG: *Archiv für soziale Gesetzgebung und Statistik*

ASP: *Archiv für Sozialwissenschaft und Sozialpolitik*

EK: *Ethische Kultur*

FW: *Das Freie Wort*

MS: *Le Mouvement Socialiste*

SSK: Ferdinand Tönnies, *Soziologische Studien und Kritiken*, 3 Vols., Jena, 1924–27

S-L: Unpublished letters from Werner Sombart to Otto Lang, in the International Institute for Social History, Amsterdam

T-P, P-T: Letters from Ferdinand Tönnies to Friedrich Paulsen and from Paulsen to Tönnies in *Tönnies-Paulsen Briefwechsel, 1876–1908*, edited by Klose, Jacoby, and Fischer, Kiel, 1961

Notes

PART I

Introduction and Chapter 1

1. Frank E. Manuel, "Two Styles of Philosophical History," *Daedalus*, March 1962, p. 408.
2. Hans Freyer, *Die Bewertung der Wirtschaft im philosophischen Denken des neunzehnten Jahrhundert*, Leipzig, 1921, p. 132
3. See Marx/Engels Gesamtausgabe, Erste Abteilung, Band 5, *Die Deutsche Ideologie*, 1933, pp. 43, 67, 185, 198.
4. See Loomis and McKinney's introduction to the English translation of *Gemeinschaft und Gesellschaft*, New York, 1963, pp. 5, 20.
5. Max Weber, *Wissenschaftslehre*, Tübingen, 1951, p. 132.
6. Ibid., pp. 427, 527. On this retreat see Arthur Mitzman, *The Iron Cage, An Historical Interpretation of Max Weber*, New York, 1970.
7. Erich Fechner, "Der Begriff des kapitalistischen Geistes bei Werner Sombart und Max Weber und die soziologischen Grundkategorien Gemeinschaft und Gesellschaft," *Weltwirtschaftliches Archiv*, vol. 30, 1929, p. 197.
8. See Gottfried Salomon, *Das Mittelalter als Ideal in der Romantik*, Munich, 1922.
9. Karl Marx, *German Ideology*, New York, 1947, pp. 46–47.
10. Fechner, "Begriff des kapitalistischen Geiste," p. 211.
11. Ernst Troeltsch, "The Ideas of Natural Law and Humanity in World Politics," in Otto Gierke, *Natural Law and the Theory of Society, 1500–1800*, Boston, 1957, p. 210.
12. Roy Pascal, *The German Sturm und Drang*, Manchester, 1959, p. 304.
13. Franz Schnabel, *Deutsche Geschichte im neunzehnten Jahrhundert*, Band I, Freiburg, 1947, p. 96.
14. Helmut Plessner, "Nachwort zu Ferdinand Tönnies," *Kölner Zeitschrift für Soziologie*, 1955, p. 346.
15. Talcott Parsons, *Essays in Sociological Theory*, Glencoe, Ill., 1954, pp. 104–12.

16. Schnabel, *Deutsche Geschichte*, p. 73.
17. Pascal, *The German Sturm und Drang*, pp. 12, 19, 31, 89; and Paul Kluckhohn, *Persönlichkeit und Gemeinschaft*, Halle, 1925, p. 5.
18. Arthur Lovejoy, "Schiller and the Genesis of German Romanticism," in *Essays in the History of Ideas*, New York, 1960, p. 211.
19. Ibid., p. 220.
20. Friedrich von Schiller, *Werke*, Weimar, 1962, vol. XX, p. 323. Emphasis added.
21. Freyer, *Bewertung der Wirtschaft in philosophischen Denken*, p. 26. Heinrich Popitz, in *Der entfremdete Mensch, Zeitkritik und Geschichtsphilosophie des jungen Marx* (Basel, 1953), discusses the relationship of Schiller's *Briefe* to Hegel and Marx on pp. 28–36, as does Walter Kaufmann in his *Hegel, A Reinterpretation* (New York, 1965), pp. 46–57.
22. Schiller, *Werke*, p. 321.
23. See Jacob Baxa's introduction to *Gesellschaft und Staat im Spiegel deutscher Romantik*, Jena, 1924, pp. 17–18.
24. T. S. Hamerow, *Restoration, Revolution and Reaction*, Princeton, 1958, pp. 21 ff., 102 ff.
25. See Karl Marx, *Capital*, trans. Untermann, Chicago, 1909, vol. III, p. 954, quoted in Erich Fromm, *Marx's Concept of Man*, New York, 1962, pp. 59–60.
26. Schnabel, *Deutsche Geschichte*, p. 23

Chapter 2

1. Hannah Arendt's term. See her *Origins of Totalitarianism*, Cleveland, 1958, pp. 227–43.
2. Fritz K. Ringer, *The Decline of the German Mandarins, The German Academic Community, 1890–1933*, Cambridge, Mass., 1969, passim.
3. See Peter G. J. Pulzer, *The Rise of Political Anti-Semitism in Germany and Austria*, New York, 1964, pp. 35, 88–101; Fritz Stern, *The Politics of Cultural Despair*, Berkeley and Los Angeles, 1961, pp. 66, 90; Paul Massing, *Rehearsal for Destruction*, New York, 1949, chapter 1.
4. See Ringer, *Decline of the German Mandarins*, pp. 128–99.
5. Pulzer, *Political Anti-Semitism*, p. 99.
6. See Weber's letter to Heinrich Braun in Julie Braun-Vogelstein,

Heinrich Braun, Ein Leben für den Sozialismus, Stuttgart, 1967, p. 349.
7. See Lewis A. Coser, "The Outsider in the Academy," in *Georg Simmel*, ed. Coser, Englewood Cliffs, N.J., 1965, pp. 29–43.
8. Paul Honigsheim, "The Young Simmel," in *Georg Simmel, 1858–1918*, ed. Kurt Wolff, Columbus, Ohio, 1959, pp. 168–69.
9. *Buch des Dankes an Georg Simmel, Briefe, Erinnerungen, Bibliographie*, ed. Kurt Gassen and Michael Landmann, Berlin, 1958, p. 13; Ringer, *Decline of the German Mandarins*, pp. 151–52; Braun-Vogelstein, *Heinrich Braun*, p. 85.
10. Honigsheim, "The Young Simmel," p. 169. Also *Stefan George, 1868–1968*, ed. B. Zeller, W. Volke, and G. Hay, Munich, 1968, pp. 142–48, 240, 353.
11. Kurt Gassen and Michael Landmann, *Buch des Dankes an Georg Simmel*, Berlin, 1958, p. 282 ("Erinnerungen an Simmel von Margarete Susman").
12. See Arthur Mitzman, *The Iron Cage, An Historical Interpretation of Max Weber*, New York, 1969, pp. 1–163 passim.
13. Ibid., pp. 148–53.
14. Ibid., pp. 148–306 passim.
15. Max Weber, "Religious Rejections of the World and Their Directions," in *From Max Weber; Essays in Sociology*, ed. Hans Gerth and C. Wright Mills, London, 1952, pp. 323–59.
16. See Albert Salomon, "Max Weber," *Die Gesellschaft*, 1925, and Wolfgang Mommsen, "Universalgeschichtliches und politisches Denken bei Max Weber," *Historische Zeitschrift*, Vol. 201, December 1965, pp. 557–612.
17. Ringer, *Decline of the German Mandarins*, p. 308.
18. Ferdinand Tönnies, *Der Nietzsche-Kultus, eine Kritik*, Leipzig, 1897.
19. On Weber's marginalia in Simmel's book, see Mommsen, "Universalgeschichtliches und politisches Denken."
20. Friedrich Nietzsche, *Werke in drei Bände*, ed. Karl Schlechta, Munich, 1954, vol. I, pp. 387 ff.
21. Friedrich von Schiller, *Werke*, Weimar, 1962, vol. XX, p. 322.

PART II

Chapter 3

1. Ferdinand Tönnies, "Anmerkungen über die Philosophie des Hobbes," *Vierteljahresschrift für wissenschaftliche Philosophie*, III (1879), pp. 453–66, IV (1880), pp. 550–74, V (1881), pp. 186–204. Hereafter referred to as Tönnies, "Anmerkungen."
2. Ferdinand Tönnies, "Über die Entwicklungsphasen Spinozas," ibid., VII (1883), pp. 158–83, 333–64.
3. Ferdinand Tönnies, "Ferdinand Tönnies," in *Philosophie der Gegenwart in Selbstdarstellungen*, Leipzig, 1922, vol. 3. Hereafter referred to as Tönnies, "Autobiography."
4. Heinrich Meyer, "Theodor Storm and Ferdinand Tönnies," *Monatshefte für deutschen Unterricht*, U. of Wisconsin, No. 32, pp. 355-80. Hereafter referred to as Storm-Tönnies.
5. Ferdinand Tönnies, *Theodor Storm zum 14 September 1917*, Gedenkblätter, Berlin, 1917.
6. Ferdinand Tönnies, Friedrich Paulsen, *Briefwechsel*, eds. O. Klose, E. G. Jacoby, and I. Fischer, Kiel, 1961. Letters from Tönnies to Paulsen will be designated "T-P"; from Paulsen to Tönnies, "P-T." Dates of letters will be given as they appear in the book—day, month, year.

Chapter 4

1. See below, p. 99.
2. Friedrich Paulsen, *Friedrich Paulsen, an Autobiography*, New York, 1938, p. 288 (hereafter referred to as Paulsen, *Autobiography*).
3. Tönnies, "Autobiography," p. 1.
4. Friedrich Hoffman, "Volksleben und Volkswesen in Husum vergangener Zeiten," *Zeitschrift für Schleswig-Holsteinische Geschichte*, 75 (1951), pp. 296–319. Population statistics for the towns of Schleswig are on pp. 297 ff.
5. Tönnies, "Autobiography," p. 2.

Notes

6. Tönnies, "Autobiography," p. 2.
7. Gertrud Storm, *Theodor Storm*, Berlin, 1912–13, 2 vols., vol. II, p. 145.
8. Tönnies, "Autobiography," and G. Storm, *op. cit.*, p. 165.
9. See pp. 94–97.
10. Tönnies, "Autobiography," p. 3.
11. Tönnies, "Autobiography," p. 4.
12. See Tönnies, "Autobiography," p. 4, and Storm-Tönnies, Tönnies' letter of June 1, 1872.
13. Tönnies, "Autobiography," p. 1.
14. Tönnies, "Autobiography," p. 4.
15. Tönnies, "Autobiography," p. 5.
16. Friedrich Nietzsche, *Werke in drei Bänden*, ed. Karl Schlechta, Munich, 1954, vol. I, pp. 137–38.
17. Tönnies, "Autobiography," p. 6.
18. Ferdinand Tönnies, *Der Nietzsche-Kultus, eine Kritik*, Leipzig, 1897.
19. Tönnies, "Autobiography."
20. Tönnies, "Autobiography," p. 7.
21. Ferdinand Tönnies, *Eine höchst nötige Antwort auf die höchst unnötige Frage: "Was ist studentische Reform?,"* Berlin, 1875.
22. Tönnies, "Autobiography," p. 7.
23. Paulsen, *Autobiography*, p. 247.
24. See pp. 63 and 73 ff.
25. Paulsen, *Autobiography*, p. 248.
26. Tönnies, "Autobiography," p. 8.
27. Ibid.
28. T-P, 29/6/76.
29. Tönnies, "Autobiography," p. 8, and P-T, 7/7/76.
30. T-P, 26/11/77.
31. Ibid.
32. P-T, 30/12/77.
33. Tönnies, "Anmerkungen," 1879. See also T-P, 2/11/79.
34. Cf. P-T, 30/12/77, and Tönnies, "Anmerkungen," 1881, pp. 199–201.
35. Tönnies, "Anmerkungen."
36. Ibid., p. 202.
37. David Hume, *Dialoge über Natürliche Religion*, 1877, intro. by F. Paulsen, p. 15.
38. P-T, 30/12/77 and T-P, 17/1/78.

Chapter 5

1. T-P, 25/5/78.
2. P-T, 20/6/78.
3. P-T, 20/6/78.
4. T-P, 9/7/78, pp. 28–37.
5. T-P, 9/7/78, p. 29.
6. T-P, 21/7/78.
7. P-T, 24/7/78, pp. 33–34.
8. P-T, 16/8/78.
9. Published by Tönnies in 1889 as *The Elements of Law, Natural and Political*.
10. T-P, 21/8/78.
11. T-P, 21/8/78.
12. P-T, 3/9/78, p. 45.
13. T-P, 25/5/78.
14. T-P, 25/5/78.
15. T-P, 25/5/78.
16. T-P, 21/8/78.
17. Paulsen, *Autobiography*, p. 291.
18. Tönnies, "Political Parties in Germany," *The Independent Review*, September 1904, pp. 572–73.
19. Franz Schriewer, "Theodor Storm in seiner politischen Welt," in *Schriften der Theodor Storm Gesellschaft*, Schrift I, Heide in Holstein, 1952, pp. 27–41, p. 34.
20. T-P, 9/7/78.
21. T-P, 7/10/78, p. 51.

Chapter 6

1. Tönnies, "Autobiography," p. 11.
2. Paulsen, *Autobiography*, p. 275.
3. T-P, 9/11/80, 9/1/81, 1/2/81, 29/4/81.
4. P-T, 14/10/80.
5. T-P, 10/3/83 and Tönnies, "Autobiography," p. 15.
6. T-P, 8/2/80 and 29/8/80.

7. P-T, 27/2/80.
8. Ibid.
9. P-T, 2/3/80.
10. T-P, 29/8/80.
11. T-P, 11/10/80.
12. T-P, 21/10/80.
13. E. Laveleye, *De la propriété et de ses formes primitives*, 1874, trans. and ed. K. Bücher in 1879 as *Das Ureigentum*.
14. See T-P, 30/10/79 and T-P, 21/8/78.
15. T-P, 31/10/79. Emphasis is Tönnies'.
16. Thomas Carlyle, *Past and Present*, Book II, chapter V, in 1918 Scribner ed., pp. 79–81. The introduction to this edition by Edwin Mims is excellent.
17. See p. 41.
18. See note 13.
19. See the preface to the first edition of *Gemeinschaft und Gesellschaft* in Ferdinand Tönnies, *Soziologische Studien und Kritiken*, 3 vols., Jena, 1924–27 (hereafter referred to as SSK), vol. I, p. 43, preface to the second edition (1912 SSK, I, p. 54), and "Entwicklung der Soziologie in Deutschland im 19. Jahrhundert" (SSK, II, 93 ff.) and T-P, 2/11/79.
20. Laveleye/Bücher, *Das Ureigentum*.
21. Ibid., p. 87.
22. SSK, I, p. 53.
23. T-P, 8/2/80.
24. T-P, 2/5/80.
25. T-P, 9/1/81.
26. SSK, I, pp. 33.
27. SSK, I, p. 4.
28. SSK, I, p. 21.
29. Ibid.
30. SSK, I, p. 32.
31. T-P, 21/16/85.
32. T-P, 30/10/79.
33. See the preface to the first edition of *Gemeinschaft und Gesellschaft*, reprinted in SSK, I, pp. 34–44, esp. pp. 34–36.
34. SSK, I, p. 30.
35. Ferdinand Tönnies, "Die Anwendung der Descendenztheorie auf Probleme der sozialen Entwicklung," SSK, I, pp. 146, 242, and "Die Entwicklung der Soziologie im 19. Jahrhundert," SSK, II, pp. 88 ff.

36. Ferdinand Tönnies, "Historismus und Rationalismus," SSK, I, pp. 105–10.
37. R. König, "Die Begriffe Gemeinschaft und Gesellschaft," *Kölner Zeitschrift für Soziologie*, 7 (1955), pp. 348–420, 350–53.
38. Talcott Parsons, *The Structure of Social Action*, Glencoe, Ill., 1949, p. 689.
39. See J. Leif, *La Sociologie de Toennies*, Paris, 1946.
40. T-P,11/10/80, p. 91.
41. T-P, 15/5/81, p. 127.
42. T-P, 26/1/82, p. 147.
43. T-P, 10/5/82.
44. T-P, 10/3/81.
45. T-P, 21/10/80.
46. T-P, 6/3/81.
47. T-P, 28–29/3/81.
48. T-P, 2/6/82.
49. T-P, 5/7/82.
50. T-P, 26/3/82, p. 152.
51. T-P, 26/1/85.
52. H. F. Peters, *My Sister, My Spouse, A Biography of Lou Andreas-Salomé*, New York, 1962, p. 153. Other details in Rudolf Binion, *Frau Lou*, 1968, pp. 115–18.
53. See editor's note to Storm-Tönnies.
54. T-P, 21/8/78, p. 38.
55. T-P, 21/1/84.
56. T-P, 8/1/85.
57. T-P, 22/8/88.
58. E. G. Jacoby, *Tönnies-Paulsen Briefwechsel*, Einleitung, p. xii.
59. Ferdinand Tönnies, *Theodor Storm zum 14 September 1917*, *Gedenkblätter*, Berlin, 1917.
60. Ibid., p. 20.
61. Ibid., p. 24.
62. Ibid., p. 29.
63. Ibid., p. 30.
64. Ibid., p. 61.
65. Franz Schriewer, *op. cit.*, p. 30.
66. Ibid., p. 29.
67. See John Harms Ubben, *The Cultural Background of Theodore Storm's Chroniknovellen* (Dissertation, U. of Chicago, 1942).
68. The material on the history of Schleswig and of Eiderstedt has been

taken from: Rudolf Heberle, *From Democracy to Nazism, A Regional Case Study on Political Parties in Germany*, Baton Rouge, La., 1945, esp. pp. 34 ff., 101 ff.; Rudolf Muus, "Tausendjahre Nordfriesische Stammesgeschichte," in *Nordfriesland, Heimatbuch für die Kreise Husum und Sudtondern*, ed. L. C. Peter, 1929, pp. 140–215; Rolf Kuschert, "Landesherrschaft und Selbstverwaltung in der Landschaft Eiderstedt unter den Gottorfern (1544–1713)" in *Zeitschrift für Schleswig-Holsteinische Geschichte*, 78 (1954), pp. 50–138; Volquart Pauls, "Zur Geschichte der Eiderstedter Gerichtsverfassung," in *Zeitschrift für Schleswig-Holsteinische Geschichte*, 57 (1928), pp. 169–203.
69. Paulsen, *Autobiography*, p. 27.
70. Ibid., p. 29.
71. Ibid., p. 48.
72. Ibid., pp. 73–74.
73. Ibid., p. 75.
74. Ibid., p. 71.
75. Ibid., pp. 72–73.
76. Thomas Mann, "Theodor Storm," in *Essays of Three Decades*, trans. H. T. Lowe-Porter, New York, 1948, pp. 274–75.

Chapter 7

1. See Ferdinand Tönnies, "Historismus und Rationalismus," SSK, II, pp. 105–10.
2. P-T, 12/2/88.
3. Gottfried Salomon, *Das Mittelalter als Ideal in der Romantik*, Munich, 1922, p. 85.
4. Heinrich Popitz, *Der Entfremdete Mensch, Zeitkritik und Geschichtsphilosophie des jungen Marx*, Basel, 1953, 172 pp.
5. Quoted in ibid., pp. 18–19.
6. Quoted in ibid., pp. 19–20.
7. Johann Gottlieb Fichte, *Die Grundzüge des gegenwartigen Zeitalters*, Hamburg, 1956, pp. 14–15.
8. Ibid., p. 21.
9. Ferdinand Tönnies, *Gemeinschaft und Gesellschaft*, II, par. 34, Leipzig, 1887, p. 173. Hereafter referred to as Tönnies, *Gemeinschaft und Gesellschaft*.

Chapter 8

1. See T. S. Hamerow, *Restoration, Revolution and Reaction*, Princeton, 1958.
2. Émile Durkheim, "La Science positive de la morale en Allemagne," *Revue philosophique*, Tome XXIV, 1887, pp. 33–58; review of *Gemeinschaft und Gesellschaft*, Tome XXVII, 1889, pp. 416–22. Tönnies, review of *De la division du travail social*, in SSK, vol. III, pp. 215–17. (Originally published 1896 in the *Archiv für systematische Philosophie*.)

Chapter 9

1. Tönnies, *Gemeinschaft und Gesellschaft*, III, par. 29 (1887 edition), p. 264.
2. Ibid., pp. 265–66.
3. Ibid., p. 267.
4. Ibid.
5. T-P, 22/7/88.
6. T-P, 26/11/88 and 14/12/88.
7. T-P, 26/11/88; 6/7/97; P-T, 7/7/97.
8. T-P, 16/7/89.
9. T-P, 3/5/90; P-T, 14/5/90.
10. T-P, 26/6/90.
11. T-P, 1/3/88. Also T-P, 22/8/88.
12. T-P, 15/3/89.
13. T-P, 28/12/89.
14. T-P, 26/11/88.
15. See E. G. Jacoby, "Ferdinand Tönnies," *Kyklos*, 8 (1955), pp. 144–61; and H. Plessner, "Nachwort zu F. Tönnies," *Kölner Zeitschrift für Soziologie* (1955), pp. 6–11.
16. See the article of Cay von Brockdorff, "Persönliches von Ferdinand Tönnies," in the Tönnies *Festschrift* of 1936, *Reine und Angewandte Soziologie*, pp. 363–76.
17. Ferdinand Tönnies, "Fünfzehn Thesen zur Erneuerung des Familienlebens," EK, I (1893), pp. 1, 10.

18. Ferdinand Tönnies, "Ethisches Scharmutzel, offener Brief an Herrn Dr. Franz Mehring in Berlin," *Deutsche Worte*, 12 (1893), p. 47; "Fernere Antwort auf eine brennende Zeit- und Streitfrage," EK, I (1893), p. 37; "Die sittliche Bestimmung der Frauen," EK, III (1895), p. 26.
19. Ferdinand Tönnies, "Ethische Betrachtungen," EK, III (1895), pp. 212–13.
20. Tönnies, "Fünfzehn Thesen," p. 310.
21. Ferdinand Tönnies, "Die Ethische Bewegung," *Umschau*, No. 42 (1899), pp. 842–45.
22. Tönnies, "Ethisches Scharmutzel," p. 47; "Fernere Antwort," p. 37; "Sittliche Bestimmung der Frauen," p. 26.
23. See also T-P, 2/10/92.
24. Ferdinand Tönnies, "Der Hamburger Streik von 1896/97," *Archiv für Soziale Gesetzgebung und Statistik*, 10 (1897), pp. 673–720.
25. T-P, 16/7/93.
26. Paulsen, *Autobiography*, cited in *Briefwechsel*, p. 303.
27. *Briefwechsel*, p. 303, n. 3.
28. P-T, 12/8/98.
29. See Ferdinand Tönnies, "Die Anwendung der Deszendenztheorie auf Probleme der sozialen Entwicklung," SSK, I (1902), pp. 133–330.
30. See Ferdinand Tönnies, "Universitäts-Ausdehnung in England," EK II (1894), pp. 290–92, and "Belleville," EK, X (1902), pp. 235–36.
31. Ferdinand Tönnies, "Eine Anmerkung über Rousseau," *Der Lotse*, No. 41 (1901), pp. 502–4.
32. Ferdinand Tönnies, "Das allgemeine, gleiche und direkte Wahlrecht," EK, XII (1904), pp. 49–51.
33. Ferdinand Tönnies, "Der Königsberger Prozesse," FW, 4 (1904), pp. 361–65.
34. Ferdinand Tönnies, "Political Parties in Germany," *The Independent Review*, II (1904), pp. 565–81.
35. Ferdinand Tönnies, "Ein Rückblick auf den Streik im Ruhrkohlenrevier," FW, 5 (1905), p. 899.
36. Ferdinand Tönnies, "Politische Stimmungen und Richtungen in England," FW, 6 (1906), pp. 337–43.
37. E.g., Ferdinand Tönnies, "Condorcet," FW, 6 (1906), p. 694.
38. Ferdinand Tönnies, " 'S'Gravenhaage und Stuttgart. Zwei Weltkongresse," FW, 7 (1907), pp. 441–48.
39. Ferdinand Tönnies, "Revolution?," FW, 6 (1906).

40. Ferdinand Tönnies, "Französische-deutsche Beziehungen," FW, 7 (1907), pp. 121–29.
41. Ibid., p. 125.
42. Ferdinand Tönnies, "Das Reichstagswahlrecht für Preussen?" FW, 7 (1907), pp. 492–97; "Die Gleichheit des Wahlrechts," FW, 8 (1908), pp. 165–69; "Liberalismus und Demokratie," FW, 8 (1908), pp. 727–32.
43. Ferdinand Tönnies, "Das Jubiläum der Städteordnung," *Die Neue Rundschau*, 19 (1908), p. 1534.
44. Ibid.
45. Ferdinand Tönnies, "Die Krisis des Reichsgedankens," *Die Neue Rundschau*, 19 (1908), pp. 526–7.
46. Tönnies, "Jubiläum der Städteordnung," p. 1553.
47. T-P, 1/3/88.
48. Tönnies, "Jubiläum der Städteordnung," pp. 1553–57.
49. Ferdinand Tönnies, "Rechtsstaat und Wohlfahrtsstaat," *Archiv für Rechts- und Wirtschaftsphilosophie*, 8 (1914), p. 67.
50. T-P, 18/7/85.
51. See below, p. 184.
52. Tönnies, "Rechtsstaat und Wohlfahrtsstaat," p. 70.
53. Ferdinand Tönnies, *Der englische Staat und der deutsche Staat*, Berlin, 1917.
54. Ibid., p. 194.
55. Ibid., p. 102.
56. Ibid., p. 192.
57. See below, pp. 261–64.

PART III

Chapter 11

1. E.g., K. L. von Haller, Hegel, and the professorial rebels of 1848. See Gottfried Eisermann, *Grundlagen des Historismus*, Stuttgart, 1956, p. 31; Fritz K. Ringer, *The Decline of the German Mandarins, The German Academic Community in Decline, 1890–1933*, Cambridge, Mass., 1969, pp. 14–128. The most important studies of the Verein für Sozialpolitik are Franz Boese's *Geschichte des Vereins*

für Sozialpolitik, 1872–1932, Berlin, 1939; Dieter Lindenlaub's *Richtungskämpfe im Verein für Sozialpolitik*, Wiesbaden, 1967, 2 vols; and, in English, Abraham Ascher, "Professors as Propagandists," *Journal of Central European Studies*, 23, 1963, pp. 282–302.

2. Else Conrad, *Der Verein für Sozialpolitik und seine Wirksamkeit auf dem Gebiet der gewerblichen Arbeiterfrage*, Jena, 1906, p. 37.
3. Gustav Schmoller, *Über Einige Grundfragen der Sozialpolitik und der Volkswirtschaftslehre*, 1898, p. 52.
4. Ibid., p. 54.
5. A. L. Sombart, "Innere Kolonisation mit Rücksicht auf die Erhaltung und Vermehrung des mittleren und kleineren landlichen Grundbesitzes," in *Schriften des Vereins für Sozialpolitik* (hereafter cited as *Schriften*), 33 (1886), p. 78.
6. Ibid., p. 79.
7. Ibid., p. 87.
8. *Schriften*, pp. 90–101.
9. Ibid., p. 92.
10. Ibid., pp. 91, 97.
11. Gustav Schmoller, "Der Moderne Kapitalismus," *Schmoller's Jahrbuch*, 27 (1903), p. 292.
12. Werner Sombart, "Das Familienproblem in Italien," *Schmoller's Jahrbuch*, 12 (1888), pp. 285–96.
13. Ibid., p. 290.
14. Werner Sombart, *Die Römische Campagna*, Leipzig, 1888, p. 161.
15. Heinrich Braun, in *Archiv für soziale Gesetzgebung und Statistik* (hereafter referred to as ASG), 1 (1888), pp. 2–3.
16. Ibid., p. 5.
17. E.g., *Schriften*, 39 (1889), 2nd sec., pp. 70–73, 115.
18. Werner Sombart, "Die Hausindustrie in Deutschland," ASG, 4 (1891), pp. 103–56.
19. Ibid., pp. 108–9.
20. Ibid., p. 110.
21. Ibid., p. 117.
22. Ibid., p. 137.
23. Ibid., pp. 129–30.
24. Ibid., p. 129.
25. Ibid., p. 142–46.
26. Ibid., p. 145.
27. Ibid., p. 153.

Chapter 12

1. Dieter Lindenlaub, *Richtungskämpfe im Verein für Sozial Politik*, Wiesbaden, 1967, *passim*; Marianne Weber, *Max Weber, Ein Lebensbild*, Heidelberg, 1950, p. 458; Franz Boese, *Geschichte des Vereins für Sozialpolitik, 1872–1932*, Berlin, 1939, pp. 108–9, 113 ff; and James J. Sheehan, *The Career of Lujo Brentano, A Study of Liberalism and Social Reform in Imperial Germany*, Chicago, 1966, pp. 165–67.
2. Werner Sombart, "Statistik der Hausweberei im Schlesischen Eulengebirge," *Sozialpolitisches Centralblatt*, I (1892), p. 391.
3. Ibid.
4. "Entwickeln wir uns zum Exportindustriestaat?" *Soziale Praxis*, VIII (1899), p. 633; "Export und Kultur," *Soziale Praxis*, VIII (1899), 31, p. 834.
5. See *Schriften*, vol. 88 (1899), pp. 246–54.
6. Ibid.
7. Werner Sombart, "Ideale der Sozialpolitik," ASG, 10 (1897), p. 43.
8. Ibid., p. 44.

Chapter 13

1. See Werner Sombart, "Demagogenthum in wissenschaftlichem Gewande, eine Entgegnung," *Sozialpolitisches Centralblatt*, 2 (1892), p. 25.
2. Werner Sombart, *Sozialismus und soziale Bewegung im neunzehnten Jahrhundert*, Bern, 1897, pp. 5–6, 51.
3. Ibid., pp. 8–11.
4. Ibid., pp. 32–44, esp. p. 38.
5. Ibid., p. 54.
6. Ibid., pp. 45–46.
7. Ibid., p. 5–6.
8. Ibid., p. 51.
9. Ibid., p. 9.
10. Werner Sombart, *Dennoch!*, Jena, 1900.

11. Werner Sombart, *Sozialismus und soziale Bewegung*, p. 36.
12. Ibid., pp. 37–38.
13. Ibid., p. 40.
14. Ibid., p. 45.
15. Ibid., p. 46.
16. Werner Sombart, *Socialism and the Social Movement in the Nineteenth Century*, trans. A. P. Atterbury, New York, 1898, pp. 172–74.

Chapter 14

1. Werner Sombart, "Ideale der Sozialpolitik," ASG, 10 (1897), p. 12.
2. Ibid.
3. Ibid., pp. 14–15.

Chapter 15

1. Werner Sombart, "Ideale der Sozialpolitik," ASG, 10 (1897), p. 3.
2. Werner Sombart, *Dennoch!*, p. 6.
3. Ibid., pp. 80–81.
4. Ibid.
5. Ibid., p. 92.
6. Ibid., pp. 64, 79.
7. Ibid., p. 6.
8. Ibid., pp. 44, 58, 68–71.
9. Ibid., p. 60.
10. Ibid., p. 91.
11. Ibid., p. 65.
12. Ibid., p. 13.
13. Ibid., p. 14.
14. Ibid., p. 23.
15. Ibid., p. 71.
16. Ibid., p. 85.
17. Werner Sombart, *Der Moderne Kapitalismus*, 1st ed., Leipzig, 1902, vol. II, p. 142.
18. Ibid., 2nd ed., 1916, vol. II, p. 108.
19. Werner Sombart, *Dennoch!*, pp. 86–87.

Chapter 16

1. Werner Sombart, *Der Moderne Kapitalismus*, vol. I, *Die Genesis des Kapitalismus*, XXXIV.
2. Ibid., vol. II, *Die Theorie der kapitalistischen Entwicklung*.
3. Ibid., pp. 433–62.
4. Ibid., p. 425.
5. Gustav Schmoller, review of *Der Moderne Kapitalismus*, in Schmoller's *Jahrbuch*, 27 (1903), p. 293.
6. Ibid., p. 296.
7. Sombart, *Der Moderne Kapitalismus*, Vol. I, p. 385.
8. Ibid., p. 397.
9. Ibid., p. x.
10. Ibid., p. xi.
11. Ibid., p. xiii.
12. Ibid., p. xv.
13. Ibid., p. xvii.
14. Ibid., p. xix.
15. Ibid., pp. xx–xxi.
16. Ibid., p. xxii.
17. Ibid., p. xxiv (my emphasis).
18. Ibid., p. xxviii.
19. Schmoller, *op. cit.*, p. 297.

Chapter 17

1. Werner Sombart, *Die deutsche Volkswirtschaft im neunzehnten Jahrhundert*, Berlin, 1903, pp. 54–55.
2. Ibid., p. 50.
3. Ibid., pp. 55–56.
4. Ibid., pp. 56–57.
5. Ibid., p. 474.
6. Ibid., p. 20.
7. Ibid., pp. 399–400.
8. Ibid., p. 419.
9. Ibid., p. 70.

10. Ibid., pp. 413–14.
11. Ibid., p. 414.
12. Ibid., p. 419.
13. Ibid., p. 107.
14. Ibid., pp. 452–53.
15. Ibid., p. 454.
16. Ibid., p. 455.
17. Ibid., p. 453.
18. Ibid., p. 107.
19. Ibid., p. 108.
20. Ibid.
21. Ibid., p. 109.
22. Ibid., p. 107.
23. Ibid., p. 110.
24. Sombart, *Der Moderne Kapitalismus*, I, p. 390.
25. Sombart, *Die deutsche Volkswirtschaft*, p. 114.
26. Ibid., p. 115.
27. Ibid.
28. Ibid., pp. 465, 466.
29. Ibid., p. 467.
30. Ibid., pp. 474–75.
31. Ibid., p. 475.

Chapter 18

1. S-L 5/ix/86.
2. S-L 21–25/vi/89.
3. S-L 16/x/87.
4. S-L 30/xi/87.
5. Ibid.
6. S-L 17/ix/88.
7. S-L 6/i/89.
8. S-L 6/i/89.
9. See S-L 5/ix/86.
10. S-L 25/vi/89.
11. Werner Sombart, "Die Hausindustrie in Deutschland," ASG, 4 (1891), 103–56.
12. Werner Sombart, "Statistik der Hausweberei im schlesischen Eulengebirge, *Sozialpolitisches Centralblatt*, 1 (1892), 39.

13. Werner Sombart, "Demagogenthum in wissenschaftlichem Gewande, eine Entgegnung," ibid., 2 (1893), p. 26.
14. S-L 5/x/93.
15. Ibid.
16. Engels' letter to Schmidt of March 12, 1895, in *Selected Correspondence of Karl Marx and Friedrich Engels*, New York, 1942, p. 530.
17. S-L *Pfingsten* [Whitsuntide] 1894.
18. S-L 14/i/1900.
19. S-L 1/v/87, 2/xii/87.
20. S-L 7/xi/97.
21. S-L 23/xii/04.
22. Ibid.
23. S-L 29/vii/06.
24. S-L 2/v/09.
25. S-L 7/ix/04.
26. Emil Ludwig, *Gifts of Life*, trans. M. I. Robertson, Boston, 1931, pp. 89–90.
27. Walter Goldstein, *Carl Hauptmann, eine Werkdeutung*, Breslau, 1931.
28. Carl Hauptmann, *Unsere Wirklichkeit*, Munich, 1903.
29. Ibid., p. 13.
30. Werner Sombart, *Das Proletariat*, Frankfurt, 1906, p. 46.
31. Ibid., p. 59.
32. Ibid., p. 80.
33. Ibid., p. 39.
34. Ibid., p. 85.
35. Ibid., pp. 74–75.
36. Ibid., pp. 75–88.
37. Ibid., pp. 76–77.
38. Ibid., p. 79.
39. Ibid., p. 82.
40. *Morgen*, 2 (1908), p. 965.
41. Werner Sombart, "Unsere Interesse in der Politik," *Morgen*, 1 (1907), pp. 43–44.
42. Werner Sombart, "Politik und Bildung," *Morgen*, 1 (1907).
43. Ibid., p. 68.
44. Ibid.
45. Ibid., pp. 68–69.
46. Ibid., p. 69.
47. Ibid.

48. Ibid.
49. Werner Sombart, "Wien," *Morgen*, 1 (1907), p. 174.
50. Ibid., p. 172.

Chapter 19

1. Werner Sombart, *Das Lebenswerk von Karl Marx*, Jena, 1909, Chapter III, pp. 37–38.
2. Ibid., p. 39.
3. Ibid.
4. Ibid., p. 40.
5. Ibid., p. 47.
6. Carl Hauptmann, *Leben mit Freunden, Gesammelte Briefe*, Berlin, 1928, p. 116.
7. Werner Sombart, *op. cit.*, pp. 54–55.

Chapter 20

1. Werner Sombart, "Der Kapitalistische Unternehmer," *Archiv für Sozialwissenschaft und Sozialpolitik* (hereafter cited as ASP), 29 (1909), pp. 689–758.
2. Ibid., p. 729.
3. Ibid., p. 725.
4. Ibid., p. 741.
5. Ibid., pp. 743–47.
6. See Werner Sombart, *Die deutsche Volkswirtschaft im neunzehnten Jahrhundert*, Berlin, 1913 ed., p. 107.
7. Sombart, "Der Kapitalistische Unternehmer," pp. 747–8.
8. Ibid., p. 723.
9. Ibid., p. 748.
10. Ibid., p. 717.
11. Ibid., p. 703.
12. Sombart, *Die deutsche Volkswirtschaft*, p. 71.

Chapter 21

1. Werner Sombart, *Der Bourgeois, Zur Geistesgeschichte des modernen Wirtschaftsmenschen*, Leipzig, 1913.
2. See above, p. 191.
3. *Der Bourgeois*, p. 69.
4. Ibid., p. 271.
5. Ibid., p. 306.
6. Max Scheler, *Ressentiment*, ed. and intro. by Lewis A. Coser, trans. William Holdheim, Glencoe, Ill., 1961, pp. 129 ff. and fn. 28, p. 188.
7. Sombart, *Der Bourgeois*, p. 307.
8. Ibid., p. 308.
9. Ibid., pp. 309–11.
10. Ibid., p. 309.
11. Ibid., pp. 320–31.
12. Ibid., p. 323; see also pp. 351–52.
13. Ibid., pp. 328–30.
14. Ibid., pp. 338–39.
15. Ibid., p. 340.
16. Ibid., pp. 340–41.
17. Ibid., p. 436.
18. Ibid., p. 436–37.
19. Ibid., p. 344.
20. Ibid., pp. 346–48.
21. Ibid., p. 359.
22. Ibid., p. 415, p. 368.
23. Ibid., pp. 426, 454–56.

Chapter 22

1. Werner Sombart, *Der Bourgeois, zur Geistesgeschichte des modernen Wirtschaftsmenschen*, Leipzig, p. 78.
2. Ibid., pp. 94–95.
3. Ibid., p. 100.
4. Ibid., p. 279.
5. Ibid., pp. 271–73.

6. Ibid., pp. 96, 101.
7. Ibid., p. 460.
8. Ibid., p. 219.
9. Ibid., pp. 237–39.
10. Ibid., p. 424.
11. Ibid., p. 427.
12. Werner Sombart, *Händler und Helden*, Munich, 1915.
13. Ibid., pp. 38, 63–64, 108, 127–28.
14. Ibid., from pp. 56, 58, 62.
15. Ibid., pp. 117–18.
16. Ibid., p. 144.
17. Ibid.
18. Ibid., p. 145.

PART IV

Chapter 23

1. Robert Michels, *Political Parties*, Glencoe, Ill., 1949, p. 401. These lines originally appeared in Michels' "Einige Randbemerkungen zur Problem der Demokratie," in the *Sozialistische Monatshefte*, 1908, p. 1620. Michels' book is in many places little more than a pastiche of his articles.
2. Michels, *Political Parties*, p. 400, and H. S. Hughes, *Consciousness and Society*, New York, 1958, pp. 257–58.

Chapter 24

1. Robert Michels, "Peter Michels und seine Tätigkeit in der Kölnische Industrie und Gesellschaft," in *Kölnische Jahrbuch für Geschichte*, XII (1930), pp. 1–98. Hereafter cited as "Peter Michels."
2. "Peter Michels," p. 30.
3. Ibid., p. 31.
4. Ibid., p. 30.
5. Cf. Laurat, Pommera, and Coquet, *Grandeur et Declin de la France*, Paris, 1946, pp. 106–9, passim; Paul Combe, *Niveau de vie et*

progrès technique en France, Paris, 1956, p. 61, John E. Sawyer, "Strains in the Social Structure of Modern France," in *Modern France,* edited by E. M. Earle, Princeton, 1951. For a statistical comparison of industrial concentration in France and the other countries, see Vladimir Woytinsky, *World Population and Resources,* New York, 1953, p. 1118.

6. Cf. the two excellent papers by David Landes: "French Business and the Businessman: A Social and Cultural Analysis," in *Modern France;* and "French Entrepreneurship and Industrial Growth in the Nineteenth Century," in *The Journal of Economic History,* 9 (1949), pp. 45–61.
7. "Peter Michels," p. 53.
8. Quoted from Georg Neuhaus, *Die Stadt Köln im ersten Jahrhundert unter preussischen Herrschaft,* Cologne, 1916, Heubner, Band 1, Teil II, p. 289. In "Peter Michels," p. 53.
9. "Peter Michels," p. 10.
10. Ibid., p. 23.
11. Ibid., p. 60.
12. Ibid., p. 33.
13. Ibid., pp. 37–38, 53.
14. Marianne Weber, *Max Weber, Ein Lebensbild,* Heidelberg, 1950, p. 30.
15. "Peter Michels," pp. 8, 31, 41, 60.
16. Ibid., p. 65.
17. Ibid., p. 61.
18. Ibid., p. 97.
19. Ibid., p. 19.
20. Ibid., p. 63.
21. Ibid., pp. 20–24.
22. This word is of crucial importance in following the development of Michels' political value system.
23. "Peter Michels," pp. 62 ff.
24. "Curriculum Vitae," in Michels' dissertation, *Zur Vorgeschichte von Ludwigs XIV Einfall in Holland,* Halle, 1901.
25. Ibid.
26. Robert Michels, *Bedeutende Männer,* Leipzig, 1927, p. 148.
27. Michels, *Political Parties,* pp. 250–51.
28. Ibid., p. 317.
29. Ibid., p. 251.
30. Ibid., pp. 251–52.

31. Robert Michels, *Der italienische Sozialismus auf dem Lande*, Frankfurt, 1902, reprinted from FW, 1 (1902).
32. Robert Michels, "Les Socialistes allemands et la Guerre," MS, 18 (1906), 129–39, 138–9.
33. Robert Michels, "Die Formen des Patriotismus," EK, 13 (1905), p. 26.
34. Robert Michels, "Der Internationalismus in der Arbeiterschaft," EK, 12 (1904).
35. Michels, *Political Parties*, pp. 252–53.
36. Robert Michels, "Die deutsche Sozialdemokratie, I, Parteimitgliedschaft und soziale Zusammensetzung," ASP, 23 (1906), 471–556, 545.
37. Robert Michels, "Zur zeitlichen Widerstandsfähigkeit des Adels," *Probleme der Sozialphilosophie*, p. 151; cf. also *Political Parties*, p. 14, and "Problem der Internationalen Bourgeoisie," *Probleme der Sozialphilosophie*, p. 185.
38. Robert Michels, "Der italienische Sozialismus auf dem Lande," FW (April 20, 1902), p. 3; book review in *Die Neue Zeit*, 21 (1903), 638; "Der Einfluss des Sozialismus in Italien auf die Sittlichkeit der Bevölkerung," EK, 11 (1903), 76–77; "Die Verrohung einer Begleiterscheinung des Krieges," and "Disciplin," pp. 283 and 303, EK (1903); "Der Internationalismus in der Arbeiterschaft," EK, 12 (1904), 113–14.
39. Michels, "Der Internationalismus in der Arbeiterschaft," p. 113.
40. Robert Michels, "Der deutsche Sozialismus im internationalen Verbande," ASP, 27 (1907), 226.

Chapter 25

1. Robert Michels, "Eine Syndicalistisch-gerichtete Unterströmung im deutschen Sozialismus (1903–1907)," in *Festschrift für Carl Grünberg*, Leipzig, 1932, pp. 343–64; pp. 345–46.
2. See pp. 317–18.
3. Robert Michels, "Der Sozialismus in Italien," FW, I (1901), p. 495.
4. Ibid., p. 496.
5. Ibid., p. 498.
6. Robert Michels, "Der Italienische Sozialismus auf dem Land," FW, April 20, 1902, p. 13.

7. Michels used this phrase in reference to German Social Democracy in "Les dangers du parti socialiste Allemand," MS, 13 (1904), pp. 193–212, p. 207.
8. Robert Michels, "Ein Kommunistischer Entwurf am Hofe Ludwig XIV," II (1902), pp. 92–95; "Eine Exclusive Proletarische Bewegung in Italien um Jahre 1883," IV (1904), pp. 64–69.
9. Robert Michels, "Die Ehescheidung in Italien," *Leipziger Volkszeitung*, Organ für die Interesse des gesamten Werktätigen Volkes, 10, Jahrgang, N. 33; "Der neue Parteitaktik in Italien," *Leipziger Volkszeitung*, N. 81.
10. In *Dokumente der Frauen*: "Das Weib und der Intellektualismus," May 1902; "Ein italienisches Landarbeiterinnenschutzgesetzgebung in Italien," June–July 1902, pp. 513–8, 612–8; "Ein Kinderstreik," Oct. 1902, pp. 16–19; "Die sozialistischen Frauen auf dem Kongress zu Imola," Dec. 1902, pp. 151–55; "Die Friedensbewegung in Italien," May 1903, pp. 459–63; "Die Frau als Streikende in den Lohnkampf," Sept. 1903, pp. 752–58; "Die italienische Frau in dem Camera del Lavoro," March, April, 1904, pp. 366–73, 425–28. In *Neues Frauenleben*: "Landleute, Kinder und Frauen in Süditalien," No. 6, 1905.
11. In *Südwestdeutsche Rundschau:* "Leonardo Bistolfi," May 1902, pp. 334–39.
12. In *Politisch-anthropologisch Revue:* "Englands Gegenwärtige Kulturwerte," III (1904), pp. 53–63; "Das unerlöste Italien in Österreich," 1. Jahrgang, N. 9, pp. 716–24.
13. Robert Michels, "Endziel, Intransigenz, Ethik," EK, XII (1903), pp. 393–95, 403–4, p. 404.
14. See Michels, "Eine syndicalistisch-gerichtete Unterströmung."
15. Quoted from Michels' diary in "Eine syndicalistisch-gerichtete Unterströmung," p. 349.
16. Ibid., p. 349.
17. Robert Michels, "Nationalismus, Nationalgefühl, Internationalismus," FW, II (1902), pp. 107–11; "Der Internationalismus in der Arbeiterschaft," EK, XII (1904), pp. 113–14; "Die Formen des Patriotismus," EK, pp. 86–91 and "Rasse und Entwicklung," EK, XIII (1905), pp. 155–57, 163–64.
18. See Michels, "Internationalismus in der Arbeiterschaft."
19. Michels, "Nationalismus, Nationalgefühl, Internationalismus."
20. Michels, "Begriff und Aufgabe der Masse," FW, II (1902), pp. 407–12, p. 408.

21. Michels, "Internationalismus in der Arbeiterschaft," p. 114.
22. Michels, "Formen des Patriotismus," p. 19.
23. Ibid., p. 27.
24. See fn. 17.
25. Michels, "Rasse und Entwicklung," p. 155.
26. Ibid.
27. Ibid.
28. See Robert Michels, "Proletariat und Bourgeoisie in der Sozialistische Bewegung Italiens," ASP, 22 (1906), p. 719; and "Controverse Socialiste," MS, 21 (1907), p. 283.
29. "Les dangers du parti socialiste allemand," MS, 13 (1904), p. 197.
30. Ibid., p. 199.
31. Ibid., p. 199
32. Ibid., p. 199.
33. Ibid., p. 207
34. Ibid., p. 213.
35. "Le Congrès des Socialistes de Prusse à Berlin," MS, 14 (1905), pp. 238–51.
36. Ibid., p. 246.
37. Ibid., p 247.
38. Ibid., p. 247 (Michels paraphrasing Bernstein).
39. Ibid., p. 247 (Michels quoting Bernstein).
40. Ibid.
41. Robert Michels, "La grève générale des mineurs de la Ruhr," MS, 15 (1905), pp. 480–89; signed "Elberfeld (Bassin de la Ruhr), Fin Mars, 1905," corrected in July 1, 1905 issue to, "Elberfeld et Bassin de la Rhur."
42. Ibid., p. 484.
43. Robert Michels, "Le congrès syndical de Cologne," MS, 16 (1905), pp. 313–21, date, "Marburg Fin Juin, 1905."
44. Ibid., pp. 313–14.
45. Ibid., p. 314.
46. Ibid., p. 307.
47. Robert Michels, "Les socialistes allemands et la guerre," MS, 18 (1906), pp. 129–39.
48. Ibid., p. 136.
49. Ibid., p. 138.
50. Ibid., p. 138.
51. Robert Michels, "Le socialisme allemand après Mannheim," MS, 21 (1907), pp. 5–22.

52. Ibid., pp. 5–6.
53. Robert Michels, "Controverse socialiste," MS, 21 (1907), pp. 278–88.
54. Ibid., p. 282.
55. Robert Michels, "Eine syndicalistisch-gerichtete Unterströmung (see note 1 of this chapter), p. 332.
56. *Patriotismus und Ethik*, Leipzig, 1906, cited in Ibid.
57. Ibid., pp. 353–56.
58. Ibid., pp. 356–57.
59. On the Weber-Michels relationship, see, in addition to Michels' piece in the *Grünberg Festschrift*, Wolfgang Mommsen, *Max Weber und die deutsche Politik*, Tübingen, 1959, pp. 121 ff.; Marianne Weber, *Max Weber, Ein Lebensbild*, Heidelberg, 1950, pp. 395 ff., 402, 408, 465, 526 ff.; and Guenther Roth, *The Social Democrats in Imperial Germany*, Totowa, N.J., 1963, pp. 249–57.
60. Robert Michels, "Proletariat und Bourgeoisie in der Sozialistische Bewegung Italiens," ASP, 22 (1906), pp. 664–720.
61. Robert Michels, "Die deutsche Sozialdemokratie," ASP, 23 (1906), pp. 471–556.
62. Robert Michels, "Die deutsche Sozialdemokratie im internationalen Verbande, eine Kritische Untersuchung," ASP, 25 (1907), pp. 148–231.
63. Michels, "Proletariat und Bourgeoisie," p. 712.
64. Michels, "Die deutsche Sozialdemokratie," p. 543.
65. The speech, given April 3, 1907, was reprinted in *Syndicalisme et Socialisme*, edited by Hubert Lagardelle, Paris 1908. The *Archiv* article was printed in the second half of 1907.
66. Michels, "Die deutsche Sozialdemokratie im internationalen Verbande," pp. 229–31.
67. Ibid., p. 224.

Chapter 26

1. Robert Michels, "Streiflicht," EK, XI (1903), p. 286.
2. Robert Michels, "Die Oligarchischen Tendenzen der Gesellschaft," ASP, 27 (1908), pp. 73–135.
3. Ibid., p. 129.
4. Ibid., p. 130.

5. Robert Michels, "Zur Zeitlichen Widerstandsfähigkeit der Adel," in *Probleme der Sozialphilosophie*, Leipzig and Berlin, 1913, pp. 132–58; and *Umschichtungen in den Herrschenden Klassen nach dem Kriege*, Stuttgart-Berlin, 1934.
 6. Michels, "Die Oligarchischen Tendenzen," p. 131–32.
 7. See Robert Michels, "Begriff und Ausgabe der Masse," FW, II (1902), pp. 407–12, where Michels views the masses as the historical agents of morality.
 8. Michels, "Die Oligarchischen Tendenzen," p. 128.
 9. Ibid., p. 134.
10. Ibid., p. 134.
11. Ibid., p. 78.

Chapter 27

 1. See especially the works referred to in Chapter 25, fns. 6, 18, and 20.
 2. See Robert Michels, "Die Formen des Patriotismus," EK, 1905, p. 26; *Political Parties*, p. 248.
 3. Michels, *Political Parties*, pp. 249 ff.
 4. See p. 24.
 5. Robert Michels, "Zum Problem der Kooperation," also reprinted in *Probleme der Sozialphilosophie*, pp. 1–44. Page references will be to this edition.
 6. Ibid., pp. 2 ff.
 7. Ibid., p. 11.
 8. Ibid., pp. 13–18.
 9. Ibid., pp. 21–28.
10. Ibid., p. 39.
11. Ibid., p. 42.
12. Ibid., pp. 43–44.
13. Michels, "Das Proletariat in der Wissenschaft und die Oekonomisch-Anthropologisch Synthese," reprinted in *Probleme der Sozialphilosophie as* "Zum Problem der Behandlung des Proletariats in der Wissenschaft," pp. 98–132.
14. Ibid., p. 114.
15. Ibid., pp. 117–18.
16. Ibid., pp. 119–20.
17. Ibid., p. 121.

18. Ibid., p. 132.
19. Michels, "Zum Problem der Eugenetik," in *Probleme der Sozialphilosophie*, p. 53.
20. EK, XII (1904), p. 53.
21. E.g., "Die Formen des Patriotismus," p. 28.
22. Michels, "Englands gegenwärtige Kulturwert," p. 54.
23. This is the principal burden of "Zum Problem des Fortschritts," in *Probleme der Sozialphilosophie*, pp. 63–84.
24. Ibid., p. 63.
25. Ibid., pp. 66–67.
26. Ibid., pp. 67–69.
27. Ibid., p. 78.
28. Ibid., pp. 79–81.
29. Ibid., p. 82.
30. Ibid., p. 82.
31. Ibid., p. 74.
32. Ibid., p. 84.
33. Michels, "Zum Problem der Internationalen Bourgeoisie," in *Probleme der Sozialphilosophie*.
34. Ibid., p. 168.
35. See fn. 6.
36. See pp. 292–93.
37. Robert Michels, "Le patriotisme des socialistes allemands et le congrès d'Essen," MS, Jan. 1908, pp. 5–13.
38. Ibid., p. 12.
39. Robert Michels, "Deutsche Sozialdemokratie im internationalen Verbande," ASP, 1907, p. 226.
40. Michels, "Nationalismus, Nationalgefühl, Internationalismus."
41. Robert Michels, "La politique étrangère et le socialisme," MS, 25 (1909), pp. 321–33. Virtually the same article appeared in German as "Pazifismus und Nationalitätsprinzip" in *Politisch-Anthropologisch Revue*, 1909.
42. Robert Michels, "Der ethische Faktor in der Parteipolitik Italiens," *Zeitschrift für Politik*, III (1909), pp. 56–91. This essay is reprinted, with minor alterations, in Michels' *Sozialismus in Italien*, 1925, pp. 249–310. Reference below will be to the original publication.
43. Ibid., pp. 61–62.
44. Ibid., p. 64.
45. Ibid., pp. 67–68.
46. Ibid., pp. 78–79.

47. Robert Michels, "Zur historischen Analyse des Patriotismus," ASP (1913), 14–43, 394–449.
48. Ibid., pp. 420–23; Michels, "Die Formen des Patriotismus," EK, 13 (1905), p. 26.
49. Michels, "Zur historischen Analyse," pp. 425–26.
50. See also Michels' *Italien von Heute*, 1930, pp. 164–65, where the author cites the educational work of the socialists as an indispensable precondition for the attachment of the masses to fascist nationalism.
51. Michels, "Zur historischen Analyse," p. 449.
52. Robert Michels, "La débâcle de l'internationale ouvrière et l'avenir," *Scientia*, 19 (1916), 183–90.
53. Robert Michels, "La sphere historique de Rome," *Scientia*, 1917. For a contrary, earlier position, see Michels' "Rasse und Entwicklung," EK, 1905.
54. Michels, "La sphere historique de Rome," *Scientia*, 1917, p. 63.
55. Ibid.

Conclusion

1. Tönnies, "Autobiography," p. 34.
2. On Tönnies' concept of history, see his "Begriff und Gesetz des menschlichen Fortschritts," ASP, 53 (1924), 1–10; on his pantheism, "Autobiography," p. 35.
3. See Sombart's *Deutscher Sozialismus*, Berlin, 1934.
4. James Meisel, *The Genesis of Georges Sorel*, p. 113.
5. Michels, *Political Parties*, p. 315.
6. Ibid., p. 209.

Index

Abano, Pietro d', 322 n.
agriculture: East Elbian, and Verein für Sozialpolitik, 139–42; Werner Sombart on, 142–6; Italian, 158
Alberti, Leon Battista, 257
alienation (from self), 10–12, 14; see also Gemeinschaft und Gesellschaft; Marx, Karl, and Marxism
Althoff, Friedrich, 109, 111, 121
Ammon, Otto, 322
anarchism, anarcho-syndicalism, revolutionary syndicalism, 110, 166, 233 n., 289, 302; see also Michels, Robert
Andreas-Salomé, Lou, 93
anti-Semitism, 30, 32, 85–8, 173; in Sombart, 251–5, 258, 261
Apollonian personality, 7 n., 9, 14, 15, 20, 27
Archiv für Soziale Gesetzgebung und Statistik, 121, 146, 153, 214
Aristotle, 14, 138
Arons, Leo, 221 n.
artisans, 4, 22, 139, 187; see also Sombart, Werner
Aster, Ernst von, 339

Bachofen, J. J., 83, 144
Bacon, Francis, 25
Bakunin, Mikhail, 166
Barrault, Émile, 314
Beaconsfield (Disraeli), Lord, 56
Bebel, August, 220, 288, 300–2, 332
Bendix, Reinhard, 140 n.
Bernstein, Eduard, 174, 219, 221, 286, 297, 298, 322
Berth, Eduard, 289, 302–4
Bismarck, Otto von, 23, 29, 30–2, 49, 56, 57, 80, 111, 112, 115, 137;

"blood and iron" cited by Tönnies, 122
Bölsche, Wilhelm, 224 n., 230
Bonomi, Ivanoe, 304
Boulanger, General Georges, 109
Bourgeois, Der (Sombart) 34, 135 n., 207, 243–62
bourgeoisie, 29, 30, 243–62; Michels on German, 280, 312, 315, 331
Braun, Heinrich, 32, 220; see also Archiv für Soziale Gesetzgebung und Statistik; Sombart, Werner
Braun, Lili, 121 n.
Brentano, Lujo, 138, 139 n., 152, 286
Buber, Martin, 208, 226
Bücher, Karl, 71, 72
Buek, Otto, 304
Burckhardt, Jacob, 3, 4, 5, 12
bureaucracy and bureaucratization, 8, 13, 15, 24, 26, 29, 34, 107
Bürger, Bürgergeist, 246–53, 254, 256–8, 259, 260; see also entrepreneur, the
Burnham, James, 268 n.
Byron, George, Lord, 215, 224

Calvinism, see Protestantism
capitalism, industrial, 17, 22, 23, 28, 113; see also entrepreneur, the; Sombart, Werner
capitalist spirit, 8, 135, 170, 186–94 passim, 274; see also entrepreneur, the; Sombart, Werner
Caprivi, General Leo von, 221
Carosso, Vincent P., 135 n.
Carlyle, Thomas, 4, 45, 69–71, 94
Carrière, Moritz, 54–5
Catholicism: and rise of capitalism, 248–52, 256; in Michels' family background, 272–3, 275
Celtic peoples, 247–8
Cohen, Hermann, 304

Index

Cologne, see Michels, Peter; Michels, Robert
Combe, Émile, 109
community, 11, 12, 13, 22, 23, 24, 25; Sombart's view of, 136, 144, 162, 343; see also Gemeinschaft und Gesellschaft; Sombart, Werner; Tönnies, Ferdinand
Comte, Auguste, 83
coquetry, 328, 329–30
corporate social structure, 22
Coser, Lewis A., 109
cottage industry, 147–51, 153–5
cultural pessimism, 16, 46, 69, 87, 227 ff., 262
Curtius, G., 44

d'Annunzio, Gabriele, 326
Dante (Alighieri), 326
Darwin, Charles, and Social-Darwinism, 55, 60, 69, 73, 79, 81, 109, 123, 216, 321–4, 330
de-Amicis, Edmondo, 325
democracy, 24, 125–7
Descartes, René, 47, 216
deutsche Volkswirtschaft im neunzehnten Jahrhundert, Die (Sombart), 33, 194–207 *passim*, 222, 223
Diderot, Denis, 342, 343
Dilthey, Wilhelm, 173, 174
Dionysian personality, 6, 7 *n*., 9, 10, 14, 15, 20
division of labor, 13, 18–19, 108, 284, 309
Dostoevsky, Feodor, 31 *n*., 35
Dreyfus, Alfred, 109
Durkheim, Émile, 108–12, 341

Ebbinghaus, Hermann, 93
Ebert, Friedrich, 312 *n*.
Engels, Friedrich, 51 *n*.
England and the English, see *Bourgeois, Der*; *Händler und Helden*; Tönnies, Ferdinand
Enlightenment, the, 5, 16, 59 *n*., 107, 268, 330, 342–3
entrepreneur, the, 25, 188, 237–64 *passim*

Ethical Culture, Society for: and Tönnies, 114, 117–21; and Sombart, 161, 222 *n*.; and Michels, 281, 283, 304
expressionism, 32, 35

Faustian personality, 6, 7 *n*., 9, 10, 25, 27
Ferri, Enrico, 304, 337
Fichte, J. G., 17, 18, 19, 21, 101, 104, 105
Fledermaus, Die, 86
Florence and Florentines, 248, 256–7
folkish ideology, see *völkisch ideology* and *Volksgeneinschaft*
Fourier, Charles, 282, 314 *n*.
Francke, Kuno, see Tönnies, Ferdinand
Franz, Rudolf, 305
French Revolution, 4 *n*., 101, 107, 108
Freyer, Hans, 7, 19, 20, 339
Friedeberg, Raphael, 300–2
Friedrich, Crown Prince, 55, 58, 85
Frisians, 41–2, 103, 248; see also Schleswig; Tönnies, Ferdinand

Gemeinschaft, see *Gemeinschaft und Gesellschaft*; Sombart, Werner; Tönnies, Ferdinand; *völkisch* ideology and *Volksgemeinschaft*
Gemeinschaft und Gesellschaft (Tönnies), 11, 24, 39–41, 43, 60, 61, 64, 69, 70, 74–84, 89, 101, 104, 110, 113–17, 123, 127, 128
George, Stefan, 28 *n*., 32, 35
Gesellschaft, see *Gemeinschaft und Gesellschaft*; Tönnies, Ferdinand
Gierke, Otto von, 27, 79, 84, 101, 110, 127, 128, 157–9, 176 *n*., 341
Glaeser, Ernst, 265
Gneist, Rudolf, 28, 45, 49, 74, 82, 113
Goethe, Johann Wolfgang von, 6, 19, 326
Goldstein, Walter, 224
Görres, Joseph von, 12
guilds, 4 *n*., 22, 274
guild socialists, 12

Index

Haenisch, Konrad, 297, 300
Haller, K. L. von, 102
Hamerow, Theodor S., 4 n.
Händler und Helden (Sombart), 130, 170, 209, 260–3; see also *Bourgeois, Der*
Hardenberg, Baron, 139, 140
Hauptmann, Carl, 32, 224–6, 239 n.; see also Sombart, Werner
Hauptmann, Gerhart, 198, 224
Hegel, G. W. F., 5, 21, 58, 59, 79, 80
Heimat, 63–100; see also Schleswig; Tönnies, Ferdinand
Heine, Wolfgang, 288, 289
Heller, Johannes, 58
Herder, J. G., 104
Herkner, Heinrich, 152, 214, 219
hero-nations, 258, 260, 261; see also entrepreneur, the; *Händler und Helden*
historical school of law and political economy, 78, 79, 82, 101–3, 135, 192, 214, 217, 330, 340–1
Hobbes, Thomas, 40, 45, 47, 48, 50, 52, 53–5, 58–60, 62, 64, 69, 71–3, 80–2
Hölderlin, Friedrich, 14
Holy Roman Empire, 4 n., 12, 15
Homer, 12
Honigsheim, Paul, 31 n., 32, 207
Hughes, H. Stuart, 268 n.
Humboldt, Wilhelm von, 19, 104, 105
Hume, David, 48, 80

Ihering, Rudolf, 73, 74, 76, 79, 80
imperialism: English and German, 262–3; and workers, 335
industrial revolution, 107, 137

Jastrow, Ignaz, 32
Jews and Judaism, 251–5, 258, 260, 261; see also anti-Semitism
Junkers, 23, 31, 58, 127, 205

Kallsen, Otto, see Tönnies, Ferdinand
Kant, Immanuel, and neo-Kantianism, 17, 18, 80, 169, 171, 173–4, 189, 191, 216, 305

Kantorowicz, Gertrud, 33
"Kapitalistische Unternehmer, Der" (Sombart), 238–43, 247
Kathedersozialisten, 64, 112, 138, 212; see also Schmoller, Gustav; Verein für Sozialpolitik; Wagner, Adolf
Kierkegaard, Søren, 4
Kleist, H. von, 104–6
Kluckhohn, Paul, 21
Koigen, David, 230
Kolping, Eduard, 274
König, René, 83
Köster, Adolf, 305
Krupp, Alfred, 239

labor cooperative movement, 114, 116–17, 124
labor movement, see proletariat and labor movement
Labriola, Antonio, 325
Labriola, Arturo, 304
Lacoste, Robert, 312 n.
Lagarde, Paul de, 28, 29, 35, 47, 89
Lagardelle, Hubert, 289
Lamprecht, Karl, 214
Landsberger, Arthur (*Morgen* editor), 230
Lang, Otto, 32 n., 209–23
Langbehn, Julius, 28, 35
Lassalle, Ferdinand, 45, 46, 49, 52, 178, 181, 214, 216
Laveleye, Emile de, 69, 71, 72, 84
Lebovics, Herman, 135 n.
Ledebour, Georg, 288
Ledru-Rollin, A. A., 282
Leif, J., 83
Leonardo, 25
Liard, Louis, 109
liberals and liberalism, 22, 29, 30, 109–10, 111; English model, 113
Lichtheim, George, 31
Liebknecht, Karl, 297, 300 n., 301
Lindner, Gisela Michels, 277, 283, 304
Linz, Juan, 269
Lougee, Robert W., 89 n.
Lovejoy, Arthur, 18
Löwenthal, Leo, 31 n.
Löwith, Karl, 7 n., 12 n., 21
Lübbe, Fritz, 21

Index

Lutheranism, 5, 15, 17
Luxemburg, Rosa, 288, 300 n.

Machiavelli, Niccolò, 268
MacMahon, Marshal, 109
Maine, H. S., 72
Maistre, Joseph de, 4
Man, Hendrik de, 300 n.
Mandarins: academic, orthodox, 26, 29, 34, 339; modernist, 30–5, 133, 339; *see also* Sombart, Werner
Mann, Thomas, 100
Mannheim, Karl, 339
Manuel, Frank, 5, 15
Marcuse, Herbert, 79
Martin, Alfred von, 11, 21
Marx, Karl, and Marxism, 7, 21, 24, 51, 138, 171; alienation, ambiguous view of, 8–9; "national class," 30–1, 123; Sombart's attitude toward, 136, 144, 151–67 *passim*, 178, 191, 192 n., 211, 214–22 *passim*, 244; Michels' attitude toward, 297–8, 312
Maus, Heinz, 79
May, John D., 268 n.
Mehring, Franz, 120
Meinecke, Friedrich, 21, 79
Meisel, James, 268 n., 341
Meissner, Heinrich O., 79
Mezzadria (sharecropping system), 143–4
Michels, Peter, 271–6 *passim*, 341
Michels, Robert, 6, 21–2, 24, 35–6, 40, 107, 111, 136, 221 n., 230, 265–338, 339–44 *passim*
  major works: *Zur Soziologie des Parteiwesens in der modernen Demokratie (Political Parties)*, 267–8, 317; *Probleme der Sozialphilosophie*, 317–35
  personal background and values: family in Cologne, 271–82; anti-Prussian views, 273–6, 280, 289, 309, 312, 315–16, 331; cosmopolitanism and antimilitarism of, 274–5, 281, 286, 301, 316, 327, 331; on French and Italian character, 278, 281–2, 285–6, 290, 307, 330–8; influence on Werner Sombart, 279 n., 306, 322; on the German bourgeoisie, 280, 312, 315, 331; Marburg syndicalist group, 304–6; elitism of, 311–15, 324, 325
  as Socialist: on significance of intellectuals for socialism, 277–9, 315–17, 324, 325; on proletarian struggle, 278, 287, 296–303; early moderation of, 283–6; critique of socialist revisionism, 286–9; sympathies for revolutionary syndicalism, 289, 295–306, 327; critique of socialist leadership, 294–302, 307–9, 327
  as social scientist: on nationalism, 281, 286, 289–94, 300, 316, 318, 332–8; on universities, 283–4, 291, 318, 320, 322, 332, 334, 337, 343; implicit acceptance of natural law, 290–1, 316–30 *passim*; iron law of oligarchy, 291, 302–4, 310–14; use of Pareto's and Mosca's ideas, 311–13, 330; view of history, 315–38 *passim*; opposition to Social-Darwinism, 321–4, 330; on sexual morality, 328–30
Middle Ages, the, 12, 26, 104, 187–8; *see also* Sombart, Werner; Tönnies, Ferdinand
middle class, *see* bourgeoisie
Mill, James, 60
Mill, John Stuart, 70, 168 n.
Millerand, Alexandre, 312 n.
Mittelstand (social class), 29–31, 89, 111, 137, 183–4, 239, 244, 339
Mitzman, Arthur, 140 n., 184 n., 205 n.
Moderne Kapitalismus, Der (Sombart), 186–94, 198, 207, 222, 223, 234, 243 ff.
Molière, 326
Mommsen, Wolfgang, 7 n., 21, 140 n., 171 n.
Morgan, Lewis Henry, 84, 144
Morgen (journal), 208, 230–3
Morris, William, 12
Mosca, Gaetano, 268 n., 311–13, 330
Mosse, George, 5, 26

Index

Most, Johann, 55
Müller, Adam, 12, 102
Muther, Richard, 230

Napoleonic conquest, 20–2, 139, 271–3
Nationalismus and *National-bewusststein*, 290, 332; *see also* Michels, Robert: as social scientist
National Liberals, 51, 58, 84
National Socialism, 26, 136, 262–4
National-Social Party (of Friedrich Naumann), 287, 305
Natorp, Paul, 305
natural law, 15, 52, 66, 72, 73, 79, 83, 126
Naumann, Friedrich, 152
Niceforo, Alfredo, 305, 323, 324
Nietzsche, Friedrich, 4–6, 9, 12, 21, 26, 31, 34–5, 43–4, 46, 59, 69, 89, 135, 324–5, 340; *see also* Sombart, Werner
Novalis, 12, 14, 17, 21, 102, 103, 104

objective spirit, 7, 8
Oettingen, Alexander von, 63

Pareto, Vilfredo, 29, 268 *n.*, 280, 311–12
Parsons, Talcott, 16, 83, 135 *n.*, 174 *n.*
Pascal, Blaise, 305
Pascal, Roy, 15
Paulsen, Friedrich, 216; *see also* Tönnies, Ferdinand
peasantry, 16
pessimism, *see* cultural pessimism
Pestalozzi, J. H., 19
Petty, William, 60
Pietism, 10, 17
Plato, *see* Tönnies, Ferdinand
Plotnik, Morton, 135 *n.*, 152 *n.*
Political Parties (Michels), 267, 268, 317
Popitz, Heinrich, 104
Probleme der Sozialphilosophie (Michels), 317–35

Proletariat, Das (Sombart), 222 *n.*, 226–9, 258
proletariat and labor movement, 8–9, 22, 24, 119, 121–3, 124 *n.*, 129; *see also* socialism and Social Democrats; Sombart, Werner
prostitution, 328–9
Protestantism, 248, 250–1
Proudhon, P.-J., 282
Prussia, 5, 15, 17, 22–4, 26, 29, 30, 31, 57, 96–7, 111, 121, 130, 137, 139, 140, 142, 211, 223; *see also* Michels, Robert; Tönnies, Ferdinand

racism, *see* anti-Semitism; *Bourgeois, Der; Händler und Helden;* Sombart, Werner
radicalism, bourgeois or democratic, 26, 60, 84
Rathenau, Walther, 241–2
rationalization, process of, 6, 7, 10, 11, 24, 107
Rée, Paul, 93
reification, 7, 13, 14, 18, 24, 34
religion, *see* Catholicism; Jews and Judaism; Lutheranism; Pietism; Protestantism; Thomism
Renaissance, the, 12, 13–14, 26, 248
Rentengüter (hereditary farm leases), 141, 142, 143
Ressentiment, Nietzsche's concept of, 135
Ricardo, David, 60
Ringer, Fritz, 26 *n.*, 31, 34, 283
Ritschl, A., 44
Rodbertus, Karl, 80, 214
Roman law, 14, 72
romanticism, 5, 7, 11, 14, 15, 17, 18, 20–3, 26, 68, 101–7, 262
Roscher, Wilhelm, 47
Rostand, Edmond, 326
Rosteutscher, J. H. W., 7 *n.*
Rousseau, Jean-Jacques, 5, 14, 35, 115 *n.*, 124, 215, 216, 282

St.-Simon, C. H., Comte de, 282, 314
Salomon, Gottfried, 101, 104
Savigny, F. K. von, 101, 102

Schäffle, August, 73, 74, 79, 80, 82
Scheler, Max, 32, 107, 172, 209, 245, 249, 257
Schelling, F. W. J. von, 79
Schiller, Friedrich, 6, 9, 10, 12, 17–20, 35, 101, 104, 106, 198
Schlegel, K. W. F. von and A. W. von, 14, 21, 103
Schleiermacher, F. D. E., 17, 21
Schleswig, 41–2, 50, 61, 87, 91–2, 110, 171; traditions of local autonomy, 97–100; *see also* Frisians; Tönnies, Ferdinand: personal life and background
Schmitt, Carl, 21, 79, 339
Schmoller, Gustav, 27, 28 *n*., 110, 112, 138, 140, 142, 158–9, 172, 187, 192, 212–14, 217, 223, 244, 341; *see also* Sombart, Werner
Schnabel, Franz, 15, 25
Schoenlank, Bruno, 218, 221
Schopenhauer, Arthur, 4, 44, 90, 215
Schriewer, Franz, 103
Schulze-Gävernitz, Gerhart von, 219
Shakespeare, William, 326
Shaw, G. B., 326
Siemens, W., 239
Simmel, Georg, 8, 9, 28 *n*., 32, 34, 79, 107, 110, 111, 136
Smith, Adam, 47, 60
socialism and Social Democrats, 8, 11, 24, 25, 35, 36, 49, 51, 52, 53, 55, 66, 68, 73, 88, 110, 113 *n*., 120–4, 127, 135, 137, 274; *see also* Michels, Robert; Sombart, Werner
"Socialists of the chair," *see* Kathedersozialisten
Society for Ethical Culture, *see* Ethical Culture, Society for
Sokel, Walter, 26 *n*., 31 *n*.
Sombart, Anton, 136, 140–3, 145, 172, 223, 228, 242; *see also* Sombart, Werner
Sombart, Werner, 5–9, 13, 21–2, 24–6, 28 *n*., 30–6, 40, 107, 110–11, 132–264 *passim*, 274, 339–44 *passim*
   major works: *Die deutsche Volkswirtschaft im neunzehnten Jahrhundert*, 33, 194–207 *passim*, 222–3; *Der Bourgeois*, 34, 135 *n*., 207, 243–62; *Händler und Helden*, 130, 170, 209, 260–3; *Sozialismus und Soziale Bewegung im neunzehnten Jahrhundert*, 161–7, 220, 222–3, 233; *Der Moderne Kapitalismus*, 186–94, 198, 207, 222–3, 225, 234, 243; *Das Proletariat*, 222 *n*., 226–9, 258
   life and background: early influence of father and Gustav Schmoller on, 140–6, 158; personal life, 207–33; friendship with Otto Lang, 209–23; early ambivalence about Socialists, 210–22; friendship with Carl Hauptmann, 223–6, 230, 237, 258
   as modernist: view of capitalism, 135, 163–5, 174, 186–206 *passim*, 238–64 *passim*; early research on rural economy in Italy, 142–6, 208, 213; and publications of Heinrich Braun, 146–8, 153–5, 214, 219–20; on cottage industry in Germany, 147–51, 153–5; interpretation of Karl Marx, 151–67 *passim*, 234–8; aligned with left wing in *Verein für Sozialpolitik*, 152–3, 156–9; support for moderate socialism, 159–68, 178–82; on trade unions, 175–85, 227–8
   as anti-modernist: on the entrepreneur, 25, 188, 237–64 *passim*, 306; racism of, 25–6, 163–4, 173, 203–4, 247, 256, 257; on spirit of capitalism, 135, 170, 186–94 *passim*, 197–8, 203–4, 208–9, 243–61 *passim*, 341; influence of Tönnies on, 144, 175–6, 182–3, 185, 199, 208, 222–5, 227–30, 234–7, 241, 255, 260–4 *passim*; voluntarist interpretation of history, 161–75 *passim*, 193–4, 234–8; influence of Nietzsche on, 174, 209, 234, 237, 257; use of "Gemeinschaft," 175–7, 182–3, 195–6, 227–30, 239; on the Middle Ages, 194–8,

Sombart, Werner (*cont.*)
222; disenchantment with proletariat, 200–1, 222 *n.*; estrangement from German character, 202, 257; articles in *Morgen*, 208, 230–3; on Germany's imperial mission, 262–4
Sorel, Georges, 268 *n.*, 289, 296, 314 *n.*, 341
Spann, Othmar, 339
Spencer, Herbert, 79, 261
Spinoza, Benedict, 47–9, 64, 84, 216
spontaneity, 10, 11, 18
Stammler, Rudolf, 169, 173
Staude, John Raphael, 32 *n.*
Staudinger, Franz, 216
Stein, Baron, 139, 140
Stein, Lorenz von, 21, 73, 74, 80, 82, 101, 110, 112, 113, 130
Stern, Fritz, 5, 26, 47, 263
Stirner, Max, 21
Stöcker, Adolf, 29
Storm, Ernst, *see* Tönnies, Ferdinand
Storm, Gertrud, *see* Tönnies, Ferdinand
Storm, Theodor, *see* Tönnies, Ferdinand
Strauss, D. F., 42, 43
Strauss, Leo, 171
Stuckert, Franz, 95
Sturm und Drang, 7, 14, 15, 17, 35; Sombart's affinity with, 208, 214–21
Sudermann, Hermann, 326
syndicalism, *see* proletariat and labor movement
syndicalism, revolutionary, *see* anarchism, anarcho-syndicalism

Teschemacher, Hans, 305
Thesing, Ernst, 304
Thomism, 249–51, 257
Tieck, Ludwig, 102, 103
Tocqueville, Alexis de, 3, 69, 185 *n.*, 282, 321
Tolstoi, Leo, 304
Tönnies, Ferdinand, 5, 6, 9, 12, 21–5, 28 *n.*, 35, 36, 38–131, 136, 171 ff., 218, 274, 339–44 *passim*

major work: *Gemeinschaft und Gesellschaft*, 11, 24, 39–41, 43, 60, 61, 64, 69, 70, 74–84, 89, 101, 104, 110, 113–17, 123, 127, 128
major concepts: *Gemeinschaft*, 39, 62, 63, 69, 73, 76–83, 89–90, 96–7, 99, 106–16 *passim*, 120, 123–6, 128, 129, 171, 172; *Gesellschaft*, 62, 63, 73, 76, 106, 108–9, 112, 116, 120, 123–6, 128, 130–1, 171; *Wesenwille*, 11, 39, 48–9, 77–84, 89, 95–6, 100, 114, 124; *Willkür*, 10, 48–9, 77–83, 89, 97, 124
political and social attitudes: to antisocialist law of 1878, 49–59, 84–110; to Prussia, 50, 61, 80, 89 *n.*, 107, 110, 124–5, 127, 129; to universal suffrage, 53, 124; to England, 56, 61, 124, 125, 130, 131; to Middle Ages, 65–70
personal life and background: Frisian origins, 40–2, 50, 61, 86 *n.*, 91–100, 103, 110, 114, 171; friendship with Friedrich Paulsen, 40, 45–94 *passim*, 99, 100, 102, 103, 121, 122, 124; friendship with Theodor Storm, 40–2, 50, 61, 94–100, 103, 114; Platonic influence on, 41, 53–4, 58, 64, 87, 93; friendship with Ernst Storm, 42; influence of Otto Kallsen, 42; friendship with Kuno Francke, 45, 90; support from father and uncle, 47; friendship with Gertrud Storm, 94
personal and professional evolution: estrangement from and difficulties within German university system, 61, 114–16, 121–2, 131; utopian aspirations, 87–93; relationships with women and marriage, 93–4; compared with Durkheim, 108–12; and labor movement, 114, 116–17, 119, 121–3; and Society for Ethical Culture, 114, 117, 121

trade-unions, *see* proletariat and labor movement
Treitschke, Heinrich von, 11, 138
Troeltsch, Ernst, 15, 79, 244, 245

"Unsere Wirklichkeit" (Hauptmann), 225–6
utilitarianism, 23, 261

Vandervelde, Emile, 304
Verein für Sozialpolitik, 137–43, 146–8; see also *Kathedersozialisten*
Vico, Giambattista, 328, 340
Vienna, 233
Vierkandt, Alfred, 107
völkisch ideology and *Volksgemeinschaft*, 5, 26, 29, 30, 89, 130
Vollmar, Georg von, 219
voluntarism, 7 *n.*, 25, 75 ff., 82–3, 136; *see also* Sombart, Werner

Wackenroder, W., 102, 103, 104
Wagner, Adolf, 28, 45, 63, 73, 80, 85, 110, 112, 129, 138, 212, 213, 223

Waldeck-Rousseau, 109
Weber, Alfred, 152
Weber, Marianne, 110 *n.*, 153 *n.*,
Weber, Max, 6, 9, 10, 11, 13, 21, 28 *n.*, 30–4, 110, 111, 135, 136, 140, 152, 153 *n.*, 169 *n.*, 171, 184 *n.*, 205 *n.*, 209, 244, 248, 250–1, 257 *n.*, 268 *n.*, 274, 306, 343; goal-rationality, 7, 10–11; nationalism of, 25–6
Wesenwille–Willkür dichotomy, 10–11, 39, 48–9, 77–84, 89, 95–6, 100, 114, 124, 225; for Sombart, 199, 222 *n.*, 229–30, 235, 241
Westphal, Otto, 26
"Wien" (Sombart), 230, 233
Wiese, Leopold von, 224 *n.*, 339
Wilhelm I, 115
Wilhelm II, 55, 58, 125, 221
Willkür, see *Wesenwille–Willkür* dichotomy
Wolf, Julius, 151, 152 *n.*, 222 *n.*
Wolff, Kurt, 79

youth movement, 32

Zola, Émile, 214

A NOTE ABOUT THE AUTHOR

ARTHUR MITZMAN is professor of history at the University of Amsterdam in Holland. Born in Newark, New Jersey, in 1931, he did his undergraduate work at Syracuse University and Columbia University. He received an M.A. in history from Columbia in 1959 and a Ph.D. in the history of ideas from Brandeis University in 1963. He has taught at Brooklyn College, Goddard College, and the University of Rochester, and was formerly associate professor of social theory at Simon Fraser University in Vancouver, British Columbia. Mr. Mitzman's first book, *The Iron Cage: An Historical Interpretation of Max Weber,* was published in 1970.

A NOTE ON THE TYPE

THE TEXT OF THIS BOOK is set in Caledonia, a type face designed by W(illiam) A(ddison) Dwiggins for the Mergenthaler Linotype Company in 1939. Dwiggins chose to call his new type face Caledonia, the Roman name for Scotland, because it was inspired by the Scotch types cast about 1833 by Alexander Wilson & Son, Glasgow type founders. However, there is a calligraphic quality about Caledonia that is totally lacking in the Wilson types. Dwiggins referred to an even earlier type face for this "liveliness of action"—one cut around 1790 by William Martin for the printer William Bulmer. Caledonia has more weight than the Martin letters, and the bottom finishing strokes (serifs) of the letters are cut straight across, without brackets, to make sharp angles with the upright stems, thus giving a "modern face" appearance.

W. A. Dwiggins (1880–1956) began an association with the Mergenthaler Linotype Company in 1929 and over the next twenty-seven years designed a number of book types, the most interesting of which are the Metro series, Electra, Caledonia, Eldorado, and Falcon.

This book was composed, printed and bound by The Haddon Craftsmen, Inc., Scranton, Penn. The typography and binding design are by VIRGINIA TAN.